Praise for Blaze Union
and the Puddin' Head Schools

** 2023 American Book Fest, Fiction Book Award: Humor/Comedy/Satire **

** 2023 Readers' Favorite Book Award: Young Adult Social Issues **

** 2023 Literary Titan Book Award **

Gloriously absurd... Kosmos employs a conversational style throughout the narrative and portrays Blaze as larger than life but still relatable; the teen is fierce, determined, and angry at the injustice around her... For the most part, though, a sense of silliness carries the day, and Blaze's escapades are often delightfully funny.
— Kirkus Reviews

An absolutely hilarious story that had me laughing at the odd behaviors presented in every chapter... The perfect book for those of you who may look around and ask, "Is divisiveness becoming as absurd as I think it is?"
— Reader Views

A wittily crafted, real-life-inspired narrative that adeptly intertwines humor and social critique. It is a powerful satirical piece primarily aimed at a teenage audience. However, its message transcends age brackets... The protagonist, the spirited fourteen-year-old Blaze Union, is an embodiment of fearless resistance. This book stands out as a unique and imaginative work of satire that invites readers into a world where ludicrous norms are questioned and intellectual bravery is celebrated.
— Literary Titan

Highly conversational, this is a tale that reads with ease... Readers with an interest in stories that offer unique and intentional descriptions of the world through atypical lenses will appreciate both the design and storytelling found in this book.
— Reedsy Discovery

A wild, Swiftian piece of imagination, W.T. Kosmos has unleashed a book as funny as it is urgent, boldly taking on vital contemporary issues for young readers.
— Self-Publishing Review

Blaze Union... is a sensational tale, a story with memorable characters. It is hilarious, and the humor—as biting as it is—greets readers from the very first page... The social and political commentaries are marvelously written... and the quirkiness in the voice transforms it into a page-turning story.
— The Book Commentary

BLAZE UNION AND THE PUDDIN' HEAD SCHOOLS

by W.T. Kosmos

WISEWIT PRESS

Wise Wit Press, LLC

Blaze Union and the Puddin' Head Schools

Copyright © 2023 by W.T. Kosmos

Summary: A fourteen-year-old phenomenal guitar and football (soccer) player attempts to lead a Puddin' Head educational revolution against powerful, divisive knuckleheads, as told by a teacher seeking a cure for absurdity neurosis. For ages 12 to 128.

ISBN 979-8-9883151-2-4 e-book

ISBN 979-8-9883151-1-7 paperback

ISBN 979-8-9883151-0-0 hardcover

Cover art and illustrations by Spits Mullins

To Jasmine, Jules, Foster, and of course, Regal

We cannot solve our problems with the same level of thinking that created them.
— Albert Einstein

Never argue with a fool, onlookers may not be able to tell the difference.
— Mark Twain

We must learn to live together as brothers or perish together as fools.
— Martin Luther King Jr.

United we stand, divided we fall.
— Aesop

The louder he talked of his honor, the faster we counted our spoons.
— Ralph Waldo Emerson

Never doubt that a small group of thoughtful, committed citizens can change the world; indeed, it's the only thing that ever has.
— Margaret Mead

Your reason and your passion are the rudder and the sails of your seafaring soul.
If either your sails or your rudder be broken, you can but toss and drift, or else be held at a standstill in mid-seas.
For reason, ruling alone, is a force confining;
and passion, unattended, is a flame that burns to its own destruction.
— Khalil Gibran

CONTENTS

Sensitivity Warning...1
Map..2
Part I: The Absurd Beginning...3
Part II: Absurd Power..85
Part III: The Absurd Schools Tour....................................131
Part IV: The Absurd Awakening...273

Dear Courageous Reader,

If you are indeed courageous and hate spoilers of any kind, please skip to the next page. If you are unsure, be warned: This story is *absurd*. You might suddenly laugh, cry, shout, jump up and down, or head butt something. Let me explain.

After the book bans and seahorse protests at my school, I developed a case of *absurdity neurosis* so severe I could no longer teach! As a cure, my shrink recommended finding schools more absurd than mine. So, I visited Blaze Union and the Puddin' Head Schools. Although I am still shocked, I am grateful to be able to share Blaze's amazing story as an antidote to the absurdity spreading across our world.

I learned that knucklehead politicians divided Island Nation, stoking extreme school rivalries between the Puddin' Heads and Sweeties. Students are required to wear MegaCorp Frames and only read MegaCorp books (all other books have been banned). In class, students attempt to survive bootstraps, spoon helmet, and dynamite combat training. Students with large hands are not allowed to lead, play guitar, or play offense in soccer. This adventure also involves a cookie bomb, stick whacks to the noggin, dangerous hand-altering experiments, and a supreme prime minister no one dares challenge.

Sensitive readers may find these sorts of things too disturbing to read despite their own absurdity ailments. I'm sorry to tell you that sometimes human stupidity causes harm. I know that all of this is tough to think about; the truth sometimes *does* hurt. Thus, if you are hoping for a safe and comforting story, or a sappy romance, then please save yourself some time, close this book and find another. Life is short, you know. Besides, those kinds of stories will not alleviate absurdity neurosis one bit.

But for the brave truth seekers, read this story as quickly as your heart and mind can handle, and *before it is too late*.

Spoons up! Heigi hooga!

W.T. Kosmos
Paradox, USA, Earth, Milky Way

MAP

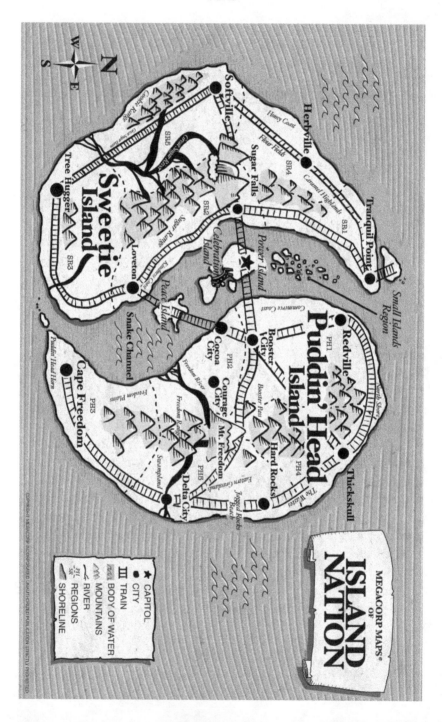

PART I
THE ABSURD BEGINNING

ABSURDITY NEUROSIS

When the first symptoms of my absurdity neurosis surfaced, I had not yet heard of Blaze Union. At this point, she was not famous, or powerful, or had a clue that she was about to catapult into an absurd journey of her own. Thus, I had no idea that our paths would cross. I had no idea that this fourteen-year-old would help cure my condition. And more importantly, I had no idea that she would inspire a ridiculous educational revolution.

Yes, we'll get to Blaze's astonishing story soon, but please allow me to first explain the origins of my absurdity neurosis, which is the only reason why Blaze and I met. Perhaps you, like me, have a few things about your school or your country that are silly, even ridiculous—which by the way *I would very much like to hear*. Maybe these silly things are indeed very funny. But perhaps you have a few things in your school or village or city that are so absurd, you not only want to laugh, you want to cry. Maybe you want to yell, "This is stupid!" Or perhaps they are so concerning, they are actually disturbing. These are telltale signs that Absurdity (with a capital A) is either laughing or lurking around the corner, ready to strike and infect you with absurdity neurosis, or the dreaded numbskull virus —much more on that later.

You see, after many years of strong public support for my school, and after I spent many years enjoying teaching and trying to do what was best for my students, some community members suddenly became suspicious and adversarial toward our school district. Sadly, they had been brainwashed by a cult leader whose only idea was to oppose anyone or anything that was not part of this cult. And get this: enough of these brainwashed followers—who had no professional experience in education whatsoever and refused to listen to anyone who disagreed—won seats on the school board to gain the majority. That meant they had the power to change things.

I'm sorry to share that despite strong opposition from many students, families, teachers, and myself, the school board went on a book banning rampage. First, they banned books that featured any color of the rainbow. Then, they banned books about climate change. Then books with human diversity, which—perhaps they did not realize—eliminated every book that included a human. Then, they banned books with unicorns, penguins, dinosaurs, and talking animals. As you can imagine, we were left with a very sad and empty library. It made me wonder what they did in that cult.

So now, on top of all the crazy things happening in the world, in my town of Paradox, USA, Earth, Milky Way, children can't read books with color, people, or talking animals? Because that would cause lower test scores? Because the school board believes that children are robots? Because they fear that children will act like penguins?

I'm not sure of their reasoning, because these brainwashed followers refuse to explain their absurd thinking. Perhaps more accurately, they can't even *see* their absurd thinking. Of course, these book bans are based in a bunch of baloney, but brainwashed people don't care much for truth or evidence. I heard these sorts of whackadoodle bans have spread to other cities and schools. Hopefully not yours.

Needless to say, it didn't take long before school morale plummeted, students were bored out of their minds, and nasty cliques, stereotypes, name-calling, and bullying began to spread like weeds. In only a few months, our school community and wonderful learning units—which we had carefully cultivated and developed over many years—withered and nearly vanished. I just wanted to teach, but that became impossible.

So, perhaps I should not have been surprised when they banned seahorses, too.

Sadly, it was partly my fault. With her family's permission, I did encourage Jasmine to share the video. Yes, I'd hoped it would go viral. Knowing what Jasmine had been through, and after the absurd book bans, and then the hurricane, we needed all the hope and support we could get. Jasmine was so proud to see her idea come to life, to make a difference.

Shortly after the book bans, the hurricane churned through the coastline. It decimated the fragile seagrass beds, coral reefs, and mangroves that hadn't already been lost to years of development, pollution, and fish trawling. The next day, seahorses—and much of their habitat—were strewn across the beach. Some of these poor creatures still gasped for breath, fighting for their lives.

Jasmine and her classmates rushed to gently return them to the ocean. But with nothing to wrap their tails around, the choppy waters just washed the seahorses back onto shore. These bright students realized that an obliterated habitat might render their kind act futile. Jasmine turned to me and asked two of my favorite questions, as if she had become the teacher. "Well, are we going to admire the problem? Or are we going to solve it?"

Jasmine and her peers pleaded to save the seahorses that had survived the storm, particularly this large one they named Regal. Typically, keeping wild seahorses is strongly discouraged or illegal. But under the circumstances, the local nature conservatory not only approved, they volunteered to help. What teacher could deny such thoughtful and passionate children?

A few days later, the wide-eyed students squealed and crowded around the enormous aquarium, gawking at an awe-inspiring surprise. Regal, who was male by the way, puffed out dozens of tiny seahorses that eventually numbered in the hundreds. We couldn't possibly count them all. Jasmine shouted that it was the most amazing thing she had ever seen. With a shaking hand, she captured the classroom's joy on video. Students danced and sang around the tank full of seahorses. Jasmine added insightful commentary, advocated for solutions, and proudly posted her video for the world to see. It went mega viral.

At first, the response was overwhelmingly positive. The nature conservatory was thrilled. A local news station ran a story. A local energy company loved Jasmine's video and agreed to donate and install solar panels in all the schools to fight climate change. The school, and most of the community, rallied, cheered, and gained new life. For a moment, I remembered why I'd become a teacher.

Yet, the video also triggered the brainwashed knuckleheads. Perhaps I should have anticipated this. The next day, a few oafs held up signs in the parking lot and yelled at students and teachers. One charged at me, apparently recognizing me from the video. "Males having babies is unnatural! It's not normal!"

I admit that while I strive to be a kind person, I struggle to be kind to adults who are being absurd. I understand how children can be brainwashed into absurd beliefs, but do adults ever have a good excuse for being brainwashed themselves? And now, adults were not only acting in absurd ways, they were messing with students. How was I supposed to teach? How could I say nothing? My emotions and surly sweet tooth got the best of me. I chomped down a chocolate bar, then corrected him, "Seahorse births are 100 percent natural. No artificial flavors, preservatives, or magic involved. As I can see that you appreciate the ways of science," I said, unwrapping and biting into the next chocolate bar, "you should know that those are juvenile, not baby seahorses. And if you want a seahorse, why didn't you just ask? We have plenty extra."

Of course, I would not have given him a seahorse. Regardless, he did not want one. Nor did he find my sarcasm one bit funny. I'm not sure if this was because he could not distinguish exaggeration from fact, or if he had a poor sense of humor. Brainwashing can really mess people up, you know.

Unfortunately, my comments and gestures—which he recorded and shared—inflamed the protesters. After a few social media posts, and sympathetic news interviews with these brainwashed whackadoodles, their numbers multiplied faster than Regal had shot tiny seahorses out of his brood pouch.

Three angry brainwashed groups eventually crowded in and around our parking lot. The Seahorse Denier group held signs and yelled things like, "Fake video! You can't fool us! Males can't have babies!" One sap—who'd driven several hundred miles and I suspect had never seen an ocean—stood beside a toppled palm tree and a mangled sign. She flat-out denied the hurricane, seahorses, video, and climate change altogether. "I don't see a hurricane—fake news! Climate change is fake news! Seahorses? Fake news!" But my personal favorite was, "Seahorses are as real as Godzilla!" This was particularly amusing—or perhaps sad—when you consider that, on this same day, Jasmine brought her three-year-old brother to see the seahorses after school. I asked him whether Regal was real or pretend. He emphatically said, "Real!" And then of a plastic Godzilla, "Pretend!" Jasmine wanted to post that video, but I said to let adults handle this skillfully.

Raising the bar above three-year-old proficiency, I handed a group of Seahorse Deniers select academic, character, and life skill competencies and standards. Although I teach older students, I could not resist making a strong teaching point. So, I gave them each a half-page handout—some with bonus chocolate fingerprints —in large font that read as follows.

Proficient Second Grade Students:
• distinguish fact and opinion, and support opinions with

reasoning and evidence
- distinguish between the truth and lying, and identify the consequences of lying
- demonstrate empathy to others who have different perspectives and beliefs

Admittedly, I did struggle with empathy proficiency, but I managed to politely ask the protesters what reasoning and evidence backed their opinions. They snarled. I asked them to explain Jasmine's video perspective on seahorses. They beat their chests and restated that seahorses aren't real. I asked if they would like to learn some seahorse facts. It is fair to say they were neither interested in learning facts nor hoping to engage in civil discourse. They pointed at their signs and shouted louder. Jasmine must have overheard this conversation and returned from school with a seahorse in a fishbowl. "What do you think that is?" she asked. They swiftly turned away, as if their unshakable beliefs had been slapped in the face. One denier pointed and said, "That's just a fish in a costume!" They ripped up my handouts, yelled to ban standards, and chased us inside.

The Save the Children group held up signs and yelled, "*Save the children!*" and "*No seahorses in school!*" One screaming couple held up a large sign that showed two words circled and crossed out with a thick marker: No Indocternation! They yelled at teachers to, "Stop doctoring lies about seahorses!"

> Facts: This couple (a) also fell into the seahorse denier group, (b) had poor spelling, (c) technically argued to indoctrinate students, because double negatives make a positive, and (d) also failed to meet second grade standards.

> Opinion: This Save the Children group engaged in actions that ultimately harmed children, as evidenced by the number of children they scared, made cry, or who didn't return to school. This is ironic, given their purported purpose. As a consequence, they should plant seagrass and mangroves while wearing *I Love Seahorses* T-shirts.

Finally, there was the Seahorse Hater group. They angrily circled and shouted. One doofus knocked down students arriving at school and ran through the building. He searched for the seahorse tank and yelled, "*Smash seahorses!*" Yes, this caused a hugely disruptive school lockdown. Yes, he was thrown in jail. But this imbecile only inspired others, who marched with frothing mouths and signs that featured cartoons of dead seahorses. One sign had an X for each eye and a tongue hanging out—which is factually impossible by the way. I decided against giving them the second grade standards handout. One provocateur—who admitted he had never eaten a seahorse, nor intended to—passed out shirts that read *Seahorse Kebab* (which is a factually accurate, albeit controversial, cuisine. I'm sure you can find a picture on the Internet). A video of the chuckling Seahorse Kebab group went viral, which drew the ire of counter-protesters.

The next day, droves of Save the Seahorses protesters arrived with a vengeance. Some flew in from the West Coast. The pro-seahorse and anti-seahorse protesters set up tailgate spots, tents, and canopies that extended from our school for at least a mile. Some pro-seahorse protesters raised awareness about global endangered seahorse populations. But to my chagrin, many pro-seahorse protesters seemed more concerned about talking—or partying and winning an actual weirdest person contest—than doing anything meaningful, supporting our school, or caring about our students' well-being. Some yelled at students and teachers to "remove wild seahorses from school!" I explained that we had a special plan, but they didn't care. Some yelled at the Seahorse Hater protesters and chanted with signs that read *Seahorses Are People, Too!* and thereby also failed to meet second grade standards.

The news had a field day. Imagine the footage. It was quite the spectacle.

But that wasn't enough absurdity for the universe to throw at me. The school board then banned all skills, competencies, and standards from school. They banned staff and students from recording, sharing, or posting videos. They banned solar panels. And they banned seahorses. In fact, they banned all animals from school —live animals, animal specimens and exhibits, stuffed animals, and toy animals—including the plastic Godzilla. Sensing a huge photo op, the governor and a senator flew down in a private jet, declared a hurricane state of emergency, and posed with the anti-seahorse protesters. They ridiculed the pro-seahorse protesters, which only caused more to show up. These politicians praised the school board for their good work, suggesting we were a model district. Then they announced in the name of freedom, that anyone—including potty trained children—who disagreed with these book and animal bans, or said controversial words such as rainbow, unicorn, or seahorse, would promptly be ticketed or thrown in jail. My principal—who had, months earlier, suggested I consider school leadership—now said this was becoming a ridiculous distraction. Besides, he had no choice: it was the seahorses or me. Well, I agreed that it was ridiculous.

So, I laughed like a lunatic. I shouted words you aren't supposed to say in school. I ran to my classroom, slammed the door, and cried a very long while. At least Regal was empathetic. You must understand that I love teaching. I love students' wild curiosity and imagination. I love watching them blossom and grow. Yes, my students are more amazing than seahorses.

My last day was very hard. Our classroom had no books, no seahorses, and no joy. Although it was comforting that the nature conservatory had carefully transported and released Regal and the seahorses into a better habitat farther down the coast, which fortunately was near my home, I've never seen such sad student faces. I promised to snorkel and share pictures (videos were banned), but Jasmine was inconsolable. I felt sucker punched in the gut by an absurd force.

That evening, I struggled mightily to suppress a terrible idea. But it finally surfaced. And it shook my soul. *Maybe I should quit teaching.* When I tried to return to school the next day, I just couldn't do it. I couldn't even enter the parking lot. My heart ached. My eyes swelled shut. I literally couldn't see. Perhaps I didn't want to see. I thought I was having a panic attack, but it was something much worse.

I am very sorry to share that I developed a serious condition. It was complex and difficult to diagnose. My shrink asked me many questions. I took many tests. At first, it seemed that I suffered from a double whammy of a *career crisis* (do I want to keep teaching?) and an *existential crisis* (what is the meaning of life given this absurd world?).

My shrink finally concluded that underneath it all, I had developed a severe case of *absurdity neurosis*. Not to be confused with an alternate personality, I had developed an alter ego that emerged in the presence of absurdity. My alter ego—indeed my entire being—desperately wanted relief. I just wanted to teach!

Yet, even worse, my sources insisted that I was not the only one. More and more students, educators, families, and citizens were suffering from absurdity neurosis. And the only cure, according to my shrink, was to face my fears and find schools more absurd than mine. Perhaps write a book about it. Imagination has wonderful healing potential.

Of course, this suggestion was ridiculous! So, I bet my colleague —who had traveled to many countries around the world—that no other school could possibly be so absurd as ours. She smiled and shared a strange story developing on Puddin' Head Island. She suggested I pay a visit.

Guess who won the bet?

ODD COUNTRY

I sincerely doubted that Puddin' Head Island had schools more absurd than mine. But I crossed countries and oceans to see if my colleague's claim was true. Besides, I needed a break.

And yes, after I met Blaze Union and understood her story, I realized that, sure, my community had too many knuckleheads. Some were elected or appointed to positions of power, where they made stupid decisions. But imagine if your school was almost entirely taught and led by numbskulls. Or most of your region. Or most of your country. Would you come to appreciate your current situation? Maybe you'd think, *Well, at least we don't live on Puddin' Head Island.* Or perhaps you would think, *Yikes, this is a warning of what could happen!* Or, *No, my school is still more absurd.* Regardless of your answer, as you read this story, I suspect that you will become more and more appreciative of the fabulous teachers and school leaders you know. I do hope you'll give them a thank you letter, a high five, a fist bump, or a hug, if your school hasn't banned such things.

You see, I owe Blaze a great deal. To be precise, she helped restore my sanity. She helped cure my absurdity neurosis. Blaze even helped me think up my pen name. I'm sure you'll figure it out by the end of this story. You are a smart person, you know.

In short, if you are craving relief from absurdity neurosis or seeking dare I say, *absurdity immunity*—and finding absurd people and places is the antidote, or the vaccine—then Puddin' Head Island is a very good place to start. But I don't want to be unfair here. I suppose every country and culture has its oddities. Clearly, mine is no exception. Nothing wrong with being odd, perhaps we all are. Puddin' Heads might, like me, find aspects of my community absurd. Perhaps they could visit Paradox, USA to cure their absurdity neuroses.

As I foreshadowed in the *Sensitivity Warning*, Blaze truly lives in a strange and confusing country. A wacky world that somehow remained relatively isolated from the rest of the planet Earth. It took me a long time to even begin to understand this country, and, in turn, my own. So, let me suggest a few simple ideas to prevent confusion. Odd thoughts and beliefs, like believing seahorses are not real, lead to odd behavior—like saying, "That is not a seahorse, that is a fish in a costume!" This is *absurd funny* because it is so willfully stupid. However, extremely odd beliefs—particularly ones that lack a shred of evidence—lead to extremely odd behavior. This is *absurd disturbing* because that is when people get hurt. But perhaps I am biased, ethnocentric, or projecting my own issues. So don't take my word for it. Notice it for yourself.

Here is a defining moment that Blaze shared with me about her older brother, Kuko, which illustrates *absurd disturbing*. A teacher asked the Puddin' Head class to watch Sweetie News. Their assignment was to identify "all the outrageous lies, whether big or small." Zuli Sweet—the famously attractive Sweetie news anchor hated by nearly all Puddin' Heads—warned of a rare thunderstorm moving across Island Nation. Despite the rain pounding the roof like puddin' bowls, the teacher yelled, "See! That report is fake news! It's a trick to make us stay inside while the Sweeties prepare to attack!" And if you, like me, already find this ridiculous, wait till you hear this next bit.

The teacher demanded that Kuko run outside with an iron spoon to thwart the Sweeties, because he had large hands. Kuko did as he was told. He was immediately struck by lightning. He stumbled back inside with smoking hair and charred, soaking clothing. Kuko whimpered, "All clear," and fell to the floor. The teacher thanked him for his courage, called an ambulance, and sent another student with large hands and a spoon outside.

Suffering migraines and memory lapses, Kuko dropped out of school shortly thereafter. Yes, this was absurd disturbing. And for Blaze, this traumatic event only served to strengthen her obsession with eliminating large hand rules from schools. And her hatred of the Sweeties.

ABSURD-CROSSED JOURNEYS

After reviewing my extensive interview notes along with news footage and hours of video clips taken from MC Frames—and, of course, consulting with Blaze—it only made sense to start Blaze's story on the day that she received her final red card, about two weeks before our ridiculous journeys would cross. This day would launch Blaze down an unexpected path of absurd challenges and opportunities to transform the schools of Puddin' Head Island—to obliterate those ridiculous rules about large hands, perhaps once and for all.

I was shocked to learn that this eighth grader had already been expelled from twenty-two schools. Blaze went into the school year intending to avoid a red card, which would mean another expulsion. And she had promised someone important that this year would be different: "Mom, really! I will stay in one school the whole, entire year!"

In fact, Blaze didn't have much choice. Puddin' Head Middle School was the only Region 2 middle school from which she had not been expelled. Another school expulsion would mean another transfer. Her family would have to move to a different region of Puddin' Head Island to find a new school. Or else, Blaze would have to drop out of school altogether, like many other kids with big hands did, including her brother, Kuko.

Blaze really did not want to be expelled again. Her family would endure even more hardship: transfer fees, new school fees, moving expenses, not to mention the costs and stress of finding somewhere else to live. Her mom might even have to find a new job. Worse, another expulsion would prevent Blaze from achieving her ultimate goal of changing the ridiculous school rules and activities, especially ones involving discrimination against those with large hands. How could she possibly change the rules of a school if she wasn't actually in one?

But this was exactly Blaze's problem: nearly all of her red card expulsions involved arguing about or fighting against rules about large hands. If you had large hands—or were considered a *Big*—you were not allowed to lead, you paid more school fees, and you always got second choice in comparison to the *Smalls*, or people with small hands.

Blaze met her best friend, Chopper, as they strolled to school.

Chopper shook his head. "Please tell me you're not bringing that guitar to school."

"We've talked about making big changes. Today's the day."

"What?"

"I'm done! I'm talking to Walka Walka. He can change these stupid rules."

"You're not answering my question."

"You didn't ask a question."

"Why the *guitar*?"

"Backup plan."

"You just got a yellow card!"

"That goal should have counted! I scored from midfield!" Blaze kicked a football (in my part of the world, a soccer ball) which hit a tree and bounced straight back. She trapped it with her thigh and dribbled it between her feet, her guitar slung over her back.

"And why should that count as a yellow card in the football match *and* a yellow card at school?!"

"Because it was a school sponsored event. Good thing it wasn't a red card."

"Ahhh! I tried to play with these rules Chopper. But I just can't. Back when I had small hands, I scored all the time! The rule that Bigs can only play defense makes no sense!"

"How long has it been?" Chopper asked.

"Three years." Blaze popped the football up with her toe, dribbled it on her knees, and blasted it off a tree again.

"Maybe you should just accept it."

"*I tried that*! But a yellow card for scoring from midfield?! I *was* playing defense. How are we going to make it to the playoffs?"

"Maybe we still can. Maybe we can win the title."

Blaze snorted. "Not with these dumb rules and me stuck playing defense."

"Yeah. But even if you could play offense, has the MC Academy team ever lost?"

"No."

"Well, what do you expect? They *all* have small hands."

"Are you serious?" Blaze yelled, punting the ball sky-high, and clenching her fists.

Chopper raised his eyebrows. "Then why are they undefeated?"

Blaze caught the speeding missile with her left foot and dribbled it in the air again. "Maybe because they all get to play offense. Maybe because the rules are to their advantage!"

Chopper burst out laughing. "Got you!"

Blaze hung her head, let out a long breath, and shoved her friend. "Funny. Real funny."

"But seriously, MegaCorp and Scarlet Pompavich would destroy us."

"Whatever. I heard her hands aren't even real. Small hands surgery."

"Still counts. Anyway, you already have a *yellow card*! A red card means no school, which means no *football*. Again."

Blaze huffed, then thought a moment. "Why is it so hard for people to change stupid ideas and rules? Maybe they're *afraid* to change."

Chopper shrugged, then smirked. "At least we aren't Sweeties."

Blaze clapped her hands and buckled over laughing. "Great Mother of Puddin', can you imagine if we played them in football? We'd win 25—0." She strummed a few chords on her guitar.

Chopper nodded. "Or more. You know, Good Hope Day is coming up soon—maybe you'll switch back to being Small. Then you could play offense again."

Blaze rolled her eyes. "That's not going to happen. And I'm going to lose my puddin' head if Maya's hand measurement is large. She actually believes that nonsense." (Maya is Blaze's younger sister.)

"They should just put me in charge!" Blaze grunted. "Of schools *and* football. It can't be that hard to be the boss. You just tell people what to do. We could make big changes Chopper, big changes. No more hand rules. No more bootstraps classes."

"Yeah, but you're not the boss."

"I know that!" Blaze quickened her pace as they neared Puddin' Head Middle School. "I can't get another red card. But I can't live like this, Chopper! Talking to Walka Walka is my best chance right now. And if talking doesn't work, then maybe a song will." She strummed her guitar again as they walked past School Boss Walka

Walka's gold-plated luxury car and rows of beat-up student and teacher bikes.

"Blaze! You know you're not allowed to lead singing!"

BOOTSTRAPS CLASS

Blaze burst through the entrance to Puddin' Head Middle School and strode to School Boss Walka Walka's office. She tapped her puddin' head three times, and said, "No. Red. Card."

She pounded on the door. The school boss didn't answer. Blaze sighed and shuffled toward the large outdoor training facility. She found a seat in the back alongside Chopper and the other students with large hands. She adjusted her MC Frames, which transitioned from clear to dark in the bright sun and concealed her intense brown eyes. She pulled the Frames off her face and cleaned the lenses on her red shirt. She ran fingers through her hair and over the flame that her aunt shaved into the side of her head. Her hair spiked in the back and flopped down the side of her head and face. Blaze slipped her MC Frames back on and heaved a deep sigh.

Everyone on Island Nation owned some version of these high-tech MC Frames: basic, limited, or elite. Due to the risk fees for Blaze's large hands, her mom could only afford the free basic government issued MC Frames. Although the basic model did not come with virtual reality, telescoping, hologram projection or a number of other features, Blaze still loved hers. They had auto dimming, they automatically adjusted the lenses to give the wearer perfect vision, and they also offered music, gaming, videos, (limited) Internet access, and new apps every day. On Puddin' Head Island, most people chose MC Frames in red with a black stripe or, like in Blaze's case, black with a red stripe.

While Blaze loved many features of her Frames, she found two aspects aggravating. One, the frown face that lit up on each arm of her Frames (to remind people she could not lead singing, the dismissal line, and so on). Two, annoying advertisements frequently flashed across her interior view.

She sighed again. Of all the stupid morning classes, she hated bootstraps class the most. Students attempted to pull themselves up by their bootstraps onto a platform without stepping, jumping, or using any muscle of their lower body. Students chose from a wide variety of boots including football boots ("cleats," in my country), work boots (low-cut, medium-cut, leather, steel-toed, etc.), and long boots ("cowgirl boots," in my country). Students were supposed to use boot laces or back straps (either was permissible).

Now, you might think this must be easy. But after you try a few times you will quickly see it is not. And then you might wonder why this course was required throughout all Puddin' Head Region 2 schools. If you were born in Puddin' Head Region 2, by the time you were five, you would know that successful bootstrapping students received big rewards. This year, students hoped to complete this rare accomplishment with a new set of wooden platforms, boots, and bootstraps.

Blaze whispered to Chopper. "Is bootstraps class: a) boring, b) useless, c) impossible, or d) ridiculous?"

"All of the above," Chopper said flatly.

Grimacing, Blaze punched her fist into her hand. She longed for a school without stupid large hand rules. A school without large hand fees. A school where Bigs didn't have to work afternoons making boots, bootstraps, and platforms in the hot workshop. (They were big sellers, particularly in Region 2.) But Blaze didn't have much choice: working afternoons offset her large hand risk fees and paid for her morning of school.

Mr. Peabody reminded the red-shirted class, "This is an important character-building skill that will help us defeat the Sweeties. You never know when you'll need it! And today we have some special guests. Let's give a big welcome to our Knucklehead Elementary students who are here to give us extra motivation!"

Blaze was shocked to see her younger sister Maya. Blaze waved, whistled, and cheered. The rest of her middle school peers mockingly clapped, rolled their eyes, or made faces at the youngsters.

Regardless of this apathetic welcome, it was indeed a special event. Puddin' Head Island students rarely had music or art lessons, let alone performances, although these classes were more common on the left side of the island. Blaze's ability to play the guitar was even more rare—a skill she'd learned from her dad.

Maya stood in the back row of her class, with the other Bigs. The small-handed guests played "Puddin', Puddin', Pop" on their recorders while the Bigs sang along. When the instrumental group reached the note "pop," they turned around and whacked their singing friends on the head with their recorders. Most of the middle school students laughed, but Blaze shot out her arms in outrage. "Really? Come on! This is ridiculous!" When I saw the MC Frame video clip, I also found this absurdly disturbing. Why would teachers encourage students to do this?

After the first song ended, Mr. Peabody said, "Okay, enough gawking! Listen while you practice pulling yourself up by your bootstraps. This is a life-long skill and mindset!"

Chopper tapped his head, reminding Blaze to avoid a red card. Blaze coaxed Mr. Peabody to allow Maya to watch her practice. Thus, Maya avoided further whacks to the head.

Shortly after another synchronized head crack, Dimbul—one of the most committed students—yelled, "I did it!" His team had used a new strategy of double laces, one pair with red and white stripes and one that was solid dark red.

Students rushed over as he stood proudly on the ten-centimeter platform and yelled different opinions. *Liar! No way! Did he really?*

Blaze said, "Whatever," but walked over with Chopper.

Mr. Peabody was also unimpressed. "Dimbul's team, while I appreciate your hard work and enthusiasm, pulling yourself up by your bootstraps requires *independent effort*. You must lift *yourself* off the ground, onto a platform by only—and once again, *independently*—pulling your bootstraps. I noticed Maki gave you a lift."

Mr. Peabody quickly displayed the video replay on a large monitor, clearly showing this assisted lift. He quashed any hint of argument. Dimbul ducked his head, gently kicked the platform, apologized for kicking the platform, and said he would work harder. The other teams snickered and mocked his team for failing.

Blaze scoffed, "Shocking!" In all her years at different schools, Blaze had never seen a successful mount. She didn't even know a single student who directly witnessed one. Supposedly, according to Mr. Peabody and MegaCorp videos of five-star students, the most recent Puddin' Head Middle School student to accomplish this feat had been Charlene Fibb, who, years ago, had pulled herself up by her bootstraps on the five-centimeter, ten-centimeter and coveted fifteen-centimeter platforms. This success propelled her to graduate with honors, receive a college scholarship, and later land a consulting job with MegaCorp.

The middle school students returned to practicing. Blaze hugged Maya and took her to rejoin her classmates. Blaze asked the elementary teacher, "How about playing a different song—maybe one without skull smacks?" Blaze was pleasantly surprised that the teacher agreed. Maybe that was why she became overconfident. Blaze pretended to pull her bootstraps. She made funny faces at Chopper. Mid-way through class—with Mr. Peabody giving pointers across the dirt yard—Blaze took two slow-motion, fake, exaggerated, floating arm pull lifts and steps backwards onto the platform. She opened her mouth in amazement. She widened her eyes. She raised her arms in a slow celebration, as if she had accomplished the impossible and a stadium of people cheered. Chopper snorted, then looked down as Mr. Peabody glanced over. Blaze quickly stepped down from the platform.

Mr. Peabody barked his favorite call and response. Acting as a military officer—with even greater enthusiasm for the benefit of his wide-eyed elementary guests—Mr. Peabody said, "Attennnn-tion! Class, did you work hard today during bootstraps training?!"

The class marched over and shouted back: "Yes, sir, Mr. Peabody, sir!"

"Class, were you afraid to fail today? Were you afraid of losing? Afraid to be weak? Or did you have the courage to be the best, to be strong, to be successful?!"

"We have the courage to win, sir!"

"Followers . . ."

"Follow!"

"And leaders . . ."

"Lead!"

"Class, why do we have bootstraps training?!"

"To be strong, to be successful! To be free!"

Mr. Peabody pointed at the red banner displayed in every classroom on Puddin' Head Island, and on his command, in unison, the class barked each of the Puddin' Head values:

Puddin' Head Island Values
- Puddin' Heads Good. Sweeties Bad.
- Hard Work and Strength
- Competition
- Courage
- Respect Authority
- Freedom
- Success

As a side note, Mr. Peabody later told me that he thought
"Respect Authority" deserved to be the first or the last value, so
that students would more easily remember it. But the education
minister on Power Island made those decisions. He took comfort in
knowing that she'd at least had the good sense to update "Respect"
to "Respect Authority" during the second revision.

After the prideful Puddin' Head chanting, Mr. Peabody
continued. "Now, class, some students think they're so smart they
can work hard, be courageous, and even be free and successful
without adult guidance or supervision. Is this true class? Can you do
this all on your own?"

"No sir, Mr. Peabody, sir!"

"Some followers forget to let others lead. Can followers lead?"

"No, sir, Mr. Peabody, sir! Followers follow, leaders lead!"

Mr. Peabody now reveled in delivering his teaching point. "But
today, one of you did not live these values during bootstraps
training. One of you thought you'd be Mr. Funny Guy. Blaze Union,
I couldn't help but . . ."

Blaze interrupted, "With all due respect, sir, I am not a funny
guy. Rather, I am a funny girl." The class boomed with laughter.

Chopper shot her a look that said to shut up and avoid a red
card. Maya curled her bottom lip and sniffled. She knew what would
happen if Blaze got a red card.

Mr. Peabody puffed out his chest and cheeks. He clenched his
fists. Then, he sighed, paused, and tapped the smiley face on his
Frames. He released his grip and said calmly, "Ahem. Ms. Blaze
Union, funny girl. Did you take your chill booster with your puddin'
today?"

"None of your business. With all due respect, sir."

"Hmph! Well, I couldn't help but notice your poor work ethic
today. Sometimes, I think you believe you can lead others. You seem
to enjoy being the class clown, distracting the class, and worst of
all, disrespecting authority—"

"With all due respect, sir, I am respectfully being respectful,"
Blaze said.

Chopper glared at her.

Blaze mouthed, "Okay, okay." She looked down to avoid

confrontation, but it was too late.

"Oh yes, keep it up! Your words, your tone, your actions—everything about you is disrespectful! I put up with a lot of things in this school: rooms that aren't maintained, outdated materials, new transfer students every week, a school boss with no experience—well, I won't go there—no planning time, no time to eat or use the bathroom for that matter. I put up with all of this because I believe in teaching for a better Puddin' Head Island and nation. But one thing I will not tolerate is disrespect."

Maya started to cry. Blaze kept her eyes on the ground, trying to resist saying something she would regret.

Mr. Peabody did not let up. "Now, you young lady already have a yellow card. Perhaps you do not even believe in the importance of pulling yourself up by your bootstraps, which builds the character, work ethic, and perseverance you will need for the rest of your life. Which prepares us to defend against the Sweeties."

Blaze could not resist. She tried her very best to ask respectfully, "Could you please explain how bootstraps class prepares us for a Sweetie attack?" It was a legitimate question.

"Are you really asking that? Isn't it obvious? Do you even *care* about being courageous or successful?"

Blaze locked eyes with Mr. Peabody. Her confident expression lacked apology.

Mr. Peabody paused. "Maybe, you should drop out of school like your loser brother." Everyone held their breath.

Blaze ran her fingers along the flame carved into her head, which now pulsed with anger. Her hands began to sweat. Her eyes widened and nostrils flared, like a bull ready to charge. She blinked several times. "Or maybe . . ." she said, pausing for effect, "you should learn how to teach."

The class let out a collective, "Ohhhh!"

Someone yelled, "Burn! Blaze one. Peabody zero."

Suddenly, *Code Blue* sirens sounded across the school.

ODD HISTORY

Before we get to the Code Blue, I am guessing that one group of readers wants to know how Puddin' Head Schools became so absurd. If so, read on. And I yes, I know—there is another group of readers screaming, "WTK! Get to the action already!" If that is you, go ahead: be a rebel, skip to the next chapter. But I fear that you'll be very confused, just like Blaze and I both were. Your choice—you can always come back and read this chapter later.

Here is a very brief history that I wish I knew before I set foot on Puddin' Head Island. I hope this summary will help guide your journey. Oh, and as protection, you might want to get a spoon hat soon. Or better, a spoon helmet.

A ridiculously long time ago, one large island emerged from volcanoes erupting in the ocean. Over the course of millions of years, volcanic forces—along with the wind, rain, and crushing ocean—shaped this island. As you can see from the map at the start of this book, a winding channel emerged and broke the island into two, with smaller islands scattered in between.

Over centuries, waves of immigrants arrived by ships, bringing along their customs and cultures. These various groups co-existed, mingled, grew, and evolved over generations. Many people on the large, western island developed kind and caring large communities that enjoyed nature and leisure. Many people on the eastern large island—perhaps in part due to the harsher climate—prized rugged self-reliance, hard work, and independence. Yet despite their differences, the island people exchanged various goods and lived in relative harmony. They formed one nation of islands, known as Island Nation.

Sounds nice, right? It was, until a sociopath scientist arrived several generations ago.

Livid to have been fired for conducting dangerous experiments on research subjects with large hands (several died), the sociopath sailed around the world to fulfill his mission and to avoid prison. After landing on Island Nation, he "discovered" a wide variety of rare and valuable medicinal, flavorful, and potent plants. (Of course, the islanders had known about these incredible plants for generations.) Perhaps some plants could shrink hands, he hoped.

This outcast scientist shared his "discovery" with corrupt friends who also happened to have small hands. Before long, ships of outcast politicians, scientists, soldiers, investors, and a ragtag circus with a few elephants and ponies arrived eager to exploit this new land. But the outcast scientist obsessed about his extraordinarily tiny hands, which confused and disturbed his corrupt comrades. After days of passive-aggressive avoidance (*I'm not staring at my hands!*), he finally shared his compelling boyhood story. As the youngest lad of eighteen children, his oldest brother one day gave him a noogie, but not the friendly one that says, *you're okay kid*, but rather the noogie with a headlock and knuckle skull scrub that hisses, *you are the bane of my existence*. When he cried, instead of intervening, his sixteen other siblings tortured him. The more he cried, the more noogies he received. The next day he ambushed his eldest brother with a revenge noogie. Alas, his tiny hands only tickled his brother's noggin. His siblings ridiculed his *itty-bitty hands*. They delivered daily rounds of noogies with seemingly monstrous hands and knuckles. Rather than intervening, his parents chuckled, "Kids will be kids." News traveled fast. Soon, his peers—all of whom seemed to have gargantuan hands—gave constant noogies, especially at recess, which became his least favorite part of the day. Unfortunately, instead of changing into a person who thwarted cruel noogies, he swore revenge on all large-handed people.

By the way, other sources revealed that his teachers were ordered to only teach the three R's: readin', ritin', and rithmetic. Not only were teachers at this school treated and trained like simpletons, they were banned from teaching about Aesop's Fables, positive behavior, and other cultures. They were banned from giving consequences for misbehavior, and in this case, stopping a relentless barrage of noogies, all of which was unfortunate for this poor child, and the future of Island Nation. Thus, this boy did not grow up to create noogie prevention inventions such as spoon hats. Neither did he become the No Noogie superhero, and thereby was denied the likely adoration of chanting fans. *No Noogie! No Noogie!* Rather, the victim who was bullied became a bully, who became a sociopath. And the rest, as they say, is history.

After hearing this passionate story, the newly arrived immigrants shook their fists and shouted, *No noogies!* But they were not cheering for superheroes; they were protesting terrible large-handed noogies. This absurd fear morphed into dread of being controlled by people with large hands. Strangely, many of the Island Nation newbies gained power by retelling the aforementioned ridiculous, yet convincing story. They promised great power to island leaders perceived to have small hands. Moreover, islanders with small hands didn't want mean noogies, and quickly warmed up to the idea that they were naturally superior beings.

Now that may seem unfair, sad, or strange, but here's something stranger: the power-hungry rulers kept Island Nation's democratic process of voting, which now included voting for the prime minister, regional senators, and other government officials. I'm guessing that Absurdity cheered when the failed sociopath scientist easily won the first prime minister election, and nearly all small-handed candidates won their elections by running a campaign based on . . . well, having small hands (which by the way, were never officially verified as small).

Despite gaining absurd power, the new rulers remained paranoid about being overthrown and ruled by large-handed people, or as noted earlier, *Bigs*. Thus, the delusional rulers created laws against people with large hands. Bigs were absolutely not allowed to lead; they must follow. Suddenly, people perceived to have large hands lost jobs, houses, and their spots in the football match or lunch line. Suddenly, everyone wanted small hands. People with noticeably large hands became resentful because they now always followed Smalls. Arguments on whether people with medium hands had large or small hands sometimes turned into brutal fights. Citizens increasingly complained and criticized the new rulers.

The insecure rulers responded by creating laws against criticizing government officials. They called people with large hands troublemakers. Some Bigs were tortured with public noogies. But the uprisings grew.

The prime minister—still traumatized from childhood noogies—devised an ingenious "distract, divide, and conquer" plan. First, they named the main islands Sweetie Island (to the West) and Puddin' Head Island (to the East). Then they turned the main islands against each other by causing problems and blaming the other island. It didn't take long after sacred desserts were destroyed, "large hands" was spray painted on houses, or people were beaten up by thugs in red or blue masks that the islands started hating each other and their differences. It didn't take long before it was us versus them, Bigs versus Smalls, red versus blue, courage versus kindness, thick heads versus zombies, and even puddin' versus cake.

It didn't take long before the corrupt rules formed a mega company that became ridiculously rich off the feuding Puddin' Head and Sweetie Islands. It was no coincidence that they built this mega company and the Capitol Building on Power Island.

The new rulers grew more powerful, wealthier, and they built elite schools. The other islands grew poorer, watched their schools crumble, and loathed each other like siblings who gave nasty noogies. Yet the rulers remained paranoid about large-handed leaders of any sort. And they had a problem: it wasn't obvious who had large hands or small ones.

So, the prime minister invented Good Hope Day. This ridiculous event started as a colossal, embarrassing failure that citizens laughed about for many years. In preparation for the first Good Hope Day, the rulers required all islanders—adults and children five years or older—to measure and record their hand size. In theory, this would allow them to calculate average hand sizes for each age. To be fair and avoid medium hand controversy, 50 percent of citizens would have large hands and the other 50 percent small hands. Of course, by now, everyone wanted to be a Small.

To keep the islands distracted and divided, the cunning prime minister did not use a national hand size average. Rather, the five regions of Puddin' Head Island and the five regions of Sweetie Island competed against each other (sort of). For example, the citizens of Puddin' Head Region 1 and Sweetie Region 1 were lumped together. The government determined the 50 percent with large hands and the 50 percent with small hands in each regional competition. Thus, on Good Hope Day, if you were a Puddin' Head in Region 1, you hoped the Sweeties in Region 1 had grown larger hands. And you really hoped your hand size was labeled small.

To make the meaning of these differences clear, the government automatically assigned people a leader or follower status, based on their hand size. Then, after Good Hope Day, they would send citizens a headband with either a smiley face (meaning "leader") or frown face (meaning "follower"), which they were then required to wear in public.

This nonsensical plan backfired badly, which of course, infuriated the rulers. Many citizens lied about measurements. Many Bigs "lost" their headbands. Others wore their frown face headbands upside down.

After decades of confusing and failed law enforcement, the third prime minister—the small-handed granddaughter of the first prime minister—shared a bold, new vision. And in less than a year, the paranoid rulers, and the mega company—now named MegaCorp—invented MC Frames. These Frames, which looked like sleek sunglasses, were assigned to each individual. Sure, MC Frames had

practical features that citizens loved, but more important to
MegaCorp, these Frames could accurately measure hand size and lit
up automatically with the appropriate smiley or frown face. Once
the MC Frames proved effective, the delusional rulers partied for
many days and nights. Their investment in technology had paid off.

Although this invention had many perks, it did not eliminate
resistance. Citizens with big hands borrowed smiley face Frames
from friends and family or stole them all the time. Then, eye
recognition software was installed to ensure each person wore their
correct own Frames. If a person wore the wrong pair, the MC
Frames would emit piercing sounds and bright, flashing lights. Bigs
countered with creative solutions. They covered their frown faces
with long hair, hats, tape, scarves, permanent markers, and so on. A
new law was passed. It stated that the smiley or frown face must be
always visible, or else citizens would be thrown in jail. And, yes,
flashing MC alarms would go off.

Eventually, after years of being thrown in jail, many citizens
gave up. Although fears of mean noogies faded, citizens accepted
that a naturally occurring difference—in this case, human hand size
—symbolized something important, indeed something that divided
people into superior or inferior groups. Of course, this was absurd!

However, in case you're wondering, my mental health had a
choppy ride as I learned about this history. At first, as my shrink
predicted, my absurdity neurosis improved. Then, it worsened as my
studies roused a terrible memory. When I was three, after being
wrongfully denied a second chocolate chip cookie, I snuck a few
bites of my uncle's cookie. As the nibbles revealed an obvious thief,
he taught me an unforgettable lesson. That night, I tiptoed and side-
shuffled across a dark kitchen, climbed on top of a chair, and
reached for that plate of mouth-watering cookies. And just as my
little fingers pulled a cookie off the plate, Uncle Brute jumped out
of the closet dressed as a giant bunny wrapped in bright lights,
banging a pot with a ladle. Perhaps Uncle Scary (as I called him for
many years after this evening) worried that wouldn't leave a lasting
impression because in the next instant, my potty-mouthed older
cousin Brute Jr. leaped out of the closet as a second bunny with
glowing red eyes, swearing and bashing pans together. Not only did
this traumatic event scare the cookies right out of me, it caused—
according to my shrink—my repressed animosity toward adults
harming children (good intentions or not) as well as my
unpredictable and surly sweet tooth. Drat! I knew what my shrink

would say: "If you want to cure your condition, then you've got to face your fears and do the courageous work." So, I strapped on my scuba mask and snorkel (at this time, I didn't have a spoon helmet), diving deeper into the history of Island Nation as well as that awful memory of the seemingly supernatural rabbits. And just as fast as my absurdity condition deteriorated, my health strengthened as I uncovered something profound: my ambivalence toward mysterious forces. Yes! This discovery explained how I'd failed to recognize Absurdity as a phenomenon just as astonishing as love, evolution, the gravitation pull of the moon, the taste of chocolate, and rabbit poop that fertilizes cocoa plants. But then, instead of finding a remedy for my condition, my courageous research and insight only led to more questions. *Why did Absurdity exist? How did it choose who or what to torment, tickle, or wrestle? Why me? Why Blaze?* And, *how could we possibly defeat this absurd force that had surely been around since the demise of the dinosaurs?* Oh, those poor creatures. Alas, all these thoughts and questions made my eyes twitch rapidly.

Speaking of odd history, Bigs were indeed hopeful they would become Smalls on Good Hope Day, especially if their hand size was near the regional average. Smalls hoped their hand size would remain small and of course, feared the reverse scenario. This happened to Blaze three years ago, amid a growth spurt.

Blaze woke up early on that Good Hope Day. She slid on her MC Frames, crossed her fingers, and watched in horror as her smiley face switched to a frown. Blaze screamed in front of the mirror. She ran outside and screamed again. "But I had small hands just yesterday!" Within minutes, people ran out of their homes to either curse with Blaze or else to smile and cheer. On that day, like every Good Hope Day, half the nation celebrated, and the other half swore, yelled, or cried.

So, at this point in our story, you and I might find much of Blaze's country and history odd, or perhaps *absurd disturbing*. But in Blaze's experience, it was normal. It was normal that large hands were bad. It was normal to prepare to fight the Sweeties. And it was normal that Puddin' Head Schools routinely expelled students with a red card for breaking school rules.

CODE BLUE

Mr. Peabody and the students rushed to the indoor classroom. Mr. Peabody clasped his hands to his head. He let out a big, annoying sigh and mumbled, "Wow, just wow. A Code Blue drill. In the middle of class. We haven't even practiced. School Boss Walka Walka, you think this is a good idea?"

Blaze was relieved. Maybe she would avoid a red card, after all.

The students head butted each other in pandemonium. Mr. Peabody composed himself. "All right, all right! Everyone calm down, and keep your courage! This is an important drill. Let me just find these new procedures." He shuffled through a stack of papers on his desk. "Ah, here they are." Mr. Peabody held up a spiral bound *MC Code Blue Emergency Procedures.*

The class stared in panic. He repeated, "Everyone keep your courage. This is just a drill. Now, it says here that Bigs grab a chair and make a large circle around the room. Smalls sit down in the middle of the room. Yes, this includes our guest visitors, too."

"With chairs?" Dimbul asked.

"It doesn't matter!" Mr. Peabody snapped. "The important thing is to cover your eyes with spoons. This will protect you from the Sweeties. They go for the eyes first."

The small-handed students trembled and ran to the middle of the room. Some scooted chairs over. Some dove to the ground. They all placed spoons over their eyes.

"Now shout, 'Puddin'! Puddin'!'" Mr. Peabody exclaimed. "This will keep those Sweeties away!"

The small-handed students, now blinded by spoons, cried or shrugged their shoulders and chanted.

"Louder!"

The students obeyed.

Blaze turned to Chopper and whispered, "What the puddin' balls?"

Chopper shook his head like he thought this safety protocol was stupid—which, I think you will agree, was indeed stupid.

"I'm talking to Walka Walka!"

"Not now. We're in the middle of a drill!" Chopper said.

"All right, large-handed students, move it! Yes, you too." Mr.

Peabody waved for Maya and the other large-handed elementary students to grab chairs.

"C'mon, Mr. Peabody! Maya doesn't need to do this. Just let the little kids leave."

"A drill is a drill."

The middle school Bigs rolled their eyes and grabbed chairs, which they dragged to form a circle around the perimeter of the room. The terrified elementary students followed.

"Hah ha!" Mr. Peabody smirked at Blaze. "I knew bootstraps practice was important! Large-handed students must pull themselves up by their bootstraps onto the chair. It says so right here!" He pointed to a section of the safety pamphlet, as if the students could read it.

The Bigs half-heartedly attempted to do so, but of course, the chairs were ten times taller than the outdoor platforms that no one could mount. One student tripped and knocked over two chairs, thumping his puddin' head.

Blaze raised her eyebrows at Mr. Peabody.

Mr. Peabody grimaced. He told the students to keep trying.

The Smalls became bored and lost energy in their chanting. Mr. Peabody cried, "Louder!" His command failed.

No one came close to pulling themselves up by their bootstraps onto the chair. Blaze and Chopper turned their backs to each other to avoid laughing. After a few moments, Mr. Peabody gave up. "Okay, just step up onto the chair! We'll work on bootstraps later. Face the outside of the room, to protect your peers. Now, clang your spoons together, and say, 'Puddin' Heads! Puddin' Heads!'"

Blaze said, "We're protecting them? What about us?!"

Mr. Peabody said, "It protects you, too. The Sweeties can't stand banging spoons."

Blaze sighed and pulled two spoons from her belt holster. She winked at Maya and leaped onto her chair. She banged her spoons with wild abandon, chanting loudly and obnoxiously, "Puddin' Heads! Puddin' Heads!"

Sparked by Blaze's energy, the Bigs enthusiastically jumped onto their own chairs, clanged their spoons, and chanted in unison. Re-energized, the Smalls yelled, "Puddin'! Puddin'!" once again and covered their eyes with spoons.

"That's it!" Mr. Peabody applauded.

Blaze caught something moving in her peripheral vision. She looked out the window and lost her breath. She stopped chanting. Goosebumps popped on her arms. Blaze held up her spoons as if ready to fight.

A small group of students wearing blue masks, blue shirts, and blue pants approached the school. They unzipped blue backpacks and reached inside.

Blaze yelled, "Sweeties! Sweeties!"

But the class was in a full uproar. Almost no one heard her.

Mr. Peabody did. He double-checked the *MC Code Blue Emergency Procedures*. "No. It's 'Puddin' Heads! Puddin' Heads!' Not 'Sweeties! Sweeties!'"

The students in blue split up and snuck toward different entrances.

Blaze pointed out the window with her two spoons. She screamed, "No, there are actual *Sweeties*! This is *not* a drill!!"

The class looked and hushed.

"Great Mother of All Things Puddin'," Mr. Peabody gasped. "Everyone back in your places! Chant as if your life depends on it! Because it does!"

Many Smalls cried and covered their eyes with spoons. They bleated, "Puddin'! Puddin'! Puddin'!"

On top of chairs, the Bigs fervently banged their spoons. They shouted like an army circling to defend against the enemy.

"What is happening? This makes no sense!" Blaze yelled. "The outside doors are all open! We're just attracting the enemy with all this noise!"

"Blaze, this is a direct order!" Mr. Peabody barked like a military commander. "Class, is this the time to question authority?!"

"No, sir, Mr. Peabody, sir!" the class sounded back. They returned to chanting and banging spoons with unwavering passion.

Presumably, in most countries, you should follow your school's emergency procedures. On Puddin' Head Island however, Blaze had other thoughts. "This is absurd!" She whispered to Maya, "You'll be safe here. I'll be right back." Then, she sprinted out the door and down the red hallways.

Chopper trailed close behind. "Wait for me!"

"Lock the doors!" Blaze yelled.

Blaze and Chopper split up and zipped passed classrooms now in full Code Blue.

Chopper darted to a nearby entrance while Blaze headed to the main one. A blue-clad student, considerably larger than Blaze, sprinted toward the same entrance from the outside. Seconds ahead of him, Blaze slammed the doors shut. The Sweetie rattled the handles and beat the doors.

Blaze pounded back. "Zombie brain eater! You won't enter our school!"

The Sweetie laughed loudly, shook a can of spray paint, and decorated the red door with the phrases *Stay on Your Own Island! Sweeties Rule, Puddin' Heads Drool* in large blue letters. The strong smell of paint wafted through the crack in the door.

Blaze ran to lock two more doors. She sped toward the sixth-grade wing and spotted Chopper. "I locked three. How many did you get?"

"Two."

"Good, that just leaves—"

A dull boom echoed down the hallway.

"The cafeteria," they said together.

After a few seconds of eerie silence, the school erupted into louder chanting and spoon banging.

Blaze and Chopper cautiously jogged toward the cafeteria and peaked inside.

Two students in blue scurried through the outside exit.

"They're getting away!" Blaze said.

"Forget it." Chopper locked the outside door and stared wide-eyed at the cafeteria walls. Chunks of chocolate chip cookie dough plastered the walls and dropped from the ceiling. They tiptoed around the piles of splattered cookie dough piles on the cafeteria floor.

"What happened?!" Blaze asked.

"Cookie bomb," Chopper said like a seasoned detective. He pointed to a line of cookie dough that led back to a table in the center. "Ignited there." A circle of splattered cookie dough rays shot out from the epicenter of the sugary explosion.

"Those soft skulls!" Blaze said. She pulled a spoon out of her belt holster and flicked a chunk of dough from the bottom of her boots. "Is it okay to touch this crap?"

"No idea. Could be contaminated. We should get out of here."

They pulled their shirts over their noses to avoid breathing cookie fumes and spun to leave. Suddenly, Blaze changed direction and scampered around more cookie dough piles toward the food line. "There's a note!"

"Enjoy your special treat! Sincerely, S2."

"Sweetie Region 2 thin-skulled, cookie-cake, brain-eating zombies! They're going to pay for this!" Blaze crumpled the note, threw it on the floor, and stomped on it. It stuck to her boot. She frantically tried to shake it off, slipped, fell, and then tore the note off her heel, swore, and tossed it against the wall.

When she stood up, she looked at the large vats of puddin'. "That's weird," she said, still holding her shirt over her nose. The cookie explosion lines changed direction on top of the puddin' vat lids. "Oh no! They got to the puddin'!"

"I wouldn't touch that!" Chopper warned.

But Blaze had already pulled off a giant lid. "It looks like they stirred something in here—a powder of some kind."

Chopper peered inside. "Booster. But why? Puddin' balls, I think those zombie thin-skulls put hand-increasing booster in our puddin'!"

"What? That's illegal!" Blaze shouted as other students and staff began to arrive.

"So is detonating a cookie bomb. I think. Or is it an attempt at a Sweetie Noble Deed?" Chopper wasn't sure.

Streams of gawking and squawking students and teachers rushed into the cafeteria. They slipped and piled up like the mounds of cookie dough. Blaze yelled, "Everyone out! Sweetie cookie bomb! Do not eat the puddin'! We think it has hand-increasing booster!"

Mr. Peabody pushed his way through the sea of students with School Boss Walka Walka at his side. "There she is. Blaze Union. Leading with big hands. Disrespecting authority during bootstraps class. Not following safety procedures. No question, that is a red card!" Mr. Peabody raised his eyebrows and grinned from ear to ear.

"What?! While you covered your eyes and banged spoons

together like a circle of soft-skulled Sweeties, Chopper and I secured most of the building! Who knows what would have happened if we hadn't locked five of the doors?"

"Okay, let's all keep our courage. We've had quite a day. Blaze, you know you're not allowed to lead." School Boss Walka Walka shook his head.

"You can't be serious!" Blaze marched past Mr. Peabody, past the school boss, and through the crowded hallways.

"Watch yourself," School Boss Walka Walka warned. "Respect authority. Respect the rules, Blaze."

"I was going to talk to you respectfully this morning about changing the stupid rules, but I can see now it would be no use."

"Blaze, no!" Chopper knew what was coming.

"Someone needs to speak the truth! This school is full of numbskull rules and numbskull teachers—maybe because: it's led by a numbskull!"

"That's it!" School Boss Walka Walka reached for a red card.

Blaze ran for Mr. Peabody's room. With a swarm of students following, Blaze grabbed her guitar and strummed. She bounded to the outdoor training facility.

Mr. Peabody shouted from the back of the crowd, "Oh no! You're not allowed to lead a song!"

BURN, BLAZE, BURN

Blaze jumped on a table. She saluted her peers and paused for a solemn moment. She knew this was her final farewell as a student in Region 2. The growing crowd, still traumatized by the Code Blue attack, quieted and stirred with nervous anticipation. Blaze ripped a chord that jolted the stunned audience into full attention. She strummed with a slow beat. Suddenly, her voice belted out a soulful, folksy song—which she had prepared— just in case this day arrived.

> *Oh, you can call me Blaze*
> *'Cause I'm about to burn.*
> *It seems I have a pattern of breaking rules,*
> *So now I need to scoot, now I need to fly.*
> *Red card again—it's time to say good-bye.*
> *But before I leave another school,*
> *I pause to ask the simple question, Why?*

Blaze held this note, which reverberated through the captured audience. Her wide-eyed classmates beckoned for more. She strummed twice as fast. The school burst into rhythmic clapping. Blaze strummed louder and louder. Her peers clapped louder and louder. Blaze strummed and danced.

> *Maybe it's me!*
> *So many schools, none where I fit.*
> *I'm like a fish out of water,*
> *A bird in a cage,*
> *A fox in a box,*
> *A tiger they can't tame.*

> *My hands are too big, but my brain's not small.*
> *So, I will not sugar coat this call:*
> *The rules here I will not swallow.*
> *They won't let me lead, but I will not follow.*

Blaze hung onto this note. Mr. Peabody and School Boss Walka Walka tried to push through the crowd. Mr. Peabody yelled at the students to stop clapping. But after a Code Blue and now a red card revolt, an unprecedented energy electrified the school. The students blocked Mr. Peabody and School Boss Walka Walka from reaching Blaze.

Chopper exhaled a long breath, inhaled, and then started a chant. "Burn, Blaze, burn!" It spread like fire. Within seconds, the entire student body erupted in unison, "Burn, Blaze, burn! Burn, Blaze, burn!"

Mr. Peabody yelled that Chopper had a yellow card and a suspension. Chopper smiled and gave a thumbs up.

With booming school support, Blaze entered into an exhilarating flow. She was leading the school! She would show them—and now she had nothing to lose. She sprang from tables and bootstrap platforms.

But maybe it isn't me.
Maybe it's the instruction.
Pull up your bootstraps, work real hard.
If you want a job, you gotta pay attention.
But I'm so bored,
I'd rather crack jokes than get a five-star mention.
I scratch my head and adjust my Frames.
School makes no sense; Thanks for the expulsion.

Half the class yawns, the other sleeps.
Dimbul drank a bottle of glue.
No class connection to reality,
or anything we'll do.
We're not even ready for a real Code Blue. (Yes, she improvised that line)

All these sad schools, maybe it's the system.
They want to blame me, but something isn't right.
There clearly is a pattern of student flight.
Breaking rules, paying fees,
And some of us can't even read.
More than once we hit the transfer door,
Seriously, even Dimbul got four.

All these rules, all these classes,
But you don't see it, like wearing broken glasses.

So, no more jokes,
Time for puddin' medication.
No more disruption,
Time for my relocation.

SCHOOL BOSS OFFICE

With her guitar hanging from the shoulder strap, Blaze extended her slightly longer than average fingers, closed them into fists, and shook them as if she had just dealt Absurdity a mighty blow. Then, she snatched a spoon from the holster and raised it straight in the air. She took a bow and hopped off the table. The school cheered and waved spoons wildly. "Burn, Blaze, burn!" They head butted and lifted each other up as if they had just won the World Cup.

The school boss yelled, "Everyone calm down and keep your courage!" He looked at Mr. Peabody, at Blaze, and then at the hundreds of students. "Put your spoons back in place! I know we've just had quite an event, but we are safe now thanks to everyone following our safety protocol. Quite amazing when we've had no practice! But clapping and cheering for disrespectful behavior is another matter entirely. This is not following the Puddin' Head values of strength, courage, or respecting authority. Anyone who continues to disrupt school order will be given a yellow card and a suspension, Big or Small!"

Students shuffled back to their classrooms. Mr. Peabody's class sat down and tried to contain their surging emotions. These were the two most exciting school events they had ever experienced.

The school boss said, "Blaze, come with me."

Blaze followed him down several red hallways. As they neared a set of vending machines, Blaze asked if she could buy a puddin' to calm down. The school boss nodded. Blaze scanned the twenty-five puddin' options and fifty booster selections. She tapped and scanned her MC Frames. Seconds later, a double chocolate puddin' and a chill booster released from the vending machine.

Blaze sat across from the school boss. "I wanted to talk to you this morning, but apparently you were too busy."

School Boss Walka Walka ignored the comment. He scooted forward in his executive chair and tapped his small hand on the large desk. The carpet had red stripes, which clashed badly with fluorescent magenta walls. Blaze thought all the red was extreme, even for a true-red Puddin' Head like School Boss Walka Walka. She poured the booster powder into her puddin' cup, stirred, and slowly spooned puddin' into her mouth.

The school boss glanced at Blaze's Frames and then at her hands. He scrolled down the large monitor on his desk. "Blaze Union. Quite the record. Twenty-two transfers. You've barely started here and already a red card. Well, I was warned. But your football talent is undeniable. And I got triple funding for taking you. But it's not worth it. You got the whole school worked up, disrespected Mr. Peabody, and even me. Look, I know you want to score goals, lead, and make schools better, but you have those hands. You're not allowed to lead. Period. So you must follow, and that makes school hard for you or seems unfair or whatever. Here's the thing: you're in control of your behavior. We don't just have these Puddin' Head values to collect dust on the wall. They actually mean something and lay a foundation to build your future. Imagine pulling yourself up by your bootstraps—imagine the opportunities!"

Blaze slowly licked her puddin'. No sense in talking to a school boss who wouldn't listen. And no way was she crying in front of this Puddin' Head.

The school boss tried again. "Well, anyway, what is your plan? What are you going to do in the future? You can't transfer to any more schools in Region 2. If you keep going down this road, you'll be lucky to find work. Nobody wants troublemakers. You could end up on the streets or in jail. Or worse, they might send you to Sweetie Island. Is that what you want?"

Blaze shrugged. "I got ideas. Like eliminating the stupid large hand rules. Like changing this boring, useless, ridiculous school. Like creating schools that are actually fair, actually respectful, and where we actually learn something worth doing. But that doesn't matter right now."

"You weren't exactly respectful."

"Maybe unfair and disrespectful people need a taste of their own medicine. Maybe bad schools should be shut down, School Boss Walka."

"That's Walka Walka!" He frowned. "Right. Uh huh. And I suppose *you* are the person to fix our schools. Funny how we have so many successful students, even an occasional large-handed one. Funny how successful students follow the rules."

"Following stupid rules doesn't make anyone smarter. But you aren't doing anything about them, so I did. Now you have a school full of Bigs who believe in something better."

"Yeah, okay. Keep dreaming. So, what will your parents think about this? You think this makes them proud?"

Blaze leaned in. "Well, my dad died in a factory accident. So I don't think he'll have a strong opinion. My mom works two jobs and doesn't have time to worry about me."

The school boss said, "Sorry for your loss, kid. Look, you're done with Puddin' Head Middle School. Maybe you had fun today. But reality will set in. It's too bad you can't try for a Noble Deed. Middle school students can't do it, and certainly not with large hands. Which is too bad, because someone should really pay those Sweeties back for the stunt they pulled."

Blaze wandered along a pathway hidden by bushes and trees. She strummed her farewell song. She swung from branches. She swore about the Sweeties, Mr. Peabody, Walka Walka, and stupid Puddin' Head schools.

After a few minutes, Blaze set aside her guitar and pulled her beat-up red-and-white football out of her backpack. She dribbled back and forth for a while then popped it up onto her toe, and juggled off her feet, knees, thigh, and head. She blasted line drives off a tree with her left foot, then her right, like a tennis pro smashing a tennis ball against a wall. She kicked faster and faster and grunted louder and louder until she was exhausted. Blaze trapped the ball and slowly dribbled to a patch of sunlight, where she closed her eyes and took a deep breath.

"Hey, wait up!" Chopper yelled.

Blaze turned and shook her head. "What are you doing? Oh yeah, you got a yellow card. Can you believe this day?"

"Yeah. Insane! Imagine if we'd stayed in the classroom, banging spoons like numbskulls."

"No doubt."

"Oh, and I karate chopped a bootstraps platform in half. Right in front of Peabody!"

Blaze snorted with surprise. "You what? Not one that I made, right? Ha! Oh, I wish I could have seen that. Wait, did you get a red card? And doesn't that hurt?!"

Chopper gently turned over his swollen hand. "Nah. I just got a suspension. Remember, max of one card per day."

Blaze's smile turned to a grimace. "Wow, I'm in big trouble. My mom's going to kill me. She can't afford another transfer, and I promised her this wouldn't happen again. We probably have to move! She'll probably have to quit her job! What am I going to do?!"

Blaze fought back tears, then screamed. "I hate school! Why is everything so boring and, so unfair? And seriously, what is up with that Code Blue? We saved the school, but we get suspended and expelled? And the hand size rules? Aren't we all Puddin' Heads? Shouldn't we fight the Sweeties instead of each other? And the bootstraps! Who wears boots anyway? It's thirty degrees out—and I don't mean Fahrenheit."

Chopper nodded. "I know, right? How can they not see that we prevented a Sweetie invasion?" He studied his sandals. "Now, it was handy to wear boots when we stepped in the cookie crap in the cafeteria. And you regularly wear football boots. Your aunt wears motorcycle boots, your mom wears boots when she goes to the factory, and farmers wear work boots . . . I mean, you have a point. The rich people don't—oh wait, there are fashion boots . . ."

"Okay, shut up! Are you messing with me? No kids wear boots —unless we're playing football or are in bootstraps class. Most adults don't wear boots. I mean, it depends on their job! But almost everyone wears sandals or shoes. We live on an island that's warm year-round! Anyway, my point is it's not physically possible to actually pull yourself up by your bootstraps!"

"Then how did all those five-star students do it?"

"I don't know. Are you really messing with me—today of all days? I guess they showed it on video and on the news, so maybe it's true. Well, anyway, *very* few people can do it, and regardless, it is stupid. Why would you ever need that skill?"

Chopper put on his best teacher's voice. "It builds character. Courage. Perseverance. And remains essential in countering Code Blue attacks . . ."

Blaze rolled her eyes. "The whole system is messed up! How can so many schools be this bad? And it's not just me! The school bosses won't change the rules! Someone needs to fight those rules." She paused, then said, "Seriously, someone should make me a school boss. I would change those rules on my first day."

Chopper nodded. "Yeah. But back to reality, where did your song come from? It had the whole school raging."

Blaze smiled proudly. "I've been writing and practicing it for a while, and today, I had nothing to lose so . . ." Blaze thought for a moment. "Oh, the 'burn, Blaze, burn' chant was spectacular. Did you get that on video?"

Chopper tapped his Frames. "Of course. I'll bet everyone did." Chopper scanned the interior of his Frames, then said. "Yep, someone posted to Mega Gossip. Look—you had the whole school fired up!"

Blaze clenched her fists with pride. Then she placed her hands atop her head as she thought about telling her mom. Panic flooded her. She closed her eyes and tripped over a tree root, swore, and stumbled into a ditch face-first, guitar smacking the back of her head. She cursed at Chopper for laughing. "I could've been hurt!" Blaze pushed herself up and noticed a camouflage canvas bag hidden under a bush.

"Hey, what's this?" She pulled up the heavy bag by the shoulder strap and unzipped it. Their eyes lit up as they peered inside. They scanned their surroundings to see if anyone had noticed. Grabbing the bag, Blaze ran to a nearby cluster of trees.

"This is fake right?"

Chopper grabbed and studied a stack of \$\$20 bills. "No, this is real. How much do you think it is?"

"I don't know—a lot. Five hundred MC bucks a stack. A hundred stacks? Fifty thousand MC bucks? What should we do?"

Chopper offered, "Well, you found it, so your call. Might I suggest the Puddin' Café to think it over? It's Two for Tuesday. Looks like you're treating."

Red flags waved in front of the Puddin' Café. As Blaze and Chopper approached, music something like hard rock played from the outdoor speakers. Blaze strummed along and dribbled her football. Chopper lugged the heavy bag of money.

Two large statues of Mr. Puddin' Head flanked each side of the café. Both statues featured gigantic heads and a spoon belt holstering an array of spoon sizes. The statue on the left wore an enormous spoon hat strapped to his chin, its handle jutting straight back—like a ball cap worn backwards. He rode a pony that was frozen mid-stride as if charging into battle, although the pony looked as though it might collapse at any moment. Perhaps the artist used the pony to accentuate the hero's super noggin while complimenting his tiny hands. The other Mr. Puddin' Head statue raised a jumbo spoon in a teensy hand, as if also bounding into battle—or, as I first imagined, ready to scoop a world-record heap of puddin'. It was next to a puddin' café, after all.

Here's a little back story on Mr. Puddin' Head. For generations, the legend of Mr. Puddin' Head grew until he evolved into a cultural icon. He allegedly used his enormously thick head to save the day by head butting Sweeties, breaking down doors, and so on. In a famous movie scene later turned into a commercial, Mr.

Puddin' Head tracks down Sweetie convicts playing billiards in a bar. After the Sweeties discover his identity, he nonchalantly slurps down a puddin' shake as they circle him. They take turns breaking pool sticks on the front, side, and top of his head, growing with frustration as they fail to knock him out. He sets down his shake. He gradually rises from his chair and dusts off his red jacket, red shirt, and leather pants. He laughs as a Sweetie breaks a bar stool over his head. Then he swiftly head butts the lot of them, knocking each unconscious. More recently, his wardrobe evolved to include a belt that secured up to fourteen different spoon sizes for you guessed it, gulping puddin' or fighting Sweeties, who at some point, had evolved into zombies (according to Puddin' Head commercials, movies, TV shows, and so on). His pathetic pony never made it to the screen; apparently, it was only statue worthy.

Blaze and Chopper stepped onto the rustic, wooden porch. Its red paint faded. The bar counter was made of long pieces of smooth driftwood grafted together like giant puzzle pieces.

They saddled up to the bar where Blaze tucked the bag beneath her feet. For once, Blaze could avoid the guilt of spending money on puddin' and the awkwardness of paying for Chopper, whose family had even less than hers.

The puddin'tender wore a red shirt and an elaborate belt with various spoon sizes. He was turned sideways, cleaning a bowl and humming as if unaware of their presence. Suddenly, he lowered the music, removed his Frames, and spun toward them, yelling, "Hah!"

Blaze said, "Moldy puddin' fart tart!" She and Chopper fell off their stools, then slowly peeked their heads over the bar.

"Gets 'em every time!" the puddin'tender laughed. Blaze and Chopper were still in shock. The right side of his body—unlike the left side of his body, which seemed normal—had various sized bumps and lumps embedded under his skin, even his right eyelid. His right ear had several holes. He nodded sympathetically at the frown faces on their MC Frames, then at their hands, and faded red shirts and khaki shorts.

"You new?" Blaze asked loudly, cautiously climbed back onto her stool, and tried not to stare.

"No need to yell. I can hear just fine from this close! Yeah, moved here from Region 3. Dropped out of school. Hard to find a job." He noticed them eying his scared and bumpy arms and pulled up a sleeve to give them a closer look. "Dynamite. But I'm the lucky one."

"What?!" Blaze cried.

"It is what it is." He looked at the time. "So, skipping school or suspended?"

Blaze and Chopper both claimed the latter.

"What can I get you?"

They read the extensive puddin' and booster menu on the wall.

Blaze was surprised at the prices. "Puddin' bowls and drinks are $$5.98 now?" (Translation: five MC bucks and 98 cents; or as Blaze said, "five ninety-eight.") "Booster is $$3.87?"

"Yep. Inflation. But do I need to remind you? It's Two for Tuesday."

"Fine. I'll take the dark chocolate wild berry puddin' smoothie with a triple boost of chill."

The puddin'tender raised his eyebrows. "That kind of day, huh?"

Chopper hemmed and hawed. "Ahhh, so hard to choose, so many choices. Uh . . . Hmmm . . . can I get a puddin' bowl of cosmopolitan topped with lemon berry, and a skull-fortifying booster?"

"Two for Tuesday—buy one, get one free. One puddin' smoothie, one puddin' bowl coming right up."

Blaze slapped $$20 on the rough, wooden bar and said, "Keep the change. And keep 'em coming."

Thirty minutes later Blaze and Chopper were beyond full. They rested their heads on the counter and moaned about overeating. Blaze looked sideways and saw an odd-looking teenager cautiously stepping onto the porch.

The large adolescent sat three seats down without making eye contact. He cocked his head and darted his gaze across the menu. He nervously pushed back on the stool, which squeaked.

Blaze and Chopper stared at this odd fellow. His thick, dark hair was pulled back in a ponytail, revealing the frown face on his MC Frames. Black tape wrapped most of his Frames, as if they were broken or old.

"Big dude with a ponytail, dressed by a four-year-old," Blaze whispered. "Socially awkward or a tourist. Who wears all red?"

Chopper coughed to disguise his laughter.

The kid did indeed wear all red: red shirt, red shorts, red socks. His red canvas shoes looked freshly painted.

Blaze broke the tension with a joke. "Nice Frames. Those a new model?"

The boy chuckled. "Yeah, these are pretty sweet."

Either this strange character didn't get the joke, didn't like the joke, or just liked his Frames. The puddin'tender said, "What'll you have?"

"Ahh!" he cried, seeing him for the first time. The puddin'tender smiled with a few missing right teeth and waited. After a long awkward moment, the boy replied, "Uh, give me a minute. Could you turn on the telly, please?"

The puddin'tender cleaned the blender and said, "Sure, I can turn on the TV, Mr. Polite Boy." He switched on Puddin' Head News with his MC Frames.

A reporter asked the locals questions about the latest Sweetie Island plot to take away Puddin' Head freedom. "Well, it's just like a Sweetie," said one person. "They think they're better than us. Sounds like being lazy to me."

The kid mumbled, "Huh? That doesn't even make sense."

The TV switched to the Capitol Building on Power Island and zoomed in on the prime minister, who placed his tiny hands around the MC podium. "We have problems! We have this radical TDLMNOP group wanting Puddin' Heads to be 'fair' and 'kind' to Sweeties—they're just Puddin' Heads who turned soft! Dangerous ideas. Probably should ban them from Puddin' Head Island. Or throw them in jail."

Blaze asked Chopper, "Puddin' Heads want to be kind to
Sweeties? What's wrong with this island?"

Chopper shook his head in disbelief.

The prime minister grimaced and sighed. "We have the Sweeties!
Or are they zombies? *Hard to tell.* We have sea monsters that could
invade anytime! Yes, we need to build that wall!" he said with
increasing enthusiasm. "A very scary wall! A wall so scary that
zombies and sea monsters won't even try to climb it! It will
surround Puddin' Head Island. It will be the greatest, scariest wall in
the history of the world! Built by the greatest prime minister to ever
live!" He held his hands high in the air, then looked confused.
"Now what was I saying? Oh yes—the Sweetie senators want to ban
everyone—including Puddin' Heads—from wearing red! They want
to destroy puddin' altogether! These terrible bills would destroy the
economy! MegaCorp would have to fire workers, and decrease
production of puddin' and booster! And that's not all! These bills
would literally sink Puddin' Head Island."

The prime minister went on with fiery passion, "I will not let
this happen! I will stop any bill that orders Puddin' Heads to be kind
to Sweeties! Not only will I stop any bill banning the color red, I will
support a bill to ban wearing the color blue! I will stop any bill to
destroy puddin'! And we will build that wall!" The TV showed a
large crowd of angry Puddin' Heads cheering.

Blaze said, "Sweeties did attack Puddin' Head schools to
destroy puddin'! My mom makes red shirts in the factory—they
want to destroy her job, too!" Blaze swallowed as she thought of
the money bag underneath her sandals.

The strange boy's mouth opened wider as he watched the news.
He suddenly exclaimed, "Wow, now that is . . . uh . . . fascinating!
Maybe the prime minister should check the definition of 'literally.'"

Blaze, Chopper, and the puddin'tender stared at him with
increased scrutiny. Blaze decided not to offer him a puddin' after all.

The news switched to a headline that read, *Breaking News!
Sweeties Attack PH Island Again.* The TV showed the Puddin' Head
newsroom. A news analyst summarized, "The Sweeties launched a
series of attacks again on Puddin' Head soil: planting invasive
wildflowers near schools, hugging trees, cookie bombing a middle
school, and starting a cattle stampede."

A reporter in boots stood near a broken fence in the middle of a cow pasture. She stated in a serious news voice, "I'm here at Freedom Farm with a breaking story. Freedom Farm raises cattle and provides land for a MegaCorp top secret booster plant program. You can see beside me this broken fence, where fifteen cows escaped last night. Luckily, they were found grazing forty meters away."

The news analyst said, "That is terrible. Looks like it's time for Puddin' Head payback. MegaCorp is sponsoring a Puddin' Head buy one, get one free red shirt and flag sale to pay for the broken fence."

The TV switched back to the reporter, who fell down trying to pull herself by her bootstraps up onto a piece of railing. She yelled from the grassy field, "I almost had it! Must keep practicing!"

Blaze yelled at the TV, "Do you Sweeties really think you'll get away with this?!" She raised an eyebrow to Chopper. "See, pulling bootstraps is stupid. Just climb on the fence already. And why is that broken fence more newsworthy than the attack on our school?"

The strange boy shifted from shock to amusement. "Everything all right?" the puddin'tender asked. "You ready to order?" The boy seemed to read the interior of his MC Frames, then tapped one temple arm as if punching in a code.

"Actually, I lost my appetite. But one question before I go. Is it true that you eat babies with your puddin'?"

Suddenly, the TV switched to a picture of a giant chocolate chip cookie. A cryptic voice said, "We interrupt your regularly scheduled program for this important Sweetie message."

"What the—" Blaze said and stood up.

"He hacked the TV!" Chopper yelled.

The large boy laughed, hopped off the stool, backflipped off the porch, and cartwheeled his way to the middle of the dusty street. Eight more adolescents wearing blue trotted from around the side of the café. They flanked the odd boy in red.

They faced the porch holding long blue cylinders. The red-clad boy tapped his MC Frames and punched a few buttons on the hologram in front of him. Suddenly, the song *Sweet Home, Sweet Cake* —sung by a large, boisterous choir—rang out over the Puddin' Café's speakers. The lead boy stripped off his red shirt and shorts and threw them to the side of the street. He now matched the others except for his red socks and shoes.

"What the—" Blaze covered her ears.

"Now he hacked the audio system!" Chopper said.

The Sweeties formed a flash mob and danced to the blaring music. They weaved in and out, danced together and apart, and flipped the blue cylinders back and forth in a synchronized, fluid, and mocking style. The lead boy turned cartwheels and flips as he neared the front porch. He stuck his landing and yelled, "Ready!"

A comrade threw him a blue cylinder as the others grabbed theirs, popped off the top, and pointed them at the Puddin' Café. Blaze could now see the cylinders were some kind of launcher.

"I think it's the same group that attacked our school!" Blaze yelled.

Compact cake and cookie dough balls whizzed from the cylinders.

Blaze, Chopper, and the puddin'tender fell to the floor as cake and cookie dough pelted the Puddin' Café. Blaze said, "They *are* trying to destroy puddin'! They *are* trying to destroy my mom's job! And they caused me to get a red card!"

In unison, the Sweeties yelled, "From Sweetie Island. Keep off our land! Grow your own puddin' and booster! To kindness, to fairness, to community!"

Cake and cookie dough balls pounded the bar. "Kindness! Fairness! Ha!" Blaze charged but cake exploded between her Frames. "Gahh!" she cried. "I can't see!"

Blaze dove behind the bar and wiped off her Frames. The puddin'tender said, "I've seen worse." He tossed Blaze and Chopper spoons the size of their legs, strapped one around his head, and whirled another one like a sword. He yelled, "Charge!!"

The puddin'tender rammed a speeding mound of blue cake, which exploded off his spoon hat. "Yeah! It worked!" he shouted proudly. Then, a dense cookie dough ball to the face knocked him to the ground. He wiped his swelling cheek and licked one finger. "Cookie dough. Disgusting!"

Blaze and Chopper huddled behind the bar before shrugging then strapping on giant spoon hats of their own. Compact cake and cookie dough balls hammered the wall and broke windows. Suddenly, the bombardment stopped. The Sweeties scampered away.

"Get them!" Blaze yelled. She tossed her football over the bar and sprinted toward the fleeing attackers with a spoon in each hand. Blaze leaped off the porch, sprinted around the corner, and dribbled in full stride. She crushed a line drive that struck the slowest Sweetie in the back of the head, knocking him down. The puddin'tender caught him, pulled a large spoon from his belt, and smacked the Sweetie on the hand. "Bad Sweeties get a hand spanking!"

The boy cried, threw cake dust in the puddin'tender's face, and escaped. Blaze and Chopper ran after him but tripped over a thin wire. The kid hopped on his bike, flipped them off, and pedaled away. The pony-tailed leader waited till the last Sweetie was in the clear. Then, he yelled, "Knuckleheads!" before saluting Blaze, turning, and shooting off.

"That's a compliment you numbskull!" Blaze shouted back. "You're going to pay for this!"

Chopper huffed, "Sweeties! We were attacked by Sweeties! Again!" He thought for a moment. "Maybe they really *are* zombies."

Over the next hour, Puddin' Head News filmed shots of the crime scene. They interviewed Blaze, Chopper, and the cake- and cookie-stained puddin'tender. Blaze slowly calmed down. She hoped the combination of the canvas bag, the Sweetie attacks, and the news would provide a distraction from her next conversation with her mom.

FACING MOM

Blaze waited nervously for her mom to return home from work. While Maya chattered and played in her room, Blaze washed the dishes and placed them in a drying rack. She swept the kitchen, living room, and her bedroom with a broom. Blaze dusted and emptied the dustpan outside. She tried to rest on her bed. She looked at the picture of her dad playing football with her three years ago, shortly before he died. Blaze held up a picture of her dad playing the guitar she now carried with her nearly everywhere. "What would you have done, Dad?" she asked.

She unclenched her jaw and called out to Maya in the sing-song voice she loved. "Oh Mayyyya. It's Mr. Puddin' Head."

Maya immediately responded, "Mr. Puddin' Head! Did you eat your puddin'?"

"Yes, I did. Two big helpings!"

"Good boy. Help! The Sweeties are attacking us with Crazy Bear and Scary Sea Monster!"

"Oh, no. I'll be right over!" Blaze grabbed the muscular Mr. Puddin' Head doll with an enormous square head you might mistake for a hammer. Blaze crawled into Maya's room. "Where are you?!"

"Under here!" Maya cried from under a red bedsheet. Using the bedsheet, she grabbed two blue-shirted zombie action figures, a fluffy teddy bear, and a plastic sea monster. She charged them toward three red dolls trapped perilously on the edge of the bed.

"I'll save you!" Blaze trumpeted rescue sounds and leaped Mr. Puddin' Head into action. And just as sure as a hammer hits nails, Mr. Puddin' Head head butted bear, sea monster, and zombies. One zombie flew across the bed with a well-placed blow to the temple, while the other sailed across the room wailing, "Ahhhhhhhh!" from a nasty head butt to the forehead.

"Now, that's a Puddin' Head!" Blaze and Maya sang together.

Still wrapped in her sheet, Maya abruptly grabbed the teddy bear, who snatched her recorder as an unlikely weapon and violently whacked an unsuspecting doll on the head. "Puddin', puddin', pop!" the teddy bear laughed.

Blaze sprang from the bed and out of character. "Wow, I totally forgot. Are you okay from class today? I can't believe they still play that song."

Maya looked down sullenly and hid under the bed sheet.

"It's going to be okay," Blaze said, peaking under the sheet. "Wait, what's that on your hands? You aren't wearing compression gloves, are you?" She pulled the cover off Maya and threw it aside.

Maya sat on her hands.

"Let me see."

"No."

"*Let me see!*"

"No!"

Blaze pulled Maya's arms straight in the air and wrestled off the white compression gloves.

Maya wrestled and screamed, "No! No! No!"

"You don't need these! There's nothing wrong with your hands! Look my hands are a little big too—it doesn't matter!"

Maya cried, crossed her arms, and hid her hands under her armpits. Suddenly, she stood up, listened, and shot out of the room, crying. "Mommy!"

Blaze's mom pulled her dented car in the dusty driveway. The brakes squealed loudly. She limped into the house without complaint, closed the door behind her, and wiped the lenses of her MC Frames. About a year ago, a driver returning from a Puddin' Head rally—intoxicated from too many bowls of adult puddin' with warrior and energy booster—had veered toward her car on her way home from work at the textile factory. She swerved and missed the car but crashed into a ditch, injuring her leg. The reckless driver sped away.

Unfortunately, Natalina Union could not afford car or health insurance, so she paid for minimal repairs and dealt with leg pain rather than seeing a doctor. She couldn't afford insurance in part because of the loss of income after her husband's death. Additionally, insurance costs dramatically increased due to high risk factors in the family: "Family Members with Large Hands," which were Blaze and Maya, and "Frequent School Expulsions," which was due to Blaze. In other words, the Union family had gone from being relatively well-off to struggling within just a few hard years.

"Ah, Blaze, thank you for cleaning up the house. You can be such a thoughtful, responsible—"

Maya blurted, "Blaze pulled my arms and took my gloves!"

"Blaze?" said Natalina, as she unpacked a grocery bag for a typical bargain dinner: hamburger, pasta, fruit, and chocolate puddin' cups.

Blaze stood in the bedroom doorway with her head down, nervously tapping her fingers on the frame.

"If Maya wants to wear those gloves, that's her choice," said Mom.

"They're stupid. And they don't work."

"You never know."

Blaze paced the floor.

Her mom turned around and said, "Are you okay?"

"What? Oh, yeah, sure. I'm fine. I just . . . had an interesting day." Blaze hovered by the door again, then paced.

Her mom sighed. "Oh, Blaze. What happened this time?"

Blaze planned to lead with the money bag or either of the Sweetie attacks, but her mom was already on to her. Blaze burst into tears. "Mom, I'm so sorry. I don't know what's wrong with me, I really tried this time, but I just couldn't help it. That school, those teachers, the school boss—they make me so mad!"

Her mom's look of disappointment sank Blaze's heart. "Blaze, don't get me started—you are responsible for your actions—not your sister, not your brother, not me, not your teachers. So you got another red card?"

"But these schools are so stupid! Did you see—"

"Did you get a red card?"

"Yes, but let me explain."

"Does it matter, Blaze? What are we supposed to do now? We probably need to move out of Region 2!"

"Can I at least explain what happened?"

Her mom sighed, sat down, and lowered her head on the kitchen table. "What did I do wrong? First, Kuko. Now Blaze. Maybe there's hope for Maya," she mumbled to herself.

Blaze raised her arms along with her voice. "You'll never believe my day. Did you see the news? The Sweeties let off a cookie bomb at our school, and Chopper and I stopped the Sweeties from getting any further than the cafeteria, so we stopped something even bigger from happening! We should be heroes but were we rewarded—or even thanked? No, no, no. No, Chopper was *suspended*! And I got another red card and another expulsion! It's so unfair!"

"A cookie bomb, huh?" Ms. Union said flatly.

"Yes! It really happened! You'll see it on Puddin' Head News!"

"That's disgusting."

"I know, right? And they dumped hand-increasing booster into the puddin'!"

"Bunch of zombies," Ms. Union said softly, her forehead still resting on the table.

"Right?! So why do I even go to school? The teachers are beyond annoying, no one can actually pull themselves up by their bootstraps, and I don't learn anything anyway! I could teach better than these Puddin' Head cavemen! Anyway, I sang a good-bye song, and the whole school sang along. It was awesome! It felt great! But did they see the leader that I am? The person who saved the school and brought us together in the midst of a great tragedy? The person who could turn this school around and end large hand discrimination? No, no, no. No, Mr. Peabody and School Boss Walka Walka didn't like that so much—you know, because *apparently,* I can't lead. So, yes, they thanked me with a red card and a kick out the door! They deserve what I did!"

Her mom slapped her hands on the table and laughed hysterically.

"So, it's the school's fault."

"Yes! Are *you* okay?"

"Oh, I'm fantastic. I was getting tired of living in this house and this neighborhood, tired of living near Chopper's family and your Aunt Serafina. Tired of the decent job I've had for years. Can't wait for a new adventure."

"Mom, I'm sorry! I can't help it! Life is so unfair!"

"Uh huh. But you know, you're wrong. You've had good teachers."

"Yeah right," Blaze sobbed.

"What about Ms. Spicer? She taught you to love reading."

"Yes, but—"

"And Mr. Sharpe?"

"Okay, two. I had two good—very good—teachers. But ten times as many bad ones! Why didn't I have more good ones? And I didn't even deserve most of those yellow and red cards! Someone needs to stand up to these stupid large hand rules! Think of Maya! She's only seven, and these rules are sucking the soul right out of her!"

"That's very thoughtful of you. But some of those yellow and red cards you *did* deserve. Look, I don't like the large hand rules either. I don't like what those schools have done to you. But it is what it is. You can't go through life worrying about things you can't change, or else you're going to live a life of frustration. Stay strong and keep your courage."

"You sound like Mr. Peabody."

"Yeah, but smarter. So, another transfer. To a different region this time."

Blaze nodded. "I guess . . . So, I do have other news. I've had quite the day." She told her mom about the canvas bag and the Puddin' Café. With a surge of energy, they discussed possibilities and decided to consult with a trusted soul.

Blaze and Maya heard the familiar motorcycle roar in. "Aunt Serafina!" they yelled as she burst through the door. They jumped into her arms, squeezed her tight, and laughed.

"Natalina, so good to see you," Aunt Serafina said.

"Serafina." Blaze's mom held out her arms, hugged her younger sister, then gave her a semi-nice noogie.

"Ah!" Aunt Serafina said and picked up a puddin' cup. "You're still eating this crap? After everything?"

"Oh, give me a break. We eat puddin' on occasion—we are Puddin' Heads after all. Live a little. You're too lean. You look like a Sweetie vegetarian," Blaze's mom said.

"Oh, c'mon . . . Well, I'm not here to argue. So, what's going on Blaze?"

Blaze explained her incredible day to her favorite aunt. Serafina had previously coached Blaze in football, taught meditation and yoga classes, and worked as a local actor, singer, and waitress at Puddin' Head Restaurant. After meditation and yoga were banned from Puddin' Head Island for being too closely associated with Sweetie values, Serafina ran for the open Region 2 Senate seat and surprisingly won. Though she was now Senator Serafina, she insisted that people use her first name.

Serafina examined the canvas bag and raised her eyebrows. She peered at a dark-gray patch sewn on the inside flap. Blaze hadn't noticed it before. "Okay, this just got real interesting," she said. In black letters, the patch read *TDJP*.

Blazed asked, "What's that?"

The adults looked at each other. Aunt Serafina rubbed her forehead and said, "Well, maybe you're old enough to know."

Blaze's mom panicked. "No, she's too young! She has enough to deal with. And not today of all days."

"What are you talking about?" Blaze asked.

Serafina removed her MC Frames and gathered everyone else's, including Maya's, and placed them in the cupboard. "No time like the present. If you can't trust family, who can you trust?"

Natalina grabbed her arm. "Serafina, no."

"Sis, it's okay."

"What's going on?!" Blazed asked.

Maya cried. Her mom handed her a puddin' cup, then some toys, and shuffled her into the bedroom.

Blaze was very confused—why remove the MC Frames?

Natalina folded her arms. "Well, you might as well tell her now."

Aunt Serafina turned to Blaze. "For several years, we've been trying to unite a group of citizens for truth, democracy, justice, and people before profit—or TDJP."

"Wait, is this the group that wants to be kind to Sweeties?"

"What? Where did you hear that?"

"On TV, I think. And don't we have a democracy?"

"Well, we do vote for senators and the prime minister. But many government positions are appointed by the prime minister rather than voted into office by citizens. TDJP would like to change that."

Blaze thought for a moment. "Appointed—you mean they just give them the job?"

"Yes. Like regional bosses appoint district bosses, and district bosses appoint school bosses."

"What? My school boss has a boss?"

"Yes. That's the district boss, who is appointed by the regional boss."

"And someone appoints regional bosses?"

"Yes. The education minister, who's appointed by the prime minister."

"Huh. That education minister has a *lot* of power to change schools then."

"Yeah. Our current one is also the football commissioner, you know. To summarize, no one voted for her or for the regional, district, or school bosses. In most cases, the community, families, and students don't even have any input on who is selected to lead them."

"That's stupid! How do we change it?" Blaze jumped on a chair and held out her arms. "I'm Blaze Union, and I'm running for education minister! Can I count on your vote?"

Her mom and aunt laughed and applauded.

"I'd vote for you. Too bad we can't," Serafina said.

"Huh. And what about the rest? Justice or something?"

"Yeah, we're still working on the JP side of things. The TD

groups mainly focus on voter rights and independent news: telling people the truth about what's really happening. The JP groups are committed to justice and fairness for people with large hands in education, health care, and the workforce. Justice goes hand in hand —no pun intended—with people being more important than profit or money."

"That sounds awesome! What *is* really happening? And why haven't I heard of this group?"

Aunt Serafina looked at the cupboard where the MC Frames were hidden. "You might call us an underground operation. It's not safe to share some of our ideas."

"What do you mean?"

The adults looked at each other.

"Some people's stories are not safe to share in public," Ms. Union said with a quiet, quavering voice.

"What do you mean? Who are you talking about?" Blaze sensed something was wrong.

Natalina started to shake and weep. After a few moments, she calmed herself and wiped tears from her cheeks. "Your father was a good man, Blaze. You know there was an accident at the puddin' factory, but you don't know the whole story. What I'm about to tell you could get me thrown in jail. You can't tell anyone else—not even Chopper. Do you understand?"

Blaze nodded.

Blaze's mom explained that Good Hope Day had been paired with the State of the Nation "celebration" that year—the same year that Blaze's hands "changed" from small to large. While Puddin' Heads didn't give two spoonfuls of puddin' about the prime minister's State of the Nation speech, they eagerly awaited the huge puddin' discounts it would bring. Massive crowds lined up before stores opened. Some camped out the night before for door-buster sales. Hospitals prepared for hundreds of trampled shoppers.

Thus, the puddin' factory required overtime. The factory line workers—most of whom had large hands—clocked two, sometimes three, shifts a day for a week to make enough puddin'. Sadly, a fatigued worker fell asleep, a puddin' pipe burst, and several very tired workers slipped into a huge vat of puddin'. Blaze's father drowned trying to save them. Someone leaked it to the news, but only Sweeties News ran the story—which was abruptly stopped in the middle of the newscast.

"Did the Sweeties make fun of Dad's death?!"

"I don't know. I do know no one was allowed to talk about it on Puddin' Head Island."

"Why not? I don't understand!"

"Your father was such a strong line leader at the puddin' factory, they finally promoted him to be a mid-level manager despite his large hands. No one had decent wages, but he had a hard time accepting that the large-handed workers were paid even less, had no choice in shifts, and had little to no opportunity for advancement. He saw the people at the top getting very rich while the people doing the actual work barely made a living. He was a person of action, like you. He was tired of TD just writing, talking, and complaining about the problems. So, he started a small JP group, which organized and attempted to join forces with the TD operation. He arranged to pay large hand fees for impoverished families using JP membership dues and some of the TD profits. That's probably what this canvas bag of money is for."

Blaze stared blankly. "Are you saying that Dad died because large-handed workers worked long hours? And that he started JP to fight stupid large hands rules? And people aren't allowed to talk about it? Why are people afraid of the truth? Why don't people change?"

Her aunt put her arm around Blaze. "I know this is a lot to take in."

Blaze cried, "Why didn't you tell me?!"

Blaze's mom hugged her and said, "I'm sorry. You've been dealing with so much since your hands switched to large. I didn't want to give you any more cause to be upset. I still think it's too early, but now you know. Your father was a hero."

Blaze sobbed and clung to her mom for a long time. She hugged her aunt and slumped to the floor. Overwhelmed and confused, she now had a deeper sense of anger and commitment grow inside of her.

After a long period of consolation, her aunt said, "Sometimes it helps to do something. Right now, I'm guessing that money you found is very important. It could impact many lives."

The canvas bag of money didn't matter as much to Blaze anymore. Yet, it was a lot of money.

She was torn. "Well, if this money is for families in need, maybe we could keep some for transfer and moving fees. Besides, how would we find the owner and their reason for needing so much money?" Part of Blaze hoped this money belonged to a scoundrel, so she could justify keeping it all.

Her aunt replied, "I have connections and can do a little searching." She paused and said, "You know Blaze, even if you were to use the money for a transfer, you may have a hard time finding a school that will accept you, even in a different region."

"What? No. Surely Region 1 or 3 would accept me. Have you seen my football skills?" She laughed. "But I don't want to be a student anymore. I want to be the boss."

Her mom sighed. "One thing at a time Blaze, one thing at a time."

By the time her aunt returned from her search, Blaze had channeled her hurt and anger into a plan. Aunt Serafina confirmed the money involved a TDJP initiative that supported families who couldn't afford school or health care. A TDJP carrier had feared he was being tracked and ditched the canvas bag. When he returned for it, the money was gone.

Blaze spent the next couple of days consumed in thoughts about her father's death, the TDJP money, and her situation. Blaze gave most of the money to her aunt, who returned it to the carrier. But she kept some money for her mom's medical needs. It was in the spirit of the money's purpose, she reasoned. So was keeping money for a school transfer. But still, she had a better plan.

Blaze paced in her room. "Chopper, it's time for a Noble Deed."

Chopper sat on the bed and shook his head. "Why cause more problems?"

"Listen. I got a red card, *again*. My family probably has to move out of Region 2. A pack of Sweeties attacked our school. Then, those same Sweeties attacked us with cake guns at Puddin' Café. So yes, it's time for a Noble Deed."

"Those do seem like good reasons. But middle school kids aren't allowed to win Noble Deeds. Bigs aren't allowed to win Noble Deeds. Even if we 'succeeded,' we would get in trouble, not rewarded."

"There's a first time for everything. Besides, how much more trouble could I possibly get into? Chopper, this is a shot at redemption. We can't let those Sweeties escape without payback."

Chopper glanced away and mumbled, "Noble Deeds are dangerous you know."

"Are you afraid of Sweeties?"

"What? No. I mean, they didn't look like zombies."

"You don't actually believe—"

Chopper put his hand to Blaze's face. "Okay, okay. Redemption sounds good to me. Nothing risky or stupid. But I think you mean 'revenge.'"

"Yeah, revenge. Isn't that what a Noble Deed is, anyway?"

"I don't know. Officially it's something about promoting Puddin' Head values. Anyway, I'm in, as long as we're back before sunset. Oh, and I need to show you something." They walked outside and Chopper grabbed his bike. "I've been working on this for a few months and finally figured it out."

On the inside of the bike frame, a large cylinder battery replaced the water bottle holder. One battery cord ran to a solar panel jutting from the handlebars. Another cord ran to a small motor attached to the vertical part of the bicycle frame, which connected to the gears. "It's a solar-powered electric bike now. It saves our energy and gets us top speed. I made one for you, too."

"Holy puddin' balls Chopper. That is *amazing*. Thank you!"

After a few spins on their upgraded bikes, they spent the rest of the evening mapping their travel plans by bike and train. Their journey would stretch from their hometown of Courage City to Booster City to Power Island to Sweetie Island. As you can see on the map, Booster City is the main hub in Region 1 in the northwest part of Puddin' Head Island, where trains bring in special plant ingredients from different islands and regions across the nation. It is also the MegaCorp headquarters of companies that research, create, and produce puddin' boosters.

Blaze and Chopper rose early and biked along dirt roads toward Boulder Pass Train Stop, the closest station to Courage City. The rising sun cast long shadows from their bikes and patches of trees and bushes. Eventually, the landscape changed to arid fields.

They passed a lone country house where a group of kids played in the yard. In bewilderment, Blaze and Chopper slowed down to watch the kids chase and smack each other on the head with sticks. In one case, a larger boy knocked out a smaller boy with what was more of a club than a stick.

"Are those kids playing or fighting?" Blaze asked.

"I don't know, but they don't seem too smart."

Suddenly, the gang of kids stopped and stared at the newcomers. Then they sprinted right toward them.

Blaze and Chopper swore and kicked it into high gear. Their solar-powered bikes easily outpaced their pursuers.

"Hey, Numbskull!" Blaze mocked.

Chopper joined in. "What?!"

"I got a great idea!"

"What's that Softskull?"

"Let's hit each other on the head with sticks!"

"Yeah! Maybe it will make us stronger!"

"Or smarter!!"

"Egg-shelled numbskulls!" they laughed and waved. They had no idea this was only a fraction of the absurdity they would see along their journey.

With the added benefit of a breeze at their backs, Blaze and Chopper arrived ahead of schedule. They stopped at a local puddin' establishment, where they gulped down a flight of puddin' samples and fantasized about achieving a wildly successful Noble Deed.

They locked their bikes at the train station and sat on an inconspicuous bench to arrange their gear. After reviewing the map projected from Blaze's Frames, they recalculated ticket prices. High-speed rail tickets were too expensive. Plus, nearly everyone boarding or exiting was (a) an adult and (b) dressed in business attire. To save money and avoid suspicion, they opted to sneak onto a cargo train.

At the Booster City stop, they peered through the crack in the cargo door. Forklifts moved pallets from the last cargo car to flatbed trucks. Each palette carried stacks of crates labeled with different cities and obscure scientific names.

"What do you think are in those crates?" Blaze asked.

"Probably puddin'. Or booster." Chopper said.

"We eat that much puddin' and booster?"

"Yes. Yes, we do."

The cargo train sped through Region 1 and then across the Snake Channel. From a crack in the door, Blaze watched the shores of her home island shrink on the horizon.

"I'm glad we have the Snake Channel. Imagine what the Sweeties would do if they lived right next to us," Chopper said.

"Yeah, the snakes keep them from swimming. The prime minister says sea monsters live in there, too—you ever seen one?" Blaze joked.

Chopper laughed. "No. And I have yet to see a credible picture, but there sure are a lot of reports of them. Funny though. I haven't seen snakes either."

"But someone built this bridge. Why are Sweeties even part of our country?"

The cargo train zipped along the dark blue channel as Blaze and Chopper changed into camo gear. They shot past the northern tip of Power Island—tall and shiny buildings, palm trees, the Capitol Building, and city streets filled with people in linen suits. The train sped back across the channel, and then, Blaze and Chopper arrived on Sweetie Island for the first time. Light, sandy beaches gave way to long stretches of rolling hills with lush green trees, bushes, and grasses speckled with patches of purple, yellow, white, and blue flowers. (Plants bearing red flowers had all been hacked down during the Great Red Cleansing years ago). A few moments later, the train slowed and stopped at their destination: the town of Sugar Falls.

Chopper lived for days when meticulous planning turned to action. He slid on his backpack, drew thick red lines under his eyes, and motioned for Blaze to do the same. They heard voices and cargo doors opening. Chopper signaled, quietly slid open the door, scanned the foreign environment, and jumped down and ran to a clearing. Blaze kept close behind.

Chopper looked back and, satisfied that no one had seen them, ran down a narrow dirt path that opened to a gently flowing stream. He looked at Blaze seriously. "We need to cross this stream. Our shoes are not waterproof. So, I know this will not be easy, but we need to lift ourselves up by our shoe straps across the stream without getting wet. We can—"

"Are you moldy puddin' fart tart crazy?! You're out of your mind if you think I'm going to even *think* about—you *know* how I feel—my shoes don't even *have* straps!"

Chopper burst out laughing.

"Okay, you got me. Wow, you got me." Blaze slapped his arm, shook her head, and regained her composure. "Now, seriously—funny how *I'm* the one being serious now—do you know how to get there?"

"Do I know how to get there? Does Peabody like puddin'? Do Sweeties like cookies and cake? Yes, just follow this stream—no crossing necessary," Chopper said with a big grin. "It will lead right to the Sugar River and Sugar Falls School. Now remember the plan: a little payback, don't get noticed, and get out quick. I calculate we have about thirty minutes."

"Yeah. Just make sure it's big. Noble. We need to send a message."

They followed the stream. Eventually, it flowed under a stone bridge and then intersected with the pathway to Sugar Falls School.

"Wow, nice school," Blaze said. "Too bad it's about to get ugly."

A two-story stone building with large blue pillars and wide entrance steps stood at the end of a courtyard that featured walking paths, gathering areas and ornate flower gardens. Each pillar displayed a Sweetie Island value written in large vertical letters: *Kindness, Cooperation, Fairness, Stewardship, Happiness,* and *Community.* The seventh one read, *Sweeties Good, Puddin' Heads Bad.* In the far distance, Sugar Falls cascaded down a mountain into the Sugar River, which eventually flowed through a field of sugar cane blowing in the breeze.

"I wonder how they'll feel about kindness after we're done with them," Blaze sneered. "And what is that?"

A five-meter-tall sphere of artistically woven sugar cane stalks perched atop a stone platform at the far edge of the main gathering area, facing the school. Students had sculpted and painted this replica of Earth in intricate detail over the course of last year.

"Looks like a huge blue ball," Chopper laughed. "It's supposed to be our world? Wow! It *is* true! They really do think the world is round! Oh, I just thought of a funny image!" Chopper lost his breath, held his ribs, took a deep breath, and finally squeaked, "of Sweeties getting a nasty surprise when they sailed off the edge of the world! Can you imagine the looks on their faces?" He howled, fell to the ground, and pounded his fist on the thick green grass.

"Wait. What? You think the world is flat?"

"Yeah, don't you?"

Blaze looked at Chopper like he was a numbskull. "Where did you learn that?"

"Region 1 geography class." He changed the subject. "Uh. Let's head over there."

They ran behind a cluster of trees, where they had a good view of the courtyard. After a few minutes, students wearing shirts of various shades of blue strolled in from all directions and entered the school. One group stopped and formed a loose circle nearby. They kicked three footballs back and forth with increasing skill and speed. Blaze and Chopper were pleasantly surprised to see the ringleader of the Puddin' Café attack. This time, he wore light shorts and a white-and-blue striped shirt.

He walked to the middle of the circle. "Okay, let's try that game again. Remember, you try to kick it past me without it hitting the ground. And I'll try to catch it."

"I'd like to kick that ball off his soft skull," Blaze said.

"Patience!" Chopper hissed.

Blaze's pony-tailed nemesis proceeded to catch ten straight passes: line drives and lobs, left and right, high and low—it didn't matter. This kid dove, jumped, and caught everything.

"Huh. Impressive." Blaze was surprised. "But what are they doing? I don't see a football goal anywhere."

"That's solid Kai," one student said.

"Thanks—couldn't do it without you. Cooperation makes us better. Although, that game does get boring."

Chopper silently gagged, then made a stupid face. "I'm Kai," he whispered. "I love cookies."

Blaze covered her mouth to muffle her laughter.

Kai punted three straight balls so high they seemed to disappear. "So, like I was saying, yes, *if* we receive a Noble Deed that might fix *our* problem. But what about Lily? What about all the others? Forty students are transferring to other schools. Our families can't afford the fees to stay or the fees to transfer." He glanced up and caught the three descending balls in succession. "Comrades, we need to organize a Sweetie army for the greatest Noble Deed in the history of Sweetie Island. I will lead this army against the Puddin' Heads before I plant another sugar cane stalk for them!"

"Did you hear that?" Blaze hissed to Chopper. "It's a good thing we got here first!"

"Technically, we are counterattacking."

"Whatever. When are these numbskulls going to school?"

"You're not allowed to lead," a Sweetie said to Kai.

"Who led the last mission to Puddin' Head Island?"

"Yeah, but that doesn't mean they'll give you a Noble Deed. Besides, Kai, how much longer can we wait?"

"Yeah, we have school fees. We have no choice. And how is a Noble Deed possibly kind or cooperative?"

"Kindness is not for Puddin' Heads. We are protecting Sweetie Island values! We need to attack Puddin' Heads until they stop exploiting us! You think they'll stop if we ask politely? If we give them a cookie? Are they treating *us* kindly? I don't think so. They're

Puddin' Heads!"

Blaze whispered, "What is that numbskull blabbing about? What a bunch of whiners. Ooh! Look at that ball. I could totally drill him in the back of the head right now."

"No! Don't blow our cover. Stick to the plan!"

Kai said, "Anyway, I'm skipping school today. Save a day of payments and a day in the field."

"What about the community circle?"

"Oh, right! Can't miss that," Kai said. The group trotted into their school.

Now if you're wondering whether the island's history of sociopath rulers turning the main islands against each other was connected to this situation, then you'd be correct. In this case, a group of MegaCorp investors—who weren't Puddin' Heads or Sweeties—had bought land in Sugar Falls a few years ago to grow and sell sugar cane, cocoa, and booster plants to meet the growing demand. It was an ideal location: near a train stop, right along the Sugar River, which could be used for irrigation. Plus, it had rich soil, largely due to the foliage of Sugar Forest, which they razed. Then, they wanted low-paid workers for their farm. Not coincidentally, student fees at Sugar Falls schools suddenly increased.

As Kai told me later, the school boss—while wearing a diamond tiara and diamond bracelets—had explained this situation to her school. "We need money to have a school, and they need students to work the sugar cane fields. Yes, I know they chopped down our beautiful trees, and a lot of this sugar goes to those Puddin' Heads, but it's paying for your education!" The large-handed students at Sugar Falls had three choices: (a) work the farm during half the school day to pay school fees, (b) pay cash for increased school fees, or (c) transfer to another school. So the Sugar Falls Sweeties blamed and swore about Puddin' Heads, who knew nothing of the situation.

Blaze said, "This is going to be fun."

Chopper nodded as they pulled their weapons from their backpacks. Blaze grabbed a two-liter canister of weed killer, pumped it several times, and waited for the last students to enter the building. She sprang out of hiding and accelerated to full speed, tapping a football out in front of her until she reached the edge of the courtyard. There, she examined the Earth sphere and blasted the football off its middle. The sphere didn't budge.

"Great Mother of Puddin'!" Chopper cried. "What are you doing?!"

Blaze cupped her hands and shouted back, "Trying to move this giant ball!"

"Ahh! Stick to the plan!" Then, Chopper changed his mind—the Sweeties deserved it. "Actually—great idea! Aim higher! Quickly!"

Blaze tried several more times, but it still didn't budge.

"Forget it! Back to the plan!"

Blaze looked more closely and noticed four wedges held the Earth ball in place. "Ah!" She nailed a football into the school-facing wedge, which spun off the platform.

"*Back to the plan*! We don't have much time!"

"Okay! Okay!" Blaze abandoned the football and sprinted to the center of the grass circle. She squeezed the canister nozzle and sprayed a large, invisible PH in the grass. Then, she ran up to the pillars and pulled out two cans of red spray paint. Under the *Kindness* column, Blaze wrote: *is for suckers*. Under *Cooperation*, she wrote: *losers*. Under *Fairness: is getting even*. Under *Happiness: is a bowl of puddin'*. She drew a huge smiley face.

Blaze didn't know what "stewardship" meant, but figured it must involve a ship, so she sketched a sinking ship with stick passengers wailing *Wahhhh!* on that column. Under *Community*, she sprayed stick figures holding hands and crying. Under *Sweeties Good, Puddin' Heads Bad*, Blaze scaled the column and wrote *Bad* over *Good* and *Good* over *Bad*. She galloped across the grass and tossed the spray cans in a flower bed. She clapped her hands, retrieved the football, and snorted with creative delight.

Chopper grinned and adjusted a band of the second sling shot, now tethered to a tree. "How long until that weed killer works?"

"About four hours." Blaze glanced at the darkening sky. "Unless it rains." She sprinted to gather the other footballs.

Chopper placed two paint balloons in the slingshot pouch. "Think I can hit the giant blue ball? Hey, what are you doing with those footballs—"

Suddenly, singing rose from the school. Blaze and Chopper ducked as streams of teachers and students wearing MC Frames rushed out of building. Classes with four-to-ten-year-olds sang and clapped as they flowed from the left side of the building toward the main courtyard. The youngest students carried blue balloons that bobbed up and down. An older group of students and their teachers came from the right. They sang, danced, and shouted "Hey, hey!" as they pumped their hands in the air. The two streams of teachers and students paraded around the courtyard circle and split into marching concentric lines. They continued circling, singing, clapping, and dancing to two different songs.

"Wow, this just got a whole lot better. Are you thinking what I'm thinking?"

Chopper furrowed his eyebrows, "What? No, we should wait. Too risky."

"Ah, come on! Imagine the payback. This is a legit Noble Deed opportunity! And we don't have much time: it won't take long before they see the spray paint."

The songs ended and everyone silently raised their arms in the air. They turned and bowed to the giant blue sphere, chanting in unison, "All hail Mother Earth. We are one." They rose and started a slow clap over their heads. The students opened a pathway and faced each other. A new stream of adolescent students flowed out, cheering something indecipherable, beating their chests, and marching to the center of the great gathering circle. The large group wildly cheered back at them, beating their own chests vigorously. This back and forth cheering continued, intensified, then ended in silence. The large group repeated turning and bowing to Mother Earth, rising and facing each other, and creating a pathway that stretched from the school steps to the blue sphere.

A student with tiny hands waltzed out of the school and stopped at the top of the steps. The majorette twirled a blue ribboned baton with white gloves, then marched down the steps and into the courtyard. The crowd rhythmically clapped as she passed, growing louder and louder with each high step. She stopped to bow before Mother Earth. The crowd clapped louder, chanting, "All hail Mother Earth! We are one!" Kai shot out of the school, leaped into cartwheels, skipped down the steps, and sprang into more cartwheels, back flips, and handsprings with increasing speed while the crowd boomed, "We are one! We are one!"

Chopper had to ask, "Why is that big-handed, pony-tailed soft skull allowed to lead?"

Blaze said, "He's not. That's why they have the kid in front with the blue stick. You know, like the time I sung on stage at Puddin' Head Middle and everyone sang with me, but it wasn't 'leading' because Dimbul sang the first line."

Kai stuck his landing in the middle of the great circle and yelled, "Who are we?"

The school roared back, "We are one community! We stand together, fall together, learn together, fail together!"

"What do we stand for?"

"We stand for kindness! For fairness—"

As the enthusiastic call-and-response continued, Blaze admitted, "That is pretty cool. But even cooler is my new arch enemy—Kai, king of cake and cookie crybabies—is about to go down. Looks like our lucky day."

Chopper laughed. "Cookies, prepare to crumble." He replaced two red paint balloons in the pouch of the giant slingshot, aimed, and fired.

The balloons sailed from the tree patch, taking different trajectories over the courtyard. The first burst on a teacher's arm. His coffee cup fell on the ground and shattered. Red paint splattered across students, who tried to wipe it from their faces and MC Frames. The second balloon flattened a bed of white, yellow, and blue flowers. They bent under the thick red paint.

Blaze pulled back another balloon in the massive slingshot and let it fly. It landed a direct hit on Mother Earth. Red paint sprayed students and teachers. A group of five-year-olds fell to the ground, letting go of their balloons, which rose at once into the sky. The youngsters pointed and cried.

Students on the other end of the courtyard squawked about the spray-painted pillars.

Confusion shifted to panic. "We're under attack!" Some students fainted. A teacher yelled, "It's the curse of the Red Cleansing! We should never have cut down those flowers!" Students stampeded— some into school, some away from it, some froze and cried with fear, and some were trampled. Nearly half the school dropped to their knees and bowed to the red-stained Mother Earth. "All hail Mother Earth! We are one!"

Chopper grabbed his backpack. "Mission accomplished, let's get out of here."

Blaze clenched her fists and furrowed her brow. "No—go big or go home! *Noble Deed!*"

"*Mission accomplished.* Stick to the plan—quick payback, don't get caught!"

Courageous Reader, you may, like me, find that these actions crossed a line into absurd disturbing. But remember that the Sweeties had attacked Blaze twice. Blaze believed Sweeties had made fun of her father's death. And Blaze blamed the Sweeties for her brother's fate and many of the problems on Puddin' Head Island. What would you have done?

Blaze said, "We're fine. Full payback." She pulled back on the slingshot and released three small balloons. One lofted into a high arc and exploded on the school. Drip lines slid down the wall like the tears of youngsters calling for their balloons and mommies. The other two sailed closer to the ground. One hit the leg of a running fourth grader. When his legs tangled, he took an abrupt nose-dive, toppling five other students like bowling pins. The third balloon tracked and hit Blaze's adversary in the back of his head. Kai fell to the ground, wiped off his MC Frames, and jumped up as red paint streamed down his back. He searched for the assailant.

Blaze buckled over laughing.

"Ohhhh! Ohhhh! Perfect shot, Blaze! Now, let's get out of here!"

"Not yet." Blaze burst from her hiding spot, kicking three footballs toward Mother Earth.

"What the moldy puddin' crust balls are you doing?!" Chopper yelled. "*Let's go!*"

"Run! I'll catch up."

Blaze sped toward Mother Earth while Chopper high-tailed it back to the pathway, peering over his shoulder.

Kai yelled, "Get up!" But it was no use. The panicked group of students continued chanting and bowing to Mother Earth.

Blaze pounded three consecutive shots two-thirds up Mother Earth. It budged and then rolled toward the terrified students—who did not see it coming. It sped off the platform and rolled over scores of Sweetie hands.

"My hands are flattened!" one cried.

"Mine too!" bawled others.

A disillusioned fourth grader looked at his throbbing, smashed hands. "Mother Earth didn't protect us?" he wailed incredulously.

"Like I've been saying—but no one has been listening—Mother Earth doesn't protect us, *we need to protect Mother Earth!*" Kai pointed at Blaze, then Chopper (by now far in the distance), and finally called out a term that he overheard teachers chuckling about recently: "*Code Red Puddin' Head!*"

"What do we do?" the students cried.

Kai told me later that he had no idea. Here's what he chose: "*Get them!*"

The entire school turned toward Blaze. Blaze flipped off Kai, saluted the student body, and charged toward the escape route.

A confused second grader said, "But that wouldn't be kind!"

Kai looked at the *Kindness is for suckers* pillar and Sweeties wringing their hands in pain. "Kindness to us doesn't mean kindness to them! Charge!"

In my country, safety and security experts would likely recommend staying safe and calling the police in this situation. These Sweeties, however, did the opposite. A mass of teachers and students—most of whom had never met a Puddin' Head—sprinted toward Blaze and Chopper. They yelled ideas they imagined as fitting punishment: *Feed them salad! Bite their toes! Paint them blue! Make them eat cake and cookies!* In fairness to the advancing Sweeties, the experts in my country would probably be alarmed at the *MC Code Blue Emergency Procedures* written for Puddin' Heads, too. Then again, I wonder what Island Nation experts and citizens would think of my country's emergency events?

Chopper cursed and ran. With a burst of adrenaline, Blaze rushed after him. The train whistled and the assailants ran like deer through the woods. Blaze yelled, "Did you see that? *Noble Deed!*"

"Not if we miss this train, you numbskull!"

It began to rain. The Sweetie mob quickly reached the narrowing path. Clumps of students slipped, tripped, and piled up. The swifter students chased Blaze and Chopper like a pack of wild dogs. The slower and younger students fell back, shouting, "Get themmmm!"

Chopper and Blaze slogged through the final stretch as the train pulled away. Chopper broke into the clearing and spotted the caboose. He gave a last burst of speed, jumped, and grabbed a wet handle. Though Blaze sprinted through the driving rain, she could not close the gap. She stopped and pleaded, "Just go!"

Chopper scrunched up his face and hung his head. He clenched his fists, screamed, and jumped off the train.

AS USUAL

Chopper's gaze scanned the dark waters of Snake Channel from the cargo train door. He elevated his swollen ankle on an empty booster crate. When recounting this part of the journey, Chopper told me with a laugh, "Even after everything that we did, those Sweeties still bandaged my ankle. Don't get me wrong, though. They did get us back."

The school mob tackled them. They bound their hands with rope. After a minute of shouting and arguing, the mob carried them back through the woods to the school, singing and chanting in the rain. "We are one! We are one!" Sweetie News reporters arrived and started live coverage. Kai gave patronizing advice about learning a lesson while the Sweeties painted the Puddin' Heads' faces and hands blue, and drew on their foreheads with thick marker.

Then, they loaded the Puddin' Heads onto the next train.

Chopper finally spoke. "You know, we've been friends a long time. I have always backed you—"

Blaze interrupted him. "Why did you jump? You should have stayed on the train and tried for the Noble Deed!"

She tried not to laugh at Chopper, whose forehead displayed a cross-eyed face with a large tongue sticking out.

"Friends don't leave friends behind! But maybe I should've . . ." Chopper paused, "because you are so selfish."

"Selfish?!"

"Only thinking of yourself. As usual."

"As usual?!"

"Yes, you took that last shot! You kicked the giant blue ball. And I think some students got hurt."

"That was an accident! But seriously, how cool was it?"

"It would've been cool if we hadn't gotten caught! And if no one got hurt! It was completely unnecessary. And stupid! And that's why you missed the train and, why we got caught—and you know it! Our chance for a Noble Deed is gone—and for what?"

"Hey, hey, easy there. This was your idea, too."

"I stuck to the plan! Not to mention all the yellow cards, the red cards—all the schools I followed you to."

Blaze looked puzzled. "What? Oh c'mon. You like skipping

school. It's fun. And this was amazing. When have we ever done anything like this? I mean, yes, we got caught, but did you see the look on—"

"*You* got caught. It doesn't matter now."

"Look, I'm sorry, okay! I'm just so mad at school—and the Sweeties, and Kai, for what they did! Ahh! If only I'd caught the train in time."

Chopper stared blankly, unmoved. Eventually, he wriggled his wrists free from the rope and untied Blaze. "You know, I need some time alone. Away from you."

"Are we breaking up?" Blaze tried to laugh. Their relationship was clearly not romantic.

Chopper shrugged without a smile, "Something like that."

The two rode home in silence, managing to scrub off most of the blue paint—though not the permanent marker faces. As they neared their hometown, Blaze said, "I'm going to peel off here. Maybe see you in a few days?"

"Doubt it," Chopper replied.

Blaze didn't know how she would face her mother. So, instead, she headed to Mount Freedom. "What am I supposed to do now?" she cried. Blaze beat her hands on the handlebars. The solar panel fell and shattered on the road. Eventually, the electric battery died. "Why did those Sweeties have to attack us?" Loneliness and rage surged through her. She pedaled with wild abandon until she reached the base of Mount Freedom.

MOUNTAIN VIEW

Blaze ignored an MC Frames call from her mom. As she slowed her bike, an advertisement for hand-shrinking puddin' booster flashed across her MC Frames. Blaze screamed and first threw her Frames to the ground, then her bike. She wiped back tears and ran toward the trail head. She raced up the grassy switchbacks, swearing, kicking rocks, and snapping branches.

After an intense ascent, Blaze slowed and guzzled water from her backpack. She kicked a dirt clod, which exploded. "This better not be contaminated," she said begrudgingly. Those kind Sweeties had filled her water bottle before sending her and Chopper packing.

The switchback neared a cliff. She stopped, tossed a small rock, and watched it plummet toward the jagged rocks below. Blaze counted its descent to the ground: one, two, three, four, five, six. She stepped out to the edge and cringed as she remembered the past few days. Her thoughts spiraled down a negative abyss.

She screamed and howled. She beat her chest, raised her arms to the sky, and bellowed the kind of long guttural sounds she imagined her ancestors made as they climbed this same mountain centuries ago.

Blaze yelled, "What is the point of this life anyway?!" She scanned the horizon, locating her tiny town. She thought of her mom, Kuko, Maya, Chopper, and her dad. She stared down the cliff with her mind racing and heart pounding.

She closed her eyes and tried to clear her mind. "Whyyyy?" she yelled across the great ravine. "Why do these stupid things keep happening to me? Why did the Sweeties ruin my life? Why don't schools change these stupid rules? Why doesn't anyone change?"

Suddenly, a strong gust of wind shot up the cliff and blew her backwards. She slipped on a pile of stones and tumbled to the ground. Out of nowhere, an ethereal voice emphatically stated, *Own. Your. Journey.*

Blaze lay there for several minutes, shaken and confused. *Own your journey*, she mused, then took deep breaths, and rolled onto her side.

What was that voice? I get captured by Sweeties, and now I'm hearing voices? Am I going crazy? What does this mean?

She sprang to her feet with her mind on fire. *Own my journey? I'm*

*on a journey? Like a vacation? No, Mom doesn't take vacations. Journey to
what?* She looked down the cliff again. *Owning? Am I not owning mine?
Of course, I'm owning my journey—who else would own it? That's absurd!*

She looked across Puddin' Head Island, then Power Island, then
Sweetie Island. Suddenly, she had an insight. "Of course! I've been
such a numbskull!" Her mind calmed and focused. Blaze spun
around and trained her eyes on a new destination: the summit of
Mount Freedom. She channeled her negative emotions into a zeal
for climbing. Her body, heart, and mind relaxed into a steady upward
stride as she passed a lake. Waves of negativity calmed to ripples,
then to a peaceful stillness. Blaze owned each step, each slip, each
ache, each breath, each gasp for air, each thought, and each emotion
fully, without complaint, and without judgment. After a long stretch
of this state of flow, Blaze gazed at the mountain peak and felt at
peace, as if the universe had rekindled her soul's purpose—as if she
knew what to do.

The sinking sun cast long shadows as she descended from the
summit. She rounded a switchback and glimpsed a person walking
down a narrow trail that branched from the main pathway.

Blaze followed. The person froze, grabbed a spoon, and spun
around as if ready to fight.

"Blaze? You scared me! What are you doing way up here? And
this late?"

"Aunt Serafina! What are *you* doing up here?"

"Uh . . . what is that on your forehead?"

"It's a long story. I've had quite a day. Wait, why aren't you
wearing your Frames, either?"

Serafina tilted her head. "Are you okay?"

"I've just made some stupid mistakes, as usual. But I'm learning
to own them."

"Wow, you are growing up."

"So . . . what *are* you doing up here?"

"I'm, uh . . . leading a retreat. We're taking a little break right
now."

"What kind of retreat?"

"Uh . . . an outdoor retreat. Exercise, getting outdoors, taking
time to clear the mind. You know?"

Blaze said, "Actually, I think I do." But she sensed her aunt was hiding something. "What's going on? What aren't you telling me?"

Her aunt hesitated. She pursed her lips and finally looked at Blaze. "Since you're so grown up . . . remember that time you tried to drive my motorcycle and tipped it over?"

"Yes."

"And the time you jumped on the bed and swallowed a five-cent piece and I had to take you to the hospital?"

"Yesss . . ." Blaze said, hoping she'd get to the point.

"And we kept those secrets because you seemed to have learned your lesson, and why upset your parents?"

"Yesss!"

"So, can I trust you to keep a secret, even from your mom?"

"*Yesss!*"

"Remember what we told you about TDJP?"

"Yes."

"We're having a TDJP retreat right now. A big one."

Suddenly, a man appeared behind her. "Serafina, there you are. We're ready." He noticed Blaze. "Whoa! Who's this?" he asked suspiciously.

"It's okay. This is my niece, Blaze. She was just out for a hike."

"What happened to your face, kid?"

"It's a long story."

Aunt Serafina said, "This one's going to be a leader. She wants to change schools. She wants to be the big boss."

"Is that right? We could use some change on this island. Good luck, kid."

After the man left, Serafina said, "A group of us meet in secret on Mount Freedom, very selectively adding new members. We even have a few senators now, besides myself."

Blaze said, "I should head back. But maybe your group would accept an eighth grader?"

Serafina smiled. "Hmmmm. I'll have to think about that and ask the group. Education is a big focus—we could use someone with inside knowledge. Okay, I have to get back, too."

"Yeah. I don't want Mom to worry. I'll keep all of this between you and me—but I want to learn more!"

Blaze quickly reached the bottom of Mount Freedom. She wasn't ready to talk to her mom yet. So, she called Chopper as soon as she started pedaling home.

"Chopper, I am so sorry for botching the Noble Deed! You're right—I was selfish. I wanted to get even with those zombie soft skulls, but I took it too far. I should have listened to you. I should have stuck to the plan. Thanks for being a good friend. I hope you can forgive me some day."

"You were a numbskull."

"Yeah."

"And I can't get this stupid face off my forehead."

"Me neither." Blaze laughed, then cried. "I'm scared, Chopper. I know what I want to do, but I blew it. I don't know what's going to happen."

"We'll figure something out. We always do."

"I hope so."

"And do I need to remind you of our pact? We have big changes to make."

"Yes, yes we do. Thanks for talking."

Blaze reached her hometown after dusk, emotionally and mentally drained. She longed to quickly assure her mom that she was okay and fall asleep as soon as her head hit her pillow.

That hope faded as she rode into her neighborhood. A large crowd, flashing police cars, and Puddin' Head News surrounded her house. A last burst of adrenaline rushed through her. *Why are they here? What do they know?*

Suppressing the urge to nap in the ditch, Blaze jumped off her bike and leaned it against a neighbor's house. She tried to sneak through the crowd, but someone spotted her in the shadows.

"There she is!"

The crowd ran toward her, erupting into cheers. "Blaze! Blaze! Blaze!"

Terrified and exhausted, Blaze turned to run and then stopped. They were *cheering* for her? Blaze turned suspiciously back. The crowd swamped her.

They hoisted her up over their heads and chanted her name.

They broke into "Puddin' Heads! Puddin' Heads! Puddin' Heads!" and carried her toward the news cameras. Blaze removed her MC Frames and slid them into her back pocket.

A bright camera shone in her face, and a news reporter looked for Blaze's hands, but she'd hidden them behind her back. "How does it feel to be a Puddin' Head hero?"

"A hero?" Blaze asked. "For what?" Obviously, the reporter couldn't have heard what happened.

The crowd burst out laughing. The reporter responded, "Ah, a humble hero. Say, what's the deal with the face on your forehead? And where are your MC Frames?"

Blaze stammered, "I was worried the crowd might break them, so I—"

Just then, Blaze's mom pushed through the crowd like a mama bear racing to her lost cub. She lifted Blaze's feet off the ground with a hug that knocked the wind out of her. "You're here! Great Mother of Puddin' Head Island, you're here!"

Blaze gasped for air as her mom read her face. "Are you okay? What happened to your forehead?"

Blaze cried, then laughed. "Yes, I'm okay."

Maya shot through the crowd, squealing, "Blaaaaazzze!" and jumped into her arms. "Are you the real Mr. Puddin' Head?" The crowd laughed and let out a collective sigh. Then, re-energized, they shouted and pumped their fists. "Sto-ry! Sto-ry! Sto-ry!"

The reporter appealed to the crowd. "So, Blaze Union. Tell us about the Battle of Sugar Falls."

Blaze caught Chopper out of the corner of her eye. His face beamed with pride. His slightly raised eyebrows seemed to say, *I got your back* and *you owe me.*

Blaze smiled and closed her eyes with relief. She surely had the world's greatest friend. She choked back tears—now of joy—and introduced herself to Puddin' Head Island. "You have no idea what a day this has been. And none of it would have been possible without my dear friend Chopper . . ."

The next morning, Chopper pushed through the growing crowd outside of Blaze's house. He peeked in through her kitchen window, then banged on the door. After the third attempt, Blaze opened the door, squinting, as if emerging from a dark cave.

"Chopper, why are you waking me up so early on a weekend? Do you have any idea how tired I am?"

"Early? It's 9 a.m. More importantly, have you seen the news?! Or your Mega Gossip account? You have over a million followers!"

"What?! That's nearly half the island!" With a jolt of energy, Blaze opened Mega Gossip—which of course, was the MegaCorp social media platform—with her MC Frames. Indeed, she had 1,213,975 followers. Seconds later, ten more joined.

"Why are so many people following me?" She looked outside. "Whoa! The crowd is still here?"

"You're the feature story on Puddin' Head News. There must be a couple thousand people out there."

A man pressed his face against the window. "She's up! Blaze is here!" The crowd erupted. "Blaze, Blaze, Blaze!"

Blaze yanked the curtains closed. "This is insane! What happened? *What did you tell them?*"

"It was more what I showed them. I posted some action scenes from Sugar Falls and tagged you. I figured you wouldn't mind." He winked.

Blaze smiled. "Cool!"

Chopper grinned and said, "Yeah, they turned out great. I know you'll be very disappointed, but I left out the end."

"Ha!"

"Anyway, the news contacted me and ran the story."

Blaze watched the videos and buckled over laughing at the paint balloon taking out the kid running. Then the Earth sphere rolling over the Sweeties.

"Ugh, I feel a little bad about those little kids. But awesome recording!"

"Thanks! Guess what? That giant blue ball rolled over two hundred students' hands, causing them to swell."

"Yeah?" Blaze said nervously.

"And today is Good Hope Day. The news just reported that in Sweetie Region 2, more than two hundred kids flipped from small- to large-handed. And Puddin' Head Region 2 has over two hundred kids who switched from large- to small-handed!"

"Whaaaat thaaaa? No way! I mean, no one was hurt, right?"

"I don't know."

Blaze tore off her MC Frames. "Wait, mine still have the frown face."

"Check your stats."

Blaze slid her Frames back on and said, "MC Frames, hand size specs." She read the stats on her interior frame. "I moved from the 66th percentile to the 65th. It doesn't matter. I hate these hand-size rules and they need to change! But what about you?"

"I stayed at the 58th percentile. But there are a little more than two hundred kids feeling lucky—thanks to you."

Blaze ran to Maya's room.

"Where are your Frames?"

"I don't know."

"Where are they!"

"I lost them."

"There they are." Blaze pulled them out from under the bed.

Maya started crying.

"Oh, Maya, I'm sorry. But hand size doesn't matter! Now take off those ridiculous gloves!"

"No! Blaze, *stoppp!*"

Blaze marched into the kitchen and stuffed the compression gloves in the trash. "Ahhh! No more." She blocked Maya from the trash and met Chopper's eyes. "You're such a good friend. I owe you huge. Thank you."

"Eh, it was nothing." He cocked his head quizzically to the side. "Do you hear that? Is that what I think it is?"

Blaze let go of Maya and ran outside. Three kids with smiley face Frames jump-hugged Blaze. "Thank you! Thank you! I have small hands!"

The faint sound of a helicopter grew louder, and soon a sleek black MC helicopter flew in fast.

Chopper raised his arms, jumped up and down, and stammered, "*What?! No way! Wow, wow, wow!!*" Wide-eyed, he shook Blaze. He yelled over the noise of the whooshing helicopter blades, "I think that's the MC Falcon 8400 XPTT! It's landing here!"

Blaze hollered, "Is it an attack!? Maybe it's the Sweeties! Should we run?"

"No! It's a government chopper! I think they're coming to see *us.*"

The helicopter hovered over Blaze's house before landing on the street. People poured out of their homes to watch the excitement. A tall man wearing a black silk suit and red tie jumped out of the passenger side. A teen girl dressed in black pants and a black designer T-shirt followed. Her black, white, and gold-streaked hair blew wildly in the wind from the helicopter.

Blaze and Chopper stood stiffly as the man stuck out his hand. The girl stepped in front of him. "Daddy, *I'm* in charge of Noble Deeds!" She barked over the helicopter noise, "I'm Scarlet Pompavich, I coordinate the MegaCorp Noble Deed program. This is my father, who is the minister of advertising and media and also the co-CEO of MegaCorp."

Blaze and Chopper nodded in astonishment.

"You two have done excellent work. I am happy to announce that you have a very good chance of being awarded a Noble Deed. The prime—I mean, the supreme prime minister would like to meet you and make the official decision. If you two don't have anything better to do, we can leave now," Scarlet said, gesturing toward the helicopter.

PART II
ABSURD POWER

CHOPPER RIDE

"What?!" Blaze squeezed Chopper. "We did it! We won a Noble Deed!!!"

"Yes!!" Chopper pumped his fists.

"Well, not officially yet," Scarlet Pompavich said. "Wait, is that a *frown* face on your MC Frames? That can't be right. Large-handed kids can't win Noble Deeds."

"Scarlet," said the minister, "The prime—I mean, the supreme prime minister said he may make an exception. They have a very large following. Blaze in particular." (FYI: the "supreme" prime minister was the great grandson of the first prime minister.)

"Well, isn't that something?"

Chopper asked, "Uh, don't we need our parents' permission? They're working right now."

"Oh, don't worry. We already notified them. It's fine."

Blaze and Chopper shrugged. "Okay, let's go!"

They climbed into the back seat, stuck on helmets, and strapped on seat belts. They shot into the air and watched the crowd below.

"So, you two want to go straight to the Pompavich residence? Or would you prefer to a see what this bad boy can do in a quick sight-seeing tour?"

"Sight-seeing tour!"

The pilot turned the helicopter and blasted toward Mount Freedom, which they reached within minutes.

The minister said, "Blaze, I believe you were here last night." Suspicious yet impressed, Blaze wondered how he knew.

"Let's see how fast we can round this mountain."

The pilot steered the helicopter toward the south side of the mountain. She turned into a tight semi-circular about one hundred meters above the trees. The two friends looked down at the rapidly passing mountain landscape. A group of hikers looked up, and Blaze recognized her aunt.

Blaze put her finger to her lips, signaling Chopper not to say anything. The pilot spotted them and dove. She blared a piercing siren and sprayed them with liters of puddin'.

Alarmed and confused, the group slipped and fell to the ground, making more than one obscene gesture. The pilot boomed with laughter, "Sweet tart nature lovers!" Scarlet and her dad laughed.

Blaze lurched forward as her seatbelt tightened. "Why'd you do that?!"

The pilot laughed. "Because I can."

Blaze whispered to Chopper, "There are a lot of things I can do, too. Like throw her out of this helicopter. But that doesn't make it a good idea."

"What did you say?" asked the pilot.

"Nothing."

They headed north as the topography changed from trees to grassland to arid lands. Occasionally, they zoomed over a town or small city. Fighting nausea, they endured dramatic turns, dives, and climbs. After fifteen minutes, the pilot turned west and sped to Power Island.

They flew over the downtown Capitol Building, shiny glass business buildings, and rows of shops. They soared over neighborhoods lined with palm trees, decorative stone streets, a golf course, and dozens of mansions with swimming pools and manicured lawns.

The pilot said, "Okay, we're almost there. You can see the Pompavich home."

On the horizon, sat a large stone house with a cobblestone path, immaculate terraced walls, and vibrant plants and trees. Chopper exclaimed, "Wow, that's your house? I mean mansion? Uh. . . what do you call it?"

Scarlet laughed. "No, that's the air purifier building. It pumps filtered air into our mega-mansion, the secretary's house, and the guest house. It takes out the impurities, reduces the humidity, and cools or heats the air to a perfect temperature."

Blaze shook her head at this obscene wealth. When they reached the Pompavich mega-mansion, Blaze mustered a non-defensive question.

"You live on an island with fresh ocean breezes. Why do you need purified air?"

Scarlet chuckled. "Well, you'd be surprised at the amount of pollution the factories produce. You're probably just used to breathing dirty air. Now, let's get on to the good stuff. We have some time for a quick tour before we give you a special gift from the prime—Ahh!" she groaned. "*Supreme* prime minister. And then we'll head to the Capitol, where he wants to meet you personally."

BLAZE VERSUS SCARLET

They stepped off the helicopter and entered the mega-mansion. The minister said, "So, would you like to see the game wing, the outdoor shooting range, the football facility, or—" He suddenly stopped abruptly, as though mesmerized.

A woman in a white business suit and stunning diamond necklace strode toward them.

"Are these the little Puddin' Head heroes?"

"Indeed. Blaze and Chopper, meet the one-and-only Mrs. Pompavich, better known as the education minister and football commissioner.

"Whaaaaat?" Blaze skipped up next to her. "You're in charge of education *and* football? Like, you make the rules?"

"That's right."

"Huh. So, you decide on things like red cards and bootstraps classes?"

"Yes. I set the rules and parameters for anything required island-wide. And I approve, revise, or deny the rules that regions recommend to me."

"So you could eliminate bootstraps classes?"

"I could, but why would I?"

Blaze ignored the question. "So, you're a very important, powerful person."

"You could say that." The education minister smiled slyly.

"Are you so powerful that you could eliminate *any* rule?"

"Try me."

"Can you eliminate hand size rules?"

"Ha! I'm not quite that powerful! I would have to bring that amendment to the Senate, and they would never pass it. And even if they did, the prime—I mean the supreme prime minister would need to sign it. And that's never going to happen."

Blaze thought for a moment, then asked very seriously, "How do I get your job? Puddin' Head Schools need to change."

The minister of education stepped back, and her smile faded to a frown. "Puddin' Head Schools are just fine," she said emphatically. Then, a strange thing happened. The education minister contorted her face, then farted. "Oh!" she said, but rather than apologize, she took a few steps and acted like nothing happened.

Blaze shot a gleeful look at Chopper.

"What a bold question," the education minister continued, with nostrils flared. "Reminds me of someone else I know. Well, you need to be appointed by the supreme prime minister himself."

Blaze refocused. "People don't vote for you?"

"No. What a waste of time and resources. Now, I need to go—"

"Wait, I'm serious. How *do* I get your job? Do I need to teach? Be a school boss? Regional boss?"

"Ha! I haven't taught a day in my life. You need connections, a lot of money, and to win the supreme prime minister's loyalty." She reached out and tapped the side of Blaze's MC Frames. "So good luck with that kid." She jumped into a waiting limo and drove off.

Blaze raised her fist, but Chopper pushed it back down before she could raise her middle finger.

"Ha! Blaze is ambitious!" he yelled awkwardly.

Scarlet cocked her head at him. "Okay . . . Anyway, don't mind her. She can be a real b— Uh, I mean . . . *piece of work.*" She smiled at her dad and winked at Blaze.

"Back to my question," Scarlet's dad said. "You can see the game wing, the outdoor shooting range, the football facility, or the racetrack. You'll have time to see one while I take care of a little business."

Blaze and Chopper asked a few questions, discussed, and chose the football facility. The minister called a driver.

A man dressed all in white drove up in a golf cart.

"I'll drive," Scarlet said. "What time do you need them back, Daddy?"

The minister raised his eyebrows. "Honey, we have a driver. I don't think—"

"What *time*, Daddy?"

The minister sighed and looked up at the vaulted ceiling. "You have one hour."

"Excellent. You two, jump in."

Blaze and Chopper slid into the middle row of the golf cart. Scarlet slammed her foot on the pedal, honked loudly, and swerved back and forth as she drove.

Blaze checked out Scarlet's Frames, which had the smiley face.

Scarlet's scarred, strange, small hands gripped the steering wheel.

"Are you checking out my hands?"

Blaze blushed. "Huh? What? No, I was—"

"Yeah, I used to have large hands and the frown face. But Daddy paid for surgery." Scarlet waved. "Ta da!"

Each of fingers and her thumbs were shorter. In case you're wondering, the surgery removed the intermediate phalanges and then grafted the distal ones onto the proximal ones.

Blaze looked at Chopper as if to say, *it's true!*

Scarlet said, "It's amazing what modern medicine can do. And it cured my temper. At least most of it."

Blaze slid down in her seat and dropped the subject as they passed an Olympic sized indoor pool. Just outside the ten-meter-high glass windows, another large winding pool was surrounded by a beautiful stone patio, palm trees, an outdoor bar and grill, and posh seating areas. Blaze imagined rich and powerful people smoking cigars and talking about money, the next best puddin', fancy cars, private jets, helicopters, and hovercrafts.

They drove past a dining room the size of a skinny football pitch (in my country, "soccer field"). A long table spanned the room surrounded by decorative chairs made with banyan wood. Scarlet explained that the table could descend into the lower level so that staff could quickly set it and place the food. Then, it would rise back up to the dining room, with the food at the perfect temperature. However, a month ago, a dignitary intoxicated with adult puddin' had fallen into the hole while the table was being set —ruining a rare platter of baby elephant steak. Now, guests had to wait until the table was fully ascended before they could enter the dining room.

Blaze whispered to Chopper, "Someone has way too much money! Imagine what we could do with it instead!" Then she noticed something odd. "What is that sticking out of Scarlet's pocket?"

Chopper glanced down. "It appears to be a rock with a tail."

Blaze shook her head. "What the puddin' balls?"

They drove past many empty rooms: a bowling alley; a casino with slot machines and card tables; an arcade with dozens of video games and a huge screen; a game room with foosball, billiards tables, and Ping Pong; a movie theater; and tennis courts. Strangely, several rooms had a thick canopy of very tall tree trunks and thick branches that lined the wall and covered the ceiling like an excessive and pretentious decoration.

"What's up with all the wood?" Blaze asked.

"My mom just likes banyan trees." Scarlet shrugged with no idea that the banyan tree deforestation that provided these decorations would also create a future enemy.

Finally, they arrived at the outdoor training facility. Sunshine beamed down through the open retractable roof. Stations, equipment, and football goals were set up throughout the facility.

"You any good?" Scarlet asked.

Blaze cocked an eyebrow. "You might say that."

"We'll see." They walked to a station that had video cameras, large screens, projectors, and a regulation-size football goal. The goal didn't have the typical net, though. Rather, a much larger mesh screen stood behind it, with an automatic return shoot.

Scarlet walked behind a stand and crouched down as if hiding something. She pulled something from her pocket, petted it, nuzzled it, and shoved it back inside. She popped up like nothing had happened, waltzing around to the stand, scanning her MC Frames on the reader. She said, "MC Frames, practice round, rectangles."

"What was that?" Blaze asked.

"What?"

"Do you have a pet mouse or something?"

"I have no idea what you're talking about!" Scarlet said. "Oh, you're afraid of playing me in football!"

"What?"

"You're trying to distract me!"

"Huh?"

Five balls rolled out from underneath the mesh screen.

A hologram projector spotlighted a thin rectangle on the right half of the goal. "Try to hit the rectangles. You get one point for each accurate shot and an extra point each time you do it in less than two seconds. Let me show you."

Scarlet tapped her MC Frames to start. She kicked a ball through the rectangle. A screen showed one point for the goal and one bonus point.

"Wow, this is cool!" Blaze said.

Chopper hit seven of ten with five bonus points for a total of twelve points. Blaze nailed nine of ten for eighteen total points, missing the last small rectangle by centimeters.

"That's surprising. Your MC Frames are accurate, right?," Scarlet asked.

"What's that supposed to mean?"

"Nothing. MC Frames, next player."

Scarlet drilled ten straight balls through targets that varied in size and location. She alternated left and right kicks with ease. "There you go, twenty points."

Blaze hated losing, especially to someone with fake hands. "I'm just warming up. How about a rematch."

Scarlet shrugged. "Sure."

They played twelve more games from different distances and angles with different levels of difficulty. Each game ended with the same result. Chopper came in a distant last. Blaze only missed one or two shots, even on corner kicks. Scarlet was nearly flawless. With each loss, Blaze became angrier and demanded yet another match. Still, Scarlet won every single game.

"You should feel great. That was actually impressive—especially for being a Big. Usually no one scores a single goal on those corner kicks. You scored seven."

Blaze punted a ball to the other end of the facility. "Losing has nothing to do with hand size! Now, how about that racetrack?"

Scarlet drove them to the racetrack and gave them a course map, helmets, and a race car suit. "In case of you crash. Or catch on fire." She explained the safety rules as well as racetrack tips, challenges, and lap records. Blaze jumped in the red car. Scarlet took white. Chopper was stuck with blue.

They drove the first lap at a leisurely pace, with Scarlet yelling more tips and cautions—the sharp turns, the jump, and how to maximize speed around curves without tipping over.

"All right, let's race already!" Blaze said.

They lined up and Scarlet shouted over the engines, "Don't feel bad when I win by a kilometer!" She smirked, raised her eyebrows, and slid on her helmet. The large traffic light flashed from red to yellow to green. The racers slammed on the pedal. Scarlet easily won several single-lap races. Despite her own times improving, Blaze grew increasingly angry. The three agreed to end with a ten-lap race.

Chopper said, "I know you want to win, but don't get yourself injured. She has probably been driving this course since she was two. This is your first day. Just have fun."

Blaze rolled her eyes. "Whatever. I can beat this fake-handed soft-skull."

"Like you did in football?"

"Shut up." Blaze stayed with Scarlet during the opening straightaway. But on the first turns, Scarlet pulled slightly ahead, with Chopper fading behind after lap one. Each lap, Blaze sped faster around the curves and turns. Midway through the third lap, she continued to close the gap. By the final round, Blaze and Scarlet had nearly lapped Chopper and were closing in.

Scarlet slowed down, waiting for the right time to pass him, giving Blaze the chance to catch Scarlet. They sped a car length behind Chopper. On the next turn, Blaze shot through a small gap between Chopper and the inside lane, screaming, "Haaa! I'm going to win!" But as she did so, she inadvertently bumped Chopper's tire. Chopper panicked and swerved into Blaze.

Blaze slammed on her brakes. Chopper swore at her and over-corrected his steering. His car flipped in the air, landed on its tires and skidded off the racetrack, nearly tipping over. It dug out huge divots of grass and mud, which caked Chopper's face and chest as he cursed.

Scarlet crossed the finish line with victory arms raised. She turned around, winked at Blaze, and raced toward Chopper.

"Sorry you lost again."

"Whatever! I would have won if Chopper didn't hit me!" But seeing Chopper's expression, Blaze said, "Are you okay? I mean, you're—"

"No, I'm not okay! *You* almost killed me! Not cool, Blaze. Not cool!"

Scarlet agreed. "Yeah, that pass was really unsafe. Aren't you two friends?"

Chopper said, "A very good question." He looked past Blaze and said coldly, "I think it's time to head back."

Blaze hurried after Chopper. "Look, I'm sorry! I needed to win and knock that fake-handed, spoiled brat off her pedestal."

"Needed to?"

"Yes!"

The three returned to the main entrance, where the advertising minister waited. He unsuccessfully tried to hug his daughter then handed Blaze and Chopper each a slim metal box. "The pri— The supreme prime minister wanted you to have this gift."

Chopper opened the box, and his anger turned to excitement. "Wow! Wow! Are these the PH Silver Night Limited Edition MC Frames? The ones with telescoping, ultra-range, and mega-boost?!"

"They are indeed. What else would you expect from the supreme prime minister?"

Chopper shot Blaze a dirty look as he tried his on.

Scarlet shrugged, "Yeah, they're okay. But they have glitches. And you can't buy or experience virtual property with them."

"You pay money for imaginary property?" Blaze asked.

"Oh, it's not pretend. It's virtual and so awesome! I bought this virtual mega-mansion for a mere million. I can decorate it and throw parties and everything. And it has a pony farm."

"You paid a million MC bucks for imaginary property," Blazed said flatly. "Meanwhile, thousands of kids can't afford school."

"It's virtual, and that makes it real! It's not imaginary!"

Blaze shook her head and whispered to Chopper. "Someone has a little too much time and money on her surgically altered hands."

Scarlet grunted, "You're such a sore loser!"

Blaze smirked and opened her own box. She slid on the new Frames, scanned her hands, examined the frown face, and glared at Scarlet. "Perfect. Until next time."

The minister said, "Okay, chop chop! Let's go. You don't want to be late for the supreme prime minister."

SUPREME PRIME MINISTER

The media minister led Blaze and Chopper through a security checkpoint and suddenly stopped. He snuck behind the minister of education who was giving orders to a group of staff members. He kissed her on the cheek with a flirty eyebrow raise.

"Ahhh! Elroy, you know I hate surprises! And what have I told you about public affection!"

He tried to grab her hand. "Baby, I was just—"

"Seriously! Ahhh!" Mrs. Pompavich clenched her fists and stormed off.

Mr. Pompavich shrugged and continued through several more security checkpoints. He introduced Blaze and Chopper to a dozen staff members along with a Puddin' Head senator, and the minister of agriculture. A sprightly man bumped into Mr. Pompavich.

"Oh! Excuse me, Minister Pompavich. I'm so sorry!" he said.

"Ah, Mr. Blunt. No worries. How are you?"

"Good, good. Say, I just saw Mrs. Pompavich. She loved those flowers, and, I must say, had a *very large* smile on her face."

"Really?!" Mr. Pompavich said excitedly. "I mean, really?" he said more controlled.

"Yes. I just heard her talking about them in her office."

"*Send more flowers,*" Mr. Pompavich mumbled to himself. He looked at Blaze and Chopper. "Ah! I need to take these two to see the prime—I mean, the supreme prime minister."

"Oh, I can do that for you."

"Could you? Thank you so much!" Mr. Pompavich sprinted down a hallway.

"I hear you two are up for a Noble Deed?"

"Yeah!" Blaze said. "I guess if we win, we go to MegaCorp Academy or something. But I'd rather be a school boss. Or the education minister." Blaze studied Mr. Blunt, who seemed intrigued.

Mr. Blunt locked eyes with her as if searching to see if she was the real deal. "Well, I hear he does like bold ideas. And flattery." Mr. Blunt winked and took them to the waiting area.

The assistant brought them puddin' shakes and puddin' cups. She skimmed the morning agenda, then noticed Blaze and her Frames. "Interesting. The prime minister wants to see you Blaze. Alone."

"What about Chopper?"

"Alone," she repeated firmly.

"Okay, okay."

A few minutes later, the assistant escorted Blaze into a large room. "Mr. Prime Minister, Blaze Union is here to see you."

"That's supreme prime minister!" a man yelled from the far end of the room.

Although the secretary said the correct title of prime minister—which by the way, I will also use unless overcome by sarcasm—she apologized and shouted back. "Oh, right, sorry Mr. *Supreme* Prime Minister!" She mumbled under her breath, "Silly, cumbersome, unofficial . . ."

"What are you saying?" he yelled.

"Nothing, sir." She gave Blaze a wide-eyed, fake smile and closed the door.

Blaze switched on binocular view and zoomed in. The prime minister wore a dark suit with a red tie and a ridiculous gold necklace. He sat behind a large gold desk stacked with gold coins. He gulped down a puddin' shake and clasped his tiny hands atop his head. He cocked his head toward the wall, the ceiling, then Blaze. Suddenly, he smacked his hands on the desk, paused, and slammed his head between his hands. Blaze jumped. Surely, he'd cracked his skull.

"Oh yeah!!" the prime minister yelled. "Puddin' with adult power booster! That's the stuff!"

Unfortunately, the heavy gold necklace anchored him to the desk. The prime minister twisted his head and grunted, "Ah! Kinked my neck!" He struggled to lift the necklace off his shoulders, which thudded onto the floor and his foot. "Puddin' balls!" he shouted, grimacing and hopping on one foot. Suddenly, he slammed his head onto the table again, rubbing his neck. "Fixed it!" he said in semi-relief. He strained to stand up and waved Blaze over.

"Not what I was expecting," Blaze said to herself. She switched back to normal view, walked past a sitting area with couches and chairs, and sat in a small, red-and-gold cushioned chair. The prime minister walked around his desk, sat on the corner, folded his tiny hands in his lap, and looked down at her.

"Nice Frames. Like 'em?"

"Yes, they're amazing," Blaze said, still stunned by the head slam.

The prime minister raised his eyebrows as if to prompt her. He flipped a gold coin a few times and whistled.

"I'm still learning what they can do."

The prime minister kept flipping the coin and whistling. "I think you want to say . . ."

"Huh? Oh, right. Thank you!"

He nodded.

Blaze joked, "Do they shoot missiles?"

"Ha! Swagger. I like that. Well, they—the manufacturers—said weapons are too dangerous. But I disagree. We've got the constant threat of sea monsters and zombies—you just never know. You're a Puddin' Head, right?"

Blaze looked at her red shirt. "Uh, yes." She decided against telling him that she'd been joking.

The prime minister nodded again. "Blaze. I've seen the video of your tremendous bravery at Sugar Falls. I don't normally give Noble Deeds to middle school students, and certainly not large-handed ones. But how many followers do you have now?"

"More than 1.3 million, Mr. Prime—, I mean, Mr. Supreme Prime Minister."

He peered outside and muttered, "Huh. Amazing." He turned back to her. "I'm going to give you a Noble Deed that will be celebrated across Puddin' Head Island. As a reward for your courage and leadership, you can attend MegaCorp Academy, which I'm sure you know has world-class facilities, teachers, and students, including Scarlet." He laughed. "A little different than your schooling experience. And to sweeten the deal, I'll throw in surgery to shorten those hands. No cost."

He cocked an eyebrow. "This is a game changer Blaze. One that will open up possibilities and fortunes beyond your wildest dreams. You can play offense in football again. More importantly, every MC Academy graduate is guaranteed entry into Power Island University, an internship at MegaCorp and, ultimately, a lucrative career. You just visited the Pompavich's home, right? Imagine owning a piece of property like that." One of the prime minister's tiny hands shot out like a snake in search of a meal. "So, can we make this deal right now?"

Blaze pushed herself out of the chair. "Uh . . . Wow, generous offer. I would love to play offense again. But shouldn't everyone be allowed to play offense? Uh . . . never mind. I'll think about the hand surgery. I have this phobia of—"

The prime minister interrupted. "The surgery is included, and . . . . A prerequisite. I mean, we can't have a student with large hands disrupting the academy."

"Huh." Blaze ran her finger along the gold-lined seam of the armchair and changed the topic. "What about Chopper? Can he join me at the academy?"

"Blaze, this is a once-in-a-lifetime opportunity! We don't give Noble Deeds out like puddin'. The waitlist is long, so creating a seat for you is already a special favor and one I can't wait on. I'm sure your friend Chopster is a lovely person, but he's not academy material."

"Chopper? You don't even know him! He's the reason I'm here. Besides, I was thinking of a different reward."

The prime minister grunted, then rubbed his neck as if soothing the pain. He was not used to losing a deal. "Blaze, you have a chance to join the elite and powerful and to reach your full potential. You could be an example—a leader, Blaze. Someone to make this nation stronger and more powerful. But how could you lead with those hands?"

"I made it this far. Maybe hand size doesn't matter."

The prime minister jumped off the desk and grabbed Blaze's shirt with his tiny hands. "Are you messing with me? Are you part of that TDLMNOP group?"

"TD what?" Blaze asked.

"Do you know who I am? Do you understand the opportunity I'm giving you?"

A shiver ran down Blaze's spine. She repressed her primal instinct to bite his miniature hand. She paced, remembered what Mr. Blunt said, and then, surprisingly, laughed. "Ha! Of course I know you're the supreme prime minister. Yes, I understand this opportunity. But I was thinking of a better reward—partly for me, but more to recognize your great power and to improve Puddin' Head Island, if not the whole nation."

The prime minister shook his tiny fists. "Are you messing with me?!"

"No, no. Listen. Think of what you just said. Me joining the elite, the powerful, making this nation strong. You are a powerful ruler. But what if we thought bolder? You know, with all my followers, and Chopper's followers, we could really boost your fan base."

The prime minister dropped his arms and smiled. "I like where you're going." A bead of drool slid from the corner of his mouth.

"I mean sure, Chopper and I *could* go to MC Academy. But with all our followers, why waste us on one school? Thousands of kids—and probably their families—don't like school. Some of them hate it. Imagine if Chopper and I were in charge of all the schools and made them better. And *you* were the one who made it happen. Imagine how that would boost your ratings!"

"Ha! You are ambitious. But your *hands*."

"Exactly. You could be the first and only supreme prime minister who got the entire population to love him, that includes, you know, all the people with large hands, too!"

"Huh?"

"What's your popularity rating?"

"I don't know."

"Really?"

"Uh, 45, 46 per cent? Okay, 43 this morning." He rubbed his neck again.

"Exactly. You're so much better than that. This could double your rating."

"Maybe. Interesting. But no, the Senate—and certainly the education minister—wouldn't like this idea."

"Oh, I thought *you* were the supreme prime minister."

The prime minister pounded his tiny fists on the desk. "I am! I *am* the supreme prime minister!"

"And who decides the Noble Deed winners?"

"I do!"

"And who decides the Noble Deed rewards?"

"I do! I do that! I decide!" He pumped his tiny fists in pride.

"Exactly!"

The prime minister paced with great confidence, except for a toe limp, and muttered compliments to himself for several moments. Then, his expression shifted to a frown. "Wait a minute, I'm the one negotiating here, not you." He slammed his head on the desk again. "You need to tell me your decision tomorrow in front of the Senate!"

"Put your Frames in here," Serafina said. Blaze and Chopper exchanged glances but placed their Frames in a thick metal box on the desk. Serafina did the same and shut the lid.

Mr. Blunt walked into the Capitol Building office without MC Frames, swept out his arm, and snapped his fingers. "Let's go."

"Mr. Blunt?" Blaze asked.

"Shh," Serafina said, motioning. "Quickly. We don't have much time. Just be honest. I have no idea if this will work."

Mr. Blunt led them down a corridor, into a tiny office, through a hidden door, down a narrow hallway, and into a dark room. Senator Serafina guided Blaze and Chopper to the front of the room, illuminated by a faint ceiling light.

Many shadowy people murmured.

"Why can't I see anyone?" Blaze whispered.

"So you don't recognize anyone. It's for your safety," Senator Serafina said. She turned to the room. "Are we ready?"

"Spoons up!" the TDJP group called. They raised their spoons, which were barely perceptible in the darkness.

"Blaze and Chopper are aware of TDJP. I vouch for them. Now, we need to decide whether to back them for the Noble Deed reward. Some of you had questions."

"Blaze, it is unheard of for middle school students, as well as students with large hands, to win the Noble Deed. But if you do win, what do you seek for your reward?"

"To become the next education minister," Blaze said confidently.

The room gasped.

"It's true!"

"This is ridiculous! They are children. Blaze, you're what? Sixteen?"

"Fourteen," Blaze corrected.

"Preposterous! This will never work!"

"Give them a chance!"

"Absurd!"

"Ambitious! I like her!"

"I love your haircut! Who did the flame?"

Blaze smiled. "Actually, my aunt here—"

"Ridiculous!"

"This child has been expelled twenty-three times. How can she run the nation's educational system?"

"I thought we came here to ask productive questions," Senator Serafina said. "Now, who has one?

"Blaze, for those of us who are senators, why should we support you—a child—as education minister? We could be ridiculed. Our careers could be ruined. The prime minister could turn on us."

"Well, you can trust me. I returned the TDJP money bag, didn't I?"

"It's true—she did. People before profit! Sort of. We can trust them! How many politicians can you say that about?" Several people applauded.

"And I want better schools for all students, small- and large-handed."

"Schools for all kids—how novel!" More applause.

"What about Sweetie students?"

"What? Of course not!" Blaze said.

The room sighed in relief.

"Integrity and courage are great, but they aren't enough. The time is not right! We don't have enough power. Anyway, it's the prime minister's position to appoint. Sorry, kids. MC Academy is probably your best option." Several people grumbled in their agreement.

Blaze said, "I'm not going to that school! They want to lop my fingers before they'll accept me!"

The room gasped. "Monsters!"

Senator Serafina said, "Yes, this is risky, but the time is never right. These two cannot do it alone—they need our support."

After a moment of silence, Mr. Blunt said, "No one is voting on this. This is an appointed position. Sure, the prime minister may be annoyed if we back them, but he'll probably forget."

"Not if he thinks we're tricking him!"

"You all know who we have now." Mr. Blunt said. "Better these kids than Pompavich!" The room mumbled in agreement, then cheered.

"Fine," someone said. "So, what is your plan, Blaze?"

"The first order of business is to eliminate hand-size rules from schools," Blaze said without hesitation.

"She is ambitious!"

"There's the J in 'Justice'!"

"She has fire in her belly. I like her!"

"Think how many TDJP papers we could sell with these headlines!"

"Ridiculous! The prime minister will never go for it!"

"Oh, but I'd like to stick it to him! And who wouldn't love to see the look on Pompavich's face?"

The room snickered.

"We want to change those ridiculous hand size rules. That is change for justice!"

"We can't change the rules until there's more public support! We need to change people's minds first."

"People's minds won't change until we change the rules!" They argued back and forth as if debating whether the chicken or the egg came first.

Blaze whispered to Chopper, "Do these people ever stop talking?"

He shrugged.

"Blaze, don't mention eliminating large hand rules. He won't appoint you. And we can't be on the prime minister's bad side. He'll destroy us!"

"But we've been talking about making this change for years!"

"Talking?" Blaze said, slowly raising a spoon. "What about acting, doing something? Now is the time. Now is our moment. Now is our chance for real change."

"Blaze, you can't change national rules without power. You need to be appointed first." Senator Serafina looked at Blaze with great hope. "Yes, becoming the next education minister will give you great power to effect national change. How are you going to persuade the prime minister to appoint you?"

"You mean the next co-education minister," Blaze said, putting her arm around Chopper. "The prime minister seemed very interested in new education ministers. And he hasn't even heard me sing. Now, are we spoons down or spoons up?"

The room cheered, "Spoons up!" and waved them wildly in the air.

BIG ASK

Blaze strode through the MegaCorp plaza with her guitar strapped to her back. She brushed past people walking to work or eating breakfast at outdoor cafés. Chopper tried to keep up. They paused for a moment to admire the Capitol Building, which looked like a giant castle. Inside, the large public visiting area displayed portraits of small-handed senators, ministers, and MegaCorp executives. A marble statue of the prime minister gesturing with his tiny hands stood in the middle.

Blaze looked at the statue and cupped her hand to her ear. "Do you hear that, Chopper? The prime minister is going to put us in charge of Puddin' Head Schools."

Chopper laughed. "I still don't know about this. Like they said, it's risky. Just accept the academy. Or suggest something more realistic. A lifetime supply of puddin', perhaps."

"You okay getting your fingers lopped off?"

"Maybe he'll forget about that part."

"*Right*. Chopper, this is it! We have TDJP support. We won't have this opportunity again!"

"We?"

"Yes! Don't you want to change Puddin' Head Schools?"

"Well, yes, but I wouldn't know where to start. What do we know about running a school—let alone many schools? I don't really want to be the education minister. That's a lot of responsibility. A lifetime of free puddin' sounds better to me."

"What about our pact? Big changes! You don't want to lead with me?"

"Maybe I could be your boss of staff."

"Perfect."

They walked down a marble corridor lined with framed paintings of people with tiny hands.

Blaze couldn't help herself. "That one doesn't even look like he can hold a spoon."

Chopper laughed again.

Moments later, Mr. Blunt greeted them as if nothing had happened the day before. "Welcome to the Senate chamber. They are ready for you."

Ministers and senators looked down upon Blaze and Chopper from elevated rows of tables with monitors. A few MegaCorp executives, the school boss of MegaCorp Academy, and Scarlet sat in guest chairs near the front. The Puddin' Head senators wore red. The Sweetie senators wore blue. Everyone else wore black and white.

In the center of the floor, the prime minister clasped his tiny hands around the sides of the podium. "Today is a special day. Wait, where is Minister Deadwood?"

"He's late, Mr. Prime—Mr. Supreme Prime Minister. His daughter is sick, and he had to—"

"Well then, he's fired! Anyway, as I was saying: Today is a special day. Today, I am awarding a Noble Deed to two courageous Puddin' Heads, who promoted Puddin' Head Island values through an epic battle that has already become legendary. And their fan base grows by the minute! Scarlet Pompavich, Island Nation Noble Deed coordinator, will speak to their heroic achievements."

Scarlet paraded to a mic stand near the podium. She tucked black, white, and gold-striped hair behind her ear and enthusiastically recounted the Battle of Sugar Falls. Video highlights flashed across the large screen in the front and the table monitors. "These courageous students are most worthy of a Noble Deed. Per the supreme prime minister, they can attend MegaCorp Academy, tuition free."

"He's offering the MC Academy to me, too!" Chopper whispered to Blaze. "He didn't say anything about chopping off fingers."

"I got this," Blaze said.

"Or there's an opening for the Minister of Agriculture!" the prime minister laughed hysterically. Some senators dressed in red fake laughed. He continued, "Anyway, this is a celebration— congratulations to these two Puddin' Heads!"

The Power Island and Puddin' Head senators, including Senator Serafina, cheered. The Sweetie senators booed.

"This is an outrageous Noble Deed! A blatant attack on Sweetie Island," one Sweetie senator yelled. The other Sweetie senators clapped and shouted in agreement.

The prime minister returned to the podium. "Oh, the question is not whether this is a Noble Deed. That has already been decided. It was a clear case of promoting Puddin' Head Island values. Your students can do the same. Don't you have a contender? The question is: What is the Noble Deed reward?"

"I thought the reward *was* attending MegaCorp Academy. When did that change?" said one senator.

"Don't these students have large hands? How are they even eligible? What will this say to people with small hands?" Most of the senators and ministers and executives stood up. They pointed and yelled back and forth at the thought of a student with large hands winning a Noble Deed.

"Enough!" yelled the prime minister. "Nobody needs to advertise that. Listen, you thin skulls, this Noble Deed is exceptionally good for business. Sales of Puddin' Head and Sweetie products are at record highs. And more importantly for everyone in this room, your approval ratings are all up, as well! Thanks to these two. Scarlet, get us back on track."

The room fell silent. The MegaCorp executives grinned from ear to ear.

"Yes, Mr. Supreme Prime Minister," Scarlet said. "Without further ado—, Blaze, I believe you have a little acceptance speech?"

"He let us both into the academy!" Chopper reminded Blaze. "Just accept and let's get out of here before he changes his mind."

"We can do better." Blaze winked at him and stepped up to the podium, strummed her guitar, and leaned into the mic stand.

"You all listen to so much talking," Blaze said, frowning at Scarlet. "Instead of a boring speech, I thought you might appreciate a song." Blaze strummed a few chords and then belted out lyrics that captivated her audience.

Thank you for this Noble Deed,
It is a true honor indeed.
Puddin' Head pride could show.
Your popularity could grow.
Your followers could crow.
For the right reward, you could be adored.
For the right reward, you could be adored.

The Puddin' Head senators and various ministers scooted forward in their seats. The Sweetie senators crossed their arms, groaned, and rolled their eyes. Puddin' Head senators began to clap along. One stood up and yelled, "Yes!"

But the MC Academy? It is a risky bet,
This sad offer people might soon forget,
You can call it a reward.
Perhaps you will be adored,
But many surely will be bored.
For this reward, citizens may snore.

The Puddin' Head senators most certainly did not like the idea of boring their citizens. They frowned and slid back in their seats. Then, a (TDJP) senator said, "These heroes deserve something much better than the MC Academy!"

The minister of education turned around. "Ridiculous! The MC Academy is the best school on the island."

"Just give them a bowl of moldy puddin' and send them home!" said a Sweetie senator. Her colleagues chuckled.

And what if families remember,
Their kids are not a member,
Of a school that's cool.
No, they belong to schools that drool.
And who will they hate?
The ones who chose their fate.
No, for this reward, you will be abhorred.
Worse, you could be gored.

Puddin' Heads and Sweeties began shouting back and forth. One Sweetie senator cried, "Gored! That would be terrible!"

"We'll have a violent mob after us!"

"*Do* our schools drool? I thought our schools were good."

"I don't want to be hated!"

"We can't send them to the MC Academy!" For a brief moment, Puddin' Head and Sweetie senators agreed on something.

The minister of education waved for calm. "This is just a silly song! All of our schools are good!" Suddenly, she grimaced and ripped another loud fart. Undeterred, she raised her arms and shouted, "This child is just making things up!" She tooted again.

"Aw, c'mon!" several senators complained and fanned their hands. Scarlet tried to step in front of Blaze, but Blaze paraded around the room, singing with greater passion, whipping up the crowd into a frenzy.

Perhaps instead, schools need a change,
Your reward could last the long range.
Imagine a vision of all schools better,
For this, you need a new trend setter.
Someone to turn our schools around.
Your rising stardom will astound.
For this reward, citizens would roar.
For this reward, citizens would roar.
For this reward, citizens would roar.

The ministers and Puddin' Head senators rose to their feet and clapped along. Some senators danced in the aisles. One (TDJP) senator stood on his seat, tore off his suit jacket, and waved it like the towel of a fanatical football fan. Even some Sweetie senators nodded along. One started to clap but stopped when her colleagues gave her a nasty look.

If you only have the aspiration,
The sense for a wise calculation,
To make us the next ministers of education.
Puddin' Head pride will show.
Your popularity will grow.
Your followers will crow.
For this reward, you'll strike a chord,
with a cheering horde.
For this reward, your ratings will soar.
For this reward, your ratings will soar.
For this reward, your ratings will soar.

Sweeties couldn't resist snapping their fingers to the beat. The ministers, Puddin' Heads, and MegaCorp executives piled into the aisles and clapped with explosive energy. The (TDJP) senators danced and shouted for an encore. Blaze played again—this time

with everyone singing loudly together. The minister of education
tried to step to the front but was knocked down by a twirling
senator. The crowd demanded another encore and sang with wild
abandon, pumping their fists, and high-fiving. Two Puddin' Head
senators body-slammed each other and fell to the ground. They
sprang to their feet, head butted each other, and roared with
laughter.

Education Minister Pompavich glared at Scarlet before charging
the floor and snatching the mic from Blaze. "As the education
minister, I am appalled by this request and this childish behavior. If
we are all done acting like *children*, let's get back to the matter at
hand."

The crowd booed. "We want more! We want more!"

She turned to the prime minister. "Mr. Supreme Prime Minister,
can we please end this perfunctory ritual and give these children
their Noble Deed rewards? Despite the senators' apparent
enjoyment of this ridiculous rhyming, chiming, nonsensical rabble
babble—ha ha! Two can play this game! Our schools are in good
shape!" Suddenly, she grunted, pointed at Blaze—as if trying to
distract the prime minister—and farted. With exaggerated passion,
she said, "The academy is a most worthy reward for this Noble
Deed. Although I don't know that this large-handed buffoon even
deserves a balloon for this silly tune." She slapped her leg, clearly
proud of her rhyming skills, while also ignoring the fact that she had
been outperformed by an eighth grader.

Her argument was not persuasive.

The Puddin' Head senators, ministers (except one), and
MegaCorp executives chanted, "Ed ministers! Ed ministers!"

The Sweeties came to their senses. "We can't have large-handed
Puddin' Head children in charge of all schools, including those on
Sweetie Island! This is an outrageous thing to consider!"

"But we'll be gored if we send them to the academy!"

"Bah! Give them a puddin' sucker and send them home."

"What? Didn't you hear? Sales are up. Our ratings are up. This
song is true! Make them the new minister of education!"

The prime minister bellowed into the mic, commanding the
room. "Hah ha! I love the energy!" He looked at Blaze. "A
tremendous performance! Tremendous! Look at the excitement
you've created."

The education minister clenched her fists and pleaded, "Sir, Mr.
Supreme Prime Minister, I beg you—do not do this. Large-handed
ministers of education? Think about it. It would be an utter failure.
And what message would it send?"

"Good point," said the prime minister.

The Puddin' Heads and Sweeties shouted back and forth. A Puddin' Head senator said, "It makes sense—two children equals one adult!"

"Oh, come on!" a Sweetie senator said. "Seriously, can you imagine two Puddin' Head kids leading our entire educational system? They haven't even finished middle school, let alone been a teacher or a school boss."

The Sweeties and the education minister buckled over laughing, slapping their tables and legs.

Blaze pointed to the education minister. "Neither has she."

"Burn!" said Chopper.

"I'll bet she hasn't even set foot in a Puddin' Head or Sweetie school," Blaze added.

"But . . . uh . . . that doesn't matter!" said Education Minister Pompavich defensively. "I run a very successful MC business that has made a fortune selling painted rocks—"

Senator Serafina raised a spoon and said with great resolve, "Mr. Pri—I mean, Mr. Supreme Prime Minister, inspire people with your leadership, sir. You can't inspire with any old reward. Send a message, Mr. Supreme Prime Minister!"

A MegaCorp executive scurried to the floor. She whispered to the prime minister, who smiled and slapped her on the back.

The prime minister addressed the floor, once again clasping his tiny hands around the side of the podium. With a few puffs of hot air, he made a decision that would dramatically change the educational course of the nation. "Blaze and Chopster, this was a special Noble Deed, indeed, and you deserve to lead. Ha, I can rhyme too! You will lead our national educational system. Congratulations."

The Puddin' Heads jumped up and down, danced, and cheered. The Sweeties stomped, cursed, and shouted. The education minister swore, strutting out of the room. The MegaCorp executives grinned and nodded.

Blaze squeezed Chopper in a hug. "We did it! We did it!" she shouted. "*We did it!*" Chopper nodded and grinned. He tried to say yes, but he couldn't breathe.

The prime minister raised his tiny hand to quiet the crowd, but no one could see it. He stood up on his tippy-toes, waving to no avail. Finally, he shouted into the mic, "Listen up! This is a great day, but . . ." He glanced at Blaze and Chopper. "If you mess this up, it's on you. And your big hands."

PUDDIN' REWARDS

The next week, Blaze and Chopper returned to the Capitol Building to start their new jobs and waited in the public gallery. The presumptive former education minister walked out of the elevator, looking at them first with surprise, then contempt. "Huh, fifteen minutes early. I figured you slackers would be late. Anyway, Mr. Blunt will meet you shortly for orientation."

"Who is Mr. Blunt?" asked Blaze in surprise.

"The assistant to the education minister," Ms. Pompavich laughed. "I'm sure he'll take good care of you." She smirked and strode to a meeting.

Blaze snorted.

"Ha!" Chopper laughed. "What's her deal?"

"Jealous. Mad. Wouldn't you be, too, if you'd lost your job to two eighth graders?"

"Okay, but why is she laughing?"

"She's passive-aggressive. Or she thinks we'll fail."

Chopper raised an eyebrow. "So nice of her."

Mr. Blunt skipped out of the elevator. "Blaze. Chopper. Congratulations, and welcome to the Capitol Building and the education ministry. I hope you do good things and don't mess it up. You can ruin a whole lot of schools in a minute, you know."

Chopper swallowed. "Thanks. I think."

"Oh, we're going to make some good changes," Blaze said. "Don't you worry. Now, can we please see our headquarters and meet our staff?"

"Sassy, aren't you?" said Mr. Blunt, playfully wagging his finger. "We'll take the stairs," he winked and leaned in with a fun whisper, "It won't take long."

Mr. Blunt skipped up a flight of stairs and down a hallway. He opened a door with a grand gesture and announced, "Here we are. Your magnificent headquarters and army of staff."

The small, empty room had two desks and chairs, one phone, and one filing cabinet. A beam of sunshine streamed through the one small window onto a dead plant. It sat on the only other piece of furniture in the room: a beat-up stool that looked like a yard sale bargain.

"This is it?!" Blaze exclaimed.

"This is it," said Mr. Blunt, waving his hand like a fairy godmother. "Sorry. I'd hoped for more, but here you are."

"Is that a phone? What are we, cavemen?"

"Where's the staff?" Chopper said.

"This is it."

"This is it? *This is it! This* doesn't make sense! How are we supposed to be the education ministers with this setup and no staff?" Blaze kicked the desk, which fell apart. The phone fell to the floor.

Mrs. Pompavich threw open the door and strode into the room, laughing boisterously. Scarlet trailed behind. "Oh, you thought *you* were the education ministers? Ha! No! One of you is the associate education minister and the other is the staff."

"What?!"

"You didn't really think the supreme prime minister gave you that power, did you?"

Blaze stammered, "Yes, he did! I mean, I *thought* he said . . . No, I *know* he did! He said we would lead the whole educational system!"

"Help lead," Scarlet lied. "It's a great job. First of its kind. I mean, what kid gets to do this? Definitely a most worthy Noble Deed reward."

"So in other words, you work for me," said Education Minister Pompavich. "Mr. Blunt will fill you in on the details. I disagreed with giving you a budget, but I suppose you have to do something."

"This is a mistake! I'm going to see the prime—I mean, the supreme prime minister!" Blaze charged toward the door.

"He's out of the building today, but I can see if he can talk." The education minister tapped her MC Frames and put the call on speaker.

"What do you want, Pompavich?"

"I have Blaze and her sidekick here."

"Blaze and Chopster? Nice! How are the accommodations, team?"

"Mr. Supreme Prime Minister, I think there has been a mistake. I remember you said—"

"Look, kids, you got what you wanted. You get to help lead our entire educational system. Now who's the associate education minister?"

"Sir—"

"Well? Is it Blaze or Chopster?"

Before Blaze could respond, Chopper said, "Blaze, sir."

"Great. Done. We gave you a big budget, so don't mess it up, and maybe you *will* be education minister someday." He laughed and hung up.

"Any more questions?" Minister Pompavich said.

Blaze hung her head. "No."

"Good. I'll leave you to it." Mrs. Pompavich grinned and swiftly left the room.

PLOTTING

"Yes, that is your budget," Mr. Blunt said with a raised eyebrow.

"One hundred thousand MC bucks! Wow, are you kidding me?!" Blaze pushed Chopper with excitement. "Can you believe it? Imagine what we can do."

"Yeah!" But Chopper thought, *"What can we do?"*

Scarlet laughed. "Righttt . . . So you have a little money. You'll want to use it wisely to maximize PR. Maybe pay for large-handed kids' transfer fees or lunches or bootstraps or something."

Blaze gave Scarlet a look. "Uh, yeah. Let's pay for the things we hate about school. Or—oh, here's a better idea—we could give all the money to the Sweeties. Gee, we really appreciate how you attacked our school. Here's some money to do it again."

Chopper snorted. "Burn!"

"No need to get defensive. I was just making suggestions. What's your idea, big hands?"

Blaze puffed, "I've got lots of ideas. Better than yours."

"Yeah?"

"Yeah." Blaze circled the small room, put her hand up as if to share one of these grand ideas and then put her hand back down. "I just don't want to share them yet."

"Shouldn't we do some research first?" Chopper asked. "Or make a plan before we start spending all this money?"

"Plan? We need action! But wait, as my boss of staff, aren't you in charge of Scarlet? And Mr. Blunt?"

"No," said Scarlet. "I support this operation independently."

"Certainly not," scoffed Mr. Blunt. "I report directly to Education Minister Pompavich, who is also in charge of you. I'm afraid you have a boss of staff with no staff to boss!"

Blaze shrugged and said to Chopper, "Anywayyy . . . we've got money to spend."

"I really feel like paying for bootstraps is an excellent choice," Scarlet argued again.

"No way! Chopper, get her out of here!"

"What? No, I should be consulted on all matters of—"

"Yeah, you're going to need to go," said Chopper.

"I am the Noble Deed coordinator," Scarlet cried. *"You don't get to—"*

Mr. Blunt stepped in front of her. "You know, they need some time to think. I'm sure they'll consult you when they're ready."

"Well, they better. For their own good. And my reputation!" Scarlet stomped off, slamming the door.

"You're welcome," said Mr. Blunt. "So, what *do* you want?"

Blaze appreciated his candor. "Well, if you must know, our schools suck, no matter what the education minister says. At least the Puddin' Head ones do. I'm sure the Sweeties ones are worse, even if they look nice on the outside, but who cares? We're going to turn the Puddin' Head Schools around." Blaze leaned in, ready for a fierce debate.

Instead, Mr. Blunt asked, "Why?"

Blaze studied his face and relaxed her shoulders. "Why do you want to know?"

"It's important that I know who I'm working with," Mr. Blunt said. "I want to know what fuels your flame, so to speak."

"Good one," Chopper said.

Blaze locked eyes with Mr. Blunt. "Okay. You really want to know?" She shared her boring, painful, stupid school experiences. No Puddin' Head deserved schools like that. For a moment, she teared up saying she would never let this happen to Maya, too. There must be a better way.

Mr. Blunt's face suddenly shifted to a look of hope. "You do care. That explains why you returned the money bag. And why you wanted this job."

"But isn't the education minister going to get in the way? And Scarlet? They're going to control everything!"

"Not necessarily. You just need to be smart."

Blaze locked eyes with him again. He smiled genuinely. "Might I suggest your first action go well if you want to stay in power? First impressions are important. You know, for the Noble Deed coordinator, the education minister, the Senate, the TDJP members who backed you, and, of course, for the prime minister."

"Huh. Right. Well, let's have some fun with hand size rules, and send a message. Who would argue with fun?"

"Oh, Blaze," Chopper said, shaking his head. "Here we go."

Blaze and Chopper brainstormed ideas you might expect from this pair of eighth graders. They ruled out canceling school for the rest of the year (Mr. Blunt said they did not have that authority—plus, families would be furious), paying transfer fees for students with large hands (surely they would run out of money), sending Sweeties stink bombs wrapped in dried puddin' skins (too impractical), paying bad school bosses and teachers to quit (a selection and money problem), and a number of other items deemed too risky, expensive, or ambitious.

"I still think we should ask the people what they want,"

Chopper said.

"They don't *know* what they want. They accept these stupid schools. Some probably like them. Look, I've been to twenty-three schools. I know what they need. Besides, I'm the boss and bosses tell people what to do. Let's start small. I like this one." Blaze pointed to a piece of paper with scribbled notes.

Minutes later, Chopper recorded a video of Blaze in front of the Capitol Building.

After Blaze explained her new role, she got to the point. "Island Nation, as the associate minister of education, I am issuing an order to make our schools better. For this week, to make up for many years of unfairness, Bigs will always be first in line. Smalls will bow to Bigs every time they meet. In addition, we'll have a contest for the best impersonation of Sweeties during bootstraps class. Everyone who submits an entry will receive a free week's supply of puddin'. The winning school will receive free puddin' for the rest of the year!"

Moments later Mr. Blunt asked, "Are you sure you want to send this?"

"You can really send it to every student and school staff member?"

"Straight to their MC Frames."

"Send it." Blaze high-fived Chopper. "We're sending a powerful message to schools, Chopper! This is just the first of many blows to stupid hand-size rules! We'll accomplish more this week than the education minister has in years! Or ever!"

"Yeah!"

"I just may be the next education minister yet!"

"Yeah! And I'll be a real boss of staff!"

Mr. Blunt said, "Uh, you may want to see what happens, before you ask for promotions."

FREE PUDDIN'

"Can someone tell me what in the humungo hands is going on?!" Minister Pompavich paced the room. "Do you know how many calls my office has received in the last twelve hours from angry parents, school bosses, district bosses, and regional bosses?"

Blaze and Chopper shook their heads.

"Mom, I had no idea—" Scarlet said.

"You are the *Noble Deed coordinator*! They are here for a *Noble Deed reward*! How can you not have known about this? Get it together!" Minister Pompavich glared at Mr. Blunt. "And you authorized this message?!"

"Just following orders, Ms. Education Minister. Don't shoot the messenger."

"Ahhhh! And you two big-handed buffoons, this was your idea? Let's just reverse generations of tradition and let the Bigs lead in line? And force Smalls to bow to them! Did you actually think this would happen?"

Blaze and Chopper tried to maintain straight faces.

"Do you know what happened?!"

"We've seen some of the news," Blaze said, trying very hard not to laugh.

Schools across the nation—Puddin' Heads and Sweeties alike—had reacted to Blaze's video in different ways. Some ignored it as spam. Some school bosses immediately dismissed it as a prank and went back to business as usual. But many schools erupted into chaos.

After decades of discrimination, Bigs cheered and dashed to the front of the lines. Some students tried to stand at the front of the line all day—even when there were no lines to have. Bigs repeatedly reminded Smalls to bow to them. At one school, half the student body wildly chanted, "Bow! Bow! Bow!" for over an hour. The Smalls revolted. Smalls blocked or pushed Bigs who tried to get to the front of the line. Virtually no Smalls bowed, despite the direct order. In many Puddin' Head schools, fights broke out between the Bigs and Smalls. In many Sweetie schools, Bigs and Smalls yelled at each other, then tried to hug it out before yelling at each other again.

"The whole nation is in pandemonium! This is what happens when Bigs try to lead! It doesn't work!"

"Right," said Blaze coolly. "More like this is what happens when Smalls get a taste of what life has been like for Bigs. They can't handle it! *They* got violent! All the more reason this whole educational system needs to change!"

"Puddin' Head Schools are just fine!" the education minister said. And yes, she grunted and farted.

"Did you just—" Blaze started to ask.

"No, no, no." The education minister waved her hand.

Blaze backed away and whispered to Chopper, "What *is* her deal?"

"This is most definitely *not* in the spirit of the Noble Deed," Scarlet said. "In fact, it's the complete opposite! You're supposed to promote your island values and the Noble Deed—not turn your own people against each other!"

"This is an utter failure." The education minister winced. "All three of you should be fired."

"You can't fire me! I'm your daughter."

"And you can't fire us, because the prime—I mean, the supreme prime minister appointed us." Blaze crossed her arms. "And we *are* promoting Puddin' Head values: competition, freedom, Puddin' Heads good, Sweeties bad. All of them, really. Have you seen some of the early video entries for the competition?"

"No. I've seen and heard enough. This is ridiculous. I couldn't care less about your stupid competition. I've already sent an MC Frame message to disregard your message. And yes, I will talk to the supreme prime minister about having you removed from office!" Once again, she stormed out of the tiny office, slamming the door.

"Nice. Now I've got your huge mess to clean up!" Scarlet cried. "You may end the Noble Deed program altogether!"

"No one asked for your help, princess. Besides, we'll be fine. Just wait till all the videos come in. You'll have plenty of promotional material. And schools will cheer once they receive their free puddin'. Check these out." Blaze calmly set her MC Frames on the table as a projector.

Scarlet perked up. Blaze projected several video clips of the Puddin' Head entries. One video showed students pretending to be zombies eating boots. In another, students clumsily fell into their bootstraps platforms and cried like babies. Puddin' Head Middle School students took it to another level. They marched around the school, threw hundreds of boots strung together up into trees, and smashed and burned platforms like zombies. They captured School Boss Walka Walka, tied him up with bootlaces, and carried him above their heads while chanting, "Eat school boss brains! Eat school boss brains!"

Scarlet grabbed two handfuls of her hair and screamed. "You think this is a *good* thing?!"

"I call it progress. Puddin' Heads good, Sweeties bad. Competition. Seems like promoting island values to me."

"What about respecting authority? They tied up the school boss!"

"Can't have them all. Still great publicity. So far, Puddin' Head Middle School is in the running for a year's worth of puddin'."

"Ahhhhh! How am I supposed to manage *this*!" Scarlet sprinted two laps around the room screaming, lost her balance, and whacked her head on the wall, momentarily passing out. After a few moments, she regained consciousness and yelled, "Ahhhhh!"

After Scarlet stumbled out of the room, Chopper said, "I don't know about all this. Maybe we took it too far."

But Blaze was too giddy to listen. Her first taste of power had been so delicious. "We'll be fine. We have power; let's use it!"

"Yes, but we don't want to lose it!"

"I agree with Chopper," said Mr. Blunt. "You don't want to lose power."

"I'm confused. Am I listening to two Sweeties? I didn't come this far to do nothing! I'm here to make changes!"

Over the next few days, Blaze and Chopper reviewed more than one hundred video submissions for the competition. More than half were from Puddin' Head Region 2. And nearly half were disqualified because they did not include boots or bootstraps. The only two Sweetie entries—from Sweetie Island Region 2—were immediately thrown out for impersonating Puddin' Heads as numbskulls whacking their heads on trees and requesting cake instead of puddin'.

Blaze sent a jingle response to the Sweeties.

Eating brains made your skulls thin.
So sorry, your submission did not win.
But as promised, enjoy a week of free puddin'.

Chopper howled. "Oh, I wish I could see the look on their faces!"

Blaze and Chopper, of course, selected Puddin' Head Middle School as the winner of a years worth of free puddin'. And true to their word, every group that sent a submission—even the ones that were disqualified—received a week's worth of puddin'.

A few days later Blaze reflected on their accomplishments. "That was a very successful first week. Look what we did!" She pumped her fists in pride. "We made the Puddin' Head News!"

Chopper projected the news onto the wall with his MC Frames. "Can't wait."

NEWS BLAST

At first, Puddin' Head News—which broadcast to the entire
Puddin' Head Island—buoyed their success. It showed clips of
dozens of schools and students celebrating and gobbling down free
puddin'.

"Oh, yeah, Chopper! Welcome to the big time!" Blaze hopped in
the air. "We're going to change the whole educational system!"

Chopper cupped his hands together. "Go, Blaze, go!" he
hollered. "Go, Blaze, go!" Blaze waved her hands and danced a little
jig.

Bartle—a lead anchor of Puddin' Head News known for riling
up millions of viewers—seemed to nod in approval. (Allegedly, he
was a descendant of pirates and negotiated a lifetime, unlimited
supply of puddin' and booster as part of his salary.) But then, as fast
as Blaze and Chopper had risen, Bartle sank them like a ship blasted
with cannonballs. "Free puddin'—seems like an amazing start to a
Big as the associate minister of education. Well, not so fast, my not-
so-gullible Puddin' Heads. Oh, just a few tiny problems—no bigger
than Blaze's hands." He drummed his small fingers across the
counter, revealing scars from botched surgery.

"Let's start with the waste of taxpayer money. Rumor has it they
blew their entire budget. And now, there may be a puddin'
shortage." He paused and drummed his fingers once more for effect.
"But, hey, maybe it was worth it. We can go a few days without
puddin', right? Perhaps all these Puddin' Head students became
more courageous. Perhaps they learned to fight Sweeties? No, in
fact, fights broke out *between* Puddin' Heads. That's right! Puddin'
Heads turned on each other. Puddin' Heads injured each other.
Why, you ask?" He drummed his fingers again. "This Blaze Union
thin-skull tells schools to— get this—allow Bigs at the front of the
line. Wait, it gets better. And Smalls should bow to Bigs for an entire
week! Fights, chaos. What a mess." Bartle shook his head in dismay
and kept drumming his fingers.

"Puddin' snot!" Blaze yelled.

"Wait, maybe I'm not being fair. Maybe they learned to respect
authority. Well, let's look at this clip." He tapped his fingers as the
clip rolled. "As you can see, these students tied up their school boss
and marched him around like a prize pig ready to be sacrificed!

Why? Well, this numbskull and her sidekick, Chopster, created a competition making fun of bootstraps classes for free puddin'. But bootstraps classes are only a part of Region 2's curriculum! So yeah, the students in Regions 1, 3, 4, and 5 were mad as a Puddin' Head with no puddin'—no puddin' pun intended!" Bartle slapped his leg, winced at the pain in his fingers, then chuckled.

"Lies!" Blaze said. "All Puddin' Heads have bootstraps class! At least, I thought they did. Well, maybe not. Maybe some of it is true —but not like he's saying! He's twisting the facts! And he's a Puddin' Head!"

"And learn how to pronounce my name!" Chopper said. "Remember, Blaze, I did recommend—"

"Shhh! I want to hear this!" Blaze said. "Wait, what's that noise? Do you hear that?" A faint chanting emerged from outside.

"Hold on, fellow Puddin' Heads." Bartle stared at the teleprompter. "We have breaking news. Protesters are circling the Capitol Building."

Blaze and Chopper ran to the window. Puddin' Heads from Regions 1, 3, 4, and 5 marched around the building, demanding that every school receive free puddin'. They carried signs and chanted, "What about us? Free puddin' now!" Puddin' Head News and Sweetie News reporters spilled out of vans to capture the action.

"Puddin' Heads, we have protesters marching on the Capitol for being denied puddin'. That's right—wait, wait. Oh, wow. If that wasn't insulting enough, wait till you hear this. We are just now learning that Blaze and Chopster not only denied puddin' to tens of thousands of Puddin' Heads, but they also sent free puddin' *to the Sweeties*! The most ridiculous use of taxpayer money in the history of Puddin' Head Island!"

Bartle squinted at the teleprompter again. "Oh my, it's getting worse. Now, Sweeties are attacking the Capitol!"

Blaze pressed her face to the window. "No!"

Sugar Falls students carrying boxes of puddin' circled the Capitol Building. They whipped puddin' cups, which exploded on the walls and littered the lawn.

"Isn't that the Sugar Falls kid? What's his name—Kai?" Blaze asked.

"That's him!" Chopper said. Kai directed students to different areas of the Capitol Building, where they continued launching puddin' cups. "Somebody needs to take him out!"

Initially stunned and confused, the angry Puddin' Head crowd charged the Sweeties. They grabbed the unused cups of puddin' and wolfed them down as the Sweeties bolted away. Some licked puddin' off the side of the Capitol.

Bartle was shocked. "What a disaster! Will we run out of puddin'? Will the Sweeties take over? Are these two numbskulls really Noble Deed winners? Should these kid Bigs be fired?" Bartle slammed his tiny, deformed hands on the table and tried very hard not to wince. "Will this be the shortest term of office in the history of Island Nation? The supreme prime minister will decide."

"Eat a moldy puddin' bowl!" Blaze yanked spoons from her holster and whipped them at the news projection. They clanged against the wall, and like Blaze's hopes, plummeted to the floor.

GO BIG OR GO HOME

Blaze and Chopper met Mr. Blunt at the office early the next morning.

"Okay, so things didn't exactly go as planned," Blaze said. "But remember, for one day we Bigs—some of us, anyway—got to lead. We humiliated the Sweeties. And look at our success with Region 2! We sent a powerful message, but now we need to think bigger. That's why everyone was mad: They didn't get puddin'."

"We blew our entire budget! *We don't have any more money for puddin'!* And yes, everyone *is* mad at us." Chopper crossed his arms and sighed. "We are so fired."

"He's probably right," said Mr. Blunt.

Scarlet charged through the door. "What was that yesterday? I'll tell you what it was—the complete opposite kind of impact that Noble Deed winners should make! Puddin' Heads *and* Sweetie protesters—and Sweeties attacked the Capitol! Because of you! You *are* going to sink the entire Noble Deed program!"

"Relax. We have it under control."

"You have it under—" Scarlet gasped. "You're delusional! My mom is on her way over here right now, probably to fire all three of us! We'd better come up with a plan."

"We? Uh . . . *you* are not the associate minister of education."

"Or the boss of staff," Chopper reminded her.

"It doesn't matter! Don't you want to change schools? We need to work together. You need to do something noble, not chaotic. Something small, simple."

"Uh, no. Like I was saying before you so rudely interrupted, we need to go big or go home. *Especially* if we're going to be fired. Let's take the opportunity while we still can."

"Blaze, this sounds like a terrible idea. But what do you have in mind?" Mr. Blunt asked.

Suddenly, Minister Pompavich kicked open the door and froze like an angry statue. She shifted her gaze, first to Mr. Blunt, then to Scarlet, then Chopper, then Blaze. "After the Bigs jumping to the front of the line and forcing Smalls to bow debacle, you somehow managed to crap a larger, monstrous pile of curdled, moldy, puddin' skin poop."

"Gross," said Chopper.

"That is gross." Mr. Blunt grimaced and pinched his nose.

"Indeed," said Minister Pompavich, still frozen, but lifting one eyebrow slightly. "Beyond puddin' puke worthy."

"Mom, are you okay?"

"Oh, I'm fine, fine, fine. Joy is beaming from my heart, and rainbows are shining from my butt. Up is down, and down is up. Make a mockery of the entire education ministry, create Bigs versus Smalls chaos in schools, cause an attack on the Capitol, blow your entire budget in your first week on the job. Do you get fired? Oh, no, no, no. You get a raise!"

"What?" Blaze, Chopper, Mr. Blunt, and Scarlet said simultaneously.

"Maybe he wants to fire me," the education minister mumbled to herself. "Maybe I should just quit. Ah, what am I saying? *I* am in charge here." She turned to Blaze. "I don't understand why you still have a job. But it comes with a warning—pull a stunt like that again and you *will* be fired! Oh, what do I know?! You *probably* will be fired."

"So I'm still the associate education minister?" Blaze looked at Chopper. "See—we still have jobs!"

They triumphantly high-fived.

"*Why* do we still have jobs?" Chopper asked.

"Well," Minister Pompavich clucked, "it seems that puddin' sales along with Puddin' Head and Sweetie products and merchandise sales reached all-time highs. It turns out that the Sweetie attack on the Capitol was," she mumbled, "good for business. On both islands."

"What?"

"Good for business. People bought more stuff. Puddin' Head and Sweetie senators' ratings are up." She mumbled to herself, "Only mine are down."

"Huh. Okay," Blaze said.

"And, of course, the *supreme* prime minister restored your budget, and even added a little extra."

"Nice!" Chopper smacked his fist into his hand. "Let's go!"

"But the senators and supreme prime minister said you took it too far with the Bigs versus the Smalls distraction. I'm serious—

another stunt like that and you *will* be before the supreme prime minister fighting for your job." Minister Pompavich gave a creepy smile, slamming the door behind her.

Blaze, Chopper, Scarlet, and Mr. Blunt spent the next hour discussing what to do next.

"Blaze, we don't have enough money to send puddin' to every Big in every school in every region." Chopper shrugged. "Sorry."

"He's right. Not even close," said Mr. Blunt. "Besides, what would it accomplish? What do you really want?"

"We don't have time for that."

Chopper crossed his arms. "Blaze, it's a good idea. A student survey could give us important information about what students in different regions think about education and what they've experienced."

"Yes, considering what just happened with the school puddin' fiasco, I advise slowing down a bit," Mr. Blunt said. "Survey results could help guide your decisions."

"Advice taken and rejected. You sound like a bunch of Sweetie tarts. Right now, we still have jobs. Who knows for how much longer? Let's just go for it. Tell people what to do, or they'll tell you what to do. Speaking of which, I've been drafting lyrics for a new song."

By the next day, Blaze had recorded the music video, *Burn the Trash*.

"Are you sure you want to send this?" Mr. Blunt asked again.

"Yeah, send it. Hopefully schools get the message."

"You do remember what happened last—"

"Send it!"

Ten minutes later, the education minister called Blaze on her MC Frames. "Did you not hear a word I said?! 'Play football if you don't like school'? 'All school bosses are fired'?! 'Burn the trash!' Are you *kidding me*? Stay there, I'm coming over."

"What did she say?" Chopper clasped his face, then grabbed Blaze.

"I don't think she liked the video."

After fifteen minutes of Blaze and Chopper pacing, arguing, and blaming each other, the education minister burst through the door. This time, she wore a wide-eyed smile—like a hungry Puddin' Head ready to devour a bowl of puddin'. "I'm going to enjoy this."

She turned on Power Island News. The news anchor, Cliff Shadow, was in the middle of a rampage. "Students are, get this, protesting anything in schools that are 'unfair, boring, or useless,'" he said, using air quotes, "across Puddin' Head Island. Bigs apparently are 'leading' hordes of students to protest 'unfair, boring, or useless' classes by leaving school and playing football—get this

—without large hand rules."

"Yes!" Blaze pumped her fists.

Alas, Blaze was about to receive a painful lesson in leadership. In fairness to her, no one had really taught her how to handle so much power, or even gave her useful guidelines for that matter. I mean, you have an eighth grader as the associate education minister of an entire country. What did the prime minister think would happen? But then again, look at his education minister.

Cliff continued. "The video message Blaze Union sent less than thirty minutes ago—again, for those of you just joining us, Blaze Union is the associate education minister—stated that all school bosses who have allowed 'boring, unfair, or useless' classes are fired. And judging by the fact that thousands of students are no longer listening to their school bosses and that our normally proud, noble, and orderly schools have descended into chaos, we can reasonably conclude that students believe their school bosses have been fired. Oh, and Sweetie Island is not much better, but for a very different reason. Blaze told them—" Here, Cliff Shadow burst out laughing. "Oh, I'm sorry, this is so absurd, what can we do but laugh? Blaze Union told them that Sweetie Island must create student football teams to play the Puddin' Heads in a Sweetie versus Puddin' Head football tournament!" He buckled over laughing. "And we all know how much Sweeties love competition!"

Blaze jumped on top of a chair and pumped her arms. "Wooo! Now, that's what I call leadership!" Blaze high-fived Chopper.

"Are you tarting nuts?" Everyone froze at the educator minister's surprise profanity. "Do you think these are good things? Is this the impact you want to have? To send schools into chaos? You don't even have the authority to demand any of these things! But somehow, those Puddin' Heads and Sweeties believed you."

"Hey, it's not that bad! Someone needed to do something. Those school bosses needed to go! Someone needed to lead, so I did!"

"What's that? This just in," Cliff Shadow said, looking very concerned. "We have at least 158 reports of burning trash." Video clips displayed burning school desks, books, MC Emergency Procedures pamphlets, and various other materials.

Minister Pompavich switched off the news. Her eyes bulged. Veins popped in her forehead and neck. "*You think this is okay?!*"

Blaze was surprised. "No, uh, well . . . maybe not that part. I . . .

I . . . I didn't tell them to do that! I didn't say *literally* burn trash. I meant it *metaphorically*! See, that's another reason we need better schools!"

"It was in the title of your song! And it doesn't matter what you meant! What matters is what happened!"

Blaze stammered, but this time, she had nothing to say. It was hard to argue with that one. Chopper looked down and whistled.

Minister Pompavich paused and then raised her eyebrows. "Oh, I see what's going on here. You want to change people's minds about Bigs. Maybe you fancy an educational revolution. You have a little chip on your shoulder because life is so unfair. Well, boo-hoo. You had the power to do something good and you blew it. And, you proved once again, we cannot trust Bigs to lead. And, yes, I'll clean up your mess. Why you were even hired is still beyond me. Now that the school bosses know they still have a job, do you know how many Bigs got red cards, thanks to you?"

"What? I never said that was allowed!"

"Oh, you didn't think that part through?"

Blaze hung her head. "I . . . I . . . What I meant was—"

"I . . . I . . . I . . . What's wrong? A Sweetie got your tongue? 'I meant, I meant.' How many times do you need to learn the hard way? I'd fire you if I could—but that doesn't matter. There is no way the supreme prime minister is going to put up with this."

WORST NIGHTMARE

"I told you firing school bosses was a bad idea!" Chopper shook his head as the duo approached Scarlet's mega-mansion. "You took things way too far. Now, you're enemy number one for many school bosses across Island Nation."

"If they were any good, they wouldn't have a problem. The rest of them deserve it."

"You know what your problem is? You don't *listen*! You really do have to learn the hard way, don't you?

"Whose side are you on?"

"Don't you get it? We are fired!"

"Maybe. But like I said, if schools weren't unfair, boring, and useless, then school bosses would have nothing to worry about. Maybe students went too far when they started burning things. But that's not my fault. Now, skipping school to play football with fair rules—*that* is sending a powerful message. If school bosses aren't going to lead change, then I will."

"You aren't going to have a job!" Chopper rubbed his forehead and sighed. "Why are we going here again? Couldn't they just send us a message saying we're fired and get it over with? And, why aren't we going to the prime minister?"

"I don't know, but I don't like it."

The house manager escorted them to MC Conference Room D, which had a round table large enough for at least fifty people. Scarlet, who sat several seats apart from her mother, stood up and yelled at Blaze and Chopper as soon as they entered. "How could you! You nearly destroyed the Noble Deed program! Maybe I'll be in charge of a Dumb Deed program now. I knew I should have supervised you—"

Minister Pompavich held up her hand. "Scarlet, please. Don't waste your energy on these numbskulls." She smiled, but without the vindictive glee you might expect.

Blaze and Chopper looked at each other, puzzled. "Should we sit down?" Blaze finally asked.

"Sure."

They sat next to each other, several seats away from Scarlet. Minutes passed without a word. Blaze finally broke the silence. "Did you hear the one about the Puddin' Head and the zombie farmer?"

"Shut up!" the education minister snapped. "Our guest should be arriving soon."

"Okay, then." Blaze rapped her knuckles on the table. She shot out two fingers from her other hand, which turned into walking legs. The knuckles and fingers lined up for a race. Despite an early knuckle lead, the full-length fingers won easily with long strides. She whispered to Chopper, "Big hands win again. I wonder why?"

Chopper snorted.

Minister Pompavich slammed her hand on the table. "Shut up! And control your hands!"

"Technically, I am." Blaze flared her nostrils and said, "So, are we getting fired or what?"

The education minister glanced at the door and grunted. "Well, not exactly." She clucked and laughed and grimaced. She walked slowly around the table. "You see, as destructive as your second video was, Blaze, there is a puddin' skin lining."

"Uh, I don't think that's the right metaphor," Blaze said.

Mrs. Pompavich frowned, dismissing the comment. "You see, we have a record number of red cards and transfers, increased support for school bosses reigning in chaos, and skyrocketing sales of Puddin' Head and Sweetie merchandise for a football match that, ironically, will never happen."

"So we still have jobs?"

"Sort of."

"Wait, are you saying that red cards—" Blaze stopped as the door swung open, and the surprise guest walked in. He saluted Chopper, then Blaze, who both dropped their mouths so low they nearly hit the table.

Kai stood in the doorway.

"It's been a while, knuckleheads." He slowly removed his Frames and cleaned the lenses with his bright-blue shirt. Kai slid the Frames back onto his face, then spoke calmly, with a tinge of sarcasm. "Blaze, I just really want to thank you for inspiring me with your amazing videos. Wow! What an impact those had on my home island, and on me personally. I mean, a lot of my people say we Sweeties should just mind our own business. Live and let live. You know, keep to ourselves. But I thought, why should those two Puddin' Heads have all the fun? So, I applied for your job. Turns out, I won a Noble Deed, too."

PART III
THE ABSURD SCHOOLS TOUR

WORST NIGHTMARE, CONTINUED

"What?! *You're* taking my job?" Blaze stood up.

Chopper held her back. "Easy! Let's see where this is going."

"Well, not exactly." Once again, the education minister clucked, laughed, and then grimaced. "Here's the fun part. In all his wisdom, the prime—I mean, the *supreme* prime minister. Oh, is he so supreme. He has awarded an impromptu Sweetie Island Noble Deed to Kai for the attacks on Puddin' Head schools, and the Capitol."

Scarlet beamed with pride.

Kai smirked. "And I suggested replacing you as the associate education minister. You know, for Island Nation fairness."

Minister Pompavich gave a very fake smile. "Yes, you did. But the prime—Gaaah! The *supreme* prime minister liked this idea of two rival associate educational ministers very much."

"Wait, what? I didn't sign up for that! No way am I working with this Puddin' Head!" Kai said.

Blaze said, "What? But the prime minister is a Puddin' Head!"

"I know," the education minister said.

Blaze waited for an explanation. "Kai is a Sweetie!"

"I know!"

Blaze still waited. "Sweeties attacked the Capitol with puddin'!"

"I know!"

Blaze glared. *"None of that makes sense!"*

"I know!" The education minister raised her eyebrows and opened her eyes wide, as if agreeing the whole situation was absurd. "He's hoping for some Sweetie votes. Puddin' Heads will vote for him no matter what he does. And the rivalry is good for business." She sighed.

"No way Chopper and I are working with this Sweetie pie!" Blaze said, pointing at Kai. She paced, then realized she still had a job. She took a deep breath and exhaled. "All right, here's an idea. We'll just work separately. You deal with the sweet tarts," she said to Kai, "and we'll deal with the Puddin' Heads."

"Watch it!" Kai charged at Blaze, but the Pompavich pair held him back. After a moment, Kai shifted and agreed. "Actually, I can live with that."

"Sorry, folks, supreme prime minister's orders: you have to work together, stay together, and use the same budget to promote Noble Deeds."

"Yes! We're back in business!" Scarlet said.

"No, no, no, no, no, no, no!" Blaze stalked around the table, nearing the education minister. "Not happening! *Not happening!*"

"Like it or not, it *is* happening!" The education minister cocked her head centimeters from Blaze's face. "Unless . . . you want to resign?"

"Yeah right. No way I'm letting this fart tart mess with Puddin' Head Schools!" Blaze reached around the education minister to point at Kai again.

"Don't make this worse!" Chopper pulled Blaze back.

"That's it!" Kai pushed past Scarlet and her mom, stiff armed Chopper, and leaped to tackle Blaze. Blaze side stepped the sailing Sweetie, who landed with a thud and grunt.

"Whoa, sweet tart. I thought Puddin' Heads were the ones with anger issues."

"You attacked my school, gave my sister and half her class pancake hands, and then created pandemonium across our entire school region. Twice!" Kai looked at the education minister like a possessed zombie. "I'm not working with this numbskull!"

Blaze shook her head calmly. "Pancake hands? Silly Sweetie, Puddin' Heads eat puddin', not cake."

"*You're dead!*" Kai chased her around the table.

Minister Pompavich laughed maniacally. "Figure it out! You're on your own!" She kicked a chair, cursed in pain, gave everyone the evil eye—daring them to laugh—and limped out of the room.

After several minutes of chasing Blaze around the room, over fallen chairs, over the table, up and down hallways, and through any open door Blaze could find, Kai finally gave up. He slid down a hallway wall, exhausted.

"Kai, I'm just too fast," Blaze panted. "There's a reason they call me Blaze." She collapsed on the floor, a safe distance from him.

"Whatever, knucklehead."

"That's a compliment, you numbskull. Question: If you did catch me, would you eat my brain?"

"Are you for real? No more than we're going to play sports ball or football or whatever you call it. Competition is the root of all evil. That's why we're in this mess!"

"You can't be serious. You started this by attacking our school! How is that not competitive?"

"That's not competition, puddin' for brains. That's retaliation for years of school oppression. You think we want to step foot on Puddin' Head soil? You left us no choice. Just like you left me with no choice but to take this job—because Puddin' Heads are evil."

"Oppression? What the sweet tart babble are you talking about?"

"It's too complicated for your thick skull to comprehend."

"Again numbskull, you compliment where you mean to offend."

"If being stupid is a compliment, then yes, I guess I do."

"You're so ignorant. Obviously, it's better to have a knucklehead or a thick skull than a thin one! And obviously, no one wants to be a numbskull!"

Kai rolled his eyes. "That makes perfect sense, *numbskull*. Just like your attack on Sugar Falls—how is that a Noble Deed? Your whole island is messed up."

Scarlet chimed in. "Hey, that was our most popular Noble Deed!"

"How was *yours* a Noble Deed?" Blaze protested. "You put hand-increasing booster in puddin'!"

"Nontoxic. You smashed small children's hands!"

"That was an accident! And *you attacked us first!* You know our schools would be fine if it weren't for you Sweeties. *You* are the root of all our problems! Most of our day is spent preparing for a Sweetie attack, with Bigs doing the stupid work. No Sweeties, no problems."

Kai belted a hearty laugh. "Have you considered going into comedy? *We're* to blame? Puddin' Heads are the source of all of our problems! Sweetie Bigs spend half their day making puddin' and booster for you lazy, spoon-wielding freaks just so we can pay for school."

"Lies. Blaming your problems on someone else—just like a Sweetie."

"Look in the mirror. Maybe Puddin' Heads should try to actually *learn* something in school instead of head butting and smashing each other's pathetic brains."

Blaze chortled. "Where do you hear this nonsense?"

"Facts are facts. I saw it on Sweetie News."

"I mean, head *tapping*, sure. Yes, a few of us may get carried away with the occasional head butt. But smashing brains? C'mon."

"So, you're only half numbskulls?"

The house manager arrived with beverages and stood next to Scarlet. "Oh, yes—thank you! Can you two just chill for a minute? Thirsty?" They nodded and the house manager handed the guests fizzy drinks in large golden spiral glasses with fruit speared onto gold cocktail sticks.

Blaze and Kai each took a big swig and agreed on something for a second time: "Wow. That is *good*." Blaze slid a piece of pineapple into her mouth.

"Right?" Scarlet said. "Listen, I know there's a way we can work this out."

"That's debatable," said Kai. "Large-handed numbskulls and problem solving don't exactly go together."

Blaze raised an eyebrow. "You don't really believe that crap about large hands, do you? I see your frown Frames."

Kai shrugged. "About as much as I believe I'm a zombie who wants to eat your brain. But you're missing my point: Puddin' Head numbskulls and intelligence don't mix."

"Is that right. You got a good idea smart tart? Yeah, I didn't think so."

Chopper glanced at Scarlet and turned to the arch-enemies. "Scarlet's right. We need to figure this out."

Scarlet beamed once more. "So, what are we going to do?"

Chopper said, "I hate to break up the love fest, but we need to focus. How are we going to promote Noble Deeds on both islands to earn money for our budget? No money, no resources. Not much we can do."

Kai frowned and chugged the rest of his drink. "Who's this guy again?"

"Chopper," Blaze said. "My boss of staff."

"You have staff? How come I don't have staff?"

"Yes, I have staff. You're looking at him. Anyway, that's a good question, Chopper." Blaze stood up and slowly paced. "Here's an idea—the ultimate Noble Deed, big money."

"Do say more," Scarlet pleaded.

"What if we do have a football match between the main islands —Sweeties versus Puddin' Heads? I mean, we would crush them, but still, imagine the crowd. It would be like two fantastic, island-wide Noble Deeds."

Scarlet wiped at a trail of drool from the corner of her mouth. "Love it! That would take the Noble Deed program to a whole new level!"

"But no large hand rules. That's non-negotiable."

Scarlet was too excited to argue. "I'll see what I can do!"

Blaze high-fived Chopper. "Yes!!"

"Don't you numbskulls listen to anything I said? Sweeties don't compete. It's evil. The root of all problems. No and no. Next idea."

Blaze retorted, "Listen, I know you're afraid to lose to the Puddin' Heads. And to watch me score goal after goal with a roaring crowd. That makes sense. But football is really about cooperation and teamwork. You obviously don't compete with your own team— or your own island, in this case. It's the ultimate cooperation, really."

"Ahh . . . I just realized: They call you Blaze because you're so full of hot air!" Kai frowned, thought for a moment, and hesitantly forced out his next words. "Anyway, let's just say we did this cooperating team thing. We would win, if we wanted to. We just don't compete."

Blaze saw an opening. "Yeah right. I can see it now, a bunch of cookie- and cake-eating, uncoordinated, sweet puffs rolling off the couch and onto the pitch. Our schools may be crappy, but we would crush you like a sad, little train of hand-holding ants."

"What? That's a stupid metaphor. What do you have against ants? If this game takes cooperation, teamwork, and community, I'm sure we'll learn quickly. Cooperation wins, naturally. So, if this game were to happen—which is still only hypothetical—what are the rules of football?"

The group explained the rules and answered Kai's questions. He asked one more: "And what happens when the Sweeties win?"

Blaze smiled. "Well, think of it this way. I'm sure we could fill a stadium. Between tickets, concessions, and merchandise sales, that's a lot of money that could go toward improving our schools."

Scarlet drooled again. "The size of my live audience—I mean, the crowd! That would be amazing."

"Winner takes all? Takes the entire education budget, makes all the decisions?" Blaze offered.

Kai did not hesitate. "Game on."

"Yes!" Blaze and Chopper cried.

"I love this idea!" Scarlet said. "But wait. Remember, you're only associate education ministers. Mom already said you can't just give your money to the other side."

"Well, that's an easy fix. The winner gets to tell the loser what decisions to make."

"Fine," said Kai.

"I don't see how that's different."

Blaze stuck out her hand. "Shake on it."

"You don't want to head butt?" Kai laughed. Then, they squeezed hands as hard as they could.

"Yes!" Blaze shook off the pain, raised her arms, and did a spoon-waving celebration dance. "Finally, every Puddin' Head child will have a good, fair school. Every child! No kid will experience what I did. Step one, win. Step two, eliminate large hands rules."

Chopper shook his head. "I hate to pop the hot air bubble, but Blaze, we already tried that. The schools just plunged into chaos, and now things are worse than they were. You can't just win a soccer game, sing a song, send schools money, and watch them magically turn into amazing, fair schools for all students."

Laughing, Kai nodded in agreement.

"Whose side are you on, Chopper?" Blaze asked.

Chopper held up his index finger and continued, "We're just guessing here! We have little idea about what schools are like in the other regions. Maybe things are better than in Region 2. Maybe the education minister is right, and most schools *are* good. Maybe in some regions, school is free for all students, the teachers and school bosses are amazing, and classes are fun."

"Yeah!" Scarlet said.

"Yeah right!" Blaze said. "Maybe Bigs are just as likely to lead as Smalls. Maybe these schools are fabulous. But more likely, they have all the same problems as Region 2. Or maybe they're worse!"

"Maybe, but that's my point. *We don't know!*" Chopper emphatically raised both index fingers. "And if we don't know anything about these schools, how are we supposed to know how to spend the money?"

Blaze cocked her eyebrow. "All right, what's your idea oh wise one?"

"As I've already suggested—but you didn't listen—I think we start by surveying all the students across all the regions. Then, we go on tour and actually see and talk to them, maybe even see some schools in action." Chopper drummed his fingers together, smiling and drifting his gaze toward the ceiling, as if dreaming. "Imagine that data set."

"Where did you learn this stuff?" Blaze asked.

"I lived in Region 1 for a while, remember?"

Blaze was impressed with her boss of staff. "Okay. I can go with that. But more importantly, we need to recruit players for the Noble Deed game. Scarlet, I'm sure you realize this tour would be a phenomenal way to promote an epic Noble Deed Match."

"Oh yeah!" Scarlet did a little dance. "You know, there is a huge Top Boss Award Banquet coming up in a few weeks. Maybe we can promote it there."

"A few weeks? I'm not waiting that long," Blaze said.

Chopper was intrigued. "Tell me more about this banquet."

"Once a year, regional, district, and school bosses gather for the Top Boss Award Banquet that Mom runs. They talk about school stuff, pass out awards, and name the year's top boss."

"Does this include Sweetie bosses?" Kai asked.

"Of course."

"Huh, interesting," Chopper said. "Maybe we could help the bosses. You know, we could present a report of what we found out from our surveys and tour so they can learn what's working, and maybe how they could improve. And, we could promote the Noble Deed game. Imagine the connections they must have."

"Wow, that sounds great!" Scarlet beamed. "I'll see what Mom says."

"We're doing this for both islands right?" Kai said. "I want to survey and tour the Sweetie regions for the same reasons. I'm sure I can recruit an outstanding team to beat the Puddin' Heads at their own game. And you know what? I want to see your Puddin' Head schools, too. I need to understand the source of all our problems. It'll be entertaining if nothing else."

"Yes, of course!" Scarlet said.

"Well, I'm not touring Sweetie Island. What a waste of time!" Blaze said.

"You don't have a choice, remember?" Scarlet said. "You are co-associate education ministers and that includes traveling together."

Chopper pulled Blaze aside. "This is actually a good idea. We'll get to know the enemy."

"Are you seriously concerned about losing to the Sweeties in football?"

"Of course not. But we can't have Kai learning all about Puddin' Head schools while we know nothing about Sweetie schools. We could learn what they teach their students about Puddin' Heads. How they plan to defeat us. It's like we're undercover but they'll be too stupid to realize it!"

"Okay, but isn't Kai going to do the same thing?"

"It doesn't matter. There's no way that Sweeties are going to win the Noble Deed Match. He'll have no power to do anything with what he learns."

"Ha! This is why you're the boss of staff. Hey, one other idea. This data collection thing. The education minister keeps saying all schools are good—which we know is a ridiculous lie. Assuming that many other schools are crappy, couldn't we use this report to show that? To prove that schools aren't so good?"

"Sure. But again, we don't *know* if other schools are good or not."

"Let's just assume they are."

"I'm not falsifying data. I'm not going to lie!" Chopper said emphatically. "The facts will speak for themselves."

"I'm not suggesting we lie! We won't need to. I'm saying, hypothetically, if many schools are indeed bad . . . what if the prime minister was there? With that presentation in front of all the education bosses, he'd have no choice but to fire the education minister. And then, after we win the Noble Deed Match . . . well, we know who he should pick as the next education minister."

"Genius!"

They returned to the others. "You know what would boost this Noble Deed Match to epic levels, Scarlet?" Blaze said. "Inviting the supreme prime minister to the Top Boss Award Banquet!"

"Ohhh! That's a great idea!"

Blaze turned to Kai. "Game on, arch-rival."

Later that day, a news bulletin flashed across the MC Frames of millions of Puddin' Heads and Sweeties.

*** *Education Minister / Football Commissioner Announces First Epic Puddin' Head vs Sweetie Noble Deed Football Match* *** *Associate Ed Minister Rivals to Tour Island Nation Schools and Select Top Football Players* *** *Each Player of Winning Team to Receive Noble Deed and Mega MC Bucks for Their Home Island Schools* ***

Courageous Reader, to sustain yourself on the *Absurd Schools Tour*, I suggest you grab (a) stacks of thank you cards to write your fabulous teachers and leaders and (b) some delicious snacks. I recommend spicy honey kale chips. And if you got that spoon helmet, strap it on, because you're going to need it.

MAKE IT RAIN

Scarlet drove the team down a cavernous hallway while Blaze and Kai argued about whose schools were worse. Scarlet wove the golf cart back and forth, singing, "Noble Deed Match! Noble Deed Match!"

Suddenly, loud laughter and squealing emanated from one of the rooms.

"Who's that?" asked Chopper. "And what are they doing?"

Scarlet blushed. "Uh, I think it's my parents. Let's keep going."

"Scarlet, what's going on?" Blaze asked at an obnoxious volume.

"Yeah, Scarlet. What's going on?" Chopper was even louder.

"Yeah, Scarlet. What's going on?" Kai couldn't resist.

"Shhhh! Uh. He he he. Strange. Oh, wait. Yes. Of course. It's the end of the quarter. This is their pay day celebration. Business has been good!"

Blaze jumped out of the golf cart and ran to the noisy door.

"No!" Scarlet cried. "Wait!"

Chopper and Kai followed. Scarlet pulled over and ran after them. "Fart tarts!"

Blaze snuck into the *Fun Room* and the troupe quickly followed. It had a balcony loft and a slide and was filled with beanbags and pillows. At two corners of the room, attendants loaded cannons with large buckets of money. The cannons shot waves of money; $50, $$100, and $$500 bills hung in the air and fluttered to the ground in layers so thick Blaze couldn't see to the far end of the room.

Scarlet's parents stood on the balcony, dressed in tuxedos. Smiley faces glowed on their upgraded MC Frames. "Make it rain! Make it rain!" they shouted and slapped through stacks of bills, which floated down onto a massive growing pile on the floor below. Scarlet's mom shrieked and slid down the slide, splashing up a wave of bills before disappearing into a sea of money. She jumped out of the enormous pile, hugging an armful of cash. She cheered, "Jump! Jump! Jump!" and splashed more waves of bills.

Scarlet's dad jumped off the balcony loft. "Wheeeeee!" He spread his arms and legs into a belly flop, splashing money in all directions. He tackled Mrs. Pompavich, laughing as he pulled her under.

"Ahh! I hate being tackled under money! It makes me

claustrophobic."

Scarlet said, "Diving from the balcony is so fun. Oh! The winner of the Noble Deed Match should get to do this when my parents aren't here. But let's get out of here before they see us."

Blaze, however, boiled inside and ran into the hallway. As soon as Scarlet stepped out, Blaze yelled, "Are you serious right now? You're okay with this? It makes me sick! Kids and families can barely afford school fees. Some students can't afford school at all and drop out! And your parents are diving into *a literal swimming pool of money!*"

Scarlet was shocked. "There's nothing wrong with being rich. They earned it and can use it however they want! I'm helping you all out here. We wouldn't even have a Noble Deed program without them! Now, you can take my help or leave it!"

"I'd rather be poor than take money from a rich b—"

"Hey! This might be fun." Chopper tried to laugh and signaled for Blaze to cool down. He whispered, "We need her, Blaze."

It didn't work.

Scarlet shot out her hand. "Oh, that's how it is, huh? You know, you haven't even thanked me for *anything*. You are so stubborn!"

"No, I'm real."

"Yeah, I see your real colors. Your arrogance is unbelievable."

"Snob."

"Puddin' Head."

"Yes, I am, pony princess."

Scarlet chomped her gum, quickly glancing at a lump in her pocket. "I don't have a pony! Now you're just making stuff up, you big-handed hot head."

Blaze was taken aback. "Wow. You're going there, eh? Well, at least *my* hands are real. Your Daddy and Mommy paid for yours. Everything about you is fake."

Chopper buried his head in his hands. Kai smiled and waited for more.

Scarlet didn't back down. "At least *I* know a good thing when I see it."

"Yeah, you can see a good thing for *you*. But you can't see injustice, because you live in a rich bubble, protected by your fancy house and your fancy school. And I bet you *do* have a pony! I can't wait to take you on this tour and pop your sad, tiny bubble."

"First of all, I *don't* have a pony, because I'm not allowed to have real pets!" Scarlet paced, turned her back to Blaze, and pulled something from her pocket, stroking it like a lucky rabbit's foot. She shoved it back in her pocket and spun around. "More importantly, who nearly destroyed the Noble Deed program? Who almost got fired and almost destroyed any chance at making schools better? Twice! Why are we in this mess in the first place? It's not because of me, *hot tart*."

"Hot tart? That doesn't even make sense!" Blaze adopted a grand voice. "I'm Queen Scarlet, and I'm *so* important with my rich gown made of the world's finest diamonds. Here, let me bestow MC bucks on you poor, needy sobs."

"What? I don't even wear gowns. Or dresses!" Scarlet dramatically pointed to her T-shirt, shorts, and sandals. "You don't know me! And you're seriously out of your mind! Which is too bad, because this Noble Deed Match could be epic!" She popped a bubble with her gum, then tore it out of her mouth, and threw it against the wall.

Chopper pulled Blaze aside. "Do I need to crack your thin skull? Stay focused. Who cares if she's rich? It's to our advantage; we need resources to pull this off."

"Did you see all that money? Imagine what we could do with it! And someone needs to teach her a lesson."

"Do you have any idea how many resources it will take to make this Noble Deed Football Match happen? Pull your puddin' head out of your butt and think about what you want. You can't do this alone, and you know it."

Blaze frowned, grunted, and walked in a circle, muttering under her breath, before eventually dragging her feet over to Scarlet. "I'm sorry. It's very hard to see a few people with so much money. You're right. We do need your help. Besides, there's no way I'm going to pass up the opportunity to crush the Sweeties in this epic Noble Deed Match."

Kai said, "Enough of this mushy talk. Let's get this tour started already."

Everyone laughed awkwardly. They had no idea what they would see on this tour or who they would meet. Guess who arrived the very next day?

WORST SCHOOLS NOTE TAKER

On a clear night I flew into Puddin' Head Island, which was lit by thousands of spectacular stars. My colleague suggested I stay at the Puddin' Hut Motel, which had deals on longer-term stays, and was conveniently located in Courage City. My colleague had connections with TDJP and Mr. Blunt, who set up my initial meeting with Blaze and Chopper the next morning.

Blaze and Chopper were busy and, frankly, had bigger priorities than attending to the strange health conditions of a foreigner. Fortunately, the swelling in my eyes had gone down. My MC Frames hid them a bit, especially when dimmed. Yes, mine also lit up with a frown face. I never did get used to the constant, subtle looks, but my above average hand size seemed to reassure Blaze and Chopper. The arms of my Frames also lit up with a bright, circled V, signaling I was an island visitor. Surprisingly, this status seemed to make me nonthreatening. Indeed, Blaze's mom and Chopper's parents took one look at me, asked a few questions, shrugged, and readily agreed to an educator joining the journey. Blaze loved the idea of someone writing a book about the absurdity of Puddin' Head schools, which she believed without question, even though so far, she had only seen Region 2 schools. She also liked the possibility of becoming world-famous.

I was ready to start, but sensed something bothered the pair.

Chopper didn't mince words. "You need to lose the beard, to blend in."

Blaze nodded in agreement. "It does look ridiculous. Is that squirrel hiding in there?"

I laughed to disguise my disappointment, and to prove I had a sense of humor. Besides, who was I to argue? I was willing to do anything to cure this absurdity neurosis! "What about the mustache?" I asked, immediately regretting this idea.

They shook their heads no.

"Even more odd-looking," Chopper said.

"Maybe if he wore a spoon hat?" Blaze offered.

"No. We don't have time for distractions."

I dodged one there. "How about a goatee?"

Chopper frowned. "Maybe a thin one. And uh, we have a major

school tour that will involve considerable traveling, biking, and walking. Think you can handle that?" He raised an eyebrow as though skeptical of my physical prowess.

Curse my surly sweet tooth! I could lose a kilo or nineteen, but I said, "Sure. I'm in shape—I snorkel, swim, and walk the beach. I'll be fine." Perhaps I embellished the swimming part. Regardless, I was suddenly overcome with a desire to prove myself. I executed nine perfect jumping jacks, dropped to the ground, and pounded out eight full push-ups to demonstrate my dedication. Gasping for breath, I stood up and said, "See. Now, where is this puddin' I've heard so much about?"

Blaze and Chopper exchanged glances, laughed, and took me to the Puddin' Cafe, which I very much enjoyed. Chopper said that my notes might be helpful for data gathering. He henceforth introduced me as "a note taker," which perhaps was intentionally boring to minimize suspicion. Shortly thereafter, I couldn't help but wonder: had I become Chopper's only staff member to boss?

The day before the tour started, Blaze, Chopper, Kai, and I met at Scarlet's house. Yes, I sported a short, rugged goatee, which better fit my mood anyway. Plus, I started my morning with eight push-ups. Chopper explained that I was a visitor who had heard about an epic Noble Deed Match (which was technically true, after I learned about it). He said I was also interested in learning about Island Nation schools. I would be taking copious notes throughout the tour, and maybe write a book about it.

Kai and Scarlet looked at the V on my Frames and shrugged.

Chopper was all business and reviewed the plan. "Team, our twenty-day tour starts tomorrow. We'll spend two days at each of the five school regions on each island. On the first day, we'll have football tryouts centrally located near a train stop. We'll review survey results and select a school to tour for the second day. I've already sent the tryout schedule and survey to all middle and high school students on both islands. As a reminder, we kept the survey short, asking only six questions." He displayed the survey.

1. My school is affordable.
   a. agree
   b. disagree

2. My school is fair.
   a. agree
   b. disagree
3. What I learn at school is fun, useful, and interesting.
   a. agree
   b. disagree
4. Why did you choose your answers?
5. What do you like most about school?
6. What would you like to change about school?

"Since we're already here, let's look at the data for Puddin' Head Island Region 1. Then tomorrow, we'll just have the tryouts." Chopper set up a slide show on a large screen. "As predicted, that short survey led to an excellent response rate so far. About 85 percent. I haven't reviewed all the open-ended responses yet, but from what I've seen so far, let's just say there is a very wide range of experiences and opinions.

Puddin' Head Island, Region 1
Student Survey Results

	All Students Agreeing	Bigs Agreeing	Smalls Agreeing
School is affordable	60%	20%	90%
School is fair	56%	10%	92%
School is fun, useful, and interesting	28%	8%	40%

Response Rate = 85%

"The numbers speak for themselves," Chopper said. "As you can see, there is a huge difference between the answers of Bigs and Smalls."

"I knew it! I knew it!" Blaze yelled. "Looks like there is trash to burn and bosses to fire."

"NO BURNING TRASH!" Scarlet and Chopper said together.

"And you're *not* allowed to fire school bosses!" Scarlet quickly added.

"I was kidding. Chill. But clearly all the schools on Puddin' Head Island are unfair and boring." Blaze whispered to Chopper, "This disproves what Minister Pompavich says—there's no way these schools are good! She's going to be fired!"

"Not according to Smalls," said Kai. "But that's not surprising."

Blaze looked at him with suspicion, confused that they agreed. "Yeah. But who are the Bigs who *agree*? And why isn't the percentage of all students the average of Bigs and Smalls?"

"Good questions," Chopper said. "As for your second question, technically that is the average. Fewer Bigs responded to the survey."

"Probably because they aren't in school," said Blaze.

"Could be. A lot of the Bigs open-ended responses complained about frequently receiving yellow and red cards, which is also what they want to change. As for your first question, a few schools had much higher percentages of Bigs and Smalls agreeing with these items."

"Weird!" Blaze scrunched up her face, trying to understand how that was possible.

The team took an hour to review and discuss the survey data, including open-ended responses. They identified themes, which led to more questions.

"What's up with this obsession with testing?" Kai asked. "What are tests?"

Blaze chuckled. "You don't know what tests are? No wonder you Sweeties are so stupid."

"They obviously haven't helped your numbskull."

"Yeah, whatever. Anyway, this seems like a whole other level of testing. Maybe we should check it out."

Chopper said, "Testing is definitely a theme. That leads us to our action item. After the football tryouts, which school should we tour? One with high agreement, moderate agreement, or low agreement, which is basically a very low percentage of Bigs agreeing?"

Blaze answered swiftly, "Low agreement. Let's go to the worst school to see it first-hand. I can't wait to fire—I mean, talk to, the school boss."

I felt optimistic about finding a cure for my absurdity neurosis.

PH1 TRYOUTS
PH1, Day 1

We got off the train at Booster City, the major hub of Puddin' Head Island. Scarlet said, "Leaders first!" and pushed her way to the front. The team walked to a nearby football pitch while I fumbled with my notepad and practiced taking videos with my MC Frames. Two of Scarlet's attendants trailed behind, lugging bags of footballs and cones. Kai, Scarlet, and I wore black shirts. Kai had recognized it was too dangerous to wear blue but refused to wear red. I'm sure you will be shocked that Blaze and Chopper "chose" red shirts.

Later that morning, hordes of Puddin' Head Island Region 1 students—large- and small-handed alike—swarmed out of train cars toward the pitch. Some came to try out for the Noble Deed Match; some came to play offense for the first time (Bigs); some came to skip school; and some came to see Blaze.

On this first tour stop, the team was unprepared for the teeming masses. Bigs especially wanted pictures with Blaze, autographs, high fives, etc. After one fan—recently transferred from Region 5—attempted an enthusiastic head butt, Scarlet ordered an attendant to manage the line. He created a sign that read: *Autographs, Photos, and Videos Only. Head Butts Are Strictly Prohibited.*

After reveling in this celebrity attention, Blaze jogged over to start the tryouts. A large, cheering crowd trailed behind, snapping pictures with their MC Frames.

Chopper had organized a tight, three-part tryout sequence.

Coaches Blaze, Chopper, Kai, and Scarlet took different sections of the pitch. They timed and rated students on basic soccer drills including dribbling, passing, heading, and shooting. Some drills were performed individually. For example, dribbling between an increasingly difficult series of cones or shooting at goals from different distances and places on the pitch. Other drills were performed in pairs—such as passing between cones and then attempting to score a goal.

Unfortunately, roughly 95 percent of players were eliminated by the end of Round 1. "Are you going to say it, or do I need to?" Kai asked Blaze as a student tripped over the ball, fell onto a cone, and cried as he waddled off the pitch.

Blaze pursed her lips and muttered, "You mean that most of

these 'players' look more like sweet puffs than Puddin' Heads?" It was hard for me to disagree.

"If this is your turnout, Sweeties might win by fifty!" Kai slapped his leg and let out a deep laugh.

In Round 2, the few remaining students scrimmaged each other, with the coaches rating their skill set. In Round 3, the top players had two chances to try to score a goal on Kai as a goalie. Then, they had two chances to stop Scarlet from scoring a goal as a defender or goalie. Likewise, they got two chances to try to stop Blaze from scoring a goal. On this day, virtually all students failed miserably. Only one student, Orion, came close to succeeding in Round 3. Orion tracked Scarlet, and then Blaze like a hunter, and he almost stopped them both from scoring. Blaze and Chopper selected this promising defender for the team.

"Should we be worried?" Chopper asked Blaze.

She said, "These tryouts were disappointing. But there's no way we are going to lose against the Sweeties. I guarantee we'll have enough players from Region 2 alone. But today does make me wonder what is happening in those Region 1 schools."

The next day, we took the train to the Redville Depot. "Tell me again, Scarlet. Why can't you get us a helicopter?" Chopper asked.

"I told you, we have no transportation budget. Not allowed. Just be glad I scored these train passes."

At the train stop, Scarlet nudged past Blaze and jumped on her electric bike en route to Red Ribbon Middle School. The rest of us —including her attendants—rode behind on traditional bikes, except for Chopper.

"Can't you make more solar bikes?" Blaze begged.

"Can't afford the materials. Maybe you shouldn't have broken yours."

"Ahh!" Blaze said, watching Scarlet zoom farther into the lead.

After a few kilometers, we pulled into a driveway with perfectly parallel lines that connected to two perfectly symmetrical rectangular parking lots. Straight sidewalks merged into another straight sidewalk that led to the only entrance at the exact center of the school. It looked like a giant warehouse with flood lights and security cameras every five meters. A huge banner—announcing, *Red Ribbon Middle School*—hung perfectly centered above the sliding door. I'll bet you can guess what color it was.

"What *is* this place?" Kai asked.

A tall fence with barbed wire surrounded the school. Blaze said, "We're about to find out. If they let us in." She pressed the buzzer, explained who we were, and the large gate swung open. We had barely set foot inside before a security guard yelled for us to stop and demanded to see identification.

"Somebody forgot their chill booster this morning," Blaze quipped.

The school boss, wearing a red suit, strode out of the school to meet us. She redirected the security officer. "It's okay—these are special guests, not spies." Then she looked at me. "Who's this? I thought this tour was for teens."

"Official note taker," Chopper said.

The school boss glanced at the V on my Frames, shrugged, and took us on a brief tour, stopping in the cafeteria, where the first wave of students was eating lunch. Tired, unhealthy-looking students lined up anxiously for the large self-serve puddin' machines. They didn't notice us.

The machines were spaced exactly two meters apart along the square room's perimeter. They stood next to narrow, rectangular tables holding equidistant baskets of booster shakers and large and medium puddin' bowls. At one table, two students with large hands sold Red Ribbon T-shirts.

"Hey, no student labor until afternoon," Scarlet said to the school boss.

"We're close enough. And remember, we're now a Red Ribbon school, so the regional boss lets us bend the rules. At least, that's what my district boss told me."

On one wall hung a large *Puddin' Head Values* sign. On the opposite wall, a large, rectangular red sign announced, *Defeat the Sweeties: Eat Puddin' and Crush the Test.* Except someone had drawn a thick line through *Sweeties* and wrote *Zombies* over top of it.

"Whoa. Quadruple spoon holsters," Chopper said to Blaze. Each student wore a thick belt that held four spoons on each side, ranging from small to very large. Some students—at the front of the lines—wore fancier belts with protective pockets. In contrast, students at the back of the line wore belts with button straps to secure spoons that dangled and jangled with each step.

"Yeah. And look who's stuck in back of the lines," Blaze said, angrily pointing to the frown Frames.

Kai stared at a table of booster shaker baskets. Some baskets had munchy booster, while others had focus booster. He grabbed a focus shaker from a basket and examined the tiny print on the bottom. "See! I told you. *Made in Sweetie Island Region 2.* It says it right there!"

Blaze snatched the shaker from Kai's hand. "Let me see that." But she couldn't deny what she read. "Weird. Maybe Sweeties are useful after all." She fake chuckled.

Kai clenched his fists. "You don't know what you're laughing —"

The school boss held up her hand. "Shh. You don't want to miss this."

Students sat equidistant from each other with two bowls of puddin' and booster centered in front of them. A student with small, pudgy hands stood up and drew the large spoons from her pocket holsters. "Spoons out!"

The entire cafeteria drew their large spoons (not the very large ones), clanged them together twice, and yelled back, "Spoons out!"

"What do we have?"

"Courage!" *Clang, clang.*

"Who will we defeat?"

"Zombies!" *Clang, clang.*

"How will we defeat them?"

"Eat puddin'!" *Clang, clang.* "Crush the test!" *Clang, clang.*

The student leader holstered her large spoons and walked over to a thick chime nearly a meter in length. She held up a very large spoon. "On your mark."

Students hovered their spoons, waiting.

The Small whacked the chime, which rang across the cafeteria with a mesmerizing tone.

Students plunged into large bowls of puddin' like Olympians swimming for gold. Left spoon, right spoon, left spoon, right spoon. Some students finished early, licked their spoons, wiped them on a napkin, placed them back into their belts, folded their hands in their laps, and closed their eyes as their peers finished.

The chime softened. The student leader—apparently reading a timer on her MC Frames—counted down. "Twenty seconds . . . Ten seconds." One struggling student blurted, "Sweetie tart!"

"Focus!" the student leader commanded. "Five. Four. Three. Two. One. At ease, comrades."

Students holstered their spoons, and quiet conversations bubbled up across the cafeteria. The school boss walked around and provided valuable feedback to the hard-working students. *Clean bowler! Ah, missed a spot there. Nice work. Amazing—not a sign of puddin'! Ah, c'mon now Gigi, that must be three spoonfuls left. Try raising your elbows a little higher next time.*

"Seems like a good school boss to me," Chopper said, deadpan. Blaze stared blankly, too mad to roll her eyes.

Then, a strange thing happened. One by one, student heads began drooping. Some tried to shake themselves awake. Some softly repeated, "Zom-bie, zom-bie, zom-bie," as if meditating. One kid's head fell back as he snored.

"Focus!" yelled the student leader. "Be strong. Condition your mind. Push through your laziness and sloth. Two minutes."

"What the—" Blaze muttered. She rapidly tapped her foot. Chopper tugged her arm. "Shh."

Kai crossed his eyes and made a low whistle. "You're all numbskulls," he whispered.

Moments later, the student leader drew a medium spoon like preparing for duel. "Spoons out!"

Students whipped out two medium spoons. "Spoons out!" *Clang, clang.*

"On my mark." She rang a smaller chime this time, and students dove into the medium-sized bowls of puddin'. Left, right, left, right. Students easily finished before time was called. The school boss nodded approvingly, but did not provide feedback this time, as if students knew they'd met expectations.

After securing her medium spoons, the student leader—who, like the rest of the students appeared re-energized, almost spunky—once again pulled out two large spoons, but this time, she held them between her thumb and index finger. She tapped lightly on the table twice and then clanged the spoons. *Tap, tap, clang. Tap, tap, clang.*

A boost of energy shot through the cafeteria as students joined in, with each round growing louder. *Tap, tap, clang. Tap, tap, clang!* Suddenly, the student leader waved her spoons like an orchestra conductor. The whole cafeteria, in a perfect unified crescendo, chanted, "Crush the test!" with the tapping and clanging rhythm. "Crush the test! Crush the test!"

Students marched out of the cafeteria while some Bigs stayed behind to clean up. Trying to suppress his laughter, Kai said, "Well the only remaining question is, what are the gigantic spoons for?"

Blaze smiled sarcastically. "Oh, those are for the Sweeties. We didn't tell you that?" She tapped the large spoons on her own belt.

"Huh? I don't get it."

Blaze smiled then frowned. "Sometimes, I don't either."

A small group of government officials entered the cafeteria. The school boss explained she had important data to review and gave us guest passes. She told us to explore on our own and reminded us that video recording was prohibited. "We wouldn't want you stealing our testing secrets! Many of our graduates go on to become top data analysts for Good Hope Day, school statistics, and MegaCorp sales. In fact, some of our top students are already working on real-world projects, getting real-world experience. Most citizens have no idea how important these accurate numbers are to the running our nation. But some do, which becomes a big draw for prospective students. At the same time, some students can't hack it and transfer. It's not for everyone."

After she left, Blaze said to Chopper, "Some of these students calculate whether we have large or small hands on Good Hope Day?"

"Sounds like it."

"Ahhh!"

The team split into two groups to tour classrooms. I followed Blaze and Chopper down a hallway. Blaze sped around the corner and accidentally plowed into Orion, who yelled, "Zombie!" Blaze screamed, grabbed a spoon, and whacked Orion on the hands before recognizing him. "You scared the puddin' out of me!"

"Fart tart!" Orion rubbed his hands in pain. "Sorry," he said sadly. "I'm glad you ran into me, though. I saw you in the cafeteria and thought—I was hoping—that perhaps you could answer some of my questions . . . Ah, never mind." Orion hung his head.

Chopper was too excited to notice his sadness. "Good to see you, football teammate. What's worth seeing? The students seemed excited at lunch. I don't understand why your survey results were so low."

"Yes, I've been hunting for answers in the data, and in the stars —I do like star gazing— but nothing seems to help," Orion said softly.

"Huh?"

"Did you know that we orbit a lifeless star millions of kilometers away? Isn't that depressing?"

"Uhh, I'm not sure," Blaze said. "So . . . we're here for this tour —"

"It's going to burn up one day."

"Listen, I wish we could help, but we don't have a lot of time," Blaze said glancing sideways at Chopper. "Are there any classrooms you recommend we see?"

"Ah, never mind. I do enjoy football. And I don't have a yellow card, yet, so I could be of some assistance. As for your small questions, yes, lunch is a better part of our day. Yes, I think you'll quickly understand our survey results. You might start with this room."

We walked into a testing results room surrounded by machines, filing cabinets, and large monitors. A teacher rushed over. He calmed down after Orion explained he was giving a Red Ribbon tour on official government business.

Large-handed students anxiously copied, stapled, counted, and compiled multiple choice tests into separate stacks—one per classroom. Others ran completed tests through a machine and spat them out the backside. Indecipherable codes lit up on a display window. A student neatly placed tests into a labeled folder and then stuck them into a filing cabinet. Data monitor students ticked off electronic checklists projected from their MC Frames. A large screen displayed a spreadsheet of classroom testing progress.

"What are the colors for?"

"The green cells mean 'not done,' yellow means 'in progress,' and red, means 'done,'" Chopper said matter-of-factly.

"How do you know that?"

"I used to live in Region 1, remember? But I've never seen anything like this."

"And look at who's doing all the work," Blaze said angrily. "That might explain our survey results."

A student recognized Blaze and wobbled over. "Take me with you!" He cupped his hands and hissed to nearby peers, "It's Blaze Union—she's here to save us! We made the football team!" A handful of students quietly put down testing materials and meandered over.

"What? No, we're just here to learn. This has nothing to do with football."

More students noticed and crept over.

"Uh, we should go. Now." Orion motioned for us to leave. "Let's visit some classrooms."

"I don't think they like it here," Blaze said to Chopper.

We quietly sat in the back of a large classroom. Orion gave the teacher a thumbs-up and the teacher nodded.

"As I was saying," the teacher told the class. "You must crush this test. Do not let the zombies weaken your mind or your body. Brains and bodies made from puddin' are excellent deterrents against zombies. Crushing tests will strengthen your brain—and especially Bigs' brains—against zombie hypnosis."

"Sir, we've already taken three tests today," a student said. "Can't we just read or something?"

"I don't believe what I'm hearing. Yellow card!"

"Can we go outside, and take a walk, or get some fresh air?" another student pleaded.

"Yellow card! You know we've banned physical education and recess. We don't have time for that!"

A tubby student with small hands stretched and yawned. Two bolts in the back of his chair snapped, sending him sailing backwards with the attached desk landing on top of him.

"Thickening up for a Sweetie attack. Excellent work." The teacher paused and looked at another student, who was leaning down to help his friend off the floor. "I know that's not a hole in your Puddin' Head red T-shirt because we sell brand new shirts every day."

Blaze clenched her jaw and asked softly, "Who is this guy? Mr. Peabody's brother?"

Chopper muffled a laugh, but Blaze was simmering.

"I'm sorry, sir," said the student who had large hands. "My parents don't get paid until Friday. My other shirt was dirty."

"That's no excuse! If you have no pride in Puddin' Head red, then I'm giving you a—"

The class responded, as they had many times before, "Card that's red."

"No! My parents can't afford another transfer!"

"Class?"

"Too bad, so sad!" they chimed in unison.

"Red card!"

The student burst into tears and ran out of the classroom. The class chanted, "Too bad, so sad! Too bad, so sad!"

Blaze stood up and started for the teacher, but Chopper grabbed her arm and pulled her out of the room. "Focus. Keep your eyes on the prize. We're just collecting information right now."

"I have enough information!"

Suddenly, a student meandered toward the classroom. She looked at Blaze like a ship that had lost its captain. She slowly drew two large spoons and clanged them twice as if dreaming. Suddenly, she smacked her head against the wall. And did it again. *Clang, clang, wham! Clang, clang, wham!*

"What the—" Blaze cried. She escorted the student onto a bench.

"Why are we here?" Orion asked no one. He yelled, "Nurse!" without a hint of panic. Then, he turned to Blaze. "It happens."

"This is ridicu—" Blaze stopped. A glassy-eyed student waddled past them with a pencil sticking out of his hand. A teacher down the hallway poked her head out of her classroom to yell, "That's a red card!" The blank-faced student smiled as if finding temporary relief.

My eyes began to twitch, and the smell of chocolate puddin' called my surly sweet tooth.

"Nurse!" Orion yelled louder, but strangely seemed unmoved. *"I'm talking to the school boss!"*

"Blaaaaaze! No!" Chopper tried to grab her but missed. Blaze tore past the head banger, past the pencil stabber, down the hallway, past the secretary, and into the school boss's office. She was too fast for me to follow, so I relied on her MC Frame video (yes, she was recording). Alas, my surly sweet tooth led me to the cafeteria—I don't recall how many puddin' bowls and boosters I tried. But I do know my twitching eyes made it hard to see.

"What kind of school is this?!" Blaze cried, knocking a stack of tests to the floor.

"Looks like we're done for today, folks," the school boss said, and the government officials quickly exited the room. "What's the problem?"

"What's the problem? *What is the problem?*! This is the worst school I've ever seen—and that's saying a lot! Not only are your classes boring and useless, but the large hand discrimination is out of control. Students are literally injuring themselves. And should I mention that nearly every student is, shall I say, unhealthy? *On purpose!* How could they possibly play football?"

"I don't know who you think you are. And you're being a bit judgmental, don't you think?"

"Judg—*I'm* judgmental?" Blaze paused to think. "It's not the students' fault! I'm not blaming them—I'm blaming you! How could you let the Sweeties do this to you? No exercise?! How could you think this mad testing will defeat the Sweeties?" Blaze paused another moment, as if lost in thought. "Wait . . . are you on their side?" she asked seriously, before recomposing herself. "Anyway, aren't you the one in charge around here?"

The school boss rolled her eyes. "Okay, Ms. *Associate* Education Minister with large hands. Yes, the last time I checked, I'm the person in charge."

"Oh, you did *not!*"

"Listen, I'll speak with the district boss. But she has been very clear: I need to keep improving our test scores. She wants all schools in our district in the 90th percentile. Otherwise, *I could be fired.*" The school boss mumbled to herself. "We always seem to hover around the middle, though. We crept up to 52 percent last year, which gave us a Red Ribbon Award, but we just can't seem to get much above 50 percent."

"*Arrgggh!* Chopper—where is my guitar?"

Chopper stood in the doorway. "We didn't bring your guitar."

"*Then we're out of here!* Don't worry, we *will* do something about this!"

S1 TRYOUTS
S1, Day 1

The next day Blaze, Chopper, and I traveled together to Power Island. Fortunately, my eyes had stopped twitching.

"Can you believe that school?" Blaze said. "No bootstraps, but those tests!"

Chopper nodded. "Yeah, that was disturbing."

"However," Blaze said with a smile, "the survey data and our school visit clearly show a lot of Region 1 schools aren't very good. And that's good for our report. And that's good for my chances of becoming the education minister."

Scarlet met us on Power Island. Then, we headed west by train to Sweetie Island and stopped near Sugar Falls to pick up Kai. He proudly wore a blue shirt, while the rest of us had settled on neutral black so as not to disrupt this part of the tour with any signs of red. The morning sun lit up the Sugar Mountains on the horizon.

"Beautiful!" Scarlet cried.

Chopper couldn't help it. "Yeah, this stop seems strangely familiar. It's almost like we were here recently on a special visit."

Blaze laughed. "Yeah, me too. *Have* we been here before?"

"Yes, you numbskulls were definitely here. Do I need to remind you how you got home?" Kai said with a grin.

"Gah!" Blaze said. "I blocked that from my memory."

We switched trains and traveled north, with the Sugar Mountains to the west and the Snake Channel to the east. Power Island and Celebration Island faded in the background. We arrived at Tranquil Point, the Region 1 stop that was farthest to the north. Scarlet once again pushed herself to the front. "Leaders first!" She jumped off the train and sprinted ahead of Blaze to an open field of sand and grass.

"Ahh!" Blaze sprinted to catch her, but Scarlet had too much of a lead.

"We'll have to make our own football pitch," Chopper said, finally catching up. "No goals anywhere on this island, right, Kai?"

"Yep. Keeping score is not a thing here."

"I can't imagine. So odd!" Blaze booted a football at Scarlet, who ducked just in time.

"Watch it!"

Blaze ran after the ball as Chopper set up a screen and displayed the survey results. "Hang on, Blaze! You may want to see this, too." She trotted back and the team examined the data.

Sweetie Island, Region 1
Student Survey Results

	All Students Agreeing	Bigs Agreeing	Smalls Agreeing
School is affordable	65%	30%	96%
School is fair	56%	14%	94%
School is fun, useful, and interesting	65%	48%	78%

Response Rate = 87%

"Well, there you go," Kai said, looking at Blaze. "Looks like we have similar opinions about school. And the reason we aren't at 100 percent is because of you knuckleheads."

"Thanks for the compliment, Sweetie," Blaze said. "Don't blame us for your problems. Obviously, you have a Bigs problem on your hands, too, no pun intended."

Chopper laughed. "But you do have a much higher percentage of students agreeing that school is interesting, fun, and useful. Somehow, I doubt that's because you enjoy testing."

The team discussed the survey results and read the open-ended survey responses. "Apparently, a lot of these schools are very relaxing," Scarlet said.

"Yeah, for some students. But many students—especially Bigs —don't find school fair or interesting. Look, someone said, 'Lying around all day might seem fun, but it gets boring fast.' What does that even mean, 'lying around all day'? They must be exaggerating."

The team reviewed the survey results from individual schools and selected one with extreme results to visit: Chill High School. "Well, it does seem stress-free," said Kai. "But why are so many students bored?"

"We'll find out tomorrow," Chopper said. "Now, where are all these Sweetie football superstars?"

Everyone looked toward the train station.

Blaze raised her eyebrows at Kai. "Yeah, where is my competition? Maybe they got scared."

"They're not scared! They don't believe in competition. But hopefully some will show up because they'll be working as a cooperative team."

Scarlet paced, tossed a cone across the pitch, and stomped her feet. "*You hope? You hope* some people will show up?!" She spread her arms in disbelief. "Where are they? How are we going to have a Noble Deed Match without another team! And if we don't have a football match, what will that mean for the Noble Deed program?"

"Calm down." Blaze tapped her football back and forth between her feet, then knees. "You're acting like you won't get a pony for your birthday."

"I told you, I'm not allowed to have a real pony!" Scarlet turned and touched her pocket as if lost in thought for a brief moment. She quickly swiped a tear from her eye and threw a cone at Blaze, then one at Chopper. "Aren't you worried? Haven't you thought about what this means for you? No Noble Deed Match means no sales. No sales means no money for education. And you'll probably be fired."

"They wouldn't do that . . ." Blaze thought for a moment. "Yeah, you're right. They probably would. Kai, I need someone to play against!"

"*We* need someone to play against," Chopper corrected. "Or we'll have to resort to having a Puddin' Head championship tournament."

"How is *that* a Noble Deed?" Scarlet cried. "It's not the same at all!"

"And no way am I letting all that money go to Puddin' Heads," Kai said. "We'll just need to do a better job of recruiting. Might as well start tomorrow."

We departed the train at Chill Village, and of course, Scarlet beat us to Chill High School.

Multiple wooden cottages dotted the high school campus. Stone pathways cut through patches of grass and flowers rising out of the sandy soil.

"Well, this is cool," Kai said. "But where's the main office, or house, or whatever? Where are we supposed to check in? I've got some recruiting to do."

"Why don't you ask those kids?" Blaze suggested. "They don't seem to have anything to do."

Kai approached a handful of Bigs, awkwardly introduced himself, and asked what they were doing.

"Uh, chillin'. Duh."

"Why aren't you in school? And where is the main office?"

The students exchanged glances. "We got red cards, *obviously*. And we don't have a 'main office.' We have learning houses."

"Weird!" Blaze was fascinated. "So where's the school boss? The person in charge?"

"Huh?" one kid said. "Oh, you mean Poppy. She doesn't come around much. But if you see her, definitely don't make her mad."

Chopper said, "Okay, folks, time is a-ticking. We need to recruit and tour. How does your communication system work? How do we make an announcement to everyone?"

"Chill, bird. Don't get yourself in a flutter."

"Bird? What? I'm just asking if you have a PA system or a way to talk to the whole school?"

The kids looked even more confused.

Chopper rolled his eyes. "Well, luckily, I came prepared." He pulled a megaphone from his backpack.

Blaze shook her head. "How could you possibly have known to bring that?"

"We obviously needed it for the huge turnout at football tryouts!" Chopper laughed.

The host students looked annoyed. "Football? Listen, we don't understand what is happening right now, so we're just going to scoot over there." They gave the team a disapproving look, stuck their hands in their pockets, and shuffled to a picnic table underneath a large banyan tree.

"Can I use that?" Kai asked. Chopper handed him the megaphone.

"Testing, test—" His voice boomed across the campus. We covered our ears. "Sweet Mother of Nectar, Honey, and Sugar!" Kai exclaimed. He held the megaphone away from him as if it had suddenly turned into a rocket launcher.

"Yeah, you might want to turn that down a bit. It can reach 120 decibels."

Kai turned it down and tried again. "Hello, fellow Sweeties. I have an important announcement." Cottage doors swung open. Students poked their heads out like anxious, curious rabbits. One said, "Testing? He wants to give us tests!" but was drowned out by the megaphone.

"As you know, we are here today to visit your wonderful school —or, uh, houses, I guess. I'm sure we'll learn important things."

A student yelled, "Chill out, bird! You're' ruining my relaxation!" But like the rest of the Sweeties, her voice was squelched by the reverberation from the megaphone that echoed off cottages.

"Thank you for completing the survey. You've provided us with valuable information. We have more questions that we hope you can answer." By now, students' curiosity had shifted to anger. Some hopped up and down like irate bunnies.

One said, "He's really a Puddin' Head dressed up as a Sweetie!" Another covered his ears. "Shut up, bird! *You're stressing me out*!!"

"I can see from your faces that you're eager to give us a tour," Kai boomed. "But first, I have a special request. We need football players for the Noble Deed Match." Chill students hopped up and down faster and faster. Some cursed at Kai. "Winning will provide Sweetie schools with significant funding and stop the oppressive Puddin' Heads from ruling us."

Blaze cocked her head at Kai.

"What?" Kai said. Chill students yelled that he must really be a Puddin' Head because who else would be so rude and unkind?

But Kai didn't hear them, perhaps because his ears were also ringing from the megaphone. "Your enthusiasm is contagious!" Kai said. "Even if you know little about football, please join me for these vital tryouts. Sweetie Island is counting on you." By this point, Chill students huddled together and wailed, commiserating over their stress levels that were making this the worst day of their lives.

To the team's amazement, about twenty students did show up for tryouts. Chopper started to explain the drills, but a student interrupted. "Whoa, bird. Don't you think we've had enough stress today? We simply came here to share our football talent."

"Yeah? Please show us." Kai couldn't wait to see.

A student waved her finger and counted to three. The a cappella group snapped their fingers and sang.

Football, football, football.
We can hear you blare.
There is no need to shout,
It's more than we can bear.
You're stressing us out,
But maybe you don't care.

The Chill students hung onto the last note, cheered, and group hugged. "Well, what do you think? We just made it up. But pretty good, right?"

"Yeah," Kai winced.

Blaze fell to the ground laughing. "I don't think we need to worry about the competition—I mean, cooperation!"

"That's not helping!" Kai said. He passed a football to one student, who stared blankly as it bounced off his leg.

"Well, pass it back," Kai pleaded. The student whiffed and slipped. Blaze and Chopper rolled and slapped each other, howling with laughter.

"They've never played football before—what do you expect?" Kai turned back to the Chill group, still hopeful. "But do any of you know how to kick, pass, or dribble a football?"

"See, I *told* you that's what a football looks like," one student said to the others.

Another frowned at Kai. "Won't kicking it hurt our feet?"

Scarlet shook Kai. "*Ahhhh!*" She grabbed the megaphone. She grabbed Kai by one arm. And much to his surprise, Scarlet yelled,

"*Ahhhh!*" in his face. He flopped onto his stomach, cursing, and plugging his ears.

Scarlet walked in a slow semi-circle and continued yelling. Sound waves knocked down the Chill group, one by one. They cried, shook, and covered their ears. Blaze cupped her own ears and bounded away. Scarlet tossed the megaphone to the ground. "What are we going to do? How are we going to have the Noble Deed Match!"

Blaze jogged back and looked at the traumatized, wide-eyed Chill students strewn across the ground. "Chill, bird," she said to Scarlet. "Tryouts are over. It's time for the tour." She laughed and turned to Kai, who unplugged his ears. "And I suggest you leave the megaphone here."

CHILL BIRD
S1, Day 2, Continued

We entered a cottage that had the word *Chill* carved above the door. At the sight of Kai, some students dove onto couches. Others ran into a corner, squatting like scared rabbits trying to hide.

A teacher wearing a flowing blue dress and blue MC Frames with a smiley face accepted a cup of tea and turned to the students. She said sweetly, "It's okay, Sweeties. We've had a rough, stressful morning, but we can do this. Look, they don't have the noise blaster." Students raised their heads and stared at Kai suspiciously.

"Are you sure, Teacher Quelly?" one timid student asked.

The teacher smiled. "Yes, I'm sure."

So, the students resumed their activities. Peaceful music wafted through the cottage. Some students napped. Some stretched. Others flapped their arms.

We followed the teacher who led students into the Chill Bird Room. It had beautiful wooden floors. Sunlight streamed through the windows and onto plants hanging from wooden beams. The walls were painted with serene birds. Bigs served tea before making some for themselves. We quietly found spots in the back of the room.

"Does everyone have their sweet tea with relaxing and hand-shrinking booster?"

"Yes, Teacher."

"Does everyone have their stress-free compression gloves on?"

"Yes, Teacher."

"Breathe in. Breathe out," the teacher said softly. "Your life is free of stress. You are happy. There are only quiet sounds now. Flap your arms slowly. Spread your wings—you are flying through the sky. Wind is blowing against your face and through your hair. Stand on one leg. Now, flap your left arm. You are gently floating down a lazy river. Flap your right arm. You are drifting on a cloud."

"These birds are very fast, yet lazy and stupid?" Blaze asked.

Kai gave her the stink eye.

Chopper's head drooped. He scrunched and shook his face, but yawned nevertheless. "I'm getting sleepy."

"Now, we must practice shielding ourselves from the evil, stressful Puddin' Heads." Suddenly, the teacher shouted, "Quack like a duck!"

The students quacked like a flock of frightened ducks, which jolted Chopper out of his stupor. "What the—"

"They're calling for their lost teacher," Blaze whispered to Chopper. "Teacher Quacky." I agreed with Blaze on this one.

Chopper snorted.

One student—who, yes, was standing on one leg, flapping her right arm, and quacking like a duck—lost her balance, and tipped over a teacup.

"Yellow card!" the teacher snapped. "Can I get a Big to clean up this mess? How stressful! Now, everyone, hop on one leg. Remove that stress! Keep quacking and flapping like you mean it!" Students quacked and flapped like a cooperative and committed flock.

We exchanged glances.

The teacher abruptly switched to a slow flap and a soft, sugary voice. "Now, find a comfortable stance for your most important defense mechanism. Enter a *chill bird trance* of stress-free protection. Breathe in. Breathe out. Close your eyes. Scrunch your face. Stay in this trance as long as possible. You will feel no stress, no pain, no unhappiness. You will see that there is no unfairness, competition, or unkindness in the world. These negative ideas exist only in your mind. Let no one else get a yellow or red card today. For those of you with large hands, focus on shrinking your hands until they are small."

Most students squeezed their eyes shut or flapped their arms as if really focusing or preparing for takeoff. But a few rolled their eyes.

"No Puddin' Head can harm you while you're in this chill bird trance. Flap your arms when you feel moved. If you reach an advanced trance, look for a genie in your mind's eye. This genie may grant you three wishes."

"What did she just say?" Blaze asked Kai incredulously.

"I have no idea. I told you—you Puddin' Heads have really messed up our schools."

"How can this possibly be our fault—"

"Shhh!" the teacher scolded them.

One student, who was a Big, practiced flapping his arms while quietly hopping or standing on one leg. But he kept sniffling. Each time he muffled a sneeze the teacher became more agitated. Suddenly, he bellowed, "*Aachooo!*"

"Yellow card!" the teacher barked. "You're stressing me out!"

"But I have allergies. I can't help it!"

Spying the spreading pool of tea on the floor, the teacher cried, "Ahhh! And clean up that mess on your way out!

He dragged his feet to the spill, wiped it up, mumbling and shaking his head. "Oh, Teacher. I did see the genie. And I wished for math today."

"Red card!" the teacher barked. "You know there's no math today! The genie would not grant a math wish. Today, you will chill."

"Apparently they don't have a one card per day rule," Chopper said to Blaze.

"Oh, come on—I like math," he said obnoxiously. "And the genie said it was a good choice."

"Actually, I would like to do math today," another student said sincerely.

"Yellow card!" The teacher was handing out yellow and red cards like cookies.

"Who knows what five rows of six ducks plus one flapping teacher equals?" the sarcastic Big asked. "One stupid class!"

"Math—ahhh!" students cried.

"Has anyone seen the genie?" the Big yelled to his class. "Anyone? Anyone had a wish granted?" He scanned the room and waited.

After a moment of silence, a student said, "Quack! Quack!"

"Ahhh!" the Big said. "I didn't think so!" He threw the tea saucer and cup in the trash and stomped out of the room.

"Look how stressed the Puddin' Heads made him!" the teacher said. "He was not in the chill bird trance. Now relax Sweeties, and find the genie," the teacher said softly. "No academic subjects today. And never will you take a test."

"No, Teacher Quelly!" a student blurted.

"Yellow card!" the teacher said. "Tulip, what have I told you about interrupting *chill bird* practice? How can we practice when students interrupt? We don't take tests! Tests are for those mean, lumpy headed, lewd, and loud Puddin' Heads! Sweeties, what would tests do?"

"*Stress us out!*" the students cried.

"And how will you find the genie if you're stressed out? And if you can't find the genie, how will you be happy? How will you shrink your hands? Look, I know we may have a large-handed

Puddin' Head here among us," she glared at Kai, "and this has been an extra stressful morning but pull it together, Sweeties. This is exactly what those Puddin' Heads want: to stress you out and control your mind. But the Puddin' Heads cannot harm you while you're in your chill bird trance. Relax. Sweeties, what Puddin' Head immunity are we building?"

"Chill skill!"

The teacher lowered her voice to a soft whisper. "That's right." She paused and squeezed her eyes closed.

I darkened my Frames to hide a rapidly developing eye twitch.

"Now practice by yourselves. In a few moments, Bigs will treat us to delicious tea and sweets."

"What?" Scarlet mumbled. "No child labor before noon."

"Shhhh!" the teacher hissed. Then, she calmly went on, "Breathe in, breathe out. Flap your arms. Please continue."

Blaze grimaced and shook her head. "You Sweeties are nuts!" she whispered to Kai.

"We're nuts?" Kai whispered back. "Constant testing is nuts! If Puddin' Heads didn't take tests, Sweeties wouldn't be stressed!"

"That makes no sense. Obviously, Puddin' Heads are taking stupid tests because the Sweeties confused them!"

"*That* makes sense?" Kai thought for a moment and mumbled to himself. "Sweet Mother of Honey! What if Puddin' Heads took over Sweetie Island? Or Puddin' Heads were in charge of Sweetie schools, and made us—"

The teacher rang a chime and stared at Kai.

"Sweeties, are you relaxed?"

"Yes, Teacher," the class responded, although this was hard to believe.

"Very well. May you stay in your chill bird trance, may your hands shrink, and may you have a stress-free, happy day."

The students bowed to the teacher, practiced for a few more minutes, and scuttled into the lounge. Blaze paced back and forth and was the last to leave. In the lounge, an assortment of small bowls with fresh tea, booster powder, and breakfast snacks sat on hand crafted wooden tables. Students quietly lined up, with Smalls in front, Bigs in back. Three Bigs stood behind the table.

Blaze watched with growing agitation as the first student in line took a teacup and requested chamomile tea, honey, and relax booster. A Big poured steaming water, a dollop of honey, and a spoon of booster powder into the cup and stirred. He then placed the cup on a saucer, filled a tea ball with tea leaves, placed the strainer in the cup, and handed it the student. The student thanked the Big, grabbed a muffin, and sat on a couch to enjoy.

Teacher Quelly said, "Let us be good hosts. Our guests can get in line, too. But stay in your chill bird trance." She smiled and clarified, "Puddin' Heads in the back, of course."

Kai pointed at Blaze, skipping to the front. The teacher shook her head and sent him to the back of the line. But Blaze didn't laugh. She waited until everyone had been served, and while I chomped down chocolate muffins, she asked the Bigs servers a few questions.

"When do you get a turn?"

"After we clean up."

"Why are you working?" The three students looked puzzled, so Blaze tried again. "Did you choose to make the food, set the table, serve the tea, and clean up? Do you take turns—you know, with the Smalls?"

The students laughed. "Not exactly. We 'chose' these jobs to pay our large hand fees."

Blaze pulled Chopper into the corner. "I hate the Sweeties, but I —" She paused.

"What is it?"

"They have stupid large hand rules, too. Just like the Puddin' Heads! I think these hand size rules must have spread from Sweetie Island! It's ridiculous! But also, why do I care about these Bigs? They're Sweeties!"

"Keep your eyes on the prize, Blaze."

"Right. Right! Yes, this is just more evidence of crappy schools. More evidence to get Pompavich fired."

After nibbling on undeniably delicious treats, we started to leave. But Blaze saw a teacher slip off her MC Frames and enter the yoga room. Blaze waved us over and we snuck into the room to watch.

Students arranged their yoga mats and stretched. The teacher noticed. "Ahh! Puddin' Heads, I presume! And the loud one! And you are?"

"A note-taker, for the tour," Chopper answered for me.

"Right. Yes, you're the ones doing the tour. For the education minister, right?"

"Uh, sort of," Blaze said.

"We're doing it to promote the Noble Deed Match!" Scarlet said.

"Ah. Sports ball. I don't suppose you know anything about TDJP . . ." She trailed off as if lost in thought. "Ah, what I am thinking? Well, maybe some good will come of this."

"Did she just start to ask about TDJP?" Blaze whispered to Chopper.

"I think so."

"They have TDJP on Sweetie Island?"

Chopper shrugged.

The teacher pointed to a table littered with MC Frames. "If you're okay with it, we don't wear Frames in this class." To the team's shock, indeed, not a single student wore Frames.

"What? That is definitely against the r—" Scarlet started to say.

Blaze shoved a hand in her face. "Oh, we're good with that!" Blaze threw her Frames onto the table. Kai did the same, but Scarlet refused. Chopper said, "No thanks, I'm good." He shot me a look, then whispered to Blaze, "I'm recording everything." My eyes twitched like a blinking light bulb, so I heeded the boss of staff, kept my darkened Frames on, and slid to the back of the class. I was beginning to conclude that my shrink's suggested cure wasn't working.

More students streamed into class and set up yoga mats. The teacher asked one student how her sister was doing. She whispered to another that she'd loved the poem he'd written, which reminded her of snorkeling. The class warmed up with some light stretches. Students shared what they'd learned last time. One showed an advanced pose she'd invented. The class applauded, and some tried it themselves. The teacher guided students through new yoga moves, providing beginning and extension options, as well as exercises for inner awareness. She quietly walked around the class, acknowledged strong poses, and gave tips for improvement.

"Am I in the same school?" Blaze asked Chopper. "I hate to say this, but uh . . . this is actually a pretty good class. And the teacher doesn't make them wear Frames!" Blaze swallowed and shook her head in disbelief.

Suddenly, the school boss burst through the door. She wore a thick silver necklace, on which shiny diamonds formed the name *Poppy*, which swung from her neck and was wider than her chest. The school boss waved her matching, diamond-studded compression gloves and acted surprised to see the black-shirted guests. "Oh my! Is this the Noble Deed tour group!"

The class gasped.

"School Boss Poppy. What a pleasant surprise," the teacher said, clearly both surprised and annoyed.

The school boss ignored her. "So, which one of you is the big boss? I mean, the associate education minister?" she asked excitedly.

"That's me," Blaze and Kai said at the same time.

"Oh, right—there are two of you!"

"Are those real diamonds?" Scarlet asked.

"Of course! I hope you've liked our school so far."

"This class seems promising," Blaze said.

"Excellent. Oh, by the way, I'm one of the rare school boss, district boss, and regional boss leaders all wrapped up into one! Some say," she said, flexing her fingers, flashing her sparkling gloves, and popping the diamond Poppy, "I could be the first Sweetie education minister. I don't suppose you could put in a good word for me to win the Top Boss Award? Or to be the education minister? I mean, when there's an opening, of course."

"What the—" Scarlet sputtered. "You're talking about my mom's job!"

"Oh? Wait, you are . . ."

"Scarlet Pompavich. The Noble Deed coordinator!"

"Oh my. I'm in the presence of so much greatness." The school boss smiled widely. Then, she noticed the students for the first time. Her face twisted. Her mouth widened in anger. "What the bitter, sour, rotten fruit cake? Where are your MC Frames?"

The class gasped and sat on their hands.

"How embarrassing in front of our very important guests! Jules, please explain what is happening."

"We are preparing for yoga, School Boss Poppy."

"Don't be coy with me. That's not my question, and you know it! Why are these students not wearing their MC Frames?!"

"With all due respect, I've found—and the students have found —that we are more focused and grounded without the Frames. You know, without those advertisements constantly interrupting the flow."

"Oh my, oh my, oh my!" The school boss paced, her diamond necklace swinging so haphazardly that a student ducked to avoid getting clocked in the head. "Jules, I've heard that you are a very good teacher. So, I am, embarrassed. I mean, disappointed." The school boss stared at the students' hands and looked confused. "How can you tell? How do you know who gets first choice, where students sit, what they do?"

"This is the first time you've visited my classroom in five years, and those are your questions?" the teacher asked flatly.

"You know what I'm asking! You're being very rude in front of our guests."

"I'm more concerned about my students."

"How can you possibly know?"

"You mean, do I know whether students have big or small hands, School Boss Poppy?"

The class held its breath.

The school boss snorted loudly. "Yes, of course that's what I mean!"

"Of course I know! I know because *they* know, and they know because it is impossible *not* to know on this island," the teacher cried indignantly. "But I will not follow any stupid rules that treat any child unfairly or make them doubt their potential! All students deserve to be treated fairly, to belong, and to reach their hopes and dreams!"

"What the—" Blaze could not believe what she was hearing. Energy surged through her soul. She was at a loss for words. Yes, Blaze had had a couple of good teachers. But she'd never heard a teacher—was this really happening?—question hand size rules. *Are there more teachers like this?* Blaze wondered.

A similar question crossed my mind. For a moment, my eyes stopped twitching.

The class exhaled loudly. One student said, "Ohhhhhh."

Scarlet yelled, "What?"

Kai hollered, "Yeah!"

Blaze and Chopper applauded and high-fived.

The school boss tried to regain her composure. Students were watching. The Noble Deed coordinator (and daughter of the education minister) was watching. The associate education ministers were watching. "You're stressing me out!" she cried defensively. "You need to work on your . . . on your . . . Self-care practices."

"Wow! You have no clue!"

School Boss Poppy lost it. "How can you not care about students' hand sizes!"

"Because their hand sizes shouldn't matter!"

The class said, "Oooohhhhhhh!" and began jumping up and down like very excited rabbits. Some flapped their arms.

"I'm giving you a red ca—"

"No, I quit!"

Blaze watched with conflicted admiration as the teacher stormed out of the room. And just like that, my eye twitch was back. Blaze chased after Jules. She told me what happened next.

"Wait!"

Jules stopped, turned around, and brushed tears from her face. "Yes?"

"Why do you— How do you— How did you learn to *teach* like that?"

Jules laughed and cried at the same time. "It's taken many years. I've learned with a few trusted colleagues. Obviously, I'm still a work in progress."

"Who taught you more, School Boss Poppy or Teacher Quacky?" Blaze said deadpan.

Jules snorted. "You're funny."

Blaze beamed.

"I shouldn't laugh. But it has been hard. I often feel alone. I wish I had more colleagues who share my beliefs, who want to collaborate and learn." Jules looked up at the sky, swallowed a lump in her throat, and watched a cloud drift by. "I'm sorry, I can't talk right now. Good luck with your tour."

Meanwhile, the school boss turned to the students in an act of desperation. "Did these Puddin' Heads put your teacher up to this?" The bawling students vigorously shook their heads no. Some reconsidered and rapidly nodded.

"She was my favorite teacher!" one student cried.

"Everyone, put on your MC Frames. Now!" the school boss demanded. "Rules are rules. They apply to everyone. Students, families, teachers, bosses. Puddin' Heads. Sweeties. No one is above the rules!"

Students snapped their MC Frames back on and wiped the tears streaming down their faces.

"Now, all of you get yellow cards! You will serve as examples to the rest of the school. And if you already have a yellow card, then it's a red one! Good luck finding another school to take you!"

Many Bigs in the room cursed, shouted, and stomped their feet, or else threw tantrums on the floor. *"You're stressing us out!"*

The school boss said, *"Chill out!* Haven't you learned anything in this school? Go find Teacher Quelly! Get back into your *chill bird trance!"* Students bawled and bolted from the room.

Blaze returned just in time for School Boss Poppy to turn to the visitors and laugh nervously. "Can you believe this teacher? Or these students? Eh he. So unusual for a teacher to disregard the rules. Although, there's a silver lining with the yellow and red card data . . . Anyway, I do hope we can forget this. Unfortunate that the teacher got a red card, but fortunate that I arrived in time to handle this difficult leadership challenge with incredible kindness and skill."

Blaze missed an important clue but grasped something else. "You call that leadership?" She shook her head. "As the *associate education minister,* I should give *you* a red card for losing a very good teacher!" She held a handout to Scarlet, grabbed her Frames from the table, hung them on her shirt, and said, "Until we meet again." Then she glided out of the room as if floating on a cloud.

The team spent the train ride arguing and ignored the boring note-taker. By this point, Blaze had processed a lot of confusing thoughts. Her self almost expanded, then snapped back into place.

"Yes, Jules seemed like a very good teacher," she said. "I started to think that maybe Sweeties aren't all bad, but then I realized she must be a fluke."

"You wish!" Kai said. "On the contrary, knucklehead, Jules illustrates the Sweeties' inherent superiority over the Puddin' Heads."

"One: You keep using knucklehead and numbskull interchangeably, but they're opposites. Thank you once again for the compliment. Two: I guess your chill bird schools are just fine, then, numbskull. And you won't need any of that Noble Deed Match prize money. Not that it matters, because you can't win."

Kai shook his head. "I know your tiny *numbskull* brains can't imagine anything besides eating puddin', but the Sweeties will win the Noble Deed Match."

Blaze chuckled. "So, back to reality. Can we please agree that we learned that Sweetie Schools have much room for improvement?"

Kai said, "Yes! Because of the Puddin' Heads!"

"Is it surprising that Sweetie schools are terrible? No, because you're all a bunch of sappy soft skulls."

"Then why are Puddin' Head schools having problems, too?"

"Obviously because—"

"You're all missing the point!" Scarlet interrupted. "Of course, every school has some minor problems! That's why we need an education minister and education bosses. It doesn't matter whether Puddin' Heads or Sweeties started your stupid school problems or continue your stupid school problems. The much more important point is that we don't have any Sweetie football players. *And that means we can't have a Noble Deed Football Match*! And if we don't have a Noble Deed Football Match, then you won't have money to solve your stupid school problems. So, someone please tell me *why we're going back to Puddin' Head Island*!"

The boss of staff countered, "Because that is the tour plan, we communicated this plan, we are sticking to the plan, and *we will see all regions of both islands in the order of the plan*! We'll return to Sweetie Island, but not until we visit, recruit from, and tour Puddin' Head Region 2. Now, calm down and chill, bird."

Blaze and Chopper buckled over laughing. Scarlet and Kai did not.

"Now, let's look at these Puddin' Head Region 2 survey results. Based on my intel, we have a lot of recruits and a big day ahead of us."

Puddin' Head Island, Region 2
Student Survey Results

	All Students Agreeing	Bigs Agreeing	Smalls Agreeing
School is affordable	50%	10%	80%
School is fair	56%	20%	85%
School is fun, useful, and interesting	58%	30%	80%

Response Rate = 92%

Blaze couldn't believe the data. "How is this possible? Sure, I could see a few numbskulls agreeing. But 50 percent? I'm shocked."

"Like I said, maybe people have a different experience from you, even in the same region. Maybe the world doesn't think like you, or revolve around you. Apparently, a lot of Puddin' Heads do disagree with you." Chopper dodged a high five from Kai. "That's why I said *we needed survey data and evidence.*"

"Okay, okay, okay. I get the point!" Blaze said. "Chill, bird."

The team scanned the results from individual schools and skimmed hundreds of open-ended responses. Eventually, they discussed which school to visit. Scarlet made a suggestion. "Your school—or should I say your former school—is interesting Blaze. Maybe we should visit?"

"Nah. I've seen enough of that place."

Chopper had a different idea. "What about this one? Crush

Sweetie High School? That's the high school we would have attended."

Scarlet smirked. "Unless you're fired and sent back to it. But then again, maybe you'll get a permanent red card."

Blaze and Chopper did not laugh.

"Do I need to be concerned for my safety?" Kai said. "I mean, I'm good observing another round of dysfunctional Puddin' Heads, but I need to know these knuckleheads won't literally crush me."

"Bah! What harm could possibly happen to a Sweetie who attacked a Region 2 school? I'm sure you'll be fine. Scarlet will protect you. She can't afford to lose the one Sweetie football player she's got!" Blaze grinned and peered out the window as the train slowed. "Whoa! Look at this turnout! We've got our work cut out for us."

Scarlet budged her way to the front and several hundred Puddin' Heads cheered as we emerged from the train. It was a very efficient day of rigorous tryouts, and the Puddin' Head team grew. Seven scored a goal on Kai. Two defenders stopped Blaze. But no one managed to stop Scarlet from scoring. And of the eighty goalie hopefuls, none stopped Blaze or Scarlet.

Kai asked Blaze, "You worried about finding a goalie?"

"If we were playing MegaCorp, maybe. But we're playing Sweeties. We could play without a goalie and still win by fifty."

CRUSH SWEETIE HIGH SCHOOL
PH2, Day 2

Kai missed twenty Frame calls and allegedly overslept. Nevertheless, he survived Chopper's lecture on the train about the importance of keeping promises and showing up on time. We arrived at Crush Sweetie High School in the early afternoon. Scarlet raced ahead and looked bored by the time the rest of us caught up. From what I'd seen in videos, the high school building looked remarkably similar to Puddin' Head Middle School, except for three adjacent buildings—one of which seemed newly constructed. Flashing neon lights lined its edges and the entrance.

"What's *that* place?" Kai asked.

"That's a giant magnet that attracts Sweeties to the skull crusher room. Especially Sweeties who oversleep." Blaze laughed maniacally, strummed a warning tune on her guitar, then stopped. "Nah, I have no idea. But we definitely need to check it out."

School Boss Walka Walka charged out of the main building like a bull who'd spotted a matador. A younger high school boss jogged behind.

"Walka?" Blaze jumped backwards, afraid the school boss would run her over.

"That's Walka Walka! School Boss Walka Walka! You *did* show up." He bent over, catching his breath. "You have some nerve showing up in this region! Do you have any idea how many problems you've caused? Firing school bosses? What a little fart tart."

"Good to see you, too. What are you doing here?"

"Mentoring."

Blaze puffed out her cheeks and crossed her eyes at Chopper. "Makes total sense."

The young boss said, "Walka Walka, I got this." He stared down at Blaze. "She doesn't look so tough to me. What's with the guitar? And remind me, why should I care about this little tour of yours?"

Blaze ignored the part about the guitar. "Because we're sharing the best ideas we see with the education minister, who along with the prime—, I mean, the supreme prime minister, approved this monumental tour. The education minister might use that information to determine which school bosses get promoted to district or even regional bosses. Or who wins the Top Boss Award."

Chopper tipped his head to Blaze as if saying *nicely done* and *please continue.*

"When we win the epic Noble Deed Football Match, I'll have some serious resources to distribute to deserving schools."

Chopper nodded.

Kai said, "*If* you win."

School Boss Walka Walka scoffed. However, the Crush Sweetie school boss bought it. He led our tour group to the main building. "All right, let me show you what you're missing." We visited several classes including History of Puddin' Heads Defeating the Sweeties, History of Bootstraps and Award Winners, Greatest Spoon Heroes of All Time, How to Be the Best at Everything, Sweeties or Zombies? (Levels I, II, and III), and Innovations in Crushing Zombie Hands.

"Notice how almost none of the examples are Bigs?" Blaze asked Chopper.

"Yep."

"Speaking of which, where *are* all the Bigs? I've hardly seen any."

Chopper shrugged. "Good question."

The school bosses had an important meeting to attend, so they suggested we check out the Game Building—the one with neon lights. "You know the best protection against Sweeties—learn to be a winner. We train our students to compete at the highest levels; losing is not an option."

The Game Building had three large rooms that ran card games, video games, and spoon games. In the card room, students sat around tables playing card games like Puddin' Jack, Puddin' Run, Puddin' War, and Puddin' Slap.

"Hey, how about that? A school that's fun?" Blaze said.

The standard deck of puddin' cards should not have come as a surprise to me, but I did chuckle. It had 26 Puddin' Heads, 26 zombies, and one MegaCorp executive. Each card had a caricature of a Puddin' Head, zombie, or executive holding out a hand that was proportional in size to their ranking. The MC executive card displayed a person in a suit sticking out a barely visible hand tattooed with the number one. Cards with hand sizes 1-13 were considered Smalls, and 14-26 considered Bigs. The hand of Puddin' Head 26 would take up nearly the entire card. The same would be true of zombie 26.

The MegaCorp card rules were equally ridiculous. The first rule of all the games was that the MC executive card always beat Puddin' Head and zombie cards. The second rule was that Puddin' Head cards always beat zombie cards. The third rule was that smaller numbers beat larger ones. Thus, Puddin' Head 12 would beat Puddin' Head 24, which would beat zombie 1. The worst card in the deck was zombie 26.

We watched the last round of Puddin' Slap, which was the most physically interactive and also a major school revenue stream. The short version of this complicated game is that players bet money, the school got to keep some, and Smalls got the "choice" to look at their cards before the Bigs, which they always did. The player with the best card won money. But players with losing cards could also win money by being the first player to slap the hands of fellow losers. Thus, Puddin' Slap also provided crucial training for quickly slapping Sweeties, in the event of an attack.

The table had four players: a legendary kid named Slappy, another Small, and two Bigs. The dealer counted down and the players flipped their card over. They kept their left hand on the table, protected with a padded glove. A Small had the best card—a Puddin' Head 5. Slappy—with a zombie 25—drew a large spoon and slapped the hands of the two (losing) Bigs like a ninja before they could even realize what they had—a zombie 15 and Puddin' Head 20.

"This is ridiculous. How is that fair?" Blaze balled up her fists. Once again, I found myself agreeing with Blaze.

At the end of five rounds, Slappy had earned the most money, followed by the other Small. The Bigs groused about the stupid rules. One whipped his spoon across the room. It whirled and hit another dealer on his puddin' head. "Yellow card!" he squawked at the Big.

Blaze pulled Chopper aside. "Why do we keep dividing ourselves instead of working together? I thought this school was about crushing Sweeties, not crushing Puddin' Head Bigs! Where's that school boss?"

"Easy. Eyes on the prize. Eyes on the prize."

They watched Slappy win several more card games and followed him to the room with spoon games. He proceeded to clean house at Spoons, Spoon Block, and Whack a Zombie Head. In Whack a Zombie Head, students used spoons to spank plastic zombie heads that popped out of holes like deranged rabbits. The team enjoyed several games, except for Kai, who refused to play. Scarlet won three games, and Chopper and Blaze each won two.

That was child's play in contrast to Whack a Zombie Hand, which involved battle simulation. Five competitors (wielding spoons, of course) fought five Puddin' Heads who "volunteered" to be the zombies. Occasionally, a Small would choose to play a zombie, but invariably—like all the other games—Bigs were, as they called it, "voluntold."

The "zombies" pulled on thick, padded gloves with electronic sensors placed over compression gloves to prevent accidental swelling. Unlike zombie movies you may have seen, Puddin' Heads of Region 2 believed that head shots were ineffective against zombies. This would only anger and motivate them. Or worse, damage a spoon.

No, the most effective way to neutralize a zombie was with a good whack to the hand. Thus, in the game of Whack a Zombie Hand, the competitors—who wore large spoon hats to keep zombies from eating their brains—tried to strike the hands of the "zombies" with spoons drawn from their holsters. Competitors had five minutes to earn points for the number and strength of hand strikes, all of which were measured by the zombie glove sensors. The zombies, on the other hand, tried to steal or dislodge their opponents' spoons or pull their competitors to the ground by their spoon hat handles.

"I thought the test taking Puddin' Heads were stupid, but this takes the cake," Kai concluded.

"He's right! Except for the cake part," Blaze whispered to Chopper. "But what's bad for Pompavich is good for us."

You may be wondering which way the spoon hat handle faced. In preparation for an actual zombie attack, teachers encouraged competitors to practice with the spoon hat handle facing both forward and backward. The forward position technique (also known as "sword fish") used the spoon handle like a sword—or like a lance in jousting—to knock zombies down, allowing the wielder to club zombie hands with a hand spoon. A drawback to this technique was frequent whiplash. Therefore, many preferred the handle jutting out the back, which allowed a Puddin' Head to ram a zombie more easily with the (supposedly more stable) tip of the enormous spoon. A sideways spoon hat handle proved unsuccessful for reasons I'm sure you can imagine.

Although Blaze found all this absurdity to be excellent evidence that Puddin' Head schools needed to change, she hated that Bigs were nearly always stuck playing the zombies. She wanted to set an example as a fierce Big competitor, but the teacher wouldn't allow her to participate. "You're not a student here. Not going to happen." So, we watched Slappy set a new record of 1,640 points with ninety-eight hand slaps (five points each), forty-five power hand slaps (ten points each), and thirty-five hand crusher slaps (twenty points each)—which was also a new record. A single hand crusher slap was believed to completely neutralize a zombie.

"Crush that Sweetie!" a student called.

"No, it's 'crush that zombie' now," the teacher corrected.

Alas, one of these hand crusher slaps broke a Big's hand, despite the protection. He moaned as he pulled off the padded gloves, watching his twisted hand swelling like a balloon. "I miss School Leader Foster!" he cried.

Blaze was so mad she completely missed this important clue. As the nurse escorted the wailing student away, Blaze yelled at the teacher for allowing such a stupid, divisive game that "literally injured a fellow Puddin' Head."

The teacher replied, "I do what I'm told to do."

Another teacher defensively told Blaze, "Appreciate that you're in the presence of greatness. Slappy is destined for the Region 2 Hall of Fame and maybe the MegaCorp Academy." Then, an argument broke out as to whether this was possible given Slappy's repeated failure to lift himself up by his bootstraps.

"Can we go now?" Blaze asked. "I hope you're noticing Kai, that all of this—the Bigs, the Smalls, the zombies, the hand slapping—is misguided Puddin' Head preparation for Sweetie attacks."

"Ha! First, uh . . . no, we're not leaving because I am very much enjoying learning about your Puddin' Head ways. I believe we still have other buildings to see. And second, this insanity or stupidity or whatever you want to call it has nothing to do with Sweeties. In fact, what I just saw is exactly why Sweeties need to win the Noble Deed Match. We need funds to defend against these numbskull lunatics."

"We're defending against you!" Blaze cried.

Chopper intervened. "I hate to break up the love fest once again, but the next train boards in an hour. So, are we going to tour these last two buildings or what?"

"Let's go," Kai said.

Blaze said, "Sure," and slowly strummed her guitar.

BOOTS, BOOTSTRAPS, AND BEYOND
PH2, Day 2, Continued

Blaze steered them to the Boots, Bootstraps, and Beyond building. In one area, a few teachers supervised students, nearly all of whom were Bigs. They sawed, carved, nailed, and built bootstraps platforms of all sizes and elevations. In another area, students worked in various stations with machines that designed boots; stretched, cut, stitched, and glued rawhide or suede pieces for boots with bootstraps; punched eyelets for bootlaces; molded the boot shaped piece of leather to a plastic or wood foot; and trimmed and assembled the boot with a supporting layer, a midsole, and the outsole. Occasionally, they included a steel shank. The final stations included trimming the outsole, buffing the boots, applying a finishing cream, lacing the boots, and checking for quality.

Each station had a large red counter that looked like the light over a grocery checkout lane. Teachers used these to track the number of items each student completed. Every few minutes, a teacher cajoled a student to meet their daily quota, which was also a part of the teacher's evaluation.

Suddenly, a Big at the sewing station screamed. The red counter blinked 42. In his haste, he had accidentally sewn his hand to half of a boot. He ran screaming down the aisle, clutching his boot-sewn hand. A teacher yelled, "Nurse!" and then, "Yellow card for unsafe behavior!"

"What the puddin' balls?" Blaze cried. She strummed her guitar.

For a moment, the factory fell quiet. Then, a teacher yelled, "Back to work!" They all did as they were told. Blaze strummed louder and asked a Big if that was usual.

She said, "It happens." Blaze asked if she liked working here.

"I used to. But they don't give us choices like before. I just lace boot after boot, every afternoon. It gets boring, and I lose my focus, you know? It was so much better when School Leader Foster was here."

"School *leader*?" Blaze asked.

"Yeah, he hated that term, 'boss.'"

Scarlet was relieved. "Finally, a place following the rules—only *afternoon* child labor."

Blaze shot her a dirty look and spun back to the student. She strummed her guitar faster. "What do you mean, 'choices like before'? Everyone had choices? Even Bigs?"

"Everyone had choices. We took turns. Including Bigs."

"Wow, interesting!" Blaze strummed slower, quieter. "What happened to School Leader Foster?"

"He was fired. Never heard why, but we didn't have these kinds of accidents back then. Kids seemed a lot happier. We went weeks without a yellow or red card. You know, I think he was fired shortly after my parents got a letter saying all students would have more voice and choice in their education." The student paused. "Yeah, maybe that was it. I don't know, no one told us. Suddenly, this new school boss shows up one day." The student sniffled. "That seems like a long time ago. I miss those days."

"Weird!" Blaze looked around. "It seems like it's mostly Bigs working in here. Why is that?"

"Because now we get the last 'choice,'" the student said with air quotes.

"Which isn't fair."

She gave Blaze the "duh" look. "Uh, yeah."

"Do Bigs and Smalls get along?"

"Not exactly. We rarely see each other. Not exactly a puddin' haven for Bigs, you know?"

Blaze had heard enough. "Well, I know what can change all of this." She strummed her guitar slowly. Kai and Scarlet slapped their heads. Chopper gave Blaze a sideways look that said, *are-you-serious-right-now?*

Blaze winked at him, jumped onto a table, and continued to strum.

"No—Blaze, this isn't the time! Wait for the Top Boss Awards Banquet!" Chopper begged.

"I don't have time to wait, and neither do they. Sometimes, you have to do things yourself." Blaze strummed harder.

Students stopped working and the whirl of machines slowed to silence.

School's not fair when
Bigs got no real choices,
And Smalls got the only voices.

School's not fun when
You stitch your hand,
A friend breaks your hand,

Or the real leader gets canned.

But this school boss blames the Bigs?
An idea we should delete.
No, the Bigs should join the Smalls.
Surely it would be a treat,
To give Sweeties the ultimate defeat.

Who do we blame?
The Sweeties!
Who will we defeat?
The Sweeties!
Who will we beat,
In a Noble Deed meet?
The Sweeties!

Perhaps you can guess what happened next. Kai ran out of the room. Chopper shrugged, shifted and then supported his best friend. Scarlet was terrified, then thrilled, and posted video clips to Mega Gossip. At first, several hundred factory workers stood in shock. Still. Silent. Staring. Then, a few students hummed or danced. Then a few groups. And the moment that Blaze started the third round, the factory workers erupted into a boisterous chorus.

Blaze waved and led the booming crowd outside and toward the Textiles and More building. The teachers and students inside heard the commotion and left their red shirt stations, red flag stations, football stitching stations, and compression glove stations to join the fun. They merged into a swelling river of Puddin' Heads that meandered through the textile factory and back toward the main building, which they circled several times. By this time, students from the Game Building and main building—indeed, the entire student body, Bigs and Smalls alike—flowed into and sang with the giant circling river of Puddin' Heads. With the exception of Kai— who hid in a corner and regretted not staying in bed—no one could resist raising their spoons or head butting each time they sang, "*The Sweeties!*"

School Boss Walka Walka ran out of the main building with the new school boss. "Not again!" he yelled at the singing jubilee. But the triumphant crowd scooped them up and tossed them like beach balls at the mercy of rowdy football fans on game day.

Blaze, Chopper, and I discussed Crush Sweetie High School on the bike ride home. Blaze and Chopper argued that surely what they had seen was grounds for ending large hand discrimination and firing Pompavich. In addition, they agreed the new school boss should be fired as soon as Blaze became the education minister. Yet, Blaze was pleased with her musical efforts to unite the Puddin' Head Bigs and Smalls against the Sweeties. My absurdity neurosis constantly flared up and down; it certainly did not improve. I maintained hope that this tour would provide relief—after all, there was still so much more to see!

The next day, we returned to Sweetie Island and stopped at Loveton in Region 2 for football tryouts. As usual, Chopper first reviewed the survey data. The team noticed a similar quantitative pattern to Puddin' Head Island Region 2. After skimming through the open-ended survey responses, Blaze drew a not-so-objective conclusion. "Basically, Sweetie Region 2 schools have a bunch of puddin'-hating, zombie-loving, clumsy, singing flower children, who hold hands and trip over each other."

"I don't see how the data supports that," Chopper said, "but it's an interesting theory."

Sweetie Island, Region 2
Student Survey Results

	All Students Agreeing	Bigs Agreeing	Smalls Agreeing
School is affordable	59%	20%	94%
School is fair	51%	5%	94%
School is fun, useful, and interesting	67%	35%	94%

Response Rate = 84%

"Yeah, you numbskull," Kai said to Blaze. "And just wait for the tryouts."

Blaze laughed. "Anyone going to show up this time?"

"Region 2 will be different. These are my people," Kai said confidently.

To the relief of Scarlet (who of course, saw first), the surprise of Blaze and Chopper, and the validation of Kai, twenty Sweeties did actually show up for tryouts. "Looks like we have a whole team here already, and we still have three regions to go!" Kai said.

"Yeah, but can they play?" Chopper said skeptically.

As it turned out, many did have football skills. They just had no experience playing competitively. Kai pulled them aside, explained the rules, and justified competition. "It's okay because we're cooperating as a team to beat these numbskulls. If we win, our whole island will have a lot more money for our schools. If we lose, all that money goes to the island on the right." The Sweeties looked east and shuddered.

At first, the determined Region 2 Sweeties appeared to give Kai a football team miracle. They applied strong football passing and dribbling abilities to skillfully shooting goals. But the scrimmage was another matter entirely. Some refused to score on the other team. Some started to play *with* the opposing team and scored a goal for them. Some could not bring themselves to steal the ball from another player. "I just don't understand. Why would anyone do something *so mean*?" a Sweetie asked.

Chopper and Blaze pointed, roaring with laughter.

Kai snatched the bag of Puddin' Head scrimmage vests.

"Hey, that's the wrong bag, sweet puff!" Blaze chuckled, slapping Chopper on the back. "They've lost their zombie minds."

Kai gathered the Sweeties into a huddle. "Do you see those Puddin' Heads laughing at us? Put these vests on." He tossed light- and dark-red vests to the two teams.

"What? They're red."

"I know. Now, imagine you're playing against Puddin' Heads, because that's what we'll be doing in the Noble Deed Match! Do you understand what will happen if we lose? Do you know that their numbskull schools teach them that we're literally zombies? Do you think they won't steal the ball from us?"

"No!" the Sweeties cried.

"Do you want to lose to these numbskulls, watching them laugh at you, your families, and this whole island?"

"*No!*" the Sweeties cried louder.

"Do you want to eat puddin' for school lunches?"

"*Noooo!!!*" the Sweeties pumped their fists and beat their chests.

"Then get out there and play like your sweet hearts depend on it!"

The Sweeties roared for the first time in their lives and tore to the pitch. Suddenly, they transformed into fierce competitors: attacking, stealing, scoring, and celebrating goals as determined teams, as if all of Sweetie Island cheered them on.

"Whoa. Something changed," Chopper said.

"Yeah." Blaze scratched the flame on her head.

"Yeah!!" Scarlet danced wildly. "Noble Deed Match!" Scarlet did a crazy dance then abruptly shifted to a slow dance, turning her hands in tiny circles, singing, "Noble Deed Match," in a soft whisper. Then, she cupped her hands and bellowed, "Noble Deed *Maaaaattttccchhhh!*" before whirling and twirling. She repeated, "Noble Deed Match!" over and over, in different paces, pitches, sounds, and volumes, with a matching dance each time.

"Okay, already!" Blaze huffed.

Kai smirked and raised his eyebrows. "You scared now?"

Blaze rolled her eyes. "Can we just get to the last part of the tryouts?"

Although the Sweeties could not stop Blaze or Scarlet, they made respectful attempts without embarrassing themselves. Except for one student who got tangled and fell face first after Blaze juked him left, right, left, and then scored with her eyes closed. Five Sweeties scored on Kai, which Blaze contested. "You let them score on purpose!"

"Whatever. I get to choose who's on my team. And just as I predicted, we have enough for a solid team right now," Kai said. "And we'll gain more. I've heard the far left parts of the island really hate Puddin' Heads, and I can't wait to add them to my team."

"We could use a little competition, you know. Keep things interesting and avoid a blowout. But one thing at a time," Chopper said. "Tomorrow, we visit Sweet Cake Middle School."

Scarlet bolted out of the train and waited for Chopper's direction. He pointed to a pathway through the woods. After walking for several minutes, Blaze said, "This feels familiar." Suddenly, she stopped. "What the—"

Two students were securing a person sized spoon—much too big for a spoon hat—to a tree. When they saw us, they scurried away.

"Why would Sweeties have a giant spoon? They must've stolen it from a museum!" Blaze jogged over to it.

"Uh, I wouldn't— You know, never mind." Kai grinned and waited.

Blaze tripped over a small wire. Suddenly, a large tree branch shot into the air pulling up a net with Blaze trapped inside. She hung upside down and yelled. "What's happening?! Get me down!" Even Chopper couldn't help laughing. "Chopper—get me *down*!!"

"And *that*, is what we call a spoon trap," Kai laughed. "You know, I never believed any Puddin' Head was stupid enough to fall for it. Guess you proved me wrong."

The building and grounds of Sweet Cake Middle School were nearly identical to Sugar Falls Middle School, including the value pillars, flower beds, outdoor gathering areas, and fields of crops. After chatting with the idle students who couldn't pay their large hand fees or who were waiting for a school transfer, the team headed inside. Blaze wanted to talk to School Boss Patty Cake, but there was a line of students out of the office door. We left a note and started our tour.

In contrast to the competitive Puddin' Head schools, the team observed cooperative group learning across Sweet Cake Middle School. Sometimes, students learned as a whole class; other times, they learned in small groups. Typically, students were grouped by hand size. In some classrooms, students choral read books or articles together: *What are Puddin' Heads and Why are They So Evil?*; *The Flower Child Who Caught a Little Puddin' Head; Puddin' Head Attack: Advanced Defense Moves; Shrink Your Hands and Defeat the Puddin' Heads; Why We Wear Blue Every Day*, and so on.

"It's true! They are preparing to attack us!" Blaze said to Chopper. "Once we win the Noble Deed Match, we'll shut down these schools!"

However, there were clandestine exceptions to cooperative work. For example, one student attempted to write her own story. Oblivious to the work of her small group, she frantically jotted words into a secret section of her notebook. Perhaps it was her tongue poking out of the side of her mouth that gave her away. Perhaps it was the teacher who scanned the Bigs' group work more carefully. Regardless, the teacher was no fool. She abruptly broke the kind chitter of the classroom. "Yellow card!" she yelled, dramatically pointing at the *Community* value hanging on the wall. "No independent work allowed!" The student tore her story out of her notebook, crumpled it into a ball, threw it in the trash can, and stomped down to the school boss's office.

"What's up with that?" Blaze said.

"I told you, competition is evil," Kai said.

Blaze shook her head. "Silly Sweetie, that's not competition. That's a bunch of Puddin' Head haters trying to squash a kid's freedom! No way are we sending money to any of these schools!"

"Whatever." Kai rolled his eyes. "You're still upset about the spoon trap."

In other classrooms, students used local ingredients to cooperatively bake chocolate cakes and cupcakes. They smothered them with blue chocolate icing mixed with hand-increasing booster or Puddin' Head repellent booster in preparation for a Puddin' Head attack, which now seemed inevitable after the Battle of Sugar Falls. In some classrooms, students sang songs or wrote stories together about Sweeties defeating Puddin' Heads. In others, students solved math problems together. For example, *If one hand-increasing batch of cupcakes will scare away 45 Puddin' Heads, how many batches are necessary to terrify 500 Puddin' Heads?* In another class, students discussed and practiced the best ways to capture, repel, or defend against Puddin' Heads. They fiercely debated whether larger or smaller spoons made better spoon traps. Kai was pleased to offer sound advice. "Definitely go big," he suggested before Blaze attempted to give him a noogie.

A highlight of the day was a Code Red Puddin' Head classroom simulation where Sweetie Bigs role-played evil red Puddin' Heads.

One Small also volunteered for the part. The Sweeties thwarted the attackers with sweet cake and pat-a-cake chants. They smashed blue chocolate cakes and cupcakes into their foes' mouths, noses, and faces (of course, this simulation did not include the hand-increasing booster that would be used during a real Code Red Puddin' Head). But the icing on the cake was excessively kind interactions amongst Sweeties, which— according to the *MC Code Red Puddin' Head Emergency Procedures*—the Puddin' Heads would find even more revolting. *This blue icing on his face is splendid, and makes me hungry. Would you pretty please pass me a delicious cookie? Oh certainly, thank you for asking so kindly. No, thank you for choosing a lovely one with blue frosting and passing it to me so thoughtfully. Oh, you are so very welcome. Oh, you are so very kind.* And so on. The Puddin' Head actors nailed their performances and ran away. Yes, students received excessively kind compliments from the teacher, who received excessively kind compliments from School Boss Patty Cake.

Throughout the day, Scarlet responded by saying, "So interesting!" Blaze and Chopper made unkind barfing gestures— especially regarding the Code Red Puddin' Head drill, which they thankfully had not encountered at Sugar Falls. Kai made unkind hand gestures to Blaze and Chopper. I just steered clear of the cookies and cake and tried to keep my eyes open.

A bell chimed over the PA system. The teacher asked the Smalls for their choice, and they all chose inside lunch. They skipped toward the cafeteria, excited for the chocolate cake and cookie buffet. "Oh, looks like we have three spots left for inside lunch— any takers?"

One Big raised her hand. Another muttered, "That would be sweet, but I have large hand fees to pay." Thus, this student, along with nearly all the remaining Big students, grabbed a blue boxed lunch and shuffled outside.

Kai said, "Whoa, look at the time! We should head home."

Chopper said, "What? We have plenty of time." He peered outside. "What's happening out there?"

Kai said, "Nothing worth—" and then changed his mind. "Actually, you *should* see this. The most important work on the island: farming. Sweetie Island Region 2 produces more cocoa and sugar than all the regions of Puddin' Head Island combined."

"That's not true," Blaze said.

"Where do you think your puddin' ingredients come from?"

"Puddin' Head Island, obviously!"

"You'll see."

Indeed, Blaze was about to have a mini-realization, sort of. We followed a large group of Bigs to fields of cocoa plants growing in the shade of large trees. The gathering team carefully cut down cocoa pods, gathered them into baskets, and transported carts of baskets to the processing station. The preparation team removed the cocoa beans from the pods, packed them in fermenting boxes, and covered them with mats. The sunshine team dumped already fermented beans into a large, shallow bin and spread them out to dry in the sun. And the sacking team packed dried beans into burlap sacks, labeled the sacks with the destination city, and carted them to the shipping shed.

"Bigs doing the work, Smalls eating cake. I knew it! Sweeties clearly started the large hand rules!" Blaze shook her head.

Kai shook his own head angrily. "You don't get it!"

Blaze rolled her eyes and tilted her head back to lean into Chopper, "More evidence to fire Pompavich."

Another team of Bigs focused on sugar cane. The gathering team used machetes to cut down tall sugar cane grasses. The preparation team stripped the leaves and removed dirt, insects, and mildew from the shoots. The packing team packed the shoots into wooden boxes, labeled the boxes with the destination city, and carted them to the shipping shed.

We visited the shipping shed, which had gigantic bins containing stacks of cocoa sacks and sugar cane boxes. "Wait a minute. Most of this stuff is going to Booster City. That's on Puddin' Head Island!" Blaze was astonished.

"Exactly," Kai said.

"I don't understand."

"You mean, you're just now realizing that you're a numbskull?"

"No, Sweetie tart. I don't understand why Sweeties would ship all this to Puddin' Heads. We make our own puddin' ingredients."

"Exactly! You don't understand anything." Kai paced, then got in Blaze's face. "So let me explain. You don't have enough cocoa and sugar for your enormous puddin'-for-brain heads. So, we Sweeties grow these crops for *your numbskull puddin' and boosters.*

Because we have *no choice*! Which is why we need to win the Noble Deed Match!"

"You don't use cocoa and sugar for cake and cookies?"

"Well, yes, but—"

Blaze sauntered around him. "One: You're the fart tart who doesn't understand. Two: Sweeties are wasting this cocoa and sugar on Code Red practice drills—which, by the way, are *ridiculous*. Three: Sweeties don't deserve Noble Deed money, because you're the ones ruining the whole system!"

"We're doing this because of the Puddin' Heads!"

"It's your problem! And it doesn't matter, because you have as much chance of beating us in football as a lily does against a fire.

"Don't talk about my sister!" Kai dove at Blaze, who dodged the tackle.

"I'm speaking metaphorically!"

Kai chased Blaze until he was exhausted, then rode home, alone.

On the train, Blaze consulted with Chopper. "To summarize, based on Sweetie Island Region 2 survey results and what we saw in Sweet Cake classrooms, these are not good schools, right? They're not affordable or fair to Bigs, right? Was any of that 'learning' really useful? And what we saw outside . . . Okay, yes, maybe we need sugar and cocoa for puddin'. Maybe this *is* important work, but Bigs do all the work to pay for their large hand fees, which just isn't fair! Surely all of this is evidence that Pompavich needs to go, right?"

"I certainly hope so," Chopper said. "And we definitely don't want a Sweetie in charge of Puddin' Head schools."

"Yeah, Sweeties are ruining everything. Do we really need to do this whole tour? Couldn't we just skip to the Noble Deed—"

"We are finishing the tour as planned!"

PH3 TRYOUTS
PH3, Day 1

We took a very long train ride to Cape Freedom in Puddin' Head Island Region 3 for football tryouts.

"Are you sure we can't take a helicopter?" Chopper asked.

Scarlet crossed her arms. "Yes! Stop asking."

"Okay," Chopper smiled as if eager to try a new plan.

Though Blaze complained about having to review even more data, Chopper insisted. The short version is that the survey data continued the trend, with Smalls viewing their schools more favorably than the Bigs.

Puddin' Head Island, Region 3
Student Survey Results

	All Students Agreeing	Bigs Agreeing	Smalls Agreeing
School is affordable	50%	10%	80%
School is fair	56%	20%	85%
School is fun, useful, and interesting	58%	30%	80%

Response Rate = 92%

One set of open-ended responses, on the other hand, painted a new picture. "What's up with all this stuff about dynamite?" Blaze wondered.

"I don't know," Chopper said. "This will be an interesting school visit."

"Great . . ." Kai drawled. "Puddin' Heads and dynamite. What could possibly go wrong?"

Nearly a hundred Puddin' Head students in tattered red shirts and shorts arrived early to football tryouts. They looked up from their small groups to cheer as the doors opened. Scarlet squeezed herself past Blaze and through the crowd. The rest of us exited. The crowd continued cheering for a few moments, then they lost interest and bolted back to their little clusters.

"Oh yeah, look at all these Puddin' Heads!" Blaze gave Chopper a high five.

Kai did not waste time assessing the crowd. "What are these numbskulls doing?"

"Correction: These Puddin' Heads are . . . well, I have no idea. But apparently, they're very thirsty." Chopper shrugged and followed Blaze to the nearest group.

Students stood around a set of containers with various types of chips and booster. Each container featured anywhere from one to five dynamite illustrations. I quickly discerned that this spicy scale ranged from mild (one dynamite stick) to absurdly hot (like five pieces of dynamite exploding in your mouth). A large jug of water sat next to each student. Like every other group, a nurse carried a medical bag and held a stopwatch.

"Wheels, you're up." The group roared, "Wheels! Wheels! Wheels!"

Wheels sped over to Blaze and grabbed her shoulders. She stared into Blaze's eyes as if saying, *Wish me luck fighting an army of zombies!* "Spicy puddin' chips make me *faster!*" Then, the student dashed back to the center of the circle as quickly as she appeared.

"You know that kid?" Chopper asked.

Blaze turned to Chopper, eyes wide. "No."

Wheels pinched a stack of level four (L4) dynamite puddin' chips. She licked the stack, buried them into an L4 dynamite booster bowl, and held up the booster covered chips to her admiring onlookers.

"Ohhhh!" the group howled. "Wheels! Wheels! Wheels!"

"You're a Big. You sure about this?" The nurse held up her timer.

"I don't understand what is happening," Blaze said to Chopper.

Wheels nodded and pointed at the previous contestant, a Small. "I'm sure I can handle as much as this zombie lover!" The crowd jeered and head butted in excitement. Wheels stuffed the dynamite chips into her mouth, chewed, and swallowed.

Within seconds, she closed her eyes in pain, tightened her fists, and screamed, "Gaaaahhhhh!" Tears streamed down her face as she continued to yell. She stamped her feet and stared at her water jug.

"Steady!" the nurse cried.

Wheels danced around her water jug like a person on fire. Her Puddin' Head peers cheered as the nurse marked the time. *Fifteen seconds. Thirty seconds.*

Wheels reached for the jug of water. The crowd screamed, "Nooo!"

The nurse gave a harsh reminder. "As a Big, you must reach a full minute, or the immunity won't work! The longer you go, the stronger the immunity!"

"Immunity to what?" Blaze asked.

"Zombies!" the Puddin' Heads responded.

Blaze and Chopper laughed. Kai slapped his head.

Wheels yelled, burst through the crowd, sprinted to the train and back, and then guzzled half a jug of water. The nurse clicked the timer. "Ninety seconds!" Puddin' Heads body slammed, head butted, and shouted with delight.

"I don't know about this immunity thing, but did you see that speed?" Blaze said to Chopper. "And how can I pass up a chance to prove Bigs are just as good as Smalls?" She stepped into the inner circle. "Mind if I try?"

Blaze snatched two L5 chips and dipped them in L5 booster. The group jumped up and down, roaring. The other groups ran over to watch. Blaze ate the chips and smiled. The crowd went wild. Blaze blinked slowly, then rapidly. Tears grew into a steady stream that ran down her cheeks. Her face twitched, then her neck, then her whole body. She looked at a water jug.

"Steady!" the nurse cried, watching the time.

"She's a Big! She'll never be able to handle it!" a Small cried.

Blaze yelled, "Ahhhhhhh!" Then she licked her lips.

The crowd gasped. "Oh, no!" said one terrified Puddin' Head.

Blaze screamed. *"Fiiiirrrre! Lips on fiiiirrrre!"*

Suddenly Blaze rocketed into the air, landed in a squat, and threw out her hands like she was about to wrestle a zombie. She yelled, *"Arrgghhh!"* and bounded through the crowd, accelerating into a steady sprint around three fields. Some tried to follow but quickly fell behind. The smarter Puddin' Heads ran to the final turn, although forming a finish line proved difficult. They pushed and shoved and head butted each other until they created an oddly shaped, jumbled pathway.

The nurse, now on Chopper's megaphone, blurted times. "Two minutes and fifteen seconds!" Then, "Three minutes!" Puddin' Head pandemonium erupted as Blaze tore through the collapsing maze of cheering students and crossed an arbitrary finish line. The crowd surrounded Blaze and hoisted her up, cheering her name.

"*Waatttteerrrr*! *Please, someone get me some—*" Chopper tossed her a water jug and gave the thumbs up. "Three minutes and fifty-eight seconds! A new record!" the nurse shouted. As the cheering continued, Chopper quietly ate an L3 chip with L2 booster, swore, looked to see if anyone was watching, and chugged his water. Scarlet refused to eat disgusting food. Scoffing about zombie immunity, Kai tried an L1 chip and L1 booster, grasped his throat, threw up immediately, chugged a whole water jug, and then threw up again.

The large crowd hoisted up Blaze and chanted, "Blaze! Blaze! Blaze!"

Blaze yelled, "Bigs can do anything! Bigs and Smalls! We must play together to defeat the Sweeties in the Noble Deed Match!" The crowd—along with Scarlet this time—roared in excitement.

After several more rounds of dynamite chip immunity boosts, football tryouts finally began. The Puddin' Head team gained several football players. Wheels stood out for dashing past Kai for two goals, nearly stopping Scarlet, and stopping Blaze once. But in fairness to Blaze, that may have been due to a sudden, unexpected gastrointestinal issue.

"After you," Chopper said to Scarlet.

"Finally, some respect for the natural leader!" she said, gracefully exiting the train.

Two minutes later, we zoomed past Scarlet on Chopper's Solar Bikes 2.0. Yes, they had major power upgrades.

"Hey!" Scarlet cried. "I'm the leader!"

"Not anymore!" Blaze laughed and waved at Scarlet, whose audible complaining faded as she quickly fell behind. Blaze wove around our bike pack, giving everyone high fives, including certain MC staff members who might have provided some power supplies.

As we approached Freedom High School, we thought it was under attack. Loud explosions ripped through the air. The red, dry grasses of the surrounding area suddenly disappeared, replaced with overlapping circles of burnt grass and dirt as if the place had been bombed. Wafting smoke obscured our view of Puddin' Head Horn's sunny coast.

We waited for Scarlet, who arrived with a real frown face.

"Hey stranger," Blaze said.

"Shut up!"

"Forget your slow bike," Kai said. "Are we sure this is a good idea?"

Scarlet chomped on her gum. "Yeah, something's weird here." She turned to Chopper. "Are we in the right place?"

"Are we in the right place?" Chopper repeated, annoyed. "Yes! That's Freedom High School!" He gestured to a school that had certainly seen better days. The explosions suddenly stopped, and in their place, chainsaws buzzed in the background. "But I'm not sure what *that* is." He pointed to a distant gathering of students and teachers.

We walked to a hilly, looping dirt bike course several kilometers long. Newly cut log piles were randomly scattered along its perimeter. A large group of students raced by on buzzing motor bikes—skyrocketing over hills, sometimes crashing into each other, and constantly adjusting their spoon helmets. In the distance, an excavator dug new slopes and moved boulders.

Two crashed students squabbled. They walked their disabled bikes toward us, and we quickly introduced ourselves. Blaze asked, "What's that digger doing?"

"Making the course wider and deeper. You know, more challenging. And, of course, building the Wall."

"The Wall?"

"Yeah, you know, the prime minister's wall."

Scarlet chimed in. "Supreme prime minister."

"Huh?"

Blaze waved Scarlet off. "Never mind. What's the Wall for? It's blocking the view."

"You seriously don't know? To keep out sea monsters, of course! And to prevent zombie attacks!"

"Sea monsters?" Blaze asked.

"Yeah. What do you think lives in the bay?" The student pointed dramatically at Puddin' Head Horn Bay.

"Uh, fish?" Kai said, deadpan.

"And sea monsters!"

Kai smirked. "You've seen these sea monsters?"

"Sure. Well, someone saw them."

"On the shore?"

"No, you sweet tart. In the water. They haven't made it to land because we chopped down the trees and made the Wall. And we just added the prime minister statues on top—"

"Supreme prime minister!" Scarlet said.

"Soup or cream minister? He eats puddin'! And how would soup or cream scare the sea monsters!"

The woeful Wall consisted of meandering berms of dirt, sticks, branches, logs, rocks, MC red rocks with googly eyes, and odd cement patches and towers. Prime minister statues stood awkwardly on top of this uneven terrain about every twenty meters. In the distance, Puddin' Heads dumped a truckload of cement into a shoddy log tower, which quickly overflowed and streamed down the berm and off the cliff. A few students pulled a statue from a pile, lugged it up the Wall, and stuck it in the wet cement, facing the ocean.

The statues were short and poorly crafted, as if they had been created by very young, satirical, or untalented artists. These sea monster fighting statues fell into three groups. The *spotter statues* were self-explanatory. The *scary statues* made yes, scary faces and hand gestures. The *superhero statues* flexed or posed like, yes, superheroes. Several vaguely resembled a familiar leader, although it was difficult to tell due to poor craftsmanship. One crouched like it was about to blast into the air, but the squat and facial expression suggested he might poop instead—as even supreme superheroes do —but I doubt that was the artist's intention. Unless, of course, that artist was a Sweetie.

The agitated Puddin' Head continued. "And we got the freedom launchers!" He pointed to a row of large wooden catapults near the Wall. Large catapult spoon buckets were filled with red rocks with googly eyes as well as logs, rocks, and dynamite. "And that's why we have *freedom*!"

Kai crossed his arms and raised his eyebrows. He grabbed and shook a googly eyed rock. Yes, its eyes spun round and round, which *was* funny, but not to Kai. "And please do explain, how do these ridiculous rocks—"

The kid snatched the wiggly eyed rock from Kai, safely putting it back into the catapult. "Those are special MC rocks. They're the guides." He leaned close to Blaze. *"They can see things."*

Blaze smiled wide-eyed at Chopper.

"Oh, what a stimulating conversation!" Kai said. "Yes, please continue—how does chopping down trees, or these pathetic statues prevent— Oh, never mind. What does a freedom launcher do?"

The student turned to Blaze. "Is this guy a Sweetie or something?"

Blaze shrugged. The Puddin' Head pointed to the catapult spoon buckets and said, "Launches logs, dynamite, rocks, and the MC guide rocks, you numbskull."

"At what?!"

"The sea monsters! Or the zombies. Why do you think there are none around here?"

Kai nodded sarcastically. "Cutting down trees. Tossing rocks and dynamite at imaginary sea monsters. Building a wall with strange statues against a zombie attack. This whole island is full of great ideas!"

"The statues aren't for the zombies, they're for the sea monsters!

And don't forget the logs!" said the Puddin' Head. "The MC guide rocks tell everything where to go. The regular rocks get the deep sea monsters, the dynamite blows up the smaller sea monsters that don't live so deep, and the logs conk out the ones on top of the water. Most importantly, the logs confuse the sea monsters—and zombies —because logs float!" The student angrily adjusted his spoon helmet, then his MC Frames, and marched off, pushing his broken bike.

Kai paced, shaking his head. "I don't think the sea monsters are the ones confused around here!"

"I don't know about sea monsters, but a zombie attack is plausible." Blaze chuckled.

In the distance, a group of Bigs with compression gloves and thick spoon hats sawed down trees. A teacher yelled at a student standing motionless, who dangled a chainsaw loosely in her hand. The teacher shouted over the buzzing saws, "Why aren't you cutting trees?" The student grunted, refusing to speak. She dramatically pointed to her flattened hand, then the student with a flattened arm, then the spot where a student was flattened. The teacher held up a red card. The girl snatched it and tore it up. She said, "You zombie-loving, sea monster!" and stomped away.

Blaze marched over to give the teacher a piece of her mind. But then her song, *Who Will We Defeat?* blared over the PA system. Well, a version of it played over and over.

> *Who do we blame?*
> *The zombies!*
> *Who will we defeat?*
> *The zombies!*
> *Who will we beat,*
> *Should we have to meet?*
> *The zombies!*

It wasn't a bugle call, but it was just as effective. Students stopped working. They set down their chainsaws, left their dirt bikes, and ran toward an oval shaped outdoor stadium.

Blaze threw up her arms. "They stole my song! I mean, I like it, but someone stole my song!" She looked at Scarlet.

"What? I just posted your song to Mega Gossip." Scarlet blew a bubble and sucked the gum back into her mouth. "I didn't change anything."

Kai paced, clasping his hands on his head. "You're upset because someone stole your stupid song? Look what your song's doing! It's the anthem for any numbskull who believes that Sweeties are literally zombies!"

Hordes of students began filling the stadium. They sang along, hooting and hollering. The school boss enthusiastically announced the winners of yesterday's races. The audience hooted louder.

"We have to see this," Blaze said.

Only Kai disagreed.

"Aren't we supposed to have an escort on this tour?" Scarlet asked. Chopper raised his hands mid-stride, pursed his lips, but didn't answer.

Kai shook his head. "Yeah. This was a bad idea."

Several hundred students sat scattered throughout the stadium seating. We took seats near the racetrack. Some kid shouted, "Nice spot!" His group near the top of the stadium howled with laughter. Another kid yelled, "Yeah, and nice hats!" The group doubled over laughing.

Scanning the stadium, we realized that everyone wore large, thick spoon hats. And everyone sat in the middle or top sections.

"No way am I wearing one of those ridiculous spoon hats!" Kai wagged his finger, letting us know he was serious. "And why is no one sitting near the track?"

"These Puddin' Heads don't know a good seat when they see one," Scarlet said. But Blaze, Chopper, and I moved near the raucous group that had just mocked us. After a brief conversation, we strapped on spoon hats. Kai and Scarlet laughed and righteously stayed put.

The school boss announced the drivers, runners, and the freedom launcher. The crowd cheered each one. At the starting line of the dirt track with undulating hills, five drivers climbed into red go-karts with giant spoon tops and doors (handles facing backwards, presumably for the aerodynamics). They revved their engines.

"Are all the drivers and runners Bigs?" Blaze asked.

"Can't tell," Chopper said.

Wheels and about twenty other runners strapped on spoon helmets and lined up around the go-karts. In comparison to the crowd's spoon hats, the runners spoon helmets appeared to be thicker and secured with higher quality double straps instead of one strap. Nearly all runners wore their spoon handles facing backwards. The runner with his spoon handle facing forward also only wore one article of clothing: a bright-red pair of underwear. He banged a spoon against his helmet and yelled, "Freedom! Sweeties can't tell me what to do!"

Another runner tried to slip away, but a teacher blew a whistle, motioning for the student to turn around. They argued, and the teacher held up a yellow card. The crowd booed as the runner flipped off the teacher, then the crowd, and walked off the track.

Wheels pulled a stack of dynamite puddin' chips from her pocket, shoved them in her mouth, slapped her face a few times, pulled two large spoons from her belt, clanged them together, and howled. The other runners clanged their spoons and howled, too. The crowd clanged their spoons and howled back. Then they chanted, "Freedom! Freedom! Freedom!"

"Am I seeing what I think I'm seeing?" Kai scooted to the edge of his seat.

Scarlet chomped on her gum. "I don't know *what* I'm seeing. How does this count as school?"

The race flagger sat next to the dynamite launcher in the crow's nest near the starting line. The flagger waved a red-and-white checkered flag. The spoon-wielding drivers and runners shot ahead. A large clock counted down from eight minutes.

Blaze had a lot of questions. The first was, "What's happening?"

A student turned to answer but accidentally whacked a friend with his spoon handle. "Spoon awareness, you sweet tart," his friend chided. "What are you, five years old?"

The student chuckled and explained to Blaze, "Basically, the competitors have eight minutes to do as many laps as possible, avoiding the dynamite blows."

"Dynamite?"

"Yeah, see that student in the crow's nest? That's the freedom launcher. A Small, of course—who wouldn't want *that* job?—gets to launch sticks of dynamite at the drivers and runners. Technically, the launcher aims right behind them—keeps them going if you know what I mean! But sometimes, there's a direct hit. Obviously, the runners and drivers avoid the dynamite or smack it with their spoons."

"What? Why?"

"Why what?"

"Why the race? Why the dynamite? What's the purpose of all of this?" Blaze asked with increasing frustration. For a moment, she thought of Orion, and his big questions.

"Are you serious? To prepare for a Sweetie attack!"

"Zombie attack!" his friend corrected.

"Whatever. This is excellent preparation on so many levels. The launcher gets to practice accuracy. The drivers and runners build

stamina, toughness, agility, courage— you know—everything you
need to fight the Sweeties—errr . . . zombies."

"And just double checking—*Who* is racing? Bigs or Smalls?"

"Bigs, of course. Would you choose that job?"

Blaze slapped her head, forgetting her spoon hat, and winced.

"Well, there is one exception—that kid in the red underwear is a
Small. But don't worry, our runners are safer than before. We're
good learners. We lowered the dynamite explosive power. Plus, it's
only fired in the last two minutes. More importantly, our spoon
helmets are stronger now. Have you seen our spoon factory?
They've nearly perfected the dynamite-grade spoon helmet—doing
some good work there. Yeah, in the old days, entire karts used to get
destroyed. A few years ago, we lost three runners in a race. Oh, and
the quick fuse blew up the crow's nest. That was bad. I mean, sure,
things still happen, but it's so much safer now."

"What the—" Blaze mumbled. She thought of the
puddin'tender, closed her eyes, lowered her head, curled her hands
into fists and looked away, fighting back tears.

"You okay?" the student asked.

Chopper said, "Yeah, Blaze. Are you okay?"

Three go-karts spun around the corner, spraying a wave of dirt
and dust into our section. The crowd cheered. A few Puddin' Heads
skillfully smacked away the bigger clumps with their spoons. Kai
and Scarlet dove for cover.

Blaze snorted, took a deep breath, and wiped a tear away. "I'm
just . . . taking it all in . . ." she said, trying to suppress her rising
anger. "So, what's the deal with Wheels?"

"Ah, Wheels! See that turn?" He pointed to the far end of the
track. "That's where the dynamite exploded next to her parents.
Ever since that day, she's just been . . . well . . . running."

"Moldy fart tart . . ."

"Yeah."

"The drivers and runners—they're going to be okay, right?"

"Yeah, probably."

At first, the event seemed absurd funny. In the first five minutes
of racing, go-karts wove in and around runners, runners smacked
each other's hands with spoons, and Wheels built up a ridiculous
lead. A series of fireworks shot into the sky, making the crowd go
wild, and the two-minute countdown began. The freedom launcher
wore a spoon helmet, spoon armbands, a spoon chest covering, a

spoon back-plate, and spoon leg-guards. "I'll bet that's what Walka Walka looked like as a kid," Blaze said. The freedom launcher ordered another kid, wearing similar armor, to light and load dynamite sticks into a swiveling catapult bolted to the floor of the crow's nest. "And there's little Peabody," Blaze joked.

In the next moment, absurd funny mutated into absurd disturbing. The freedom launcher took aim and sent sizzling dynamite sticks hurtling toward the racers. The drivers peered through their windshields or through the small window of their spoon doors. Convex spoon mirrors allowed for a wide rear view. The runners eyed the crow's nest as they sprinted across the lap line —which was the closest spot to the crow's nest. Some runners crossed it looking backwards. Others crossed it and then ran backwards shifting their spoon helmet in the opposite direction— keeping a close eye on the freedom launcher.

To my relief, the freedom launcher was quite skilled at dropping exploding dynamite right behind runners and drivers—not too close, not too far. Yes, the runners were motivated and moving! My eye twitch was going crazy. I dimmed my Frames and considered leaving or intervening while I still could—surely, my eyes would swell shut at any moment. Thankfully, I had no access to chocolate. My shrink had definitely prescribed the wrong treatment plan; if exposure to this level of absurdity didn't work, what possibly could?

Blaze grabbed Chopper. "This is insane! I'm talking to the school boss! We need to stop this. We should be united against the Sweeties, not blowing each other up!"

"Just hold on. It's almost over. And remember, they've improved everything, so it's much safer now. Besides, this is excellent data."

Another dynamite stick exploded behind a panicked runner. Blaze yelled.

The launcher catapulted a stick too far into the stands, blowing up a set of chairs. Kai and Scarlet gaped at each other before sprinting up the stairs and plopping next to Chopper. "I'm still not wearing a spoon hat!" Kai panted.

The launcher shot the next stick toward the far end of the track. But then, she sensed trouble. She grabbed two large spoons from her holster and pounded her spoon hat like a fanatical drummer. The school boss scrambled to the microphone and yelled, "Incoming!"

The crowd gasped.

Blaze stood up.

One runner—the pantless, freedom-loving, true-red Puddin'

Head—watched in horror as the dynamite descended right toward him. If only if he was faster, or perhaps had turned his spoon helmet around for better aerodynamics and speed. Alas, he lost the trajectory, tripped, and fell face first. I'm sorry to say that he got a nasty whiplash as soon as his spoon helmet handle hit the dirt, flipping him over and scraping his back down to his ankles. The crowd gasped at what seemed inevitable.

Suddenly, Wheels—who was about to lap this hapless runner—sped up and grabbed a hand spoon as smoothly as an Olympic relay baton pass. She leaped into the air and smacked the dynamite stick far away. A second later, it exploded. The crowd went insane, clanging hand spoons and whacking spoon hats. Wheels holstered her spoon without breaking stride. The crowd cheered, "Wheels! Wheels! Wheels!"

Blaze shook Chopper. "What just happened?"

Fireworks exploded as time ran out. Blaze and Chopper fought off a rowdy crowd of spoon-wielding Puddin' Heads like spoon-sword fighters. "I guess I needed spoon combat training after all!" Chopper quipped. Kai and Scarlet covered their heads and bolted.

Blaze finally escaped the crowd. "I'm going for the mic. Someone needs to talk sense into these numbskulls!"

"Blaze, no!"

"Where did that school boss go?" Blaze hurdled rows of chairs and sped down an aisle toward the crow's nest.

Suddenly, sirens pierced the air. Everyone froze and lowered their spoons. The school boss announced, "This is a Code Blue. We are under attack. I repeat, this is a Code Blue. This is not a drill. Take your stations. Now!"

Blazed pulled up short. The spoon waving crowd rallied and ran to the exits. Blaze pushed through the chaos to find us outside. We were frozen with confusion and staring toward the coast of Puddin' Head Horn.

BLUE ROBES
PH3, Day 2, Continued

Sweeties wearing thin blue robes walked calmly and slowly through the pandemonium. Blue hoods covered their heads. Some Sweeties sat cross-legged in a small circle. Some tied themselves to the few remaining trees. Others scaled trees and tied themselves to the upper branches.

Our team ran to the edge of a cliff not yet blocked by the Wall. Two large sailboats were anchored in the harbor. Rowboats of blue-robed Sweeties landed on shore. A line of Sweeties steadily hiked along the beach and up the narrow path toward Freedom High School.

One said, "Careful not to step on the bugs! Careful not to breathe them in!"

"Another Sweetie attack on Puddin' Head soil!" Blaze said to Kai. "This is why Puddin' Head schools are so messed up! We keep preparing for your stupid attacks!"

"We wouldn't attack you if you didn't mess with us! Let's go see why they're here."

One blue-robed Sweetie waved his hand in circles; perhaps he was the leader. He wore a belt with two slots that held not spoons, but banyan sticks.

"This looks like another Noble Deed!" Scarlet clapped her hands.

"We are not here for a Noble Deed," the presumptive leader said.

Puddin' Heads circled. Apparently, Freedom High School hadn't read or practiced the *MC Code Blue Emergency Procedures.*

"What?" Scarlet cried. "But this is the perfect—"

"Hah ha!" Kai interrupted. "They're so excited about the Noble Deed Match, they came early for football tryouts!"

"We are not here for games."

"My turn," Blaze said. "You're here to learn how to change your stupid schools?"

The blue-robed Sweetie paused, as if annoyed. "I am Root-Woot, protector of creatures and trees." He swiftly spun his arms in opposite directions and took a step back. He stopped in what seemed to be a fighting pose. "We are not here to change our schools. We are here to change yours."

The Puddin' Heads from Freedom High growled like they were angry—or very hungry.

Blaze turned to Chopper. "They're wearing hoods and covering their MC Frames. You can't tell who has large or small hands. Why aren't Frame alarms going off?"

"I don't know."

"I have to find out." Blaze reached for Root-Woot's hood. This was a mistake. The blue-robed Sweetie swiftly snatched her hand, twisted her wrist, locked her arm, and spun with her motion as if they were dancing together. Blaze shouted, her body contorted, the Sweetie let her go, and she flew to the ground. Root-Woot returned to the grounded martial arts stance. "Don't touch the hood," he said.

Thus erupted wild speculation among the scared, confused, and growling Puddin' Heads about who or what was under the blue robes and hoods. *That was a total zombie move! Look how they walk and talk—they're already dead! Why aren't they scared of the MC guide rocks?! They're going to eat our brains! No, those are sea monsters! The prime minister was right—I told you sea monsters are real! We should have finished the Wall! No, you numbskull. These are just silly Sweeties! Look—they're wearing blue!*

Blaze leaped to her feet and dusted herself off. She spotted the shaking school boss and tapped him on the shoulder. He jumped about a meter in the air. "Don't you see what's happening?" she demanded. "Puddin' Heads—big hands and small—are talking together as *equals* about how to defeat the Sweeties. That's what "Who Will We Defeat" is about. Puddin' Heads need to work together!"

But the school boss held a different set of beliefs. He bolted away with the other sea monster believers.

"He ran away! The school boss literally ran away!" Blaze said to Chopper. "That's the *opposite* of leadership!"

"Great Creator of Trees—they cut down banyan trees!" Root-Woot cried, scanning the deforestation. "It *is* true!" He wailed, then began an indecipherable chant, waving his arms.

The remaining Puddin' Heads all had different theories, each leading to a different set of actions. The zombie believers smacked the alleged zombies on the hands. Sweetie believers spanked their uninvited guests over the heads with spoons—and sometimes, they spanked their hands, too. Those who'd lost all their senses wildly smacked any hand they saw, including their own.

Strangely, the blue-robed Sweeties did not fight back, resist, or even cry. In great confusion, the Puddin' Heads soon stopped the spoon flogging. It was hard to say who was angrier, Kai or Blaze. Kai grabbed the megaphone from Chopper's backpack and put it on full blast.

"Who is your leader?" he roared.

Many Puddin' Heads and Sweeties dropped to the ground, covering their ears.

One blue-robed Sweetie said timidly, "We don't have a leader, because we don't believe in leaders."

"Then whose idea was this?" Kai boomed. The Sweeties covered their ears again. The Puddin' Heads covered their ears and then raised their spoons, ready to defend against the blue attack.

Several Sweeties sheepishly pointed at Root-Woot—apparently the non-leader leader.

"Just checking again. Do you play football?"

"No. Why do you keep asking the same question?"

"Technically, I didn't ask that question—" Kai started.

Root-Woot waved his hand in annoyance. "We are tree huggers —students from Tree Hugger High School. We live along the southern coast of Sweetie Island Region 3. We come for one purpose—to change your schools. We come in peace."

Blaze turned to Chopper and said sarcastically, "Is he for real? These *blue-robed Sweeties* are going to change Puddin' Head schools?"

And thus began a gentle wave of Sweetie sharing.

"We come with loving kindness."

"We are nature lovers."

"We protect a dwindling herd of elephants."

"We bring no harm."

"We hug trees."

"Good luck with that!" a Puddin' Head said, pointing to the hundreds of tree stumps. The Puddin' Heads snickered and eyed the few standing trees, which Sweeties were now hugging and climbing.

Root-Woot spun his arms in circles once more.

A Puddin' Head smashed a mosquito on her arm with a spoon. "Oh dear. Poor creature!" Root-Woot said.

The Puddin' Heads snarled. "Weird!" one said. "I don't like them, or their blue robes!" Several Puddin' Heads grunted, waving their spoons in agreement.

A Sweetie climbed into a catapult spoon to speak above the din of the crowd. "We're here to peacefully protest your inhumane destruction of the wondrous natural world," he said clearly, calmly, and softly. "And to see if you have stolen elephants."

The tree huggers scanned the land but saw no sign of elephants. They protected a small herd of elephants that now roamed Sweetie Island Region 3. They'd been transported by a circus decades ago, but the owners found them worthless on Island Nation and too difficult to care for. They happily gave this burden to the tree huggers.

"Elephants?" The Puddin' Heads looked very confused.

The tree hugger continued. "Never mind about the elephants then. As I was saying, day after day, we see explosive refuse, dead fish chunks, and hacked tree trunks and limbs floating westward, polluting our coastline and beautiful ocean. This makes us very sad."

"I can't believe they cut down the banyan trees!" a Sweetie lamented from atop a tree branch.

"See!" Kai said to Blaze. "This started with the Puddin' Heads!"

"You must stop. It is not right," Root-Woot said, still waving his arms in opposite directions.

The Puddin' Heads raised their spoons and chuckled. Many eyed Root-Woot suspiciously, then Kai. An uneasy chuckle shifted into rumbling across hundreds of Puddin' Heads.

"Enough! This is not funny!" Root-Woot said. "Your ignorant ways must cease! We will protest until you stop this meaningless destruction!"

Now, the Puddin' Head laughter turned into simmering anger.

"And plant trees!" cried another Sweetie.

"They're trying to tell us what to do!" a Puddin' Head said indignantly. "They're trying to take away our *freedom*!"

"This isn't going to end well," Blaze said to Kai. "I mean, did they really expect a warm welcome?"

Root-Woot kept waving his hands in circles, as if trying to hypnotize the Puddin' Heads. "Do not destroy nature. Love nature. Care for nature. Love plants. Care for plants. Love bugs. Care for bugs. Love trees—"

"Zombie mind tricks!" the girl with the flattened hand shouted, perhaps trying to make up for her red card. "These *are* zombies dressed up like Sweeties!"

"I knew it!" cried several Puddin' Heads.

"No, they're talking sea monsters!" said one of the few remaining sea monster believers.

The Sweeties had prepared for such a moment. They sat cross-legged, closed their eyes, and softly chanted, "*All we need is love, all is well, all we need is love.*" Even the ones in the trees. Although one did fall onto two unsuspecting Puddin' Heads, who provided a good hand spanking in return.

Suddenly, a familiar boss emerged from the trail leading from the coast. She huffed and puffed, pausing to catch her breath. Dressed in a blue robe with the hood down, her obnoxious diamond necklace still swung in the sunlight. Puddin' Heads and Sweeties raised spoons and hands to block the blinding rays reflecting off the sparkling diamonds. "Sorry I'm late!" she gasped. "Looks like I arrived just in time to save the day!"

For a moment, my surly sweet tooth—still plagued by absurdity neurosis—thought about challenging her to a cookie eating contest.

"You've got to be kidding!" Blaze said.

Kai smacked his forehead. "Could this get any worse?"

"Who are you?" asked Root-Woot.

"Sweetie Region 2 Boss Poppy, at your service." She shot her arms into the air, drew in a long breath, and exhaled as she lowered her arms back to her sides. "Now, how does it go? Ah, yes. If we could all just close our eyes, take a few deep breaths, flap our arms, and enter the *chill bird trance.*"

"Sweet tart!" Kai tried to guide Root-Woot away. But just as Kai said, "You need to leave. Nowww—" the non-leader leader grasped Kai's wrist, locked his upper arm, spun low, and sent him flailing through the air.

Poppy continued, oblivious. "Deep, relaxing breaths. Inhale, exhale."

"We will stay until our wishes are granted," Root-Woot said, then returned to chanting.

"Leave while you still can!" Kai shouted from where he lay on the ground. He could see what was coming.

The blue-robed Sweeties linked arms around trees and chanted. Regional Boss Poppy closed her eyes, exhaled, and shared her words of wisdom. "Puddin' Heads will stop chopping down trees. There is no injustice. Puddin' Heads will stop blowing up fish. All is well." She opened one eye to see who was following, which was no one.

A launcher yelled, "Feed the zombies to the sea monsters!" He released the gigantic catapult spoon and the cross-legged, blue-robed Sweetie sailed through the air. Puddin' Heads whooped with rising delight. The Sweetie's scream faded as his arc peaked and he fell far away. From the cliffs of Freedom High School, a tiny Sweetie splashed into the water without a sound.

Blaze watched carefully and got her answer. "Ah, they aren't wearing Frames!"

The Puddin' Heads cheered and waved their spoons.

Kai looked at Blaze and Chopper in panic. "Who cares if they aren't wearing Frames! You need to stop this. This has gone way too far!"

"Uh, we're not the ones invading an island," Blaze pointed out.

Inevitably, the spoon smacking started again. Puddin' Heads cheered and head butted the Sweeties, then each other, with their spoon hats. I could barely see.

"You give us no choice!" Root-Woot said. "Use their own energy against themselves!" he shouted to his comrades. Suddenly, the blue-robed Sweeties spun into a defensive stance: knees slightly bent, arms extended, and hands open.

Puddin' Heads stuffed dynamite chips into their mouths, jumped up and down, and attacked with spoons. The Sweeties deftly redirected the blows, contorted wrists and elbow joints, and deployed an impressive repertoire of throws. They spun like graceful dancers, flinging Puddin' Heads into each other. But strangely, they never once initiated an attack.

There was one odd exception: Root-Woot pulled the banyan sticks from his belt and whirled them like swords. "Who wants to play?!" he challenged. Root-Woot blocked a series of spoon attacks, then swiftly played the drums on too many spoon hats to count, as if he had transformed into a samurai drummer. With their spoon hats ringing like bells, Puddin' Heads fell like chopped trees to the ground.

"What the—" Blaze and Chopper said together.

"Sweet Mother of Honey!" Kai cheered.

The Puddin' Heads looked at each other in confusion. "I thought we had zombie immunity?"

Regional Boss Poppy deflected spoon whacks with her diamond compression gloves. "Okay, that's it! I tried to be kind and block you with the *chill bird trance*. But I can see that I need to start handing out some serious red cards!" She looked at Blaze, Chopper, Scarlet, and Kai. "You're so lucky I'm here!"

"Who does she think she is?" a Puddin' Head asked.

"I am the Top Boss!"

Puddin' Heads grunted, hefted her over to a catapult spoon, and released her on a joy ride into the ocean. She flapped her arms and yelled, "I am a chill bird heeeerrrrooooo!"

Alas, the spinning blue-robed Sweeties were outnumbered. They flung Puddin' Heads until their swollen heads and hands could take no more. Root-Woot pounded out a last round of drums on spoon hats and finally called it. "Run away!" They burst toward the coast through a sea of hopping-mad, true-red Puddin' Heads.

Things could have gone much worse if Kai hadn't bought them time by booming over the megaphone, "Let them go!" The Puddin' Heads cupped their ears and turned, waiting for a good reason someone would stop the fun. An awkward silence followed.

"Why?!" one Puddin' Head shouted.

"Uh, because . . ." Kai dramatically lifted a fist up high and paused. He pointed two fingers at the sky, then at the crowd. He paused, wearing a very confused expression. He did a very odd-looking chicken dance. He glanced at the Wall, widened his eyes, and nodded as if he'd just had a great epiphany. He pointed his index fingers at each other, then made binoculars with both hands. He scanned the horizon and opened his mouth in surprise, as if he saw a giant sea monster, or was about to reveal a master plan.

"He's trying to tell us something!"

"He has no idea! They're getting away!"

"Rocks! He's saying launch the rocks!"

"No, that's not what I'm saying!"

"Logs! Launch the logs!"

"No, you knuckleheads!"

"Ha! See, we're getting close. Okay, okay. Dynamite! Launch the dynamite!"

"Bunch of numbskulls!"

"I got it!" one exclaimed, clapping his hands. "It's so obvious—launch everything!"

The Puddin' Heads roared.

"No! That's not what I—" But it was too late.

The rowdy crowd ran to the catapults. Skilled and unskilled launchers climbed into the catapult seat, swiveled, and released a barrage of logs, dynamite, rocks, and, yes, guide rocks that rained down into the ocean. One rock shot through Root-Woot's rowboat, which sank as Sweeties bailed and swam for the next rowboat. Dynamite sticks exploded in the water. Sweeties cried as they tried to row around the dead fish that floated up to the surface. Kai tried to speak, but a Puddin' Head ripped the megaphone away from him and bellowed, "Freedom! Nobody tells me what to do!"

Kai pinched his nose, and sneered, "Including when to bathe?"

The stinky student started a clever chant on the megaphone. "Fire! Freedom! Fire! Freedom!"

Many Sweeties, including Regional Boss Poppy, hadn't yet made it to the large sail boats. They rowed frantically as exploding dynamite, logs, and rocks crashed down around them.

Kai looked at Blaze. "Someone is going to die! Do something!"

"The sweet tarts attacked us!"

"Attacked? That was a peaceful protest."

Scarlet popped a large bubble. "Wow, this is good stuff. Definitely a Noble Deed, whether they want one or not. Talk about island pride. I'm going to rack up some serious Mega Gossip views for these posts."

Blaze stuck a finger in Kai's face. "You still don't get it! What just happened is exactly why Puddin' Head schools are so messed up. Bigs are risking their lives preparing to fight the Sweeties, who are trying to take our freedom."

"Are you insane? How is launching—"

Three Puddin' Heads grabbed Kai and said, "We'll take care of this." Chopper and Scarlet tried to intervene, but the Puddin' Heads hauled him to a catapult nevertheless.

"Your people started this!" Blaze called as Kai sailed into the ocean. The crowd cheered. Kai shook his now barely visible fist. Blue hooded Sweeties scooped him into a rowboat. Freedom dynamite, logs, and rocks pummeled the water, sending waves that nearly tipped the boat.

"Okay, they're getting carried away," Scarlet said anxiously. "We can't lose the Sweetie football captain! Do you want to play a Noble Deed Match or not?"

Blaze wasn't a monster. She was just confused and hadn't learned any of her big lessons yet. She snatched the megaphone. "Puddin' Heads, today is a very proud day. Did you notice Puddin' Heads Bigs and Smalls working together? Did you see what we can accomplish when we work as equals?"

The Puddin' Heads looked at each other in confusion, and then cheered with pride. A Big hugged a Small, then gave him a noogie.

Blaze raised a spoon and sang, "Who did we meet?"

The Puddin' Heads stared blankly. Blaze sang it again. This time they got it, but their response wasn't the one Blaze had anticipated.

"The zombies!"

"Uh . . ." She shrugged and went with it. "Right. Who did we defeat?"

"The zombies!"

"Who did we beat!"

"The zombies!"

"But they're getting away," some Puddin' Heads cried. The crowd turned back to see the frantically rowing Sweeties. "Sink them all!"

"Sink them all! Sink them all!" the crowd repeated. Puddin' Heads loaded more freedom ammunition into the catapults.

"No, no—wait!" Blaze hollered into the megaphone. "Actually, uh, that's a terrible idea."

"Huh?" The Puddin' Head crowd spun around.

Blaze didn't want to lie, but she couldn't think of a better alternative. "If you kill the Sweeties— or zombies, or small sea monsters, or whatever they are—in the ocean, that will only attract the *very large sea monsters* right here to Freedom High School. They love Sweetie and zombie blood. They can smell it for miles."

The crowd didn't understand, but this was Blaze Union talking.

"Well . . . we don't want that, do we?"

The crowd shrugged and said, "No!"

"And besides, there's a much better way to teach those zombie Sweeties a lesson."

"There is?"

"Oh yes, there is." Blaze led the original version of "Who Will We Defeat?" with a very rowdy Puddin' Head crowd.

When reflecting on this part of the tour, Blaze later told me, "Of course, what happened at Freedom High School was absurd. But it was fantastic evidence that this school was no good, Tree Hugger High was puddin' mold, and Pompavich needed to go. Yeah, some Puddin' Heads took things too far, but I was finally uniting the Puddin' Head Bigs and Smalls alike, for the epic Noble Deed Football Match. I thought we had seen the most absurd schools in the nation, but I was wrong."

Surprisingly, Kai agreed to continue the tour. Unsurprisingly, he put Blaze in a headlock, giving a not-so-nice noogie. They wrestled and pushed and swore. Catching his breath, Kai said, "Your no-brain, numbskull, zombie-and-sea-monster-believing Puddin' Heads have only made me more committed to destroying you in the Noble Deed Match!"

"Bah!" Blaze said, rubbing her head. "Your sad Sweetie team is as likely to win the Noble Deed Match as the Region 3 tree-hugging zombies will return to protest at Freedom High. Speaking of which, are we touring Region 3 for your recruits?" She buckled over laughing.

"They weren't interested!"

The wrestling continued. Scarlet and Chopper finally separated them.

"Let's end the tour," Kai said. "We have enough players. What's the point? Let's play football already."

"Fine with me!" Blaze bent over to catch her breath. "The sooner the better."

"Nope, not going to happen," Chopper said. "We just made a major change to the plan—not touring Sweetie Region 3, but for good reason. We need to stick with the rest of the plan. We can't give the prime minister any reason to change his mind and cancel the Noble Deed Match or change the winner's reward. Besides, we still have more crucial data to collect." Then, he whispered to Blaze, "You don't want to him to dismiss our report."

"Okay," Blaze said, raising an eyebrow.

Scarlet blew a bubble and nodded. "And better publicity. More visits equals more attention for the Noble Deed Match. Imagine the entire nation getting involved. It's going to be epic!"

Kai groused but finally agreed. "Fine, but I still think that once you've seen one Puddin' Head, you've seen them all. I mean, really. How could the Puddin' Head numbskulls be any worse than the ones in Region 3?"

Scarlet stepped in front of Blaze before she could tackle Kai, "Good, we agree then! And . . . I have some awesome newwwsss.

After that ridiculously long train ride to Region 3, and because my Noble Deed coverage on Mega Gossip has been sooo amaaazzziiinnnggg, Daddy agreed to give us a helicopter for the rest of the tour!" She did a little dance and then abruptly stopped. "But *do not* tell Mom!"

"I'm sure that has nothing to do with our upgraded solar bikes," Blaze snickered to Chopper.

Before the football tryouts, we were a little surprised at the data for Puddin' Head Region 4. "Well, they do have higher numbers for Bigs, but there are still some pretty big gaps," Blaze said. "But whoa —look at Puddin' Brains High School. The Bigs and Smalls are close in agreement!"

"Yeah, their percentage agreeing is so high, it pushed up the average for the entire region. Let's check out the open-ended responses."

We learned that a new school boss had been hired after the last Good Hope Day, and as a result, a lot of students elected to transfer there. Many students were grateful for new opportunities, new possibilities, and a whole new life—particularly amongst the Bigs.

"I wonder why that is?" Blaze mused. "Maybe we should change things up and see a better school. Maybe football tryouts will give us a clue."

Puddin' Head Island, Region 4
Student Survey Results

	All Students Agreeing	Bigs Agreeing	Smalls Agreeing
School is affordable	56%	30%	80%
School is fair	78%	70%	85%
School is fun, useful, and interesting	75%	70%	80%

Response Rate = 95%

Chopper's request to pilot the helicopter got chopped down like a tree in Puddin' Head Region 3. The pilot landed on a field near Thickskull. At tryouts, we met about fifty Puddin' Head Region 4 hopefuls, most of whom were Smalls. Of the few Bigs, half of them—all from Puddin' Brains High—had their hands wrapped in bandages.

"What's up with the wraps?" Blazed asked.

"Oh, we have this awesome new school boss. We're preparing for revolutionary experiments that will change everything. This," the student said, tapping one bandaged hand with the other, "will be totally worth it."

"Okay, whatever. Can you play football?"

Yes, they could play, but only a few could play well. Blaze and Chopper placed them on the backup to the backup team. Maybe this lot was so mediocre because half of the students at Puddin' Brains High aimed for a different below-average target. And their whole school was rooting for them.

The pilot landed the helicopter near the school. Several hundred students poked their heads out of sheds and the main school entrance before resuming their activities. The school boss and five intense, grinning Smalls dressed in lab coats met us outside. One had tiny, dried red dots splattered on his lab coat, as if he'd been near a paint bucket that had fallen from a ladder.

"What, no spoon hats?" Kai said with a large, sarcastic grin.

"What?" the school boss frowned, then smiled. "Welcome to our school of excellence—or should I say, we are on our way to becoming a Red Ribbon School. I've only been here a short while. My name is School Boss Keen, but you can just call me Clever." The school boss slapped her knee and chuckled under her breath. Her minions guffawed and stuck out their teeth like braying donkeys.

"Well, Ms. Clever, you have impressive survey results. Curious to know why that is," Chopper said as he shook her hand.

"Please call me either School Boss Keen or Clever—no Ms. necessary." The school boss—who wore smiley Frames—cocked her eyebrow and brushed her lab coat, as if teaching those infinitesimal particles a lesson. "It's quite simple, really. Sometimes the most profound ideas are. You know those Sweeties are sad, but they do have one thing right. Most Puddin' Heads *are* a bunch of numbskulls."

Kai snorted. The school boss looked at his black shirt and, upon discovering he was a Sweetie, ordered him back to the helicopter or else the tour was canceled. What choice did we have?

The school boss continued, "Look, I've been around the island, traveled to all five regions."

"Puddin' Head schools are in bad shape, aren't they?" Blaze said.

"Indeed."

Blaze grinned wider than she had in a very long while.

"Region 1 Puddin' Heads obsessively take meaningless tests?" the school boss laughed. "Region 2 kids trying to pull themselves up by their bootstraps? Region 3 numbskulls launching rocks at sea monsters? And Region 5 . . . Oh, don't even get me started. So yeah, you could say Puddin' Head schools are in pretty bad shape."

Blaze high-fived Chopper.

Scarlet said, "Hey! My mom is in charge, you know."

"Yeah. Okay." The school boss rolled her eyes. "The problem with these imbeciles is that they don't have a clue how to defeat the Sweeties. The big bosses are out of touch, too. When do they actually visit schools? The answer is right in front of our eyes. So obvious. We need Bigs and Smalls to work together."

Blaze lit up like a rainbow. She nearly cried. As she told me later, "For a brief moment, I thought, *This is why the survey results are so high. Finally, someone who gets it! Finally, someone who speaks my language. Someone who can lead!* And then, you know what happened."

"It's not about the size or thickness of our skulls, as too many Puddin' Heads believe—"

"But this school is near Thickskull," Chopper pointed out.

"Ah—I hate that name! No, no, no. It's about our brains, not our skulls. The simple, intelligent solution is to reduce Bigs' hand sizes. It's not booster science. If everyone in Puddin' Head Region 4 has small hands, then everyone in Sweetie Region 4 has large hands. And we all know what happens then. It's that simple! And that's why I sent your Sweetie 'friend' back to the helicopter. Can't have them stealing our ideas!"

"Huh?" Blaze was crushed. Angry. Confused. "Is that so? And how are you going to do that? Don't tell me you use compression gloves."

"Ha! Sure, we use those. We're the leading producers on the island. But that's just a money-generating side show." She pointed to a large shed with a sign that read, Compression Gloves. "It's a temporary fix. There's not much scientific evidence that they work. If you're going to do something, you've got to do it right. Let me show you what we're working on, and why we have Bigs transferring here like we're giving away free puddin'." The school boss slapped her knee, laughing.

But then, the school boss seemed to read something on her Frames. "Oh, wait. I have something to take care of. You can wait in the cafeteria. Grab a few snacks if you want."

We shuffled into an empty cafeteria, which had the standard puddin' and booster vending machines. But no one was hungry.

Scarlet checked her Mega Gossip feed.

"I didn't come here to eat puddin'," Blaze said. "Let's see the classrooms." Chopper and I followed her down a hallway.

We overheard a teacher say, "I don't know how much longer I'll be here." Blaze stopped in her tracks to eavesdrop.

"That's why it's important that you think for yourself," the teacher said. "It's important that you know your history—the people's history, not just MegaCorp's version. Demand the facts. Demand evidence. Always consider who is telling the story and who is not, whose voice is heard and whose is missing. Now, let's examine these historic documents again. Who wrote them? How do they compare to the MC text?"

A student said, "The first prime minister was obsessed with hand size. But many islanders thought it was a joke."

"How do you know that? What's the evidence?"

"Teacher Howzin, the prime minister wrote it in his journal! And the—"

Blaze's eyes were the size of puddin' containers. She leaned closer and accidentally stepped across the threshold.

"Who's there?" the teacher asked.

"Oh, hello," Blaze said with a goofy, friendly wave. "I'm Blaze Union, and I was just in the region and uh . . . thought I'd stop by. What uh . . . are students learning?"

"Are you with this new school boss?"

"Not exactly."

The teacher hurried to scan the hallway, and regarded me and Chopper suspiciously. "We're with her," Chopper said.

The teacher whispered into Blaze's ear, "Are you with TDJP?"

"Unofficially, sort of? Officially, I'm the associate minister of education," Blaze whispered back.

The teacher motioned for us to enter. "Quickly!" he hissed and shut the door.

"Do you know what's happening to this school?" the teacher demanded. "With this new school boss? Are you supporting her new 'strategy' to change schools?"

"We just got here," Blaze said. "I have no idea what you're talking about, but you seem worried. What's going on?"

The class looked at their teacher expectantly.

"It's a long story. I've been teaching here for—"

Suddenly, the school boss burst in.

"Why is this door closed?" She snatched an article from a student. "What is this?" She studied it, sneering in disgust. "Is this article *critiquing* the first prime minister?"

The class gasped.

"We are simply analyzing history from multiple viewpoints," Teacher Howzin said.

"You know this kind of material is banned! You may only use MC textbooks—and that's it! This is an automatic red card!" the school boss barked.

"I thought you stand for freedom!"

"I am for freedom!"

"Then why are you banning the freedom to think!"

"You think I'm a numbskull? Your mind tricks won't work on my puddin' brain. Never again will you corrupt student minds! Pack your things and be gone before I return!" The teacher swore, and the students wailed. "You three, with me!" The school boss marched us back to the cafeteria, where we picked up Scarlet, and then she hustled us outside.

"What just happened? Who was that teacher? What was he talking about?" Blaze asked Chopper.

"I don't know, but I think we're going to find out."

The school boss continued at a brisk pace. "Some teachers these days," she sighed and shook her head. Of course, my eyes were going bonkers. Chopper held me back from giving the school boss a noogie, then steered me away from going back for that cafeteria puddin'. The school boss continued, "Now, as I was saying, let me show you what we've been working on. Your timing is perfect. Ah, here's the factory. I'm telling you—this will change everything!"

We entered a large building. In one section, students welded spoons of all sizes. In another, they welded axes of all sizes. In another still, they constructed a vertical apparatus that held a heavy ax blade near the top. "We've just started our new production lines. The nurses said the saws were messy and dangerous, which of course also means inefficient. So, we went back to the drawing board."

"Huh?" We looked at each other with a sinking feeling. My eyes fluttered as if preparing for something awful.

"In fact, today we move from practice to application with our newest equipment. Speaking of which, let's go check out the practice building." In the next building, we observed students throwing small, medium, and large axes at zombie targets from various distances. The zombies' hands were in various positions, though always with their fingers extended. They resembled demented goalies, diving, jumping, or stretching to block a football. The students' goal was to chop off the zombies' fingers at the tips. Some Puddin' Heads were remarkably accurate.

Blaze was confused. "I don't get it."

"Of course, if we were actually attacked by zombies, we would chop their heads clean off, not their fingers."

"I thought their heads grow back," Blaze said sarcastically.

"What? What are they teaching in schools these days?! Aren't you the associate education minister?" the school boss huffed. "No, double-headed zombies are the invention of some filmmaker. Fiction, people, fiction. Decapitation is the only way to kill a zombie. But let's not miss the point here: these Puddin' Heads are practicing for their friends, which provides them with extra motivation."

"Huh?!" Blaze suddenly wished she had her guitar.

"Well, imagine if you chopped your friend's fingers in the wrong spot."

While Blaze widened her eyes, I could barely keep mine open.

"Let me show you."

But the school boss didn't need to. Next door, a Puddin' Head screamed.

BLOODY INSULT
PH4, Day 2, Continued

We ran outside. A student held up his hand. His fingers were wrapped with athletic tape just below the first knuckle. They were wrapped so tightly the fingertips had lost circulation and were turning darker and darker.

"Now's the best time to do it, Adolfo!" one student urged.

"Yeah, you won't feel a thing. We'll aim just above the tape mark! We've been practicing for weeks!" shouted the Small running the finger guillotine. "Come on already. This baby is oiled and ready to go—I finally want to use it!"

"What the—" Blaze spun around, trying to make sense out of what she was seeing. "Nurse!"

The school boss stepped in. "They all quit, fortunately. That's why we get to do these new techniques!" The school boss grabbed Adolfo's good hand and coaxed him back inside with a pep talk. "You'll be fine. Short-term pain, long-term gain. Who's next in line? Let's get a queue going, students."

"What?!" Blaze couldn't believe her eyes. Many Bigs raised their hands, eager for the opportunity to have smaller hands. For a flickering moment, Blaze was glad Kai wasn't there to call them all numbskulls.

"No, no, no, no, no! You don't need to chop off your fingers! There's nothing wrong with you! This is *not* how we'll beat the Sweeties!"

Chopper yelled, "Yeah!"

Scarlet waived her hand wildly, as if she had something very important to say. Or like she really needed to use the bathroom.

"This *is* how we'll beat the Sweeties!" one Big cried. "Adolfo, let me go ahead of you!"

Scarlet said, "Um, excuse me! I have something very important —"

The school boss put her hand in Scarlet's face. "You all need to relax. All these kids deserve equal opportunity."

"This is the dumbest school I've ever seen!" Blaze ran into the Applied Learning Room.

"Um, I really need to say—"

"Shut up, Noble Deed Coordinator—or whatever you are." The school boss ran after Blaze. "Hey, *Associate* Education Minister, where are you going?"

Blaze charged into the building and yelled, "STOOPPP!" The ax throwers, guillotine operators, and hopeful students with outstretched arms and taped fingers stopped and stared at Blaze.

"This is all wrong! It's all lies! Cutting off your fingertips won't fix your problems!"

"Yes, it will!" yelled the school boss, directly behind Blaze. "Think about it. Your entire life will be changed for the better. And who will pay? The Sweeties!"

Scarlet tried again; this time much louder: "Excuse me! Excuse me! I have something *very* relevant to this conver—"

"Shut up! You're all welcome to leave!" The school boss pointed to the door.

Scarlet unzipped Chopper's backpack and pulled out the—you guessed it—the megaphone. *"Everyone, listen up!"*

The students dropped to the ground, clutching their ears. Scarlet turned in a slow circle and yelled, *"The hand-size reduction rules are very clear. Finger removal is prohibited! Except in cases of surgery, where the tips of the fingers are reattached and still remain. Any person without fingertips will automatically be designated a person with large hands, regardless of their hand size. Supreme Minister rule 54T5-8.* She handed the megaphone back to Chopper. "See, I told you it was important."

"Nooooo!" cried the students.

"Nooooo!" cried the panicking school boss. "That's not true! You're lying! How could I not know about this rule?"

"It was issued last year. I'm sure you got the memo." Scarlet blew a bubble the size of her head. The school boss shoved the bubble right into Scarlet's face. It burst, covering Scarlet's head like a thin, sticky face mold.

Pandemonium ensued. Students slapped and head butted each other. Some ran outside and shook their fists at the unfair sky. "Whyyy?!" they cried.

I was useless—my eyes were going crazy. Curse my surly sweet tooth! I sprinted toward the cafeteria, tweaking my hamstring. I pulled up in pain, preventing a chocolate attack, but costing me precious time.

Adolfo, who had nearly lost his fingertips, did not take Scarlet's news well. He unwound the tape from his fingers. With his good hand, he dumped oil on the wall and lit it on fire. He calmly walked to the practice building and did the same thing. Then the factory. Within minutes, the entire campus was ablaze.

The team bolted for the helicopter with flames and smoke billowing behind them. As I limped away from the cafeteria, Chopper turned to me and yelled, "Let's go!"

I swore at Absurdity and hobbled toward the helicopter.

"What have you done?!" yelled the school boss, who—along with hundreds of students—chased after us.

How would I make it? The team might be captured because of me! Then, a strange thing happened. The memory of tiptoeing and side shuffling for that second cookie at Uncle Brute's house appeared. Suddenly, I shot toward the helicopter with my torso and arms twisting in sync with one leg quickly crossing in front and behind the other. With the pain more tolerable, yes, I raced with karaoke crossovers just in front of the pursuing mob.

The school boss turned to her burning school and yelled midstride, "These are lies! And now, there's nothing left!" She raised her fist and pointed at us. "*Get them!*"

The student body charged.

"We didn't start the fire!" Blaze yelled, "Just for the record."

A Puddin' Head shouted, "We can use the blades!" A mob of Bigs cheered and sprinted.

I barely made it. We climbed aboard.

"Go! Go! Go!" Blaze yelled at the pilot.

"What is *happening*?!" Kai cried. "What *happened*? Why are Puddin' Heads chasing you?"

"No time. Go! Go! Go!"

The pilot tried to lift off, but too many students clung to the landing skid. Several rattled the door handles. Others hoisted their friends into the air. They jumped one by one, trying get their fingers between the whirling blades.

"*What are these numbskulls doing?!*" Kai screamed.

Scarlet pulled gum from her hair while chomping another gum wad like a jackhammer. "I'm not posting this to Mega Gossip!" she yelled at the leaping students. "So, you can go away now!"

Swear words popped like popcorn in the cabin as fast as the blades turned. The pilot sprayed puddin' on the school boss and students with puddin' guns, but the crowd only grew larger and angrier. The Puddin' Heads rocked the helicopter, chanting, "Crash! Crash! Crash!" as it swayed.

Blaze and her team had thwarted a version of absurd disturbing we had not hitherto seen. But I'm very sorry and saddened to report that Blaze could not save everyone from an irreversible fate. Thankfully, you are a Courageous Reader. You are unafraid of the truth, right? Here you go: one Puddin' Head—who later renamed himself Nub—achieved misguided success by reaching the spinning blades with the tip of his longest finger.

Don't say I didn't warn you about *absurd disturbing*.

The crowd cheered and hurled Nub into the students on the right side of the landing skid, toppling them like bowling pins. The helicopter seesawed, lifted off the ground, and flung off the students on the other side. One Puddin' Head dangled from the rising helicopter (both hands intact) before plummeting into the crowd.

The mob cried, but then cheered once more. You see, Nub proudly raised a bloody insult: a middle finger that was longer—no longer.

S4 TRYOUTS
S4, Day 1

Traumatized by the attack on the helicopter, we unanimously agreed we would take the train to Sweetie Island Region 4, even though it would be a lengthy trip. First, Blaze, Chopper, and I raced on solar bikes toward the Boulder Pass Train Stop.

"Puddin' Brains High School was a bit of a setback," Blaze said, pursing her lips.

"You think?" Chopper said.

"Puddin' balls! We made progress with Freedom High School and even at the Region 4 tryouts—Bigs and Smalls started working together as equals to defeat the Sweeties. Then that Puddin' Brains boss messed everything up. She fired what seemed to be a good teacher and somehow got the Bigs and Smalls to work together—but only—by convincing Bigs to lop off their fingers. Where do people get these crazy ideas about how to beat the Sweeties? Why do other people believe them? Puddin' Head schools are more complicated than I thought."

She sighed and cruised for a while, lost in thought. Then she perked up. "But this is good for our report, right? I mean, who's going to argue *that* school was good for kids? Who's going to argue to keep the stupid hand size rules now? Pompavich needs to go! That school boss needs to go! Should we let Puddin' Head News know about this?"

"No, I think Scarlet got the point across," Chopper said. "Let's add this to our mountain of evidence for our report and blow the prime minister away. Besides, they don't have anything left to cause harm."

Blaze shuddered. I took deep breaths to prevent an episode. In case you're wondering, I didn't enter any chill bird trance, nor did I see a genie.

Scarlet boarded at Power Island, riding a supercharged racing motorcycle. "What?" she said to our shocked faces, then rolling eyeballs.

When Kai got on at Sweetie Island, Blaze preemptively said, "I don't want to talk about it."

"You mean, you don't want to talk about the fact that Puddin' Head schools are—" Kai started.

"Okay, okay, no need to rehash the past," Chopper said. "We have Sweetie Island Region 4 results to review."

Sweetie Island Region 4
Student Survey Results

	All Students Agreeing	Bigs Agreeing	Smalls Agreeing
School is affordable	57%	32%	80%
School is fair	79%	72%	85%
School is fun, useful, and interesting	76%	72%	80%

Response Rate = 94%

Kai said, "Interesting. Similar to Puddin' Head Region 4." Then, he shattered any hope of moving past the past. "But, I'm pretty sure we won't be attacked by dynamite-launching lunatics or fingerless fanatics. I mean, what was that?"

"*That* was a bunch of Puddin' Heads confused by the Sweeties!" Blaze said.

"Oh, Blaze," Kai said. "Like I've said all along, the problem with Puddin' Heads is . . . well, they're *Puddin' Heads.*"

Blaze rolled her eyes, then glared at Scarlet. "One thing we know for sure is that these school bosses—these supposed leaders —should all be fired. Why doesn't your mom fire them? Yet one more reason I should be in charge!"

"Hey, School Boss Keen had excellent survey results!"

Blaze thought for a moment. "Which makes no sense. And it makes their survey results meaningless."

"Hey, now," Chopper said. "We had a high response rate. And what we saw helps explain why the results were so high."

"If you mean that Puddin' Heads are numbskulls . . ." Kai paused for effect and flashed a sarcastic smile, "then I agree."

"Yeah, you can't have it both ways, Blaze," Scarlet said. "Either the survey results are valid, or they aren't."

"Oh, they're valid," Chopper said. "And the open-ended results corroborate what we observed."

"Corroborate?" Kai said. "I guess that means the survey and the visit both show that Puddin' Heads are indeed numbskulls."

Blaze booted a football against the side door, then the other side door. "It just means that someone needs to take charge, fire the school bosses, and tell schools what to do! Can we just play this Noble Deed Match already!"

Kai widened his eyes. "Chill, bird."

"Aren't we supposed to be analyzing survey results from Sweetie Region 4 right now?" Blaze yelled.

Here's the short version: The most interesting pattern was that many—but not all—Sweetie Bigs felt optimistic about vague opportunities to reduce their hand size . . .

Now, as for the Sweetie Island, Region 4 tryouts . . .

The train slowed to a stop at Herbville. Blaze peered outside. "Oh no."

Several hundred blue-robed Sweeties had traveled from Region 3. They sat crossed legged in circles, chanting, "All you need is love. All you need is love." Apparently, word had spread that the team would be stopping in Region 4.

"Back for more, eh?" Blaze pushed Scarlet and jumped off the train. Several blue robes snarled, rubbing their swollen hands and heads. Root-Woot waved his arms in a circle, and everyone resumed chanting. Scarlet shot out of the train doing a wheelie. Kai shook his head, walking past his fellow islanders.

Suddenly, a group of Sweeties wearing face paint of various colors (except red) surrounded Kai. They wore tall, pointy hats with blue- and white-stripes, shiny blue jackets, shiny blue shirts, and shiny blue pants, as well as boots painted with bright flowers.

"It is Kai, son of Aquarius!" one called exaggeratedly.

"Aquarius?" Kai said.

"Our great leader speaks!" They bowed, rose, stuck out their tongues, danced like a flock of chickens, turned themselves around, and all fell down. They jumped up, punched the air, and cried, "Heigi hooga!"

Then, they hoisted Kai up and carried him away, tossing him up and down. "Heigi hooga!" they cheered once more. An outer group surrounded them, faced outward and, fell down, then jumped up, punched the air, and yelled, "Heigi hooga!" as if warning everyone to stay away.

Blaze said to Chopper, "Why do I feel like someone's following another stupid version of MC Emergency Procedures?"

The shiny blue group erupted into an exaggerated, synchronized dance that opened up for Kai to launch into a full sprint, followed by cartwheels, a backflip, and a round off. He nailed the landing.

"Heigi hooga!" the shiny blue group cheered.

More impressively, several thousand Region 4 sweeties wearing blue shirts cheered. Then, they jumped up and down, turned themselves around, and all fell down.

"Heigi hooga!" several thousand Sweeties sang together.

"Now that's what I'm talking about!" Kai cried. "Chopper, where's that megaphone?"

Then, the Sweetie crowd recognized Blaze, perhaps from Scarlet's Mega Gossip posts. They booed loudly and surrounded Blaze like a swarm of friendly bees, tossing her back onto the train.

"Heigi hooga!"

Root-Woot saw his opportunity, waved his arm, and blue-robed Sweeties rushed over to block the door.

"What happened to kindness?" Blaze banged on the door. Soon, she gave up, and watched sadly through the window like a kid staying in from recess. Blaze said, "Your tryouts are futile! You'll never win!"

The Sweeties grabbed bags of footballs and emptied them like it was their collective birthday. They kicked the balls and chased each other like little kids playing football for the first time—who, as anyone who has ever watched little kids play football knows, also look like friendly, bumbling bees.

"Hey! We have a protocol here!" Chopper didn't have time for giggles and games, but the Sweeties were having too much fun to care. Even Kai joined in. At one point, several thousand Sweeties gathered into a giant, smashed, and swaying circle. They draped their arms around each other's shoulders and sang in unison.

Mess with one Sweetie, mess with us all!
Hit one hand, that's our call.
Launch a Sweetie, time for football!
Sweetie, heigi!
Hooga, ho!
Football win,
Here we go!

After five rounds of this contagious singing, a large portion of the blue-robed Sweeties stood up and joined. Root-Woot, however, immediately shut them down with a fierce wave of his hand. After a few more rounds, the increasingly obnoxious choir finally stopped, then burst into another, "Heigi hooga!" and then, "Kai! Kai! Kai!" followed by, "Teach us! Teach us!"—because they had no idea what football was or how to play.

Their performance was pathetic. There were too many ball whiffs, sprained ankles, broken toes, swollen shins, concussions, and miscellaneous injuries to count. Eventually, Blaze snuck back onto the pitch and broke four Sweeties' ankles with misdirection jukes. But one blue-robed Sweetie turned out to have ridiculous, sweeping defensive skills, defending the goal like a spoon hat prevents mean noogies. He stopped Blaze twice and nearly thwarted Scarlet. And his name was Root-Woot, protector of creatures and trees.

Blaze endured several minutes of insults, but a slow-moving hive of Sweeties carried her back to the train. "Heigi hooga!" they said, tossing her back aboard. After watching Scarlet score on ten more Sweeties, the rest said thanks but no thanks. No one scored on Kai.

Kai was all smiles, which seemed odd given the pathetic tryouts. But then again, he wasn't so happy the next day, when we visited Sweetie Experimental High School.

Scarlet acted like she'd been waiting for days as we neared Sweetie Experimental High School. Fragrant herbs and spices filled the air. Hundreds of students hunched over various plots of land, gardening. One area was surrounded by a tall fence with a sign that read Keep Out: Authorized Students Only.

"No morning child labor!" Scarlet protested as she cruised by in a low gear.

The campus featured a large outdoor gathering area and four separate buildings. The school boss quickly introduced herself and the (small-handed) team leaders and walked briskly to the first part of the tour as if eager to get this over with.

"We are proud of our experimental work," the school boss explained, offering a box of chocolate chip cookies. "Try one."

Blaze and Chopper refused. Kai, Scarlet, and I weren't going to pass. They were delicious, but strangely made me feel edgy.

Scarlet munched down a cookie, widened her eyes, and cried, "*So good*!" Suddenly, she slapped Kai.

"Ow! They aren't that good! What's your deal?!" Kai said, rubbing his cheek.

Blaze, Chopper, and I exchanged glances.

"Oh my—I'm so sorry! I don't know what overcame me." She gawked at the school boss. "I must have them!"

"Uh . . . I see you like them. You can take a box at the end of the tour. I can't recall what booster was mixed with these cookies, but I do know they were developed with rabbit manure from pen nine." He pointed to a rabbit pen, then said, "No, I think they're from pen eight."

"What! These cookies are made with rabbit poop!" Scarlet started gagging. "How is that possible?!"

"No, no, no! The rabbit manure fertilized the cocoa plants that made the chocolate for these cookies. Rabbit poop in cookies, ha!"

"I knew that!" Scarlet said, grabbing four more cookies.

"Anyway, experimental cookies are a small operation. We have a much larger production of honey, herbs, and spices—over 50 percent of these goods come from Region 4. You see, a great deal of innovation and product originates from this campus."

"Spices? I thought Sweeties hate spices." Blaze said.

"Sweeties like some spices, you numbskull," Kai said.

The school boss chuckled. "Oh, our hot spices are not for Sweeties. Who would ruin their food with flaming-hot spice other than Puddin' Heads? Their Region 3 is our biggest customer."

Blaze thought of Wheels and the dynamite chips.

"What?" Kai said. "Why are you—I should say, why are *students* —making stuff for Puddin' Heads?! They're the enemy!"

"That may be, but without those sales, school tuition would be even higher, especially for Bigs."

"Uh huh. And let me guess, the Bigs are the only ones working these plots!"

"Actually, we have so many plots, the Smalls have to work them, too. But, of course, few Smalls choose to experiment with hot peppers! The Bigs have to do that. But these profits not only pay tuition, they fund our larger, shared vision and priority: our top secret experiments. And believe me, Bigs want to be first in line once we're successful. That's why so many stay. And why so many transfer here."

"What the puddin' balls is she talking about?" Blaze asked Chopper.

"No idea."

After watching the beehives and the student beekeepers from a safe distance, we followed a student leader on a tour of various plots that grew hundreds of experimental herbs. "What are these used for?" Blaze asked.

"To make food taste better. And booster, of course: chill, relax, focus, energize—you name it, we probably make it."

Chopper tested this idea. "Silly Sweetie?"

"Yep."

"Numb numb skull?"

"Yep."

"No noggin?"

"Yes."

"Skull fortifier?"

"Uh huh."

"Hand-shrinking?"

"Yep."

"Hand-increasing?"

The student adjusted her MC Frames. "Yep."

We looked at each other in confusion. "You make hand-shrinking *and* hand-increasing booster?" Blaze asked.

"Certainly. And after what we just learned about Puddin' Head Region 4, our hand-shrinking experiments are high priority. Finger chopping! I mean, really, what lengths will those knuckleheads go to?"

"Finger chopping is not allowed!" Scarlet said. "It was in the memo—"

The school boss cut her off. "I read the memo. No one is chopping fingers here. Okay, I think we've heard enough about herbs. You were asking about spices. Let's head over there."

"Why would they make both hand-shrinking *and* hand-increasing booster?" Blaze asked Chopper. "Puddin' balls! Remember the cookie bomb attack and the hand-increasing booster in the puddin'? This is where they made it!"

"Zombie thin skulls!" Chopper said. "But do you think that stuff actually works?"

"No, of course not! But it perpetuates the idea that hand size matters!"

"But maybe they've discovered a hand increaser—or decreaser—that works! That would devastate Puddin' Head Region 4!"

"We just need to destroy hand size rules! Then none of that will matter," Blaze said. "This is why I need to be the big boss!"

Suddenly, a shiny blue group charged toward the school. They sang an up-tempo version of "Heigi Hooga." The school boss called security, who chased them off. "That's the third time this month! So annoying!"

Kai asked, "What are they doing?"

"Protesting our experiments. They have something against progress. Ridiculous!"

Suddenly, a student dressed in what looked like a blue space suit came flailing out of the Special Projects Building. He pulled his space helmet off, yelling at the school boss, "It's not fair!"

"You're the one who got a yellow card!" the school boss called back. "You could be a hero!"

The student stomped his feet, kicking dirt at the school boss. "It's not that bad! The experiments are better. We're getting closer!" the school boss said.

The student jumped up and down, threw his head back, and yelled.

"You know other schools don't like transfers from our school! You can't afford a red card!"

The student stuck out his tongue and walked back to the building, dragging his feet and kicking more dirt. He frowned at the school boss before going inside, slamming the door behind him.

"What was that about?" Kai asked. Blaze didn't like it, either, but kept her expression neutral.

"Ah, kids. Sometimes they just need to be reminded of what's important." The school boss turned to a student leader. "Do you want to tell them about your experiments? Way over there."

A tall, thin Small led us toward a plot with tall, thin trees. A group of blue-robed Sweeties chanted in protest as students cut down trees.

"This is bamboo," the student leader shared. "Very durable and versatile. We started growing it a few years ago. Wow it grows fast! We've learned to cultivate the strongest variety. And we're experimenting with different uses for it."

Kai sighed. "And what *is* it used for?"

"Right now, it's extremely useful for building materials, boats, incense, and catapults. We're experimenting with other uses for it as well. Puddin' Head Region 5 just ordered a large shipment of our strongest bamboo sticks. It's fantastic money for our tuition and our experiments."

"What?! You have catapults?"

Blaze and Chopper gaped at each other.

"Huh? Oh. No, catapults are for the Puddin' Heads. I don't understand their purpose myself—must be a Puddin' Head hobby. But who cares? It's not like they shrink hands. And the profit margins are incredible. But did you hear this rumor about Freedom High—"

"Ahhhhh!" Kai yelled. "What is *wrong* with you people? *My* people!" He yanked a corner of Blaze's black shirt. "Don't you see? Don't you see this Puddin' Head oppression! This is why we have to destroy you in the Noble Deed Match!"

"Okay, okay, I can see it's getting a little spicy around here," the school boss chuckled. "Oh, look at the time. I think we're done with the tour."

"Uh . . . No, we're not," said Chopper. "We still need to see that next." He pointed to the Hot Spice Building.

"I don't think that's necessary—"

"To the spice building!" Blaze cried. We shook our heads and jogged after her.

The Hot Spice Building had an enormous picture of a dynamite stick on the door. "I suggest you put these on." A student handed us each a thick mask. I placed mine over my mouth and nose.

Inside, about fifty students gathered at different stations. Most of them were Bigs and crying from inhaling or touching hot peppers. "Why aren't they wearing masks?" Blaze asked.

"It reduces their immunity. They'll build it up over time," the student said. "And hot spices might increase or decrease hand size —we aren't sure yet. You're only here for the day, so better to wear a mask."

At one station, students chopped peppers and placed them into small bowls. In another, students tied peppers to a string and hung them to dry. At the grinding station, students ground dried peppers into powder and placed them into labeled containers. In another large area, Bigs sitting next to several jugs of water taste-tested the spicy powder and ground-up peppers.

"We have a very rigorous testing method. Each container has four reviewers, who rate each sample on a scale from one to one hundred, with one hundred being the hottest. These independent ratings are displayed on that monitor, and a result is only counted as valid if all reviewers are calibrated within three points of each other. This allows us to accurately label and package one hundred levels of hot spice jars."

"I thought there were only five categories," Scarlet said.

"Those are the dynamite categories. But we don't stop there. Each category has about twenty levels of hotness. You want to taste the difference between an eighty-five and a one hundred?"

The team violently shook their heads. "I'm good," said Kai, growing angrier by the minute. "But Blaze here, loves hot spices. Isn't that right, Blaze?"

"Nah, I'm good. Already got my fair share."

A large monitor flashed the last results as four reviewers chugged jugs of water: *Ghost Pepper. Plot 42. Sample S4-358*. Then, it listed the reviewers' names next to their hot spice ratings: *89, 91, 91, 98*. The 98 rating, along with the reviewer's name flashed in blue.

"Azalea, this is the second time," said a teacher. "I'm sorry, but no more warnings." The teacher reached for her back pocket.

"No, no. Wait, I just need more practice!" the student looked at her teacher desperately.

"Sorry. Rules are rules." The teacher held up a yellow card. Azalea smacked an open container of chopped ghost peppers, which sprayed the unmasked teacher and our tour group. Then, Azalea fled the room shouting, "*Not fair*!"

Fortunately, our masks and MC Frames saved our eyes, mouths, and noses from the ghost pepper. But the teacher caught a large piece in her gaping mouth and made the mistake of slugging down water and swallowing it instead of spitting the pepper out. She blinked, realized her mistake, and tore from the building. The rest of us frantically wiped the burning pepper pieces from our hands, arms, and legs.

I can tell you that the capsaicin oils burning my skin was no joke. The pain was ridiculous. Kai cried and dumped a jug of water down his arms. The rest of us dumped water on our arms and legs, too. Unfortunately, this only spread the burning. We sprinted from the building, ran in circles, frantically shaking our limbs, which made it worse. Finally, the tour guide gave us a neutralizing solution, which provided some relief.

Then a strange thing happened in the Special Projects Building. The space suit student flew out of the building without a helmet and a swarm of bees chasing him. With a swollen face, he stripped off the rest of his protective suit that buzzed with bees. He stared at his very puffy hands and cried, "That experiment didn't work!"

Azalea and other students poured out of the building behind him, pursued by buzzing and stinging bees. Azalea hid behind Kai. "Take me with you!"

Teachers in lab coats ran with colorful concoctions splashing from beakers. A skeletal student with MC Frames and four arms bounded away, trying to swat bees. One student's skin was the color of a blueberry. Another student had hands that seemed to be permanently balled into fists. But the most shocking student came gliding out of the building with very long, enlarged eyes, a face completely covered in fuzz, and tiny, fuzzy hands. Surely, she was changing into a bee. Bees buzzed around her as though she were their queen.

"What *is* this freak show?" Kai cried in horror. It was a terrible sight. My eyes were going crazy.

"Nothing to see here. Nothing to see." The school boss shooed away the bees and then hurried the Special Projects escapees toward the bamboo patch.

Kai chased after the school boss. I karaoked triple time to the box of chocolate chip cookies he dropped.

"Wow, Sweeties *are* the real numbskulls!" Blaze said.

Then, another strange thing happened. A bee stung Blaze underneath her right eye, just below her MC Frames. Suddenly, the right side of her face swelled up as if Absurdity itself had landed a precise blow. Her left side remained normal. She looked like half a freak show. Blaze yanked off her Frames, which now didn't fit. "I can't see out of my right eye!" she hollered.

Kai shouted at the school boss. "Are these all Bigs?!"

"Yes, but they got yellow cards!" the school boss said, running in zig zags. "Most Bigs are very happy here. With a small number of sacrifices, we'll eventually find the cure for large hands. This is our shared mission! That's where the money is. And that's how we will ultimately defeat the Puddin' Heads. Imagine, every Sweetie in Region 4—or the entire island—with small hands! The Puddin' Heads will be destroyed!"

The school boss stopped and turned to Kai. "It's not going to happen through a numbskull competitive football game."

"What is happening?" Blaze wailed to Chopper, touching her very puffy right eye.

"How is this legal?" Kai said. He turned and glared at Scarlet.

Scarlet wagged her finger. "First of all, you're required to promote the Noble Deed Football Match. Second, yes, technically, all these different methods of reducing hand size are allowed." She blew a bubble and sucked it in. "Although, I don't know about Fist Boy and Bee Girl. That could be a small hands violation."

Blaze told me that when she walked into her home that evening, Maya screamed and ran to her room. Her mom gasped and jumped out her seat. Blaze tried to explain what had happened, and her mom said this new job was becoming too dangerous—that she should simply go back to school, stay out of trouble, and find a job later, just like every other kid.

Looking out of her one good eye, Blaze argued that this was another example of why her job was so important and why the Puddin' Heads needed to win the Noble Deed Match. Her mom said Blaze would have the advantage, because the Sweeties would take one look at her face and run away. Then, she gave her a bowl of chocolate puddin' with no pain booster and handed her a bag of ice. She stacked some extra pillows on Blaze's bed and told her to sleep with her head propped up to reduce the swelling.

Blaze did not sleep well. Her mind buzzed with the ridiculous things she'd seen in Sweetie Island Region 4—especially the girl who looked like a bee. What if the school boss was right? What if the Sweeties did find a "cure" for large hands? Would it spread throughout Sweetie Island, and then Puddin' Head Island? Would everyone turn into human bees? She imagined growing a stinger. How would she wear pants? Blaze could not let this happen.

By the time Blaze and Chopper stepped onto the train the next day, Blaze was as worked up as her face was puffy.

Kai welcomed her aboard. "Nice face."

She frowned, unable to think of a witty reply. "Your island is turning into a hand-shrinking freak show."

Kai punched his hand. "Yeah, we've got some work to do," he acknowledged for the first time. "But then again, we aren't chopping off our fingers."

"Which is illegal!" Scarlet chimed in.

"Sweeties created a bee girl!"

"Which is probably also illegal," Scarlet warned.

"Blaze, I don't know why you're so upset about the Sweeties," Kai said. "Other than your face, I mean. If I were you, I'd be more upset about the Puddin' Heads. About the incessant testing. The finger chopping. The dynamite throwing. The sea monster believing. Need I continue?"

"Because of Sweeties!"

"Oh, come on, Blaze—just own it! That's what *I'm* trying to do! You think I like to see my people—Bigs, Smalls, all of them—experimenting like this, turning into bees, blueberries, and four-armed walking sticks? Of course not! And that's exactly why Sweeties need to win the Noble Deed Match, so I can take charge, and put an end to this absurdity."

"Noble Deed rivalry—woo-hoo!" Scarlet cheered.

Blaze barked a loud laugh, then winced and put her ice pack back on her face. "Yeah, let's give the Sweeties prize money to spread those brilliant ideas. Yes, I'll admit those Sweetie experiments made me sick, but that's exactly why we can't have Sweeties in charge! Anyway, it doesn't matter. You have no chance of winning."

"We'll see. I like my chances, zombie face."

"Okay, chill, love birds," Chopper said. "We'll play that match soon enough. We only have to visit each island's Region 5. The better our tour, the better our case. Now, can we review the data already?"

Puddin' Head Island, Region 5
Student Survey Results

	All Students Agreeing	Bigs Agreeing	Smalls Agreeing
School is affordable	80%	60%	97%
School is fair	53%	8%	95%
School is fun, useful, and interesting	47%	2%	95%

Response Rate = 90%

The team tried to make sense of these massive discrepancies. "A lot of Bigs are complaining about head injuries and headaches. That might explain it. But what are they doing to injure their heads?" Blaze said.

"Maybe they were stung by swarms of bees that confused their giant puddin' heads for beehives," Kai suggested.

Blaze gave him a dirty look, but due to the swelling, succeeding only in making Kai laugh. "Or maybe . . ." She tilted her head and paused, as if thinking of something clever to say. "Maybe they ate zombie brains as the secret to growing powerful and overthrowing Sweetie Island."

Chopper and Scarlet raised their eyebrows at each other. Kai regarded her blankly. "Yeahhh . . . Blaze solved the mystery. Guess we can go home now."

"Oh no. We are going to see this through," Chopper said.

Scarlet blasted off the train at Hard Rocks depot, bumping Blaze who nearly crashed, but corrected her steering, then stopped. An ambulance from Hard Rocks Hospital blared past.

"Huh, that's weird," Chopper said, staring after it. Indeed, it was. No other region on either island had its own hospital. The main hospital was located on Power Island and was too expensive for most islanders to afford (unless they went to the emergency room, in which case it came out of citizens' taxes).

More than one hundred Puddin' Head students waited for tryouts. About half of them had odd heads. Some noggins had large lumps, some had band-aids, and some were wrapped with a bandage. It was if they had been caught in a bad rock shower without an umbrella, although they appeared otherwise uninjured.

"Nice bike," one said to Scarlet. "Time for a spin." He snatched the keys, pushed Scarlet to the ground, raced it about twenty meters, crashing into a tree.

"You destroyed my motorcycle!" Scarlet cried. "And that's why you wear a helmet!"

"Ah, but look!" one said.

"Yeah, that's a nice lump," another admired.

We exchanged glances, as if recognizing a warning.

Blaze immediately noticed that many Bigs were highly motivated to join her team. They wanted to know if they could transfer to another region if they made the team and won against the Sweeties. As they would win a Noble Deed, Blaze said she didn't see why not.

Blaze and Chopper were very excited to discover a Big trio with football heading skills so unusual, it was as if their noggins had adapted to extreme conditions. These three wore no bandages or had any sign of head inflammation. Ram boasted a large, thick skull and an unusually thick neck—like she'd been born to, well, ram things. Crusher had a square head resembling that of Mr. Puddin' Head. She crushed anything that came near her noggin, including one header that drilled Kai in the knee. He hobbled off the pitch whining, "Haven't we seen enough already?" And then there was Rock Hammer—Hammer, for short. Whereas Ram and Crusher used brute force to crush headers, Hammer drilled headers not so much like a sledgehammer, but more like a precision hammer, or a woodpecker.

In contrast to their absurdly talented peers, many of the other Bigs complained of dizziness, headaches, and fainting spells. These issues became abundantly clear during the heading portion of the day, which was led by Scarlet. She kicked the ball like it had been shot out of a cannon. Some winced, some ran away, and more than a dozen were knocked unconscious.

Strangely, the ambulance medics hauled them off on stretchers while chatting about their family squabbles, or new kinds of puddin', as if they were just taking a walk in the park. Puddin' Heads falling over from head injuries seemed to just be something that happened in Region 5.

Oddly, none of this was the highlight of the day. That was another Puddin' Head who literally stood out. He was more than two meters tall, and his wingspan was wider. Somehow—fortunately for football, but not so fortunate for life on Island Nation—his hands were disproportionately larger than the rest of his hulking frame. Thus, he was nicknamed Hands. Blaze and Chopper immediately had the same thought. *Can this guy play goalie?* Their question was quickly answered.

After scoring hundreds of goals on Puddin' Heads and Sweeties over the past few days—with the best barely getting a finger or toe on the ball before it scorched the net—Scarlet initially scoffed at Hands. She lined up the ball for a penalty shot. She confidently crushed a ball into the upper right part of the goal. Then, the impossible happened. Hands took a quick step, lunged, and caught the ball with one hand.

Everyone froze. Mouths dropped open. All eyes watched as Hands palmed the football in his humongous hand. He squeezed it. It popped like a balloon. The crowd erupted into cheers, high fives, and head butts, which led to multiple concussions. Another ambulance was called.

Scarlet picked her jaw up off the ground, shook her head, and wagged her finger at the crowd, who stared back with their MC Frames. "Do not post that! Do *not* post that! My foot got caught on that patch of grass." She kicked the alleged patch and moved the ball away from it with a grunt.

Hands pointed at Scarlet. "Again."

Scarlet drilled a perfect shot into the lower left corner. Hands dove and swatted the ball like a gigantic fly swatter swats a tiny fly. The crowd went ballistic.

Scarlet suddenly grabbed her foot, plopping to the ground as if in pain. She *was* in pain—just not the physical kind. "Ah! I twisted my ankle," she wailed. "I injured it earlier today. And I . . . I thought I would play through the pain."

Blaze rolled her eyes, did a little dance, and smiled widely with the unswollen side of her face. A medic left a batch of semi-conscious Puddin' Heads, wrapped Scarlet's ankle, and gave her a pair of crutches. Scarlet insisted that the ambulance drop her off at the train station.

She pouted against her crutches during the long train ride home. Blaze hadn't stopped half-grinning and said to Chopper, "We found our goalie. Any chance those Sweeties had, just vanished." Then, she stopped smiling. "But what's up with all their head injuries?"

HARD ROCKS HIGH SCHOOL
PH5, Day 2

Scarlet was miraculously recovered by the next day. "I'm fine now!" Of course, she had a backup supercharged motorcycle. After a short ride, —which took Scarlet about 47 seconds—we approached Hard Rocks High School as an ambulance shot past us. Courageous Reader, I hope your spoon helmet is still strapped on.

The dilapidated school had boarded windows, crumbling brick corners, and a rusted tin roof. Two ambulances sat parked in the front. We coughed and waved away the thick dust in the air as we rode down the driveway.

The school boss ambled out with wide eyes and half-open arms, as if looking for someone to wrestle. If he were a clown at a three-year-old's birthday party, they might laugh at first glance. But then, they would surely cry, because even three-year-olds would sense that he was creepy. His head had two large lumps—like a camel with misplaced humps. Every so often, he would twitch his head to the side. At the same time, his right eye bobbed up and down or left and right and then returned to its original place. His mouth was open slightly and curled up on one side.

He seemed to recognize Blaze and shot out a hand to shake but misjudged the distance and poked her in the gut, where her guitar strap hung. "Arrrr! Sorry! My eyesight is a little off since that last head banger! Gotta lead by example, if you know what I mean!" Blaze shook his hand. "Name's School Boss J.RRRR."

"Does this guy think he's a pirate?" Blaze whispered to Chopper, who shrugged.

"School Boss J.R.?" Blaze asked.

"Aye. J.RRRR. I used to have a full name, but, aye, that rock bucket to the head. Shook the letters right off my name! Now, I just got two left!" He barked loudly and slapped Blaze on the back, just missing her guitar. "Oh, looks like you took one to the face here," he said, placing his dirty fingers on her still slightly swollen half face.

"Ah!" Blaze winced.

"Aye—but someone missed your head!"

We exchanged worried glances. Several Puddin' Heads, including

Ram, ran out of the school in torn red clothing and stood beside School Boss J.R. Two hobbled out on crutches.

The fastest one skidded next to Kai, shooting another cloud of dust into the air. Kai coughed as this Small smelled his shirt , laughing to the others, "Clean. Fresh meat."

Kai uneasily nudged the student away. "A little space, please."

"Why are you on crutches?" School Boss J.R. asked a student.

"Keep losing my balance."

"Ram clocked me in the knee," said another.

"*Arrrr*!" The school boss shook his head, patting Ram on the head. "Head shots. Gotta work on your head shots."

"Yes, sir— But it still builds character."

"Aye. True that." School Boss J.R. got down to business. "Listen, I heard about your little visit to Region 4. Finger chopping. School Boss Keen—what a numbskull!" The school boss slapped Ram on the back of the head angrily. "And those stupid spoon hats. Even got those in Region 3, I heard. They just don't get it do they?" Ram vigorously shook her head.

Temporarily relieved that he wasn't about to be eaten, Kai leaned in to hear this theory, as did the rest of us.

"Now, look, I'm no thin skull. I know about Sweetie attacks. The Sweetie experiments. Tryin' to shrink their hands, but that's just a distractation from the real threatation. They're over there building a nation of brain-sucking zombies, but we'll be ready. Arrrr!"

Kai sighed and hung his head.

The school boss drew a bamboo stick spoon from a sheath strapped to his back and whirled it around poorly. "Sure, you can blow up the zombies, but they're too clever to attack during the day." Blaze raised an eyebrow at Chopper, thinking of the unsuccessful, blue-robed Sweetie protest.

"Guess where that stick came from?" Kai whispered to Blaze.

"They attack at night. And we'll be ready to give them a good spankation. But not with some ridiculation giant spoon hat or helmet." The school boss laughed. "No, we're going to fight them with spoon handles and, more importantly, with thick skulls!" He held up the bamboo spoon handle.

"Thick skulls," Kai nodded with a little too much sarcastic agreement.

"Aye, thick skulls!" Then, School Boss J.R. noticed Kai's black shirt. "Why isn't this kid wearing red?"

"I told him to, but he just wouldn't listen," Blaze said.

The other students, who were mostly Bigs, jumped up and down with wide eyes, calling back and forth "Woo! Woo! Woo!" like wild animals on the hunt. They had bruised and lumpy heads, and four sported black eyes.

The kid who'd called Kai fresh meat widened his eyes like he *was* going to eat him. His friends jumped up and down, grunting "Woo! Woo!" faster. He stepped closer and lifted Kai's top lip with two fingers, exposing his teeth. "Shhhhh," he said. His friends jumped and barked with excitement, anticipating a fight.

"All right, George, calm down," School Boss J.R. said. "They're just visiting. Give them a tour. They might get us some money or something. Isn't that right, Blaze?"

She nodded.

George said, "Wait, is you Blaze Union—the one who destroyed Sugar Falls?!"

Blaze nodded again.

"Wow! Great to meet in real person! Epic battle! We just named a new level after you."

"Level?"

George noticed Blaze's Frames. "Yeah. Huh. Didn't think that was possible." George poked Blaze's face. "Ah, took a couple rocks, eh? Well, come on in and let us know how we can help!" He slugged Blaze in the arm.

She hid the pain. "Nice one. What's up with the ambulances?"

"You'll see."

We followed George and his entourage into the school. Half the rooms had dusty, dirty floors; the other half had hard dirt floors. Dull, faded paint clung to the walls, which revealed an occasional rat hole. Sunlight glowed faintly through a patchwork ceiling.

George escorted us to a rundown gym. He laughed heartily. "Ha! One of my favorites—dodge rod!"

About forty students ran wildly around the gym. Half of them —the Smalls—wielded bamboo rods about three centimeters thick. Some had spoon handles. They yelled, taunted, and tagged each other out with a swift whack to the head.

One struck his peer in the back. "Take that, eggshell-skull, cookie-eating zombie!"

The teacher yelled, "Headshots only!"

A fiery student whirled two rods like a pro. Within seconds, she struck five Bigs across the head with ruthless efficacy, exclaiming, "Yah!" with each strike. Students tried to block, run, or fight back, but she mowed them down like a scythe cuts grass. The rats fared no better. She spun and killed two that had the misfortune of poking their heads out from holes. Finally, she wielded a two-handed chop to the crown of the remaining Big's head. He fell to the ground, instinctively covered his head, and screeched, "Gahhhh! I'll get you someday!" He crawled to the wall with one hand on his head and flung the dead rats into the corner. He slid to the ground, applauding the victor with the others.

"Did you see that?" George said. "Those new bamboo sticks didn't even break!"

"Ahhh!" Kai cried.

"This kid is weird." George frowned at Kai.

"Where is Root-Woot when you need him?" Kai mumbled.

"Root what? You got a problem!"

"What? Shhh," Kai said as if annoyed. "I'm trying to learn here."

The teacher congratulated the winner. But instead of a pat on the back, she said, "Now it's your turn." She hailed the victor with a rod crack to the skull. The student winced and said, "Thank you."

FIRING SQUAD
PH5, Day 2, Continued

By this point in the story, you are likely shocked and appalled (don't say I didn't warn you!). Perhaps you think you would never crack your friends' noggins with a stick. Your teachers would never teach that. Your school bosses would never allow that. But you didn't grow up, learn to teach, or learn to boss in Region 5. This also might be a good time to—if you haven't already—write those thank you cards.

George and Ram applauded with the other students. George said, "Now that Puddin' Head's got talent. One to watch, right there."

In bewilderment, Blaze placed her hand on Chopper's shoulder. "Should we do something?" I wondered the same, but I was too stunned to do anything. Once again, my eyes were going crazy. My surly sweet tooth would have done anything for a large bowl of chocolate puddin'. Chopper gazed at the bamboo rods lying on the floor, shook his head, and swallowed. "Uh, I think that would be a mistake." Relieved, we quickly followed George to the next class.

"That was a warm-up. Now, this is hard rocks class—the ultimate skull fortifyin' and Sweetie preparation class. When those zombie Sweeties attack, they won't have no brain sucking from our thick skulls. Strongest, hardest, toughest-working kids on the island, right here, Bigs and Smalls alike.

"Not my idea of working together . . ." Blaze mumbled to Chopper.

Kai chuckled and muttered to himself. "If I were a zombie, I would suck brains through the eyes. Skull thickness wouldn't matter."

"Something funny there, pretty boy?" George barked. "What town is you from again?"

"Nothing funny here. Nope, nothing funny here. Nothing funny at all."

Sensing things could get ugly, real fast, Chopper interjected, "Kai is coming with us from Courage City. You know, on the left side of the island, eh he. We've never seen kids so tough before."

George grinned and nodded, "That so?"

Kai nodded in return and said, "I can't wait to see this class" with a hint of sarcasm, but not enough for George to notice.

George explained the basic sequence: "Skull breakdown, puddin' and booster recovery, repeat. It's that simple. Most people don't realize the skull is actufully an extra-strong muscle. Break it down, eat puddin' with skull fortifier, rest, repeat. People forget to rest—that is when your skull rebuilds itself, strong. Now the key here is you got to build up to it, one level at a time. Everybody wants to be at a level seven, well now, level eight. But you got to work for it. You can't skip from level three to level eight or guess what happens? Ambulance time."

"You said 'everyone.' Bigs and Smalls do this?" Blaze asked.

"Well, of course, Smalls have the first choice, so we usually chose a differentfully training. But we aren't as tasty to zombies, so the levels don't matter as much for us. But some of us Smalls, like me, we want the full training. You seen School Boss J.R., right? He's a Small and completed all the training, even level eight. And he hasn't stopped. Now, that's a leader by example!"

George passionately elaborated. He explained that the first three levels increase board thickness for head boarding. (Dodge rod was a warm-up—it didn't even count). At level four and beyond, students move to rock bashing, with increasing rock weight and decreasing rock bag thickness. At level seven, gifted and talented students elevated to the rock firing squad. "And the most talented now try for level eight, which we named after you Blaze, after the Battle of Sugar Falls: the flaming rock cymbals challenge."

"What? No."

"Yeah, it's true—you're an inspiratation, Blaze!"

Blaze slapped her forehead and sighed, "I don't like the sound of that."

We followed George to the firing squad outside. I struggled to keep my twitching eyes open. It was very difficult to watch the videos later. Two Bigs lined up against a dented, boarded wall. A dried-up, dirt football pitch stood in the background. One goal post was missing, and the other rusted goal looked like it would collapse in the next strong wind.

"Ughh. What's that smell? And what's up with your football pitch?" Chopper waved a nasty, rotten smell away from his face.

George pointed to a pile of dead rats stacked against a

crumbling wall. "Got to put them somewhere. Football? Ha! Hard to play without a football. School boss says we got more important things to spend money on." George smiled as he turned back to watch the gifted students. An odd assortment of stretched, worn, and over-sized clothing—stuffed with uneven clumps of padding—protected their bodies. Torn sheets wrapped their necks and faces, leaving only their noggins exposed.

George said seriously, "School boss is saving up for better gear, but we need the ambulances. School boss says you get what you get."

Several students, including Hands, stood with piles of red rocks and googly eyes beside them.

"I have to ask," Kai said. "What's up with the rocks with eyes?"

"Ha! Finally, a good question!" George said. "Those are MC guide rocks—very special! They help with accuracy and work great with the right puddin' and booster! Expensive, but totally worth it!"

Kai raised his eyebrows toward Blaze, who puffed out her cheeks. The wrapped students quivered with anticipation. A teacher said, "Now, go easy. They just reached the gifted level. *Ready.*"

The firing squad reached into their bucket and pulled out red rocks and stones with yes, googly eyes.

"*Aim.*"

Blaze sensed what was about to happen. "Wait!" Everyone stopped and turned to her. "Uh, that's not a good idea with Hands."

"Huh?"

"He's our star goalie against the Sweeties."

The Puddin' Heads looked at her curiously.

"The zombies." Now, the Puddin' Heads nodded. "We can't risk him being injured."

Everyone agreed this was a fine idea, even though no one ever played football at this school. Hands, like Blaze, had transferred to many schools and regions, and had picked up football along the way. He joined the spectators, and the teacher didn't miss a beat.

"Actually, this isn't a good idea for anyone—" Blaze started, but it was too late.

"*Fire!*"

Chopper held Blaze back as the firing squad lobbed red stones with googly eyes at their comrades. Many missed, sporadically pelting and banging the broken-down wooden boards. One squad member hit a student on the chin, causing her to wince. Another clocked a student on the side of the head, dropping him to the ground.

I passed out, collapsing to the ground. My team decided against an ambulance and rested my head on some rocks.

"Nice shot!" someone yelled. The squad relentlessly launched ammo at the brave student still standing and whimpering about her chin. "It's for your own good!"

At last, she buckled over after taking a one-two hit to the middle and side of the head. The teacher yelled, "Great shots! *Cease-fire!*" The student fell to the ground, semi-conscious. "Ah, come on!" the teacher groused. "Ah! We're going to need medical attention. Ambulance!"

Everyone ran over to congratulate the students who were crying with pain, removing the protective layers, and gathering stones. The teacher handed them puddin' mixed with no noggin and skull-fortifying booster, which they gobbled down. A minute later, the other students lifted the gifted and talented onto stretchers, carried and cheered them to the ambulance, and then waved as they sped away.

"That's some good stuff. You can see my nice one from a few days ago." George pointed to a lump on his head.

Blaze, Chopper, and even Kai—who'd thought he'd seen it all—were speechless. Blaze began convulsing and nearly threw up. I'm sorry to say we had not yet even seen the full absurdity of Hard Rocks High.

FLAMING CYMBALS
PH5, Day 2, Continued

They roused me with a pungent booster. I wobbled after George and his entourage with an odd kink in my neck. "What did I miss?"

"We'll tell you later!" Blaze said.

"We used to have sharp rocks that tore up clothes, made cuts, blood everywhere—not helpful in skull fortifying!" George explained. "But with these MC guide rocks—nice and smooth, and the googly eyes, of course—what an improvement! Yeah, we still lose kids who can't handle pain, but they got the transfer option. This school ain't for everyone. Anyway, like I said, we just started level eight, the ultimatation expert level. So, let's go see the cymbals."

Kai tried to lighten the mood. "I thought you don't play music here," he said in jest, but also wondering if they even knew about the musical instrument.

George slugged Kai in the arm. "Music? Who said anything about music? Seems like you could use a firing squad yourself."

Kai frowned, rubbed his arm, and imagined clocking George's puddin' head with a speeding rock. But, like the tree huggers, he was badly outnumbered and deep in enemy territory.

George led us back inside to a large room. "Good timing," he said. In the middle of the room, two long red ropes were anchored to a large red ring on the ceiling. At the end of each rope was a thick red rock bag. School Boss J.R. chatted with the teacher and a nurse while two Smalls climbed bamboo ladders in different corners of the room. They used a pulley to raise the rock bags, so that they now hung like two giant pendulums. A student with large hands sat in a chair directly below the ring. She choked back tears as sweat poured down her face.

School Boss J.R. shouted, "Ready!"

"Watch the temples!" the nurse said.

George said, "Have to be careful about the temples. Learned that the hard way."

"Aim." The students pulled long lighters from their pockets and lit the rock bags on fire.

"No!" Blaze cried.

"No worries—the bag and rope are flame retardantly," George said.

Blaze tossed Chopper her guitar, and sprinted to stop what was about to happen.

"Fire!"

The students let go. The fiery bags gained momentum as they swung toward each other. Blaze tackled the student a second before the flaming cymbals collided. I threw up in a trash can.

The teacher shouted, "What are you doing?" as she extinguished the flames.

"Arrrr! String up the bags again!" School Boss J.R. called.

Blaze kicked the wall. "Flaming numbskulls!" She held up a hand as if to speak, but then paced and muttered to herself, repeatedly punching her fist into her hand. She had a funny thought. *I'd take Walka Walka over J.R. any day.*

She tried to focus. "How did Sugar Falls inspire this?" she demanded. She paced and started to say, "So you think—" but then said nothing further and moved to Ram and Hands. "There are better ways—" she said, placing her hand on Ram's shoulder and Hands's elbow, as if they were warriors about to enter battle. She paced faster, now staring at School Boss J.R. "How do you—" she stopped again. "Why is it that—" Finally, she found the words.

"I've seen a lot of stupid things on this tour. Puddin' Heads driving pencils into their hands due to daily testing. Puddin' Head Smalls shooting dynamite at Puddin' Head Bigs. Puddin' Head Bigs trying to chop their fingers off. I've seen a lot of dumb things, but this is the *dumbest* Puddin' Head school I've seen yet!" Blaze was furious but focused.

"I'd ask if you think smashing rocks into Puddin' Heads is a good idea, but obviously you do! And you know what I've learned, School Boss J.R.? All roads lead back to leadership. The good, the bad, the ridiculous—they all lead back to the leaders. And bad leaders should be fired."

"Arrrr. Watch your tongue!"

"Um, technically you're not allowed to fire—" Scarlet said, but Blaze strummed her guitar.

"But since I can't do that—" Blaze stopped strumming, glared at Scarlet, glared at the school boss, smiled, and then said, "I'll sing a song." She slipped on her MC Frames for the first time in several days. She strummed again and trotted out of the room and throughout the school. She strummed louder and louder.

School Boss J.R. grabbed a giant bamboo spoon handle and chased after her. "Arrrr! I heard about your guitar playing!" But the school boss tripped over his own feet. The spoon handle whacked him on the head. And somehow, despite his elite head bashing training, *that was the crack that broke the skull*, as they say in Region 5.

The school boss snorted, shook his head, and narrowed his eyes like a bull ready to charge. He shouted gibberish, calling everyone around him zombies, sweeties, cake lovers, and words I can't repeat. This offended even George, his most loyal follower.

The school boss collided into Hands. He looked up and suddenly wailed. He abruptly shifted into his wrestling stance, jumped left, then right, and grabbed his bamboo spoon handle off the floor. Holding it like a giant steering wheel, he galloped for the door, making monster truck noises. He raced toward it full speed. The "steering wheel"—which was locked horizontally—did not come close to clearing the entrance. Both sides slammed into the door frame. The school boss slammed into his spoon handle. It lurched forward and then sprang back. The school boss grunted and laughed for a brief, airborne moment before he crashed to the ground, cracked the back of his skull a second time, and then lay there unconscious.

"Ambulance!" the nurse called.

The massive Blaze parade grew and sang, following her through the school and around the school.

You might hope by this time in our story that Blaze would encourage her fellow Puddin' Heads to pause and reflect upon or take responsibility for their absurd beliefs and behaviors. I mean, the deranged school boss was knocked out cold. This was a fantastic opportunity to crack thickheaded absurdity about hand size wide open and bring some sanity to the madness between the Puddin' Heads and Sweeties.

Blaze aimed for one but steered clear of the other. More than anything, Blaze wanted to win the Noble Deed Match and become the next big boss of education. She wanted the entire Puddin' Head Island on her side. And she knew, at least intuitively—whether you like it or not—that little unifies people around a common cause

better than a common enemy. And so, the Puddin' Heads marched
united around a bonfire of burning bamboo sticks and spoon
handles. They sang another version of a familiar song.

You think a head that's thick
Will do the trick
To beat the zombies?

Bang your head,
Stick to the head,
Rock to the head,
Thickens a Puddin' Head?

Crack your skull?
Just makes us dull!
Big versus Small?
Divided we fall!

It makes me sick.
This twisted trick.
The Sweeties are laughing!
The zombies are laughing!

Who do we blame?
The Sweeties!
Who will we defeat?
The zombies!
Who will we beat,
In a Noble Deed meet?
The Sweeties!

SWEET PERFECTION HIGH SCHOOL
S5, Days 1 & 2

By this time on our tour—with our final stop scheduled at Softville in Sweetie Island Region 5—we were exhausted. You might be exhausted from all this absurdity. But you really don't want to miss this last bit. Chopper even agreed to skip discussing the survey results, which were notably like the other regions.

As usual, Blaze, Chopper, and I traveled to the football tryouts together. Blaze was still upset. "Chopper! What was up with Hard Rocks High! And why do all these schools completely misunderstand my messages? How did I possibly inspire flaming cymbals!"

"That was strange."

"We really need to win this Noble Deed Match. Can you imagine what it would be like with Sweeties in charge?"

Chopper shuddered.

"But obviously, that isn't going to happen!" Blaze laughed. "We have so much work to do after we win."

"Yeah. When are we going to find time to plan?"

"Planning. Right." Blaze rolled her eyes. "Oh! I just had a scary thought."

"What?"

"You know how Chill High School fought Puddin' Head ridiculous testing with that bizarre chill bird trance? And Sweet Cake Middle School did that disgusting Code Red Puddin' Head? And those blue-robed Sweeties protested at Freedom High School with those zombie moves? And Sweetie Experimental High School had those outrageous experiments, that were worse than what happened at Puddin' Brains High School?"

"Yeah, there seems to be a pattern. But what are you saying?" Chopper asked.

"Well, think of what just happened at Hard Rocks High in Region 5! What are Sweetie Region 5 schools going to be like?"

Chopper shuddered again. "Good point."

While Kai found the football tryouts to be odd and disappointing, Blaze and Chopper were relieved, at least at first. The odd flower headbands that every Sweetie wore to tryouts were indeed a welcome distraction—and a sign of what was to come. Virtually no Smalls even bothered to show up, and those that did had no interest in physical exertion.

Some disgruntled Smalls had mistaken the invitation for a great baking show. Bigs had spread rumors of the most delicious free cookies and cake imaginable. Another group cried after learning this gathering had nothing to do with an alleged new crop of singing flowers.

Suddenly, two players in shiny blue jerseys rolled in, with fanatical fans. They snapped pictures, asking for autographs, and gushing about sports ball. "Who's the Sweetie around here?" one asked. Kai excitedly talked to these presumably great athletes. But alas, Kai learned this group was a theater troupe playing a practical joke.

Only a handful of Sweeties had any clue about these tryouts, and not one stood out like Orion, Wheels, Ram, Hammer, Crusher, Hands, or Root-Woot, for that matter. To say that Kai grew more worried while Blaze grew more confident was like saying that Puddin' Heads like puddin'.

The next day we headed to Sweet Perfection High School, near the west coast. We passed fields with odd flower patches. Some patches had strong, vibrant, and colorful flowers. But others had sad, drooping, and dull flowers. None were red, of course. One group of Bigs, working in a pathetic flower patch, wove pathetic flower headbands, necklaces, and bracelets, which they would supposedly sell later at the market. "Perfect!" the teacher said.

We approached a very large bird flock that followed a class planting flower seeds. It was impossible to count the variety of species, let alone the hundreds of birds that circled and squawked. Scores more flew in from all directions as if they heard about a party with free and fabulous prizes. The teacher told the Bigs—all of whom wore lovely flower headbands—to plant seeds any way they wished and to trust nature to take care of the rest. Some planted seeds in the sand, some in rich soil, some in the shade, some in the sun. And some laughed and traipsed through the field, flinging seeds into the air. Birds dove and fought for a free breakfast faster than Scarlet shot past and missed it all.

Unfortunately, the giggles and games quickly ended. More adventuresome birds—mostly, the ones late for the party—swooped to peck seeds from the students' hands. Students panicked and threw handfuls of flower seeds into the air, which caused far greater problems when seeds landed in their hair. The aerial attacks intensified. The students cried and tried to run away.

"Perfect! Love it!" the teacher said.

"What the—" Kai said, and then asked the question on everyone's mind. "What is happening?"

"I don't think they got the chill bird lesson," Blaze laughed.

In the next field, Smalls directed Bigs to cut and gather withering flowers, even though the blue-robed Sweeties protested this vulgar destruction of nature. One kind Sweetie offered a headband too close to a visitor's hood and was thanked with a surprise twirling throw into the field, which ironically smashed more flowers than had been cut. To add insult to injury, a teacher gave this kind student a yellow card.

Feeling more assured that nothing extreme or life-threatening would happen, Blaze asked Kai a question. "How do you tell the difference?"

"Between the Bigs and Smalls? You already know the answer!"

"No, between Sweeties and flowers. Because I can't!" Blaze and Chopper high-fived and bent over laughing.

Then, a stranger thing happened. We visited a building with a very large kitchen. At first, Bigs seemed to mix cake batter and cookie dough.

A Big pulled Blaze to the side. "Thank you," she whispered.

"What? Me?" Blaze said, looking very confused. Why would a Sweetie thank her?

"I've been following you. Your messages are fantastic! Smalls bow to Bigs, *Burn the Trash*—what revolutionary ideas! The Smalls didn't know what to do! And now, I finally understand. Puddin' Heads aren't the problem—Smalls are."

"What? I didn't say that."

"They are all lazy, imbeciles!"

"Huh?"

The Big dumped a container of bugs into what might have been cookie dough.

"Great Mother of Puddin'!"

"What? No, these were already dead."

"What the—"

"You think—oh come on, I'm not a zombie. I didn't kill them!" The student stirred and offered bug dough on a stick. "Oh, you want a bite?"

"Ugh!"

"Just kidding! That's for the Smalls." The Big's smiling eyes turned vengeful. "And we're just getting started."

Upon closer examination, Bigs mixed strange combinations of ingredients for cake batter and cookie dough; they had no recipes and baked in any way they pleased. Some stirred with sticks or dried flower stems, which sometimes broke into the batter. They added flower petals, grass, sand, salt, who knows what kind of booster, and yes, bugs. They slapped something resembling icing onto something resembling cupcakes and large cakes. They packed many of these for Sweetie Region 2 Schools, who'd apparently perfected their Code Red Puddin' Head procedures.

Blaze shook her head and let out a deep belly laugh. Then she pointed to a rolling pin flattening a ball of sugar cookie dough (or was it?) and whispered something to Chopper. Blaze laughed so loud and Chopper snorted so violently the disgusting kitchen production stopped for a moment.

While some Bigs snuck to a kitchen corner and enjoyed delicious cookies, other Bigs served bake disasters with ice cream to their smaller-handed peers. On a large porch next to the kitchen, Smalls adorned with pitiful flower headbands lay on comfy couches and lounged in relaxing chairs. They all wore very soft clothing, which they discussed incessantly. *Feel this shirt, it is so soft. Wow, that is sooo soft, but feel these socks. Amazing softness! Feel these pants—they are sooo comfy and soft, I could lounge all day. We're so not Puddin' Heads! So soft! But you have to touch my robe*—And so on and so forth.

"Hey! Can we like get some cookies over here! I'm literally starving!" one Small demanded. A Big with a large grin offered a platter of cookies. "And these better not taste like yesterday!" the Small warned.

A teacher frowned, as if giving her own warning. The Small chomped half a cookie, which turned out to be extra crunchy, and perhaps sandy. As his face contorted, he cried *"Grooosssss!"*

"Red card!" the teacher screeched. "That is a perfect cookie! And that was not kind!"

The Big holding the cookie platter pursed his lips and forced an odd, disappointed expression, but nonetheless pointed. "I think you have something in your teeth," he squeaked, then turned snickering.

Yes, even with yucky, baking catastrophes, the Smalls gave compliments of perfection. *I love cookies with all this salt, or is it sand, or dirt?* And, *This twig in my cupcake is delicious.* And, *Oh, a cookie with flower leaves and sticks, how scrumptious.* And, *What is this stuck in my——, I mean, I love very crunchy cookies.*

As a side note, these Sweeties refused to use spoons or even say the word "spoon." Thus, they faced the great challenge of eating ice cream with a fork, especially as it melted beside a warm, disgusting cookie. One teacher told me that after too many instances of sticky clothing from dripping ice cream—which caused much teasing and unkindness—Region 5 had compromised and allowed sporks, although they called them "rounded forks." Even the "sp" in "spork" was too closely associated with Puddin' Heads who allegedly wielded spoon weapons and wore scratchy clothing.

"You think Puddin' Heads are numbskulls?" Blaze said to Kai. "What *is* this place?"

"I don't know, but I've seen enough."

"We're finishing strong!" Chopper said.

The art building provided a pleasant surprise. A class of mostly Bigs created intricate jewelry from seashells, coral, and colorful stones. Some students learned a new technique with one teacher, others worked in pairs, and some consulted with the other teacher as they finished necklaces, bracelets, or earrings.

"These teachers remind me of Jules," Blaze marveled. "Am I in the same school? How is this possible?"

Chopper shrugged.

"Now that's what I call sweet perfection!" Kai said.

Even Scarlet was impressed. "Wow, this jewelry is amazing!" Then, she fell in love. "Is . . . that . . . a . . . *pony necklace?*" she cried, looking at her pocket.

"Yes," the teacher said.

"Made of coral?"

"Yes."

"It's . . . Amazing. How much?"

"It's not for sale."

"I must have it. I'll give you $$10,000."

"What? That's ridicu—"

"Ok, $$20,000."

"What?!"

"I'm tired of carrying this MC rock pony!" Scarlet pulled out a thin, oblong rock that was painted with a pathetic pony face, mane, hooves, and tail. Yes, it had googly eyes. "I'm not allowed to have a real pony!" she cried. "Please. Please! I'll give you $$50,000."

"Sweet Mother of Honey! Hang on." The teacher yelled, "Hey, Breezy!" and sprinted toward her colleague, talking excitedly. They pulled a student over, who nodded her head, jumped up and down, then passed out.

"Deal!" the teacher said, rushing back. Scarlet handed her a stack of money, and quickly put on her necklace.

The teacher counted the money, her jaw opening wider and wider. "Wow. You do have $$50,000."

"You can't raise the price now!"

"Right."

"Sweet!" Scarlet trotted over to a mirror, cuddling and whispering sweet nothings to her pony necklace.

Blaze slapped her forehead, then asked the teacher, "How did you learn to teach like this?"

"Learning with my amazing co-teacher. Doing everything I can to make students great artists. *All* students."

"Smalls *and* Bigs?

"Uh, yeah."

"Do you know what is happening in the kitchen?"

"Listen, we just do our own thing, ok? But I'll tell you what— I'm not eating those cookies anymore."

The accolades abruptly ended in the next class. Although some Smalls worked with their own small hands, for the most part, they directed Bigs to make clay bowls, flower vases, painted rocks, and various oddities. One group slapped red paint on rocks while another grabbed the dried ones, and glued on, you guessed it, googly eyes. Others painted pathetic rock ponies.

Kai shook an MC guide rock and cried, "Are you kidding me?!"

"What are *those!*" Scarlet plucked the lot of not-so-pretty rock ponies and carefully placed them into a bag.

"Hey, those are $$12.98 each!" a teacher said.

"No problem!" Scarlet shoved a handful of cash in the teacher's face. "And I want the change!"

One Big made a clay statue with a large and odd-looking head, enormous bug eyes, and a ridiculously thick skull as if to scare a sea monster. A peer laughed at the noggin, which indeed was intended to mock a Puddin' Head. But nonetheless, the laughter received a yellow card for being unkind. The teacher said the monstrosity was perfect, which perhaps it was, and would be sold to an undisclosed buyer.

"Please tell me those are not what I think they are!" Kai cried again.

Although nearly all the misshapen art seemed to be the work of four-year-olds, teachers adored their students' sad performance, as if they'd had no expectations, or perhaps had set only very low ones. When students asked how to do something, the teachers refused to stifle anyone's creativity. They told students that, *Every work is a sweet perfection. Don't let the Puddin' Head meanies beat you down. Whatever you make is beautiful.* Excessive flattery filled the air like nauseating bake fails. *Very nice. Perfect! Oh, that's amazing.* One sensitive Small threw his pathetic clump of clay in the trash, which truly did look like a pile of you-know-what. He got a red card, grabbed the lump of clay, hurling it into the back of a Big. Thus started a Bigs versus Smalls clay fight.

Students chucked clay and anything else they could find at each other, the teachers, and the guests. We dove under tables as artwork shattered around us. Scarlet clutched her bag, crying "Don't hit my ponies!" Then, she shared the live excitement with a Mega Gossip video group.

The teachers laughed, handing out compliments. *Great shot! Nice block! Such talent in this room!* Then, a clay clod smacked a teacher on the side of the head, knocking off his Frames. He snatched them off the floor, stuck them back on his face, and gave a red card to a Small who called a Big, "a lumpy Puddin' Head", which was unkind.

My surly sweet tooth was desperate. I grabbed a broken cookie off the floor. It must have been part of a disgusting batch, and my now angry sweet tooth spit it out.

Kai jumped out from underneath a table. *"Everyone stop!"* he hollered. The class froze. Kai pointed at Blaze. "You, be quiet. And you," he said to a teacher, "are you okay with this chaos? With your students' work? With this large hand discrimination? With these 'products' going to the Puddin' Heads!"

"All students' performances are creations of sweet perfection. Let's not label things as negative."

"You're missing the point! Do you even notice that Sweetie Bigs and Smalls oppose each other! How are we going to win the Noble Deed Match when we can't even get along!"

"Oh, my—you are so rude! I *could* give you a red card."

"No, no you cannot. And where's the school boss?"

"We don't have a school boss. We don't need one."

"Bahhh!" Blaze and Chopper laughed.

"Ahh!" Kai pointed at Blaze. "I can't wait until we win the Noble Deed Match!"

Scarlet stopped Mega Gossiping about her pony necklace and treasure trove of rock ponies. "What? Did someone say Noble Deed?"

Blaze said, "Maybe I've been wrong all along. With the bug and sand cookies for Smalls, MC guide rocks and statues for the Puddin' Heads, and teachers who actually taught students some art skills, maybe some of these Sweeties aren't all bad!"

"Your Puddin' Heads threw those guide rocks against each other's heads!" Kai said.

Blaze paused. "Right. What am I thinking? Once again, we see why Puddin' Head schools are so messed up!"

"Hey, what's that?" Blaze pointed to a sign that read *Perfection Pool* above swinging double doors. She strode to the pool and instantly felt very overdressed. Smalls lounged in or beside a giant swimming pool. About half wore blue swimsuits, while the other half wore very soft blue shorts and shirts. Many wore pathetic flower headbands. And every belly was exposed—even the Sweeties wearing shirts, which had a large, perfect hole that showcased their belly buttons.

And why is this important, you ask? Because these Region 5 Sweetie Smalls lounged outdoors with mirrors. But rather than admiring their faces, they used their mirrors for yes, navel-gazing. They compared outie and innie belly buttons. They guffawed over new navel piercings. They chattered about the latest and greatest tools for removing belly button lint, flower petals, or pieces of cookie and cake. And, of course, they snapped pictures of their belly buttons and posted them on Mega Gossip for friends, families, and followers to admire.

At first, the Sweeties did not recognize the team. "Hey, can we get some more sweet tea with silly sweetie over here?" one giggled at Blaze.

Then the whispering started. Someone shrieked. Rumors spread like frosting on a hideous hot cake. And faster than cookie crumbs fall into a belly buttonhole, Sweeties leaped out of the pool and out of their comfy chairs. They barreled toward Blaze from all directions, like she held a platter of warm chocolate chip cookies that tasted like cookies.

"Hey, now! One at a time. Plenty of time for autographs—"

They bulldozed Blaze and ran for Kai.

Kai could not help but swallow his anger and laugh at Blaze. He extended his arms. "My people!" Some Sweeties rushed past him. Others trampled him.

Scarlet's eyes widened like the giant bubble she blew.

One Sweetie just could not contain herself. She flapped her arms, stamped her feet, and screamed. *"Oh! My! Perfect! Cake! Cookie! Mother!* Are you—are you, like Scarlet Pompavich?"

"In the flesh." Scarlet waved her fake hands. On this day, she also happened to be wearing a midriff top, which proclaimed, *Do a Noble Deed!*

The Sweeties shrieked in delight. "Amazing idea—we could cut off half of our shirt! We should totally do that!" But another touched Scarlet's shirt and said, "I don't know. This is like, not very soft."

Another Sweetie tried to read her shirt. "'Doe ah moedlee bebe.' Ah, I don't know. Hey—can I get a Big over here to read this!"

"It's okay. You're perfect. I got this!" a friend reassured the high school reader. "It says, *Drink Silly Sweetie."*

"What?!" Kai said. "They didn't teach you how to read?!"

"Why would we like, read when we have Mega Gossip videos!"

Lots of questions for Scarlet followed. *Like, will you take a picture with us? Do you like my navel? What's it like to be so rich? Do you have, like, a pony?*

"I'm not allowed to have a real pony!" Scarlet cried, stroking her pony necklace, then petting the ponies in her bag, then returning to Mega Gossip.

Do you like, shop all the time? Will you friend me on Mega Gossip? Why isn't your shirt softer? Do you have, like, your own perfect swimming pool? Do you eat, like, delicious cookies and cake all the time? And so on and so forth.

"What am I hearing?!" Kai cried. "Why do you keep saying 'like' like you're a bunch of bird brains! And talking endlessly about soft clothes! Why is everyone wearing a shirt with a belly buttonhole and carrying a mirror? Is this what you—especially you Smalls—do all day? Does anyone here even know how to read? Do you know what is happening on our island?"

The navel-gazing Sweeties shrugged, frowned, and gave Kai a good mocking. "Sil-ly Sweetie! Sil-ly Sweetie!" They chanted, raising their arms up and down, until he screamed.

"Okay already!" Kai clasped his face with both hands.

"Mmmm. I'd like to drink this silly Sweetie," one said, running a finger down Kai's arm.

Kai brushed the hand away. He was in no mood for romantic giggles and games. "Does anyone have a clue about the Noble Deed Football Match? About what will happen if we win? Or lose!"

Blank faces stared back at him. His admirer unsuccessfully tried to coax him once again. Then they ridiculed him some more.

Now, Scarlet was really upset. "What? How can you not know about the *Noble Deed Football Match*?!"

"What's a Noble Deed? Eww, that sounds like work."

"Yeah! That sounds like reading."

"You all, like need to relax," another Small said dismissively. He frowned and turned his attention to something more important in the mirror.

"Yeah! Like, relax!" others whined, clearly annoyed that these rude guests had disrupted their pool time.

Blaze and Chopper laughed so hard they gasped for air. Blaze—who may have been amped for even greater exaggeration after being bulldozed—eked out some words. "Kai, I can't wait to—" she laughed, "—roll you like cookie dough—" she gasped for breath, "at the Noble Deed Match. But at least your Sweeties will have—" Blaze took a deep breath, loudly sucking in the air for effect, "—soft, comfy clothes and mirrors to admire their belly buttons!" Blaze and Chopper rolled on the ground.

Kai frowned and hung his head. "Yeah, we got some Sweetie problems to solve." He pounded his fist. "And winning the Noble Deed Match is the solution!" He thought for a long moment, slowly rubbing his head, and running his fingers down his ponytail. And if you watched closely, a small smile curled up on his face, and then disappeared.

By this point, I could barely see. My surly sweet tooth found the good cookies, which I washed down with sweet tea and silly sweetie. But instead of feeling silly, I felt yucky. Absurdity laughed as my condition crumbled.

PART IV
THE ABSURD AWAKENING

NEW HOPE

The team met to plan the big presentation for the Top Boss Award Banquet.

Blaze said, "We're in excellent shape with the Noble Deed Match. We have our teams assembled."

Scarlet danced and twirled. "Yes! This is going to be the game of the century!"

"This is also our chance to share what we've learned," Blaze said, for once cautiously aware that she was speaking to the daughter of the education minister. "We have overwhelming evidence that schools could be, you know, better—especially for students with large hands. So, let's figure out what we're going to present at this banquet."

Blaze and Chopper summarized the Puddin' Head school tours and survey data, while Scarlet and Kai listened, rolled their eyes, frowned, and yawned. They recalled the horrible state of Puddin' Head schools, the ridiculous treatment of Bigs across the island, the prevalence of yellow and red cards, the obscene cost of tuition and transfer fees, the stupid plans to defeat the Sweeties, and schools that didn't even have a football pitch. Blaze blamed the school bosses and, of course, the Sweeties. "That's why we need to win the Noble Deed Match, and why I need to be in charge."

Kai scoffed. In contrast, he provided many examples of sad Sweetie schools that were in terrible shape. Interestingly, he blamed the Puddin' Heads, and the Sweeties. "The last thing Sweetie schools need is another Puddin' Head telling us what to do. We'll find a way to win the Noble Deed Match."

Blaze and Chopper nodded sarcastically. "Yeah, that's going to happen."

"Ah! But we can't confuse these big bosses. We need simple messages," Blaze said. So, Chopper, Kai, and Blaze walked and talked and came up with a plan. Then, at Chopper's direction, I worked day and night, editing and splicing videos.

I was pleased that Blaze felt great about the presentation. "The evidence that schools need to change and to eliminate hand size rules is overwhelming—on both main islands!" she said to Chopper. "How can the prime minister not fire Pompavich and make me the next education minister after we win the Noble Deed Match?"

She scratched the flame on her head. "You know what's strange to me, though? The teachers and the school bosses. Are they *all* okay with these ridiculous schools? And how do they get to be teachers and school bosses in the first place? And what about the good teachers? The good bosses? What do they think?"

"Or did they all get fired?" Chopper said.

"Good point."

Kai was on board gathering information about teachers and bosses, but for different reasons. They debated how to identify good teachers and bosses, and made their best estimation based on the information they had. They made many MC Frame interview calls. Blaze and Chopper even met with a Puddin' Head TDJP educator group. Little did they know that Kai did the same—except his group wore shiny blue shirts and costumes.

As Blaze, Chopper, and Kai finished crafting their presentation, they felt confident they had a strong case for changing schools. They felt confident that an epic Noble Deed Football Match provided the solution. Blaze and Chopper felt confident they would win. But strangely, so did Kai.

THE PRESENTATION

The Top Boss Award Banquet took place in a large ballroom within the Pompavich mega-mansion. Regional bosses, district bosses, and many school bosses—almost all of whom were Smalls—swapped stories about how they'd handled allegedly bad students and teachers. They crowed about setting personal records for the number of yellow and red cards given. Puddin' Head bosses gathered on one side of the room, while Sweetie bosses took the other. As part of the seven-course meal, staff served delicious appetizers: puddin' for the Puddin' Heads and cookies and cake for the Sweeties, and not the yucky kind.

Out in the hallway, Blaze laughed to Chopper. "You know, I think I learned more on this tour than I did throughout all of middle school." She lifted her nose and sniffed. "Smell that?"

Chopper sniffed. "What?"

"Big changes are in the air," she said and high-fived Chopper.

The ballroom buzzed with anticipation. Then, Blaze walked in, and—as you can guess—many school bosses snarled in response.

"Where's the prime—I mean, the supreme prime minister?" Blaze asked Scarlet.

"He's usually late."

Scarlet took the stage. She opened with a few jokes and a football trick. She kicked the ball off the ceiling, off a pillar, and then a different pillar, so that it ricocheted into a small net placed above a five-layer Sweetie cake. The audience burst into resounding applause. Scarlet bowed. She proceeded to report on the Noble Deed teams and their odds of winning (92:1 in favor of the Puddin' Heads). Strangely, this was met with a standing ovation, even from the Sweetie bosses.

"Where's the prime minister?" Blaze hissed at Chopper as they strode to the front of the room with Kai. Despite hating each other, they'd agreed on a strategy.

Blaze started, "Everyone can agree that school is important. We spend millions on schools. But we know very little about them beyond our own personal school experience. Even in my case, with *twenty-three different schools*, I didn't know what hundreds of other Island Nation schools were like. Maybe you don't know much outside of your own school. And we had no way of knowing—we couldn't find anything that told us. That is, until now. What we learned may shock you."

Blaze had the audience hooked. "We surveyed students across the entire nation. And we have a ton of videos from our tour."

Chopper stepped forward. "Besides observational data, we have more than fifty hours of video footage and more than six hundred thousand survey responses. Our evidence is rock solid. You each have a copy of our report in your folder." The bosses pulled out the report and glanced at the team's summary of evidence.

Blaze and Chopper highlighted the huge differences between Bigs and Smalls and the large percentage of dissatisfied students.

The bosses shrugged and tossed the reports on the ground.

Blaze and Chopper exchanged confused glances. Blaze said, "Okay, then. Well, if that wasn't convincing, let's see a short video from our school tours." A large screen descended from the ceiling.

The video opened with a montage of Puddin' Heads stressing over testing, crying in bootstraps classes, whacking each other with spoons, launching dynamite at each other, attempting to chop off fingers, and crushing their skulls with a rock firing squad beside a dilapidated building.

"Aye! That's my school!" School Boss J.R. proclaimed proudly. He had two black eyes and very large lumps on his head.

The video continued with clips from Sweetie Island as Kai narrated. Sweeties with large hands tested flaming-hot peppers; baked and served disgusting cake and cookies; and turned into freakish, four-armed walking sticks, blueberries, and human bees. Sweetie Smalls watched, gave orders, navel-gazed, lounged on couches, and failed to read simple words. And some Sweeties—big hands or small—quacked and flapped like ducks. Sprinkled throughout the video were clips of surprised and angry students receiving yellow and red cards.

The bosses shrugged. A few cheered.

Blaze picked up the narration again. "So, what did these students learn? In short, not much. Some students learned the basics, yet many still tripped over this low bar. Many Bigs learned nothing at all, because they couldn't afford the transfer fees. Some dropped out before graduation." After a clip of a graduate saying nothing he'd learned in school was useful in the real world, Blaze said sarcastically, "Turns out, crushing rocks over one's head isn't a sought after job skill."

School Boss J.R. disagreed. "It got me my job!"

"And what do we know about how teachers learned to teach?"
The video showed one teacher spooning puddin' from a large red
container. "Look, I was a student. I graduated high school. I
watched my teachers. It ain't hard. I just follow the teacher guides.
My job is to teach. The students' job is to learn—not my problem if
they don't. Oh, sure, some cause problems, but I just give them
yellow cards." The teacher smirked. "Red card, no more problems."

Blaze continued. "Now, to be fair, students did share stories of
great teachers and great school bosses. Teachers who were creative,
interesting, fun, and who actually helped their students learn. We
saw a few of these teachers. But they were rare, like flowers that
grow in a dry field of weeds. This was confusing, so we did some
more research. We found out that just about anyone can become a
teacher."

Another teacher on the video said, "I learned to teach in a five-
week online program. But it turns out, I have to teach students in
person! It's so much harder. You can't mute students when they
misbehave! Luckily, I have these yellow and red cards."

Blaze said, "That's right. To get your teaching license, the
education ministry requires a five-week online training program,
license fees, and passing a Puddin' Head or Sweetie Island test.
That's it! And get this! Many teachers keep teaching the same way
year after year, and they keep their jobs no matter how good they
are!"

The video showed a teacher—whose face was blurred to protect
her identity—watching students crack their peers' skulls with
bamboo sticks. In another clip, an ancient teacher lectured as kids
slept. He coughed, "He he. Same lesson I used thirty years ago. I
call it my recycling program."

Blaze narrated, "On top of this, we have a shortage of teachers,
maybe because . . ."

The video cut to a teacher saying, "Well, I work for puddin', and
the working conditions suck."

Blaze continued, "Sadly, some of the best teachers quit. Other
great teachers were fired! The same is true of some of the great
school bosses."

The video ended, and the screen slid back up into the ceiling.

"And so," Blaze said with fiery passion despite the crowd's apathy, "our schools need to change. Too many students are harming their friends. This is not okay. Too many students cannot afford school. This is not okay. Too many students are learning useless skills. This is not okay. Some don't even have a football! This is not okay. Great teachers are rare. This is not okay." Blaze stared down a sea of blank faces. "Our students deserve better. We urge you to eliminate large hand rules and to make schools fair for everyone."

The crowd burst into laughter.

Unshaken, Blaze went on. "All students deserve a good education, regardless of the size of their hands. It will only make our islands and our nation stronger. These ridiculous hand size rules are not good for students, or the islands. We urge you to make schools free for all students, to eliminate school fees, transfer fees, and large hand fees. Support better teacher pay, training, and working conditions. This will make our nation stronger."

I'm sorry to say these were not crowd-pleasing ideas.

"Who's going to pay for all of that?!" a regional boss shouted.

"Yeah!" several bosses yelled. Some stood up and booed. The audience grumbled louder. The presentation seemed to be headed in the wrong direction and getting out of control.

Blaze felt like she was pushing a boulder up Mount Freedom. Were the bosses ignoring what they'd just watched? Or worse, accepting it? She scanned the audience but didn't see the prime minister. How was Minister Pompavich smiling? Fortunately, Blaze found the courage to shift to the next part of the plan. "Yes, how *are* we going to pay for all of this?" Blaze asked over the grumbling crowd. "We anticipate a record crowd at the Noble Deed Football Match. Imagine a sold-out game, with one hundred thousand more fans cheering outside the stadium. Imagine the ticket sales, the concession sales, and the merchandise sales across both islands!"

Suddenly, the bosses cheered.

"And the winner takes all! The winning team will use this money to improve their island's schools. This will be the rivalry game of the century!" The room went wild with high fives, head butts, and group hugs. Puddin' Head and Sweetie bosses jeered and taunted each other.

Blaze, Chopper, and Kai stepped off the stage, feeling slightly better. But then, the education minister took the stage and spun the enthusiasm in her favor. "Yes, yes, we're all very excited for this Noble Deed Match. And yes, no doubt it will dramatically increase our funding for education!" The room cheered. "But that's not really why we're here today, is it? We're here today to celebrate our schools and bosses! Sure, there's always a bad puddin' cup in any crate, but come on, really—what are you all supposed to do when students misbehave? *Not* give out yellow and red cards?"

This crowd of bosses—all of whom Minister Pompavich directly or indirectly appointed (and brainwashed?)—nodded their heads and chuckled.

"The prime minister sends his regrets—he had an important game of golf today. Do you know he shot thirty-six under par during his last round?"

The bosses wildly applauded.

Blaze whispered, "What does that mean?" But Chopper had no idea.

The education minister continued, "But as the supreme prime minister knows, and as *you* all know, while no school is nearly as excellent as MegaCorp Academy, all of our schools are—" she paused and raised her hands, as if knowing what would happen next, "—very good!" She clapped wildly and loudly—perhaps to drown out a mighty fart.

The bosses cheered.

Chopper stood up, waved his hand, and grimaced, "That's not true! Look at the survey data."

"Shhhh!" the bosses hissed. "They are very good!"

"And the survey data show trends of continuous improvement," the education minister reframed, winking at the audience.

Blaze whispered, "Improvement?! Improvement compared to what?"

The education minister grew more enthusiastic. "Yes, it has been an extraordinary year of bosses handing out yellow and red cards, especially thanks to Blaze Union! Our schools are very good!" she crowed again, clapped, and farted loudly.

"What?" Blaze said.

The bosses cheered.

"How about some music?" Minister Pompavich called. Suddenly, something like polka streamed from the speakers, and she became more passionate—dancing, clapping, and farting louder each time she shouted her ridiculous lie.

Suddenly the whole room was dancing and singing, "Our schools are very good! Our schools are very good!"

Blaze was fuming. "Very good schools? Good for whom?" she cried. "They can't see the truth that's right in front of their faces!"

"Or smell it," Chopper said, still waving his hand.

Regional Boss Poppy grabbed Minister Pompavich's hand, hugged her tight, and twirled her. "You know, I'm up for the Top Boss Award," she whispered.

"Fart tart! No one hugs me! I could fire you!" Minister Pompavich screeched.

"You wouldn't fire me with my performance."

"True." Then, she flung Poppy across the room. School Boss Walka Walka swiftly declined Poppy's invitation, and continued dancing by himself in uncoordinated circles. Poppy grabbed School Boss J.R., and they skipped round and round. When he finally opened his swollen eyes to see her blue jacket, he tried to push her away. She gave him a bear hug, cracking his vertebrae like a chiropractor. This now useless dancer wobbled toward a chair. Alas, Poppy spotted me at the dessert table, perhaps sensing my dance skills. And before I could hide, there I was dancing around the room with Poppy, who kept steering us toward Minister Pompavich. Although unfamiliar with this music, I quickly caught the rhythm and followed Poppy's lead. As we turned and swayed our hips every couple beats, I bobbed and weaved to avoid getting clocked by her giant necklace. Unfortunately, we turned into a hip checking wrecking ball that knocked over an unsuspecting J.R., then Walka Walka, then other dancers en route to the object of Poppy's desire.

Blaze paced and swore with Chopper in the hallway, and thus, missed this embarrassing scene. In that moment, I wished Poppy could dance with Root-Woot. Of course, I knew that was ridiculous. Obviously, Root-Woot would make a better dance partner for Minister Pompavich.

The education minister noticed us mowing down dancers and heading straight for her. She dove back onto the stage just in time, toppling the podium and yelling, "STOP THE MUSIC!" She bounced up, pulled the podium back into place, tried to compose herself, motioning for everyone to sit. She scowled at Poppy, who sat next to Walka Walka, who bounded to the back of the room, plowing through chairs. Blaze and Chopper scurried back to their seats.

The education minister huffed, "Everyone has been invited here to thank you for your outstanding work in education." The bosses beamed. "Next up, we have a long list of boss awards. And of course, the Top Boss Award!"

The bosses cheered. Poppy waved at the minister.

The education minister snorted. "And I have party favors! Each of you will receive a special necklace with a golden key—like this one." The education minister removed her own necklace and spun it around her finger. The room hooted and hollered.

"Because you have unlocked the potential of our students, you get to unlock something special for yourselves, right after the meeting. Now, without further ado, let's get to it! Our first award this evening goes to School Boss Walka Walka from Puddin' Head Middle School, Region 2, for a 21 percent increase in transfers!"

Blaze balled her hands into fists. To prevent herself from tackling Pompavich, she once more dashed from the room.

Thoughts of playing a raucous song or beaming a football off Pompavich's head filled her mind. But she had neither a guitar nor football with her.

We followed Blaze, who glared at Scarlet. "How can the education minister be handing out *awards?*"

"There are good school bosses, you know," Scarlet said.

"You think Walka Walka is a good school boss?"

"Everyone has their strengths."

"Puddin' mold fart tart!" Blaze pumped her fists.

"Where was the prime minister?"

"That's supreme—"

"*I know!*"

"He had more important things—"

"*Ahhh!*"

"In fairness, we chose to visit some of the worst schools Blaze," Scarlet said. "Remember, that's what you wanted to see."

"*You're missing my point!* Every school boss we visited was in this room. Even School Boss J.R.! How are these bird-brained numbskulls getting awards?"

"Yeah, how are these bird-brained numbskulls getting awards?" Kai deadpanned.

"That includes your school bosses, too! And where are the good school bosses in that room?! Is there even one?"

We looked at the long list of school bosses in attendance. Indeed, none of these schools were known to have good school bosses. The adored School Leader Foster—who they'd discovered had found a new job in Region 1—was not listed.

"*What* is going on!" Blaze glared at Scarlet once more.

"Listen, I don't know why you're so upset. Stop being so negative. Everyone in this room is excited about the Noble Deed Match. And right now, that's all that matters. Win the game and earn a boatload of money for your island's schools. It's that simple."

"Something's going on!"

"Nothing's going on!"

"But it doesn't make sense!" Blaze pounded her fist against a wall.

"No, it doesn't," Chopper agreed. "But while we're here . . . Scarlet, maybe you could sneak back into the banquet and bring us some food?"

We enjoyed the most delicious food we had ever eaten. Blaze and Chopper wolfed down golden bowls of puddin' mixed with all sorts of toppings and booster. They ate fillet mignon, scallops, and swordfish—though, they passed on the baby zebra, baby elephant, baby seal, and endangered seahorse meat. "Are you sure?" Scarlet asked. "The baby elephant is to die for. It's even locally produced."

Kai frowned and sighed but enjoyed sweet fruits and salads with various kinds of honey-drizzled vegetables and nuts, alongside, of course, scrumptious cookies and cake (that I had already sampled). Scarlet ate a little bit of everything. I couldn't help but focus on a buffet of desserts.

Then, over the hallway speakers, we heard the education minister announce, "And the Top Boss Award goes to. . . School Boss J.R.!"

I don't know who screamed louder: Blaze or Poppy.

Blaze calmed down a little after beating Chopper and Kai in several games in the game room. She refused to play Scarlet.

We headed outside as the banquet ended. Blaze trailed behind with Chopper. "Fart tart! Do you think the prime minister will read our report? Or care about it?"

"Not if the education minister delivers it."

"Fart tart! Well, at least we've got the Noble Deed Match. After we win, there must be a way for me to become the education minister. You know though, something's just not right here."

Valets brought around the guests' fancy cars. Staff carted out chests of various sizes and stowed them in the trunks.

"Look, it's School Boss J.R.," Blaze said.

"You mean the Top—" Scarlet said.

"Do *not* go there!"

The swollen-eyed, lumpy-headed boss ambled toward his limousine with a face that was part pirate, part wrestler, and partly saying, *my puddin' head is in pain.* He dragged his left foot, refusing the cane the driver proffered. He snapped the key necklace off his neck, leaned over the trunk, and opened the large chest. He scooped out large stacks of money, which he held up next to a diamond-studded trophy. "Arrrr!" He threw the money back into the chest, slammed it shut, slammed the trunk closed, and clutching the Top Boss Award trophy, head butted the large-handed driver, who wobbled and opened the door for him. As School Boss J.R. sped off, he stuck a long spoon handle out of the window. With a big but painful belly laugh, he cried, "Here's your tip!" and clocked the valet right on his MC Frames.

Scarlet was emphatic. "I'm going to prove you all wrong. I'm so sick of hearing there must be something strange going on. After this, can we *please* be done with this ridiculous talk?"

"Sure," Blaze said.

Kai said, "I can't believe I'm doing this."

"It'll work. Trust me."

Kai called Scarlet's mom on speaker through his MC Frames and muffled his voice.

"Hey, this is Jerry. Just checking on something."

"Why aren't you on video or hologram? And why is the ID blocked? And why do you sound weird?"

"Uh . . . I have a cold. And there's some sort of glitch with my Frames. Anyway, we got an order for three ponies, a giraffe, a baby zebra, and a baby elephant. They're here early. I need to bring them over tonight."

"The banquet's already over. And we don't eat pony!"

"No, these are live animals."

"What? No, no, no! I didn't order— Are you serious? Where would we possibly— Scarlet! I can't believe that little— Okay. How do I cancel?"

"Once the animals arrive, you can't cancel."

"No, I'm saying *cancel the order!* I'm not having *zoo animals* at this residence! An elephant, a giraffe—are you serious? Why don't we throw in a tiger, a hippo, a rhinoceros, and some clowns while you're at it?! We'll have ourselves a circus!"

Kai bit his lip hard to keep himself from laughing. He turned away from the others, who were all rolling on the floor, cupping hands over their mouths. Blaze pretended to reel in a big fish.

"No, I don't see tigers, hippos, or rhinoceroses on this order. And we don't work with clowns."

"Ahhh!"

"Sorry, can't cancel on the Frames. But maybe we can do this in person. I'll need a personal signature and an eye scan, from both of you."

"Both of us? What? Are you laughing?! What kind of business is this? Since when do you sell live zoo animals?! Who authorized this order? I *told* you not to let Scarlet make big orders anymore! I *told* you we'll never have ponies—I don't care how much Scarlet wants one! Are you kidding me?! I'll have you shut down! And we've always paid electronically!"

"Sorry. And for your convenience, I want you to know now, there will be hefty return fees."

Scarlet's mom slammed something on the ground, swore repeatedly, and yelled for Elroy to get the limo. "We'll be there in twenty minutes. And I'll have that baby elephant made into soup before it sets foot on this property! *Ahhh!*"

After the team recovered from the laughter-induced side aches, Scarlet sighed, "Oh, that *was* good! Now, let's clear up this nonsense." Then, she petted and whispered to her pony necklace, "Sorry you won't have a real pony to play with." She scanned her MC Frames on the monitor next to the private office. It unlocked and she said, "Guess I *do* have a master key. I'm telling you, there's nothing weird happening. But if there were, it would be in here."

The team entered an office large enough to hold several zoo animals. It had floor-to-ceiling tinted windows, an electronic white board wall, and a U-shaped executive desk. Beautiful wooden cabinets with white marble countertops ran along two walls, each of which displayed a large white board at its center. One white board had a neatly handwritten organizational table of Puddin' Head Island and columns for the five regions, schools, school boss dividend, district boss dividend, regional boss dividend, and total number of transfers. Each boss's name was either circled, crossed out, or had a little check mark next to it. The other wall had a similar chart for Sweetie Island.

Scarlet ran to the desk and found the team's report, flipped to the first page of the recommendations section. A single word, *Wow*, was written in the margin. "That's not a good sign," she mumbled.

Neatly stacked, gold-lined boxes glistened like skyscrapers around the room. Blaze opened one. "What the—" Chopper and Kai began rifling through them, too. Each box was labeled with the names of a school and school boss and contained stacks of $$500, $ $1000, and $$5000 bills.

"Wow, these boxes have *a lot* of money!" Chopper said, before holding up some reports he'd found in one of the boxes. "School bosses seem to be getting two different reports. One is a second quarter dividend statement, and the other is a second quarter transfer statement. I think they match the white board. And the money is based on the reports."

"Nothing weird happening, huh?" Blaze scoffed.

Each money box had a single-page report. The top of the report had boss contact information. The rest was a simple table with rows that included enrollment, transfers in, transfers out, other profits, and the number of students with yellow or red cards. The rows displayed how much money was earned for each of these categories during the quarter and the year.

Chopper read one, holding a fistful of money in the air. "In Region 5, Hard Rocks High School: enrollment = 2018 students, 187 students with red cards, 185 transfers out, two pending, 211 yellow cards, 143 transfers in, quarterly dividend $$164,000, yearly dividends $$382,500! Folks, this is only for one school, and we still have two quarters to go!"

"Well, he was the top school boss," Scarlet said flatly.

"Ahhhh!" Blaze said.

"Forty percent went to the school boss, forty percent to the education ministry, and twenty percent to the Wall."

"The Wall!" Kai said.

"Yeah, who else is going to pay for it? We're not raising taxes!" Scarlet said.

"Ahhh! What is the education ministry money used for! And School Boss J.R. got forty percent!" Blaze looked at another report, then the white board. "Wait a minute. School bosses are getting paid for . . . transfers?" She thought a moment. "That's about $$500 per transfer. But the bosses just got chests full of money! So, what's this money for?" She glared at Kai, then Scarlet.

"Those were bonuses. This seems to be quarterly payments." Scarlet smiled sheepishly. "School business is good?"

"I *knew* something was going on!!" Blaze shouted. She whipped a $$5000 bill stack at Scarlet, who ducked just in time.

Kai shook his head nervously. "Oh, Sweet Mother of Honey, this is *big*. Wow, this is *messed up*. This is big-time corruption." His mouth dropped as he leafed through a box labeled, "*Sugar Falls Middle School*." Kai scanned both white boards. "This is happening on both of the main islands! How can this be? We're supposed to put community first! We've been corrupted by the Puddin' Heads!"

He grabbed a stack of $$500 bills and said, "This is enough money to feed my entire village for months, maybe even a year! This would pay for all those school fees." He chucked the stack at Blaze, smacking her in the leg.

"Those *are* the school fees!" Blaze yelled. She whipped the $ $500 stack back at him, nailing him in the shoulder. She tossed stacks of money in the air, which thudded to the ground. "The whole system is corrupt!"

She flew around the room, opening cabinets full of perfectly organized and bound stacks of large bills. We stared at the ridiculous heaps of money. "It's millions! Think of what I could do for schools with this money!"

Kai said, "*You?* I don't think so."

Chopper said, "Millions? Try hundreds of millions. Maybe, more than a billion." Uncharacteristically, Chopper yelled and waved his arms wildly. "This is *insaaaaaannne!*"

"I'm sure there's a perfectly logical explanation for all of this," Scarlet said, backing toward the exit.

"There sure is!" Blaze grabbed two bound stacks of $$1000 bills, held them up in clutched hands, and screamed a maniacal, evil laugh that caused her peers to jump. "I am the minister of education! The education witch! I steal from kids who transfer schools! I have so much money I shoot it from cannons for fun!"

"That's not true!" Scarlet wailed.

Blaze laughed hysterically and hurled a stack that just missed Scarlet's ear.

Chopper started to ask, "Are you ok—" but Blaze leaned into him and shifted into the character of an old man intoxicated with too much adult puddin'.

"C'mon kids, when's the last time y- y- youuuu got to have a . . . have a . . . have a billion-dollar money fight?" She crossed her eyes and opened her hands wide.

It took them a moment. "We are *so* not going to have a money fight—imagine the mess!" Scarlet cried once again.

Chopper shrugged and struck Kai in the forehead with a stack of $$1000 bills.

"Lucky shot, numbskull." Kai pegged him in the chest with a $

$500 stack. Money mayhem ensued. They whipped handfuls and armfuls of money stacks at each other, while Scarlet frantically tried to stop them. I sat in the corner, eating the cookies I saved from the banquet. Within minutes, great piles of money and knocked-down boxes, lids, and reports were strewn across the room.

Chopper let out a hearty laugh. "Okay! That was fun! But we don't have much time left."

The team fiercely debated keeping the money, but Scarlet simply would not allow it. "This should go toward the Noble Deed Match!" Blaze argued.

Scarlet offered a compromise. "Okay, Okay. Yes, the Noble Deed Match should have bigger prize money. But probably not this much."

HYPE

The Puddin' Head and Sweetie football teams finally assembled. Sort of. Feeling sorry for the Sweeties and eager to avoid a boring blowout, Scarlet agreed to train them. Unsurprisingly, the main barriers that she and Kai faced were (a) getting the team to develop a competitive mindset and (b) years of inexperience rivaled only by their lack of talent, which had little chance of improving within a just few short weeks.

The Puddin' Heads on the other hand, barely practiced. Blaze didn't see the point. "Look at us," she said to Chopper. "You and I could beat the Sweeties by ourselves." Chopper was skeptical but agreed that their time could be better spent creating a plan to increase and spend the Noble Deed Match reward money.

Given Kai's direct experience with Puddin' Head extremism and spoon violence, he requested that spoons be banned from the stadium during the match. Scarlet readily agreed, fearing that no Sweeties would show up to the game otherwise, thus dramatically decreasing merchandise sales. Blaze didn't care—she just wanted to finally play.

At the same time, Blaze secretly hoped for a large Sweetie turnout. She very much looked forward to taunting those saps and drubbing them in a humiliating defeat. The more Sweeties to see it, the better. She even released an inflammatory video rendition of "Who Will We Defeat? (The Zombies!)"

But word that spoons were prohibited spread like wildfire across Puddin' Head Island. They cried, "How will we eat? What will we use in the event of a zombie attack?" and many other ridiculous fears that I'm sure you can imagine. So, they compromised. Each Puddin' Head could bring one spoon, for eating purposes only (no spoon swords, spoon hats, etc.).

In preparation for the Noble Deed Football Match, outrageous advertisements and promotions bombarded everyone's MC Frames. Puddin' Head News, of course, promoted Puddin' Head memorabilia, while Sweetie News promoted Sweetie memorabilia. Power News, of course, promoted the Noble Deed game and the sale of anything related to it. Thus, it was no accident that everyone wanted commemorative Noble Deed Match blue or red jerseys, shirts, shorts, pants, backpacks, boots, sandals, coolers, plates, napkins, toilet paper, pencils, bootstraps, compression gloves, spoons, and so on. Special puddin' and cake and cookie and booster sales went through the roof.

The Noble Deed Match would take place on Celebration Island, population fifty-eight. This island had originally been developed for the State of the Nation speech, which took place in MegaCorp Stadium. Here, the prime minister would brag about the nation's alleged accomplishments and rally supporters to vote in the upcoming election.

In his first term, the "supreme" prime minister had anticipated tens of thousands of supporters would turn out and cheer his celebratory speech and tiny hand gestures. He envisioned gushing about and thanking tremendous crowds. (This happened even at his "rallies" with fifteen people: "Whoa, look at this wonderful turnout!" he would rave to the Power News cameras.)

So, the long bridge from Power Island was expanded. The enormous MegaCorp Stadium was built. It would hold 150,000 fans, with concession stands and overflow areas. Outside grounds were prepared for 250,000 more fans. Bathroom and food facilities were constructed. Speakers and billboard screens were placed throughout the island for those who could not make it inside to witness the event in person.

In reality, however, the prime minister's first State of the Nation speech had historically low attendance. Some two hundred people had been required to go: senators, ministers, and MegaCorp executives. Although the attendance grew to two thousand the following year, the prime minister was very upset to see tens of thousands of empty seats and a virtually deserted island. He told the media minister—Scarlet's father—who was in charge of advertising the event, that he would be fired unless attendance grew tenfold this year. So, Scarlet easily convinced her dad—and by default her mom—and then the prime minister, to move the State of the Nation address to just before the Noble Deed Match. If they truly wanted a monstrous crowd, they should dramatically increase the advertising, the event budget, and they all greedily agreed.

It was not an understatement to say this would be Island Nation's event of the century. And at first, it certainly seemed that this would be the case.

STATE OF THE NATION

In my country, there is an American football rivalry so great, it is simply known as, *The Game*. The Noble Deed Match made that rivalry look silly. On Power Island, even before dawn, the crowd was huge. Hordes of people, dressed in blue or red, exited their trains hours earlier than anticipated. Visitors walked past the Capitol with red or blue backpacks, blankets, bags, and coolers, ready for an all-day celebration.

Streams of people meandered down stone streets like streams of blue and red ants. They plodded through sprawling manicured lawns and marveled at mega-mansions. Puddin' Heads in particular found this ludicrous wealth to be, as the prime minister put it, "something to aspire to." The chauffeurs of luxury cars, however, were not amused. They yelled and honked at the massive crowds blocking traffic.

When the swelling crowd reached the large bridge to Celebration Island, they instinctively split into two marching stripes—one red and the other blue. After the nearly two-kilometer walk, they entered Celebration Island through a beautiful wooden gateway. One side of the gateway displayed a sign that read Welcome Puddin' Heads with large white letters over solid red. The other side had Welcome Sweeties in white over solid blue. Puddin' Heads and Sweeties merged awkwardly under the half-red, half-blue gateway arch en route to the big game, which emptied onto the sandy island with patches of grass, bushes, and small trees. At first, only minor scuffles broke out.

The crowd rushed onto the island like water from a bursting dam. They passed a helicopter landing area and a fleet of ambulances. They ran into MegaCorp Stadium to claim the best seats on their team's side—those that hadn't already been reserved for the government, MegaCorp elite, and news. Visitors quickly filled all 150,000 seats—one half painted blue; the other half painted red. The bright sky, blue ocean, and Power Island stood majestically in the background.

Once the stadium was full, the still-rushing crowd threw down blankets to save shady spots close to the stadium or the large screens. Puddin' Heads sat to the right of the stadium and Sweeties to the left. Many Puddin' Heads missed their spoon hats. Many

Sweeties enjoyed their flower headbands, necklaces, and bracelets.

Blaze and the Puddin' Head football team enjoyed watching the fans roll in. Surprisingly, Kai stopped by the Puddin' Head sideline. "Good luck—you're going to need it," Kai laughed.

Ram looked around nervously.

"Everything all right?" Kai asked. "Afraid of the Sweeties?"

"Wait, *you're* a Sweetie? And, uh . . . no. Just . . . uh . . ., looking at all these people. This island can't sink, right?"

"Doubtful, but you never know. All these Puddin' Heads are awfully heavy. The entire student body of Hard Rocks High is here, and we know how thick their skulls are."

Fortunately for Kai, he avoided a head butt.

By the time the ministers, senators, and MegaCorp executives arrived hours later, two-thirds of the island was full, and the crowd continued to spill from the bridge. The prime minister stepped off his MC helicopter with a huge grin, head butted the side of the chopper, and yelled, "Oh yeah! Now this is a *crowd*!"

One Puddin' Head said to another, "Isn't he a great guy? So confident. Wouldn't you just like to sit down and have a bowl of puddin' with him?"

The prime minister waved to the crowd, shook hands with Puddin' Heads, and followed the path his security guards cleared to the stadium. The media minister hurried after him, enthusiastically applauding the fact that he still had a job.

The prime minister strode onto midfield. The Puddin' Heads went wild, standing, cheering, and head butting each other. The blue side of the stadium stayed seated. Some pretended to clap, but most stayed silent.

"Wow, what a crowd! A crowd fit for the greatest supreme prime minister of all time!" he cried into the mic. The Puddin' Heads shrugged, then cheered and head butted each other. The Sweeties snickered.

This pattern continued throughout the prime minister's speech. The Puddin' Heads applauded virtually everything he said, while the Sweeties grimaced, yawned, snickered, or stayed silent. There were two notable exceptions.

Halfway through the speech, he said, "Now, we all know for the sake of our national security we need to build the Wall to keep out the sea monsters. They're stealing and eating babies all the time. One disappeared just yesterday in Puddin' Head Island Region 5. We just started the Wall in Region 1 and have enough funding for half of Puddin' Head Island. But we need the Senate to approve funding for a wall around the perimeter of all the islands!"

A Sweetie yelled, "Sea monsters aren't real! We don't need the Wall!"

Surprisingly, someone from Puddin' Head Island Region 1 nearly agreed. "Can't the Wall be a bit shorter? I can't see or walk to the ocean. Maybe build some doors, too. Clear ones would be nice."

The prime minister, of course, didn't hear them. "Some of you have asked me if Sweeties are actually sea monsters. Do we really need the Wall to keep them out? We have reports of blue sea monsters walking right onto Puddin' Head shore. Lots of reports."

Half the island booed for the first time, while thousands shuddered and pulled their small children closer. The prime minister, accustomed to events with only supporters, was startled to hear this booing. He moved on to a more popular topic.

"Now, our schools. Our wonderful schools. Yes, we can improve our schools." The entire island cheered, which restored his confidence. "Our schools are doing a great job. We don't need big fixes. They have everything they need to improve! We just need to encourage them. Our education minister is doing a very fine job."

Puddin' Heads applauded. The prime minister wrapped up his speech.

Then, without the event planners' approval or say-so, Blaze and Kai strutted out to midfield.

Chopper smiled. Scarlet swallowed as Bee Girl, Fist Boy, Four-Armed Stick Boy, and Blueberry Boy shuffled to midfield along with a few other Sweetie students, the puddin'tender, and a grizzly group of former Puddin' Head students. The Puddin' Heads wore head bandages and eye patches, and had disfigured and bruised faces, cauliflower ears, missing and broken teeth, smashed noses, and dented skulls. Although Puddin' Brains High School students refused to participate, Blaze and Chopper recruited two former Puddin' Head Region 3 students who had odd features like the puddin'tender. The crowd sat, stunned into silence. Puddin' Head News, Sweetie News, and Power News cameras rolled.

Smarter than the average Puddin' Head, Blaze had learned a thing or two about politics, people in power, and how to get what she wanted. Or so she thought. She grabbed the mic, almost exactly three years after her father's death, and three years since her hands changed to large. She knew 150,000 people watched from the stadium, 250,000+ people watched on screens outside the stadium, and millions watched from their homes. "As the prime—, I mean, the supreme prime minister said, we *can* improve our schools. And today, for the first time, we thought you'd like to see the areas in which we can improve. We thought you'd like to see some of the harm that has occurred in our schools. Particularly to large-handed students like me, and Kai. Which is also why we are leading our teams."

Kai nodded in a rare moment of solidarity.

A clumsy, rough sod approached the mic, nearly tripping over his feet. "School Boss J.R. said smash rocks. Sides my head," he stammered. "Now no see, hear, walk. Smell. Think." He cried. "Like before." He sobbed, handed the mic back to Blaze, and dragged himself back to the rest of the walking wounded. The crowd gasped, moaned, and shouted as they listened to several more head-spinning, jaw-dropping, and crazy stories.

Then, the puddin'tender and two adults—who also had a battery of scars and scaly bumps only on the right side of their body—approached the mic as the wide-eyed crowd whispered to each other. The puddin'tender said, "In my days at Freedom High we didn't have those fancy spoon helmets. I was a Big that year and I told these two Smalls not to run with me," he sighed and shook his head. "But they insisted. And when we turned that corner on the track, and the dynamite exploded right beside us, well . . . we were the lucky ones. I told myself that our sacrifice made Puddin' Head schools stronger because then they got all these safety upgrades. But recently, Blaze got me thinking . . ."

Wheels's mom grabbed the mic while holding her partner's hand. "Wheels, we're so proud of you! Who knows how many kids' lives you've saved on the track? But Blaze is right, it's time for a change. There's a better way to beat the Sweeties."

Wheels jogged along the sideline waving a spoon. The Puddin' Heads nodded, furrowing their brows.

Two Sweeties approached the mic. Well, one waddled, wearing a jacket covered with feathers along with a long beak strapped to her face. The other student—a Big you might remember from Chill High School—pursed his lips, then said, "I got a yellow card for sneezing, then a red card for asking to do math! But worse, our teacher taught us to flap and quack like ducks. And now," he cried, "my friend thinks she *is* a duck!"

"Quack! Quack!" she said, flapping her wings.

More Sweeties shared stories of having cake shoved in their faces during Code Red Puddin' Head drills, being stressed out by the school boss, eating yucky cookies, or engaging in dangerous experiments. Unlike two of his comrades, Four-Armed Stick Boy was able to grab the mic. He put his other arms around Fist Boy, Blueberry Boy, and Bee Girl, and told his story. Then, he said solemnly, "And Kai is right, it's time for a change. There's a better way to beat the Puddin' Heads."

The Sweeties nodded and squeeze hugged.

Chopper hacked the video screens, showing the outrageous clips from their school tours we'd prepared for the Top Boss Award Banquet. This time, instead of shrugs, the audience gasped.

Blaze took the mic as more than a million people watched, shaken and stirred. "For some reason, these stories don't make it to the news. For some reason, some people are okay with this happening over and over." Blaze paused. "Are we really okay with this happening over and over?"

The crowd startled from its stunned stupor. "No!"

"Are we really okay with schools that launch dynamite at students? Schools that experiment on students and turn them into bees? Or crush students' skulls and spirits?"

"No!"

"Should schools continue to have large hand rules?"

"No!" nearly everyone cried.

"Should Bigs and Smalls unite?"

"Yes!" the crowd cheered and pumped their fists.

Of course, by this time, the prime minister, the education minister, and a whole lot of education bosses squirmed in their seats, and muttered, "What the—" The prime minister shouted something into his MC Frames.

Chopper switched the video screens to the big corruption reveal. The video showed the stacks and boxes of millions upon millions of dollars with name after name of school bosses, district bosses, and regional bosses, as well as their dividend amount. It showed report after report of funds going toward the Wall. As you can imagine, several hundred more "*What the—*" resounded across the nation and in a very tiny section of the stadium.

Blaze continued, "And where did these billions of MC bucks come from? School fees. Student transfer fees! Yellow and red cards! Again, mostly from large-handed students. Are we okay with this?!"

"No!" the crowd shouted. Puddin' Heads and Sweeties began to boo loudly. The cameras trained on Education Minister Pompavich.

The crowd roared, "Shame! Shame! Shame!" The infuriated education minister snapped Scarlet's pony necklace off her neck and stomped it to smithereens. While Scarlet wailed, her mom swore at Blaze and grabbed her husband by the ear. "Our schools are very good!" she farted. She ran from the stadium with Mr. Pompavich in tow. In a rage, Scarlet punched her chair, then shook her fist at Blaze. The prime minister kept shouting into his MC Frames.

"Should this money be returned to students and families?" Blaze yelled. "Should we eliminate ridiculous school fees and transfer fees?!"

"Yes!" the crowd cried.

"Should all schools be free and fair, for all students?!"

"Yes!"

Blaze, Chopper, and Kai were ecstatic. Their plan was working. The prime minister charged back onto the pitch, still shouting into his MC Frames. Suddenly, the video screens went blank. He snatched the mic from Blaze.

The cameras turned on again, this time focused on the calm, smiling prime minister.

"Wow, what a fired-up crowd!"

The crowd glowered at him.

"Yes, our schools can improve! But these young folks don't have their facts straight. None of that money you just saw was for regional, district, or school bosses—no, no, no! It was actually for the winners of this epic Noble Deed Football Match!"

The crowd exploded into applause, head butts, and group hugs.

Blaze, Chopper, and Kai pumped their fists. "*Let's gooooo!*" Blaze shouted, gesturing for the mic. The prime minister frowned, then smiled for the cameras, and handed it over.

After leading the stadium in a few rounds of shouting, "Free and fair! Free and fair!" Blaze added, "But we don't *just* want free and fair schools, do we? We don't want free, fair, and *lousy* schools, do we?"

The crowd shrugged. "No!"

"We want free, fair, and *fabulous* schools! Triple F schools!"

No one had any idea what fabulous schools could be, but who could disagree that fabulous schools must be better than lousy ones? And three Fs were easy to remember. After several rounds of shouting, "F! F! F!" the crowd settled down.

"Now that we know the winner of this Noble Deed Football Match will earn a free, fair, and fabulous education for all its students, large- and small-handed alike—" Blaze gave the prime minister a thumbs-up, "—it's finally time to play the Noble Deed Match! Enough talk. Enough hype. Folks, I'm Blaze Union, and our Puddin' Heads are about to toast and roast these sad, little Sweeties!"

Blaze dropped the mic. The Puddin' Heads went wild. They head butted each other. They waved their tablespoons and wished they had larger ones.

Kai picked up the mic. "I'm Kai of the Sweeties." The Sweeties shouted and group hugged. "Blaze talks big, but really, she's just full of hot air, more flame than fire. My name stands for a sea of water. And we all know what a sea of water does to a sad, little flame!" The Sweeties jeered and cheered. Kai looked at the sky as if it might rain.

THE NOBLE DEED FOOTBALL MATCH

One side of the stadium shouted, "Fart tart!" and the other kindly replied, "Numbskulls!" Then, "Sweet tarts!" and, "Puddin' mold!" Back and forth, back and forth, becoming less and less kind.

A cart of delicious puddin' was delivered to the favored team. They wolfed it down with wild abandon. They were too excited to notice the education minister waving with a very big smile.

The whistle finally blew. Blaze passed to Ram. Although Blaze played midfield, instead of hanging back, she immediately went on the attack. Blaze could not wait to show the country what Puddin' Head Bigs could do. Ram quickly passed back to Blaze, who dribbled and cut through the Sweetie defense like a spoon glides through puddin'. But Root-Woot proved to be a tenacious defender. Blaze dribbled left and right, back and forth, attacking and retreating, but she couldn't pass the protector of creatures and trees.

"Pass the ball!" Wheels said.

"No! I've waited too long—I'm scoring the first goal!"

She dribbled back and forth.

"Pass the ball!" said Ram.

"Pass the ball!" said Crusher.

"No! I'm scoring the first goal!"

Root-Woot kept Blaze dribbling in circles.

"Pass the ball!" said Hammer.

"No, I just need an opening!" Blaze dribbled for a frankly ridiculous amount of time. Root-Woot clung to her side. Finally, she shook him by brushing past Crusher, Ram, and Hammer, who essentially set a triple pick. Blaze found the opening, and juked Kai, who, of course, played goalie. To the shock and chagrin of many large-handed doubters, Blaze crushed a goal into the right side of the net.

"Gooaaalll!" the Puddin' Head announcers yelled. Blaze pulled a spoon from her holster and pretended to eat puddin'. "All day! All day!" she taunted.

With the exception of a few Puddin' Heads from Region 4— who still resented that we'd burned down their ridiculous hopes of finger chopping—the Puddin' Heads cheered, jeered, head butted, and waved their table spoons. Nevertheless, doubters rationalized the goal. "Eh—anyone could score on the Sweeties—even Bigs."

"No!" Root-Woot cried. He spun, jumped into a twisting flip, and landed in a defensive posture. Kai shook his head. Scarlet slapped her own. Ram rammed the goal post. The prime minister seemed to cheer by whacking his head on the seat in front of him. He shouted something to the education minister, who, as you may remember, was also the football commissioner.

The Sweeties kicked off. Blaze stole the ball, sliced through the Sweetie defense, and the crowd watched the same Blaze versus Root-Woot battle like an MC commercial stuck on repeat. "I just watched this!" a fan cried. "Pass the ball!"

This time, though, a swarm of Sweeties stole the ball. Ram stole it back. Root-Woot flew to Ram. Ram passed to Hammer. Root-Woot flew to Hammer. Hammer passed to Wheels. They simply could not shake Root-Woot.

In the now viral "pinball goal," Wheels accidentally smashed the football off Root-Woot's head. Ram rammed the rebound off Root-Woot's noggin. Hammer hammered the second rebound off Root-Woot's skull. As Root-Woot slowly spun and fell to the ground, Hammer pounded the third rebound like a woodpecker into the goal. The score was 2—0.

Root-Woot, protector of creatures and trees, could no longer defend against the nature-destroying Puddin' Heads. He was knocked unconscious and carried off the field on a stretcher.

The Puddin' Head crowd cheered, waved their spoons, and, this time, ate puddin'.

The Sweeties kicked off. Blaze stole the ball, sliced through the Sweetie defense, and scored within seconds. The score was now 3 —0. "All day! All day!" she taunted them again.

It seemed that the Puddin' Heads would indeed roll the Sweeties like cookie dough. It seemed that Blaze was finally proving to herself, and to Island Nation, that Bigs *could* lead. It seemed that Blaze was well on her way to becoming the education minister and changing schools for the better. But unfortunately for Blaze and the Puddin' Heads, the Sweeties changed strategies. They quadruple-teamed Blaze.

They stole the ball from her repeatedly. Everyone yelled at her to pass. "Fine!" she finally shouted. "Someone take some pressure off me and score! Someone has to be open!"

But such frustration confused Crusher, who head butted Hammer, then Ram. Yes, Puddin' Head fans and announcers finally got the answer to the very important question: Who would win in a head butting contest—Crusher, Hammer, or Ram? Crusher and

Hammer left the match unconscious. *But was it a fair contest?*

The remaining Puddin' Heads had barely practiced as a team, and so they struggled to pass, let alone score. The Sweeties stole the ball. The Puddin' Heads stole it back. And so it went for many minutes.

In another blow to the Puddin' Heads, they had a sudden puddin' energy crash. Strangely, the prime minister yelled, "Let's go!" to the Sweeties. But still, the Sweeties struggled to advance the ball. Finally, they had a shot on goal. But even feeling sluggish, Hands still managed to swat it away.

The prime minister shouted angrily at the football commissioner. She shouted something into her MC Frames. The Sweeties kicked off. Ram stole the ball. A ref blew the whistle and held up a yellow card.

"What?!" Blaze yelled. "That was a clean steal!" The ref held up a yellow card for Blaze. "You can't give me—" Then she stopped and looked at Chopper. "What's going on?"

This outrageous call recharged the Puddin' Heads.

"Just keep playing! Don't complain. Keep it clean!" Chopper called.

The next time, Blaze dribbled through the Sweeties more cautiously. In a rare display of teamwork, she crossed a line drive past four Sweeties to Wheels, who passed to Ram, who headed the ball back to Blaze, who sped past the Sweetie defenders and tapped the ball into the goal, past a diving Kai.

But this beautiful "give and go" goal, as the announcers called it, was recalled. The ref held up a late offside flag, which was totally bogus. Ram complained and received a yellow card. Orion said, "I'm very confused" and got a yellow card. Hammer, now rousing from the sideline, rapidly lurched her neck back and forth in frustration. For that vulgarity: a red card. Blaze could not believe what was happening. They were down to ten players.

The Puddin' Head fans booed the refs. The Sweeties cheered. The prime minister and education minister smirked. *You* might see what was happening, but no one else did.

Blaze and Chopper quickly pulled the team together. "The refs are terrible," Chopper said. "They're making ridiculous calls!"

"They're biased against us Puddin' Heads! And they're only calling yellow and red cards on Bigs! They can't stand to see us succeed," Blaze said. "But we're still up 3—0. They've only taken one shot. And I have a lot more scoring to do."

"Take it easy. Don't give them any reason to give you a red card! We can't afford to lose more players. And pass the ball!"

"We'll win by a landslide!" Blaze said. "It's time to light it up. Just follow my lead."

Blaze stole the ball again and raced through the Sweeties in the middle of the pitch with Wheels running on her right. Ram ran on Blaze's left. Blaze yelled for Wheels to back up, who complained she couldn't run any slower, but stayed a step behind nevertheless. Chopper yelled for Blaze to pass the ball. Blaze didn't consider it. She side-stepped one defender, who pretzeled her legs together and fell down in a heap. She faked left and flipped the ball right to shoot past the final defender, who spun like a top. Then, she scorched a goal past Kai's fingertips in the top left corner. He swore under his breath. Then, he studied the sky, which started to darken.

The Puddin' Heads cheered. The ref raised another bogus offside flag on Wheels, who kept her mouth shut.

Blaze did not. She wasn't going to have another goal unfairly stripped away. She yelled at Wheels for being too close. "But she wasn't really offside, now was she?" she mumbled.

"What did you say?" the ref cried.

"Nothing."

"Watch your mouth."

Blaze paced.

"You think you're hot stuff. But you're really nothing more than a numbskull Big full of hot air."

"What did *you* say?!" Blaze fired back. "You obviously missed that goal I just scored. Maybe you should fix your Frames."

Blaze watched in slow motion as the ref reached into his back pocket, pulled out the red card, and held it up for all to see. At first, it didn't register. She turned and saw that Chopper looked like he'd been hit by a puddin' truck. He pummeled his head, which he then hung down, and swore under his breath.

Unfortunately for the ref, some Puddin' Heads took football seriously. With their best player ejected from the game, they pulled the ref into their section and tossed him like a beach ball, which he didn't appreciate. Nor did he appreciate getting tossed out of the stadium, falling onto a Puddin' tent, and breaking several bones. No doubt this sent a different message to the remaining refs, who subsequently ran the pitch with hands in their pockets.

Blaze watched from the sideline and taunted the Sweeties. A

win seemed imminent. But the Puddin' Heads were down to nine players, had lost nearly half of their talent, and didn't know how to play as a team. Chopper, Orion, and Hands stopped the Sweeties from scoring, but Wheels and Ram could not advance the ball close enough for a shot on goal. The prime minister shouted into his Frames, which few noticed amid all the excitement.

Within minutes, a ref tentatively issued a red card. Eight players. Yes, that ref was also tossed from the stadium. With three more players now on the field, the Sweeties repeatedly charged, firing shots on goal. It seemed that the teams were finally even. The yellow and red cards stopped.

Chopper and Orion held their own, but the Sweetie's biggest obstacle was Hands, who remained unstoppable. Even when they made it past Chopper and Orion, Hands snatched the ball out of the air like Puddin' Heads would snatch candy from a baby Sweetie if they actually liked candy. Neither team scored another goal before the half-time whistle blew. It was still 3—0.

The prime minister was fuming. But not for long.

GO SWEETIES

"I can't believe they gave me a red card! But we still got this!" Blaze told her team on the sideline. "We're fine. Just stay focused. No let downs."

But to Chopper she cried, "Ah! We should be up by twenty by now!"

"Maybe if you'd passed the ball, we would be!" Chopper said.

Then, something strange happened. The sky turned darker. On the Sweetie sideline, Kai opened large boxes around which the Sweetie team began chanting and dancing in concentric circles, their arms draped over each other, shifting and swaying.

Blaze laughed. "What are those fart tarts doing?"

Dark skies became storm clouds. It began to rain. Nearly 75,000 Sweetie fans reached into their blue backpacks. But instead of grabbing raincoats or umbrellas, they pulled out blocks of dry ice, fans, large forks, and a few other fun items. When the pouring rain hit the dry ice in the stands and in the large boxes on the pitch, huge plumes of fog drifted across the Sweetie side of the stadium. Then, the Sweeties turned on their fans. The thick fog slowly filled the stadium. The Puddin' Heads couldn't see the Sweeties.

Suddenly, nearly 75,000 Sweetie fans and the entire Sweetie football team emerged from this dense fog, holding their breath, as —yes!—zombies. Fake teeth, painted black-and-blue faces, and painted arms and legs. They wielded the dreaded large fork that rivaled the spoon hat. Paint smeared down their faces, shirts, and legs in the rain.

Yes, the Sweeties looked ridiculous, but they scared the puddin' right out of the Puddin' Heads. These next few minutes are not recorded in the annals of Puddin' Head history with Puddin' Head pride. But, wow, did these moments make for *excellent* news coverage, which was broadcast live across all of Island Nation.

Puddin' Head children screamed as their parents scooped them up and ran. Cries of "Zombie attack! I need my spoons! I knew they were zombies!" erupted throughout the stadium. Puddin' Heads trampled each other as they stampeded for the exits. A few jumped from the top of the stadium. Puddin' Heads galloped toward and across the bridge, perhaps wishing they had ponies to ride. Puddin' Head News showed clip after clip of the Sweetie zombies, and then across Puddin' Head MC Frames and screens in Puddin' Head homes.

Blaze was not fooled. She shouted at her team through the rain. "Those are fake teeth! They're not real zombies! They're just wearing paint, for puddin' sake!" But the Puddin' Heads couldn't see the evidence in plain sight. They could only see the ingrained fear and prejudice of generations. Ram and many of the Puddin' Head players ran away. Even Hands—the mighty Puddin' Head giant—bolted like an elephant from a mouse. Only Chopper, Wheels, and Orion were left to play. Blaze stood alone on the sideline.

Chopper suggested the obvious strategy: run down the clock. They were up 3—0. With Wheel's speed and Chopper and Orion on defense, they had a chance. They were playing the Sweeties after all.

Blaze was soaked, furious, and pacing the sideline. Furious at the ref for giving her a red card. Furious at her people from running away from a bunch of flower-loving, navel-gazing, soft puff Sweeties dressed up in costumes. Furious at the now impossibility of winning by a landslide. But Blaze did not yet fear losing.

Of course, the lopsided crowd only added fuel to Blaze's fire. The Sweetie crowd spread out around the stadium, overshadowing the remaining handful of MegaCorp elite, the prime minister, and three loyal-to-the-death Puddin' Heads. The Sweetie fans laughed and cheered like never before in their lives. They created new cheers, which resounded throughout the stadium. The news organizations ate these cheers up like puddin', cookies, and cake. Here are some of the favorites:

Cheers for scoring:
Make it rain! Put out the fire!
Make it rain! Put out the Blaze!

Go Sweeties! Go Zombies!
Go Sweeties! Go Zombies!

Cheers for Puddin' Head mistakes:
Who is whin-ing? (Clap, clap, clap clap clap)
Who is cry-ing? (Clap, clap, clap clap clap)

Pudd-in' head ba-bies! (Clap, clap, clap clap clap)

What's that smell? Moldy puddin'!
What's that smell? Moldy puddin'!

Cheers just for fun:
Zombie! Kindness! Zombie! Kindness!
Zombie! Sweetie! Zombie! Sweetie!

Who is laugh-ing? (Clap, clap, clap clap clap)
Sweet-ie zom-bies! (Clap, clap, clap clap clap)

Sweeties are smart, Puddin' Heads are dull.
Sweeties hug, Puddin' Heads bang numbskulls.
Sweeties wear flowers, Puddin' Heads smell all day.
Zombies come together, Puddin' Heads run away!

Chopper, Orion, and Wheels did their best to withstand the kind
yet hostile crowd and run out the clock. Wheels chomped down
dynamite chips, dribbled down the side-lines, and sped around the
pitch as if chased by bombs. Chopper and Orion played long ball
and hoofed it to the other end of the pitch every chance they got.
But the Sweeties badly outnumbered them and eventually closed the
gap, 3—3, with one minute to go.

The Puddin' Heads risked it all, attacking with all three players.
In a dazzling display of teamwork, Orion laced a pass to Chopper,
who crossed it in front of the goal. It was impossible to be offside.
Time ticked off the big screen. Five seconds. Four seconds. Three
seconds. Blaze ran onto the pitch with raised arms, knowing what
was about to happen. Wheels sped past five defenders and blasted a
shot through the goal just as time expired.

The tiny Puddin' Head celebration—which burst across the
pitch and the handful of Puddin' Head fans left on Celebration
Island, and then erupted across millions of viewers—lasted only one
second.

The ref waved a flag.

Someone was offside.

No, wait.

Red card player incident. On Blaze.

No goal.

No overtime shoot-out.

Game over.

To Blaze's horror, to the team's shock, and to Puddin' Head Island's embarrassment, the game ended in a draw: 3—3. Blaze tried to plead and argue with the refs, but they bolted from the stadium. Thousands of Sweeties streamed onto the pitch to celebrate the impossible. They picked up Kai, a half-conscious Root-Woot, and the Sweetie players, chanting, "Draw! Draw! Draw!"

PUDDIN' BALLS

Blaze and Chopper reluctantly watched the Puddin' Head evening news. It started with the energetic Puddin' Head co-anchors, Bartle and Nutt. They wore their usual white dress shirts with rolled-up sleeves and red ties.

Nutt opened. "My lovely Puddin' Heads, tonight we are sad to share an unfortunate story. Warning: This news hour is not recommended for children. As everyone knows, Blaze Union and the Puddin' Head football team had a very important Noble Deed Match today versus the ridiculously inferior Sweeties. We almost killed this story because it's so embarrassing for one of our own."

Bartle chortled, "How fast our heroes fall."

Blaze stared wide-eyed.

They showed short clips of her red card, the Sweeties scoring goals, Blaze running onto the pitch just in time to nullify the last goal, and Sweetie fans celebrating. They showed a clip of Zuli Sweet—yes, the Sweetie news anchor and arch enemy of Puddin' Head News—mocking Blaze and the Puddin' Head team and commending the Sweeties on a kind and cooperative effort to pull out an amazing draw.

Nutt said, "Hey Bartle. Here's a tough question. Which of these two is the most pathetic? Because they're both pathetic."

Bartle snorted. "Well, we already know Zuli Sweet is pathetic, so no doubt this award goes to Blaze Union. Do you think she's gone sweet?"

Blaze screamed.

"Could be. But that's just part of the problem here. What did we expect, really? I mean, this is what happens when you put Bigs in these kinds of positions. Can't handle leadership." Nutt shook his head. "And what's up with those ridiculous demands. FFF schools? It's like they want to have their puddin' and eat it too."

"'Let's hand out free puddin'! And how about free education, especially for the Bigs!'" Bartle chuckled and slapped his knee. "But let's be fair here a minute—what's Blaze's point? What are these FFF demands?"

Although furious, Blaze saw a glimmer of hope.

Nutt responded, "They want to improve our schools, which, of course, would be a good thing. But to them, that means a free education for all students."

"Ridiculous."

"Right?"

"Sad, because these Puddin' Heads had quite the opportunity to win the Noble Deed prize money. That would have covered at least a year, I would think."

"Yeah, they really pooped their pants on that one."

Bartle snickered. "Oh, and they want a 'fabulous' education and 'fair' rules, including eliminating yellow and red cards. Eliminating large hand rules. Yeah, let's wait around and see what happens then!"

"Schools without rules! Imagine! What are school bosses saying about these Fs? Let's hear from the nation's new top boss."

"Stupid. Weak. Arrrr!" School Boss J.R. said. "That's what that rules result being. Next thing you knows, Puddin' Heads run round with flowers heads. When zombies—"

Blaze screamed again.

Bartle chuckled. "This team has gone sweet, and now they want everyone else to go sweet, too? Do we need to hear more? Yes, unfortunately we do, my esteemed Puddin' Head viewers," Bartle said seriously. "We need to hear more, because Blaze and this sugary sweet team are spreading cancerous ideas across our amazing schools. Some say they are part of the TDLMNOP group, who are poisoning our children's minds and making them go soft. Puddin' Heads are protesting across our great island in favor of Blaze's ridiculous demands right now. School bosses are reporting protests at their schools, demanding their resignations. But, fellow Puddin' Heads, this isn't the worst part. What else do they propose? They want to raise taxes to pay for all their recommendations!"

Yes, Puddin' Heads were conditioned to hate taxes almost as much as loathing Sweeties. While Nutt pretended to fall out of his chair, several million adults across Puddin' Head Island yelled, cursed, pumped their fists, and head butted each other.

"What about all the money the bosses are taking?" Blaze cried. "I can't believe we didn't win the Noble Deed Match!"

Bartle grimly shook his head at Nutt, still splayed on the ground. "I know. This is startling and serious. But that's right. They want to raise taxes to the highest level seen in decades. They want rule-free schools. They want to pay teachers ridiculous salaries. They want teachers to have 'better working conditions.' *They want to take your freedom.*" The camera shot behind the anchor desk to show Nutt looking up in terror.

Blaze yelled at the screen. "Liars! They're making half this stuff up! Why?!"

Bartle turned back to the main camera. "Puddin' Heads, this is a dangerous and credible threat to our island, and we need to shut it down. I hope we won't need to cover this story anymore. But I'm afraid we will for our island's safety. Please talk to your children. Make sure they haven't been brainwashed by these outrageous ideas. Our schools can certainly get better, but they are in excellent shape already. We don't need them to go sweet, nor do we need to raise taxes. This is Bartle and Nutt. Stay strong, eat your puddin', and have a good night."

Blaze was humiliated and furious, but somehow still had hope. "There are protests across the island?" She paced. "Maybe if we . . . no, that won't work."

Suddenly, Chopper exploded. "Why didn't we practice?! Why did you have to get that red card! We would have won!"

"The Sweetie refs were out to get me! They were looking for a reason. It didn't matter what it was."

Chopper "It did matter!"

"Hands and more than half the team ran away from the fake zombies! The whole game was rigged! We would have won by fifty if it wasn't for the refs!"

And just when it seemed like things couldn't possibly get worse, Blaze and Chopper were charged with inciting violent protests and national insubordination and were carted off to jail.

After a very long day complaining about false charges and putting kids in jail, Blaze and Chopper were starving. They reluctantly tried the moldy, crusty puddin' balls—and immediately spat them out.

Chopper said, "They're just trying to break our will."

Blaze shook her head. "Maybe they did."

Chopper refused to talk. Blaze stewed and turned the events of the previous day over and over in her mind, wishing she had another chance. Her anger turned to sadness as she realized the consequences of her actions, and what her future could be. Finally, after two days, the protests across the nation died down. Blaze and Chopper were finally released from jail—although they were due to appear before the Senate the following day, which they knew meant being fired.

A crowd of students, teachers, TDJP members, and citizens from across the island gathered outside the jail. They cheered for Blaze and Chopper, urging them to continue to fight for FFF schools. They held up signs with crossed-out pictures of compression gloves, bootstraps, obsessive testing, rock bashing, and other ridiculous school activities. In contrast, a large group of Sweeties celebrated the Noble Deed draw. They boisterously sang cheers for scoring, cheers for mistakes, and cheers for fun.

Blaze told her worried mom that she wanted to be alone. She walked slowly past the crowd. She waved off a group of children with frown Frames asking for her autograph. "I'm sorry. I failed. We lost. Please, leave me alone."

Blaze told me she could only think of one place to go.

Blaze stood near a familiar precipice on Mount Freedom. A light, cool breeze blew across her face. A colorful butterfly landed on her hand for a moment, but Blaze just fought back tears and it fluttered away. She remembered what had happened last time. She remembered who she'd been. She remembered her passion. But now, she felt humiliated, defeated, depressed.

Suddenly, a powerful anger erupted inside of her. She yelled, *"Whhhyyyyy?"* across the great ravine. *"Why is this so hard!"* The wind picked up as she cried, yelled, stomped, shouted, and swore. She held out her arms with tightening fists—as if fighting the wind, as if fighting the world.

Blaze peered over Puddin' Head Island. Her town of Courage looked minuscule. A calm sadness overtook her. She tossed her MC Frames aside and breathed rapidly as tears rolled down her cheeks. "I am so sorry," she said to the schools across Puddin' Head Island.

"I failed you. I failed myself."

Blaze shook her head and sighed. "And now here I am. The numbskull talking to the wind. Or the mountain. Or the universe. Anything that will listen. I don't understand this world. Every time I think I can make schools better, something bigger gets in my way! Why does this keep happening?! And why do these ridiculous rules exist in the first place?!"

The wind gained force. Blaze talked louder. "Why do ridiculous things keep happening over and over?"

The wind strengthened. Blaze spread out her arms and leaned into it. She thought of Orion and yelled, "What is the point of anything in this absurd world?!"

I can relate to these thoughts and feelings. Perhaps you can, too.

"I'm just a stupid person on this stupid mountain traveling on a stupid planet around the stupid sun in a stupid universe!"

Suddenly, the ethereal voice came out of nowhere once more. It asked, *Who is the problem?*

"What the—" Blaze said. "Dad?"

After a long moment with the wind still blowing, Blaze shook her head. Then, she repeated, "*Who* is the problem? What kind of question—" She thought for a moment. Suddenly, it hit her.

And she started bawling uncontrollably. She could barely get out the words. "*I* am the problem! I am the numbskull who ruined Puddin' Head schools forever. I made them worse than they were before! I didn't have the team practice! I got a red card for being stupid! I ran onto the pitch too early! We would have won that game and got all that money if I wasn't such a numbskull, egg-shelled, head-bashing, moldy-puddin'-eating, fart tart!"

Who is the problem?

"What? I just told you! I'm the problem!" The wind continued to howl. "Okay, then. The Sweeties! The lying, cheating, cake-and-cookie-eating, navel-gazing, sweet fart tarts! How did they tie us?!"

Who is the problem?

"Why do you keep asking me that?!" she yelled. "The Puddin' Heads! *We're* the problem! We hurt our own, because we're a bunch of thick headed, rock-for-brain numbskulls. We allowed those no-good, zombie-faking, sweet puffs to trick us, and then we ran away! I knew zombies weren't real but I went along with it, and they came back and bit me like *real* zombies!"

Who is the problem?

Blaze cursed and closed her eyes. The wind blew so hard it lifted her off the ground. She landed on her back, the air rushing out of her lungs. She could barely breathe or see from the torrent of dust streaming against her whole life force. For a moment, she lay unconscious—or perhaps, *more* conscious.

After a long while, another question popped into her mind. *Who benefits?* As she lay there, she retraced the events of the past month. Connecting the dots between the mega-mansion Fun Room, the private office, the school bosses, the schools, the news, the Noble Deed Match, the referees. Suddenly, in a flash of insight, a dark ignorance was illuminated.

The wind calmed. Blaze rose to her feet. "Of course! It's so obvious!" Blaze could see more clearly than before—but not yet clearly enough.

Who is separate?

"Ah, come on! What kind of question is that?! Enough with the questions!" Blaze paced and thought. She shook her head. "Who is separate? Separate from what? The problem?! Forget this, I have my own questions! About the game. Were those Sweetie or MegaCorp refs? Are they working together?! Who sent that cart of puddin'? And how could they possibly have known it was going to rain?! And more importantly, *what can I do*? They are in power. I have no power now. What am I supposed *to do about that*?"

"Those are great questions."

"Great, now we're having a conversation. I'm having a conversation with the wind. I'm hearing voices everywhere. I'm losing my moldy mind!"

"I thought I'd find you up here, Blaze."

Blaze spun around. "Aunt Serafina! What are you doing up here?"

"The question is, what are *you* doing up here? You have people waiting for you."

Blaze hung her head. "I can't. It's too hard. And what difference does it make? I'm starting to understand the problem, but I can't do anything to fix it. Puddin' Head schools are just too complicated!"

Aunt Serafina hugged her. They said nothing for a long time.

They just breathed and looked across Puddin' Head Island.

"Blaze, I've known you your whole life. You're a fighter. A lot of people lack the courage to do what you've done."

"What *have* I done? I've only messed things up. Schools are worse than before. And now what am I going to do?"

"Blaze, do you realize how many people came to the Noble Deed Match? How many people watched on their screens and MC Frames? And more importantly, how many people are starting to change their minds? Who are questioning hand size rules? Who are now, for the first time ever, imagining and supporting free, fair, and fabulous schools? Do you know how long TDJP has been waiting for this kind of momentum? This kind of opportunity?"

Blaze looked up. Tears welled in her eyes. "I know," she cried. "But we tied! And that means no money for Puddin' Head schools! I blew it."

"Blaze, you can't stop now. Sure, this was a setback, but it's not over."

"I can't! The Sweeties tricked us—Puddin' Heads literally ran away! Maybe if I would've . . . oh, it doesn't matter. Look at the refs! The whole game was rigged! MegaCorp. Sweeties. The prime minister. The news. They're all in this together, aren't they? They're too powerful. "

She threw a rock into the ravine and watched it plummet to the ground far below. "How do you do it? How do you keep going? How do you make sense out of all of this?"

Aunt Serafina didn't hesitate. "Those are great questions. Keep asking them. You know what keeps me going? You. I've watched you grow up. Even as a small child you had such energy, such a zest for life. You were always all in—no holding back. Sure, you made mistakes, but you learned from them. And one thing I love about you is your tenacious drive for justice. You stood up for Bigs even before you were one. And so, on that ridiculous, made-up Good Hope Day, when your hands 'changed' from small to large, it just broke my heart. It shouldn't matter, of course, but it does in this nation. It was one of the most absurd things I've ever witnessed. How that day crushed your spirit. Your passion turned to anger. What happened to you at school. What happened to your family. Yes, Blaze, I keep going for you. I keep fighting for the thousands of other people who just want to live their lives."

Suddenly, Aunt Serafina grabbed her. "Look at me," she said with great passion. "Blaze, you're a fighter. This is a pivotal time in our nation's history. This is not the time to lie down. This is the time to rise up and fight. Who are you fighting for?"

Blaze didn't hesitate, either. "Maya." She felt a new wave of inspiration rising from deep within her. But she still had big, unanswered questions. "But how am I supposed to do this? *How do you lead* in this absurd world?"

Aunt Serafina laughed. "Well, I'm still learning, too. But you have to start with yourself. You must be the change you wish to see in the world, as Gandhi taught."

"Own your journey," Blaze said.

"Yeah."

Blaze took this in. She thought about her mistakes. She thought about the absurdly cruel and unfair things she had seen. She asked, "But what about anger? Don't you get angry? Sometimes, I just can't take it. I just want to head butt someone. And do something. And then, sometimes, I make things worse."

"Of course I get angry! We all get angry. Anger can be very useful. It compels us to act. It can offer us insight. When you slow down and notice what's behind it, it can reveal what's important. Sometimes we're angry for the right reasons, but sometimes we're not. That's why you want to own it, but don't let it own you."

"How do you do that?"

"It takes time. I have some mindfulness practices I can teach you."

"Are those like chill bird trances?"

"What?"

"Never mind. Yeah, mindfulness sounds great." Blaze let out a deep breath. She thought a moment. "So, how *do* you lead others? Especially when they believe ridiculous things, like Smalls are better than Bigs?"

"I don't have all the answers but try leading by example. You've done that in many ways. Do you know how many people are singing your songs?" Blaze smiled proudly then looked down the ravine, across Puddin' Head Island, and then at Power Island.

"I can lead by example all I want, but it doesn't matter if I can't change the rules."

"If you have followers, you're a leader. Leadership always matters."

"But School Boss J.R. has followers—I don't want to lead like that. I want to lead positive change, for everyone."

"You want to be transformative."

"Yeah, I guess. But how do you change the people causing the problem? The people in power?"

"You're asking good questions. I wish I had simple solutions. But I've learned that those in power—especially those there for the wrong reasons—don't change or go away easily. And they'll fight to the bitter end. In this country, they have incredible power, especially to shape minds through the media. But tomorrow, you'll have a national stage. Think about how to use that. Think about what you've learned on your tour, what those schools want and need, and how to use this opportunity."

RIDICULOUS CHALLENGE

Blaze and Chopper stood before the Senate. Outside the Capitol, protesters chanted for FFF schools. Everyone expected that Blaze and Chopper were about to be fired, and yet Blaze had a glow about her, as if she had a profound awakening—or else had a brilliant plan. Blaze was surprised to see Kai walk in, too; apparently, he faced the same scrutiny—maybe even, termination.

Per the prime minister's demand, live cameras rolled. He wanted to make a national spectacle out of these losers. "I think we've all seen what happens when Bigs are allowed to play offense in football. And when they attempt to take on a leadership role." The prime minister, MC executives, and most of the Senate chuckled. Senator Serafina gave Blaze an encouraging pump of her fist. The education minister glared daggers at the trio. A video replayed highlights of the Noble Deed Match, especially the yellow and red cards and Puddin' Heads fleeing the stadium. Then it showed the protests across the nation, demanding FFF schools.

"There's no doubt that the sales from the Noble Deed Match far exceeded expectations." The prime minister smiled at the education minister and gave Scarlet a thumbs-up. "But we just can't have troublemakers spreading lies, stirring up protests across our great country and school system, and giving people false hope."

"You're the liar!" Kai said unexpectedly. "That Noble Deed Match money was supposed to go to schools!"

Blaze and Chopper exchanged looks.

"Awww. This kind Sweetie thinks I've been unfair." The room laughed. "I kept my promise. No one won. So, no one got the money!"

Suddenly, Blaze realized that was true—the Puddin' Heads hadn't gotten the prize money, but neither had the Sweeties.

"We should split the money!" Blaze said suddenly.

"That wasn't the deal!" the prime minister countered. "A great game but not my fault you ended in a draw." He frowned at Kai. "Sweetie cookie pie, you couldn't even win with eleven players against three. And after watching that game, sweet puff, you're lucky it ended in a draw. Like I said, no one won, so no one got the money."

Blaze said, "Oh, someone did get the money. But it wasn't the schools. How convenient that the refs gave out so many yellow and red cards. Know any of them?"

Chopper looked at Blaze, wide-eyed. The nation gasped. The senators were taken aback. Some pounded their desks. Senator Serafina sighed, lowered her head, and whispered to herself, "Did you learn *anything* from our conversation?"

The prime minister stood on his tippy-toes. "That's preposterous!"

"And how convenient that last goal wasn't counted, so the game could end in a draw."

"You're the numbskull who ran onto the pitch."

"You would have found another reason not to count that goal."

The nation gasped again.

"I wasn't a ref!" The prime minister *almost* took the bait, but then he looked into the cameras. "I'm so sorry that you couldn't handle playing offense and were booted from the game. I'm so sorry that you couldn't even handle staying quiet on the sideline," he said sympathetically, "and staying in your place."

Blaze raised her eyebrows, squeezed her fists, and then took a very deep breath. She re-centered. She was a quick learner this time. "You know we would have destroyed the Sweeties. But you planned a draw and selected refs to ensure that it happened. What was your cut of the profits from the Noble Deed Match? I don't think I have to remind the citizens of this country about the multi-billion MC bucks education scam. We saw it with our own eyes, stolen from hard working students and families. You're behind that, too, aren't you? You cheated us out of schools, and then you cheated us out of a fair Noble Deed Match."

"Ha! A loser always lies! And you couldn't even beat the Sweeties. I mean, look at your hands!" The prime minister burst out laughing and waved his tiny hands.

"Oh, really?" Blaze said. "Then why don't you let us do a re-match? This time *we* choose the refs."

"Yeah!" Kai said.

"Yeah!" said the millions of people watching.

"Yeah, *I'm* going to let you choose the refs. *That* would be fair!"

"Actually, better yet, why don't you let us play MegaCorp for the entire pot of the Noble Deed Match prize money? And yes, for those billions sitting in the private office of the education minister. Not just the money for bosses. The money for the Wall. The money for the education ministry. That would easily fund the FFF schools that so many students, teachers, parents, citizens, and, yes, *good* school bosses want. If you actually allowed a fair game, we would beat the pants off of MegaCorp."

The nation couldn't wait to see what would happen next. This was better than watching the Noble Deed Match. The prime minister and the room roared with laughter. Scarlet laughed the loudest.

"I don't think so!"

"I know you're scared. You know what? I'll even choose an entire team of large-handed players." The room bellowed with laughter. Many senators fell out of their chairs, guffawing.

Senator Serafina stood up. Blaze was indeed unfolding a brilliant strategy.

"Okay, yeah, that would be *some* game!" the prime minister sneered. "But it's not going to happen! What a waste of time!"

Blaze leaned in as if toward a Mount Freedom wind. "I can see that you're scared the Bigs will trounce MegaCorp. So, I'll tell you what. To give MegaCorp a tiny fraction of a chance, we'll even put Sweeties on the starting team."

The prime minister, Kai, Chopper, Senator Serafina, the rest of the room, and millions of people across Island Nation all fell silent. Then, when they picked their jaws up off the ground, they all uttered, "What the . . ."

"Imagine the sales! Puddin' Head and Sweetie Bigs versus MegaCorp. Now *that* would truly be an epic battle."

For a second, the prime minister pondered this idea. "That would be a lot of money," he said to himself, strumming his tiny fingers together. Then he returned to outrage. "That's the most ridiculous challenge I've heard in my entire life! Oh, but I would love to see MegaCorp pound the hands off you Big numbskulls! And teach you all another lesson. You don't have a puddin' cup's chance in a roomful of starving Puddin' Heads! If you win, I'll even make you the education minister!"

"For real?"

"*For real!*"

Blaze nearly toppled off the stage. Education Minister Pompavich kicked her chair and stomped out of the room. New hope surged throughout Blaze's entire being. Senators yelled back and forth at each other and at the prime minister. The nation rose to its feet, head butted, and cheered. Imagine the match!

But a team of MegaCorp executives and lawyers rushed over, whispered something in the prime minister's ear, and let him off the hook. "Uh, sorry. Never mind. I forgot why we're here. You three are fired! Oh, I love saying that!"

SOLIDARITY

The prime minister mistakenly believed that he was done with the small but mighty team. But Blaze, Chopper, and Kai—who now sported a new ocean wave tattoo on his left arm—had other ideas. After a difficult round of apologies, they engaged in a few days of intensive history study with Jules and Teacher Howzin, which included the shocking insights you read earlier in this book. This resulted in considerable swearing, head tapping, affirmations, and exclamations such as, "Why am I just now learning about this history?"

After their study session, they met a lively bunch of Puddin' Heads and Sweeties on Peace Island. This group included Senator Serafina, TDJP members (citizens, families, and educators, mostly), and several dozen student representatives from various regions. The Puddin' Heads and Sweeties had last met on this island many generations ago, prior to the arrival of the first prime minister—and prior to the names "Puddin' Heads" and "Sweeties."

Blaze had planned to discuss strategies for redoing the Noble Deed Match, but first, her leadership was tested with a number of tough issues.

The shiny blue Sweeties had serious concerns. During a round of slightly awkward introductions, Jules officially introduced herself as a TDJP member. She wore a shiny blue jacket with a matching beret that had a shiny spinner on top. She said, "Blaze, you made an impressive speech. But were you being real, being truthful? Or did you just say these words out of desperation?"

Blaze told her story and explained her shift and realization. The shiny Sweeties seemed receptive.

Jules continued, "Let's assume for the moment that you are being truthful, that you do indeed intend to become the next education minister to improve schools for the entire nation. In principle, we very much like the idea of free, fair, and fabulous schools. But free, fair, and fabulous for whom? Sorry, we just don't trust Puddin' Heads!"

"Or the education minister!" a shiny Sweetie called.

"Or the prime minister!"

"Heigi hooga!" the TDJP Sweeties said.

"Let me be clear," Blaze said emphatically. "I will lead for all students to have FFF schools. All means all. Large-handed, small-handed, Sweeties, and Puddin' Heads alike. Besides, we must work together to defeat MegaCorp!"

"Heigi hooga!"

"Nay!" a Sweetie cried. "These are just words. This Puddin' Head can't be trusted! Remember the Battle of Sugar Falls! Remember the puddin' they sent us!"

"It's true!" the Sweeties cried.

"No, I've changed!" Blaze said.

"Prove these are more than just empty words!"

"Heigi hooga!"

"Well, I can tell you I learned more on our school tours than I did in all of middle school. And the cross-island survey results overwhelmingly showed students want real-world learning. I think fabulous schools should include cross-island field trips, where students can visit, learn about, and even partner with students from other schools. If done well, it could break down these ridiculous island stereotypes. And we already have a train system."

"That *is* a fabulous idea—we've never done anything like that!"

"Yeah, Puddin' Heads and Sweeties could work together!"

"It beats taking tests!"

"Heigi hooga!"

"No, that's a stupid idea. Some schools are too far away from the trains!"

"And it'll cause too much pollution!" a tree hugger cried. "Imagine doubling or tripling the number of trains!"

"No heigi," some Sweeties whined.

"Then we have a problem to solve as a group," Chopper said. "A lot of schools already do experiments—why can't we collaborate with the railway company and design extensions? Or invent a solar-powered train? Now that would be an awesome group project!"

"We could have a competition!"

"No, it should be done cooperatively! See—they want to turn us into Puddin' Heads! They want to erase our values! They don't want us to be kind!"

A raucous debate erupted about which island had better values. The TDJP educators dressed in red argued that the Puddin' Head Island values were fine, but too limited. The nation needed to add truth, democracy, justice, and people before profit as core principles. The shiny blue TDJP group argued the opposite: The Sweetie Island values were sound but also too limited. Orion paced outside the group, as if an outcast or lost in thought.

"And you got the TDJP wrong," Jules said. "It stands for 'truthfulness, diversity, joy, and planet before profit!'"

"What? I thought there's only one TDJP!" School Leader Foster said. "I mean, what does diversity matter if there's no democracy? Ridiculous!"

"Hear! Hear!"

"What is a democracy that fails to recognize diversity? Diversity is a fact, not an opinion. Affirming diversity, combined with fairness —a Sweetie core value—is a powerful combination!" Jules said.

"Heigi hooga!"

"Ha!" said Senator Serafina, raising her spoon. "Fairness—that sounds like justice! And there can be no joy without justice!"

"What is justice if there's no joy? I'll tell you what: a bunch of angry, marching sticks who get stuck in the mud! Get it? Sticks in the mud?" a Sweetie named Blue Cloud scoffed.

"Heigi hooga!"

A Puddin' Head raised her spoon. "Sounds like silly Sweeties ignoring injustice," she scoffed. More Puddin' Heads raised spoons and yelled, "Spoons up!"

"Heigi hooga!" the Sweeties yelled back.

"*Spoons up!*" the Puddin' Heads yelled louder, waving their spoons wildly.

"*Heigi hooga!*" the Sweeties bellowed.

Orion stopped pacing, entered the middle of the fighting, crossed his arms, and sat down. The raucous debate suddenly stopped. Orion exclaimed, "I'm not mad! I'm depressed. The truth is," he said, "life has no purpose. We live on a rock that orbits a lifeless star. And we're all going to die."

"No heigi," some Sweeties sighed.

"Sweet honey tart! Who invited this killjoy?" Blue Cloud asked.

"That's a good question, Blue Cloud," a Sweetie said.

"Clouds bring rain, which makes mud," Orion said flatly.

"Are you mocking me?" Blue Cloud thundered.

"Clouds bring rainbows," Kai said.

"And lightning."

"Watch it!"

Blaze thought of Kuko, her dad, and Mount Freedom. "Yes, difficult things happen—sometimes things that make no sense," Blaze said to Orion. "But we can choose how we look at them. We can choose a different perspective. I think it's amazing that there's life at all. How did that happen? It's amazing that humans even exist."

"And the planet!" a Sweetie added.

"And trees!"

"Trees are already part of the planet, tree hugger!"

"So are people, you numbskull!"

Orion said, "Maybe." He shrugged, lowered his head, and furrowed his brow, as if trying to pout or to sink into mud that wasn't there.

Then, a strange thing happened. A synchronized flock of shiny blue Sweeties began to giggle and wiggle. They waddled in lock step to give this Puddin' Head a silly tickle. "Here comes the tickle zombie!" They stuck out their hands and wiggled their fingers, waiting. As hard as he tried, this Puddin' Head could not keep his face angry or sad.

"Okay, one time!" Orion said, half eager with anticipation, half trying to stay sad. But the tickle torture made sorrow impossible—his sadness transformed into a joyful explosion of laughter. And after he caught his breath, he begged, "Do it again! Do it again!"

"Actually, Orion's right," said a Sweetie, who I suspect hailed from Region 5. "There's no such thing as the truth. Everyone has a different truth. So, if his truth is a miserable, meaningless existence, so be it."

"Oh, come on! What's with all these energy sucks?" Chopper said.

"No heigi!" some Sweeties agreed.

"Everyone has their own truth, their own perspective. It is only about being truthful with yourself!"

"I'm not sure wallowing in misery is the same thing as being truthful," Blaze said. "Yes, sadness and anger tell us something important, but at some point, I think they're choices that we can change. We can stay stuck in the mud or do something about it."

She thought a moment. "And are you saying that your perspective is better than that of someone who disagrees with you?"

"Huh? No, that's not what I said."

"You can't have your cake and eat it, too."

"Huh?"

Blaze tried again. "I agree that there's no one 'right' perspective. But aren't some perspectives better than others? Isn't justice and fairness better than injustice and unfairness? Or is the prime minister's 'truth' about hand size just as valid as the TDJP perspective?"

"Well, uh, of course not! Not *his* version of the truth! But that numbskull lies to himself. He isn't being truthful!"

"That lunatic *is* being truthful—he believes his own lies! He denies the facts!" Teacher Howzin cried. "The importance of seeking the truth—and using facts and evidence—cannot be overstated!"

"I agree with that one," Mr. Blunt said, wagging his finger.

And so began another round of Puddin' Heads and Sweeties shouting back and forth. They debated whether it was more important to seek the truth or to be truthful, to be just or joyful. They debated whether people or the planet were more important than excessive wealth and how much profit and tax were reasonable. They debated whether it was more important to be courageous or kind, competitive or cooperative, successful or happy, spoons up or heigi hooga, and so on and so forth.

Blaze started with the low hanging fruit. "Can we at least agree to abolish the ridiculous idea of island superiority, to abolish 'Puddin' Heads Bad, Sweeties Good,' and vice-versa?"

And after a long pause . . .

"Spoons up!"

"Heigi hooga!"

"Can we agree to eliminate, blow up, utterly destroy, and end, once and for all, hand size rules, prejudice, and discrimination?"

"Spoons Up! Heigi hooga!" everyone said as the odd, unifying rallying cry. Then the shiny blue Sweeties turned themselves around and all fell down. They jumped up and punched the air. "Heigi hooga!"

Blaze paced and had a little epiphany of her own. "Can we be both courageous and kind at the same time?"

This idea hung in the air for several moments. Then, "Spoons up! Heigi hooga!"

"Can we be successful, happy, and stewards of the Earth at the same time? Can we strive to tell the truth, to seek the truth, *and* to be truthful?"

"*Spoons up! Heigi Hooga!*"

And so it went.

Then, there was a heated debate that you will likely find boring, but I happened to quite enjoy: whether to have national school standards, curricula, assessments, licensure requirements, resources, and organizations; whether these should be required, recommended, or optional; whether decisions would happen at the national, regional, district, or school level; and so on and so forth. I spared you the details.

In the end, the two TDJP groups agreed to join forces, to continue working on the framework for FFF schools, and, for the first time, to launch a public campaign to recruit new members and future senators. This cross-island group agreed to send citizens video clips of outrageous school activities, the corrupt education boss money, the unfair firing of Blaze, Chopper, and Kai, and support for FFF schools. After a fierce debate of whether the movement's symbol should be the flame shaved into Blaze's head or the ocean wave of Kai's tattoo, the former enemies said simultaneously, "Or we could have both."

My absurdity neurosis was feeling better, but it was not cured.

After a break of walking along the Peace Island shoreline, skipping rocks, and scrumptious snacks, Blaze brought the group back together to decide how to convince the prime minister to put the MegaCorp Match back on the table. Blaze argued this strategy was the best shot they had at promoting FFF schools and making them reality.

Fortunately, this debate ended quickly. The group shot down the idea of a Good Hope Day strike, where everyone would refuse to measure their hand sizes. MegaCorp would simply keep everyone's current hand size. Likewise, an MC Frames strike was unimaginable —who could live without them?

Blaze said, "Okay, I have another idea. It's counter intuitive, but it could work. What do all those power players care about?"

"Firing people!"

"Fancy cigars!"

"Eating baby elephants!"

"Navels!"

"No! Money, people, money!" Blaze said. "So, what if everyone —on all the islands—stops buying booster, *anddddd* . . . wait for it . . . puddin', cake, and cookies. We'll have a hunger strike until they agree to play the MegaCorp Match and, if we win, give us FFF schools."

"And you become the education minister," Kai said rethinking all of this.

"Yes, apparently. We'll split the funding fifty-fifty. Puddin' Head's honor."

"Right, because that's credible with Sweeties," Kai said sarcastically.

"Did you not just hear everything we agreed upon? No, for real. It's a win-win." Blaze actually looked serious.

Jules said, "I believe her."

Aunt Serafina smiled and nodded.

"All right. I'm exhausted with this whole associate education minister thing, anyway," Kai admitted. "I never wanted to do it. I just want to win this game, return to Sweetie Island, and help my people. So sure, let's go for it. But good luck getting people to give up their puddin', cake, and cookies."

"Are you *crazzyy*?!" Chopper banged his head on a tree.

"No cake or cookies? *No heigi!*" the Sweeties on Peace Island cried and—along with my surly sweet tooth—almost revolted right there.

Blaze said, "I know, I know. It will be tough. But it'll get a lot of attention and hit them where it hurts the most. We can do anything for a few weeks."

The cross-island team launched a new message: *No MC Match? No puddin', no cake.* They debated about including cookies and booster, but decided that would be too many words. A rapidly growing and well-organized TDJP network promoted the hunger strike. Nearly 80 percent of people across both islands stopped eating puddin', cake, and cookies. And booster. At least, most kinds of booster.

It worked. MegaCorp started losing mega money.

The MC board and senior executives faced their biggest fear: a drastic drop in puddin', cookie, cake, and booster sales. These accounted for nearly 40 percent of MegaCorp revenue. Worse, rumors of happier and healthier people on both islands spread like brushfire. And although many people indeed felt healthier after weeks without their puddin', cake, cookies, and booster, others had withdrawal symptoms of shaking, anxiety, depression, sleep loss, uncontrollable yelling, panic attacks, nervous breakdowns, and random head butting. I might have been one of those people.

For several days, it was unclear who would give in. Mr. Blunt shared stories of MC senior executives freaking out and shouting that if this habit became a long-term trend, it could bankrupt whole divisions of the company. One executive jumped out of a window. Another cried and rolled on the floor: He would have to sell one of his mansions!

Finally, facing relentless pressure from MC executives, the prime minister agreed to play the MegaCorp Match. He took no chances of losing, though. He bought the MC team whatever they needed. Most importantly, world-class football players were flown in from all around the world to coach and train the MC team. Blaze, Chopper, Kai, Orion, Hands, Hammer, Crusher, Ram, Wheels, Root-Woot, and the lot of Puddin' Head and Sweetie footballers seemed outmatched and doomed to fail, for a variety of undeniable reasons.

BRIGHT IDEA

The highly unexpected football team—which now consisted of
Puddin' Heads and Sweeties—had a problem. Despite broad
support during the hunger strike and interest in FFF schools,
actually playing on the same team—or cheering for the same team
—was an entirely different matter. Generations of prejudice,
distrust, and animosity were not easily overcome.

The Sweetie-turned-zombie trick at the Noble Deed Match did
not help. Polling now showed over 60 percent of Puddin' Heads
believed Sweeties were indeed zombies, which fortunately had
dropped from 85 percent prior to Blaze's ridiculous challenge to the
prime minister. But nearly 100 percent of Region 5 believed this
zombie nonsense. Moreover, nearly 90 percent of Sweeties believed
Puddin' Heads were test-taking, head-bashing, tree-cutting, Sweetie-
catapulting numbskulls, although this was down from 100 percent
just weeks earlier.

However, while Blaze and Kai still felt little affinity for each
other, they now shared a common enemy and purpose. Without
Scarlet's resources, Blaze, Chopper, and Kai debated what to do.

"To beat MegaCorp, we need our best players. And even then,
we'll need to play a near flawless game in order to win," Blaze said,
"Hands is the only person who can shut down Scarlet. But Hands is
terrified of zombies after that stunt at the Noble Deed Match. So is
most of Puddin' Head Island. I don't know if they'll even come
back to Celebration Island, let alone enter that stadium again, or
agree to play with Sweeties." Blaze locked eyes with Kai.

"We did what we needed to do."

"And yet you didn't even win!"

"The refs were biased!"

"In your favor!"

"They weren't going to let either of us win, and you know it."

Blaze paced and took a deep breath. "Anyway, like I was saying,
with the Puddin' Head talent, we can win this game—"

"Puddin' Head talent anddd . . ."

". . . and Sweetie support."

"Collaboration."

"Sure, yeah, whatever. You have, well, you and Root-Woot. But back to my point. *We need Hands to win this game.* We need Orion, Wheels, Ram, Hammer, Crusher, and every one of our best players. We need overwhelming crowd support. We need every advantage we can get. We need to energize both islands to rise up and work together."

"Fine. So, are you going to admire this problem? Or do you have a solution?" I liked this question, too.

"I have a solution. You just aren't going to like it. You see, if we can get Puddin' Head Region 5 on board with FFF schools and supporting a lineup of Puddin' Heads and Sweeties, everything else will fall into place."

Kai cocked his head. "What the—"

The team brought a high-tech audio-visual projector because Hard Rocks High didn't have one. In consultation with George, we decided to meet after school. Kai managed another flawless MC Frames tap with School Boss J.R., who believed he had an important meeting with the prime minister regarding a zombie and sea monster mission.

Nearly all two thousand students stayed and packed into the dimly lit, rundown gymnasium, excited to meet Blaze Union and to watch a special FFF schools video. All wore faded shades of red. Even Kai took no chances and wore red, too. The students cheered wildly when they appeared in the video, but they had confused and mixed reactions to some of the FFF recommendations, going nearly silent about eliminating rock smashing and cymbals.

When the video finished, only murmurs and whispers could be heard. Kai couldn't take it and yelled, "Well, what do you think?"

A student from the back yelled, "Well, pretty boy . . ." and the audience erupted into laughter, breaking the tension. Just as quickly, though, the tension returned. "You fancy people got a lot of fancy words. I was with you, but then you said for Hard Rocks High to stop throwing rocks. *That is a problem.*"

Laughter turned into a collective jeer. "Ohhhhhhhhh." The student cracked his knuckles and walked up to Kai, staring him down.

The student body rose to their feet, shouting, "Fight! Fight! Fight!" Some jumped up and down, shouting, "Woo! Woo! Woo!" The chants echoed off the walls, and bits of ceiling fell on students, which fueled their enthusiasm for an all-out brawl.

George took the mic, held up a spoon, and yelled, "Hard Rocks High!" The student body raised spoons and called back. George beat his chest and grunted chants that the student body returned ritualistically. "Before we get carried away, I want to introduce you to Blaze and Chopper, who led the Battle of Sugar Falls!"

Blaze and Chopper waved. The audience switched to thunderous applause. Blaze took the mic.

"Puddin' Head friends, before you decide if you're going to beat us into puddin' surprise or join our FFF mission to crush MegaCorp like an eggshell head, let me say a few more fancy words. If you

don't like them, you can stone us to death and eat us for dinner."
The audience let out a long laugh.

Kai was terrified.

Blaze continued, "You know this group right here has read the
feedback from thousands of students. We've traveled to schools all
across this nation. Puddin' Head schools, including yours." The
audience cheered. "And Sweetie schools." The audience booed. "I'm
not going to give you a long list of information and
recommendations. What I'm going to do is tell you a little of my
story, because it's part of a bigger story happening across this great
nation. It's a story I still don't understand, but what I do know is
school just does not work for too many of us."

Someone yelled, "Puddin' Head News said you turned sweet!"
The student body grumbled in agreement.

"Just hear me out. You can't believe everything you hear on the
news. I'm not a Sweetie!" Blaze said.

Kai nodded, trying to hide his growing fear.

Blaze told her difficult experiences and transfers across schools,
connecting them to the negative things she'd seen at Hard Rocks
High. "I'm fortunate to be in my position. It doesn't make me better
than anyone else, but it does give me an opportunity. That's what I
want for everyone—free, fair, and fabulous schools. For you, your
brothers and sisters, your family—for everyone. Because when we
have great schools, we have great opportunity. That's what my team
wants. That's why we traveled hundreds of kilometers to be here. I
know deep down everyone here wants FFF schools, too."

Blaze took a deep, confident breath. "Now I can see your
puddin' heads nodding and I know you are with me. But I'm going
to tell you two ideas that don't make sense about your school—
about most schools across this island. Two ideas that need to
change. I'm not going to sugarcoat it; I'm going to give it to you
straight, because I know you're tough and can handle it. I recently
learned where these ideas came from. I learned that someone tricked
us! Someone duped us all in to believing these ideas. And I know no
one here likes to be a sucker. Am I right?!"

The student body yelled, "Right!"

"I mean, if someone slapped your sister in the face and said it
was a good idea, would you ask them to do it again?"

The student body was energized. "No!"

Kai spotted the nearest exit. One hundred rowdy, true-red Puddin' Heads stood in the way.

Blaze spoke with passion. "The first idea that someone tricked us into believing is that Bigs can't lead. They can't play offense, they can't be first in line, they can't make choices. But who scored the goals against the Sweeties? Bigs or Smalls?"

"Bigs!" the student body roared.

"And that's one reason we need fair schools. We need to eliminate the large hand rules. We need to eliminate hand size rules, once and for all! And the Bigs are going to prove that this idea—that Bigs can't lead—is ridiculous. And we're going to do it by whupping MegaCorp!"

The student body cheered as if they wanted this to happen but didn't really believe that it could.

"See now, I knew you could handle that. You want to hear the truth." Blaze planted a seed. "You know what else is the truth? They laugh at our name, 'Puddin' Heads.' We weren't always Puddin' Heads, you know. Maybe we should call ourselves 'Freedom Fighters,' because that's part of our history, part of who we were, and who we want to become again. People fighting for true freedom."

The student body exchanged glances. Some cheered. Some nodded. Some shrugged. Some head butted. "Now, some of you might be thinking it's the Sweeties who tricked us, who duped us, who are laughing at us, which brings me to the last idea that must change across this entire island."

The Puddin' Heads leaned in.

"Everyone here knows how much Puddin' Heads hate the Sweeties. And I was no exception."

"Battle of Sugar Falls!" someone shouted.

"Yes, the Battle of Sugar Falls was proof of my hatred of the Sweeties. But now I have to live with the fact that, because of me, a bunch of Sweetie kids now seem to have permanent pancake hands —including someone's sister." She looked at Kai, who nearly pooped his pants. He doubted Hands, Crusher, Hammer, George and two thousand other Puddin' Heads could take much more.

"But the strange thing is, what you just saw on the video is far worse. And here's the strangest, stupidest part of all: students are harming themselves, their friends, and their fellow Puddin' Heads.

And they think it's a good idea! They think harming themselves is fighting the Sweeties. But they've been tricked. In fact, *you've* been tricked!"

Hands and more than two thousand Puddin' Heads frowned in anger and confusion.

Blaze was on a roll. "In some tall, fancy building on Power Island, people in their fancy suits and fancy offices are laughing at us. Yes, MegaCorp tricked me! And they tricked you. They're laughing at us for head boarding and rock smashing. You know why? Because it keeps them in power. It keeps our minds imprisoned."

Hands and two thousand Puddin' Heads grunted with greater anger and confusion. Blaze and Chopper nodded like, *yep, we've been duped.* Kai cautiously nodded, too. "Now I give you credit. You're the toughest school I've ever seen. But you know what I learned about being strong? About being free? You know what's stronger than taking a rock to the face? Admitting you're wrong. Changing your ways even when it's hard. Freeing your mind to discover what you know deep down is true. That's what being strong is, my Puddin' Head friends. That's what it means to be a Freedom Fighter."

Blaze talked about getting to know the Sweeties. "Sure, they do some bizarre things. They do things I don't like. They have their problems. But believe it or not, they're humans just like us. They eat, sleep, have fun, make mistakes, and want FFF schools. But once again, someone tricked us into believing Sweeties are the enemy. They manipulated us into believing crazy ideas like the Sweeties are zombies and will eat our brains. And that's why we lost the Noble Deed Football Match! We ran away like a bunch of scared numbskulls. Yes, Sweeties *are* different, but that doesn't mean they're all bad. Look, I'm still not crazy about this, but we need them in the MegaCorp Football Match. They can help us win."

The student body sat stunned.

"And to prove we can work together, one of those Sweeties is the co-captain of the cross-island football team." Blaze held up a spoon and gestured to Kai. "And he's right here. Puddin' Heads, meet Kai."

REINTRODUCTIONS

Kai—now the widest-eyed person in the room—changed his mind. He started for the door. But Chopper and Ram held him back before he could take another step. Chopper leaned in to whisper, "You have to do this if we're going to win."

The crowd picked up on Kai's energy, yelled in panic, and pumped their arms. If it hadn't been for Blaze's speech, mass confusion would have ensued. Nevertheless, some Puddin' Heads still panicked. *Sweetie in the house! Zombie in the house! No, he's wearing red! That's the same footballer who turned into a zombie—he's just trying to trick us again! Don't let him bite you!* Some lost their moldy minds and shook each other. Rows of students head butted each other unconscious.

Three crazy-eyed students approached Kai. One said, "How about a taste of your own medicine, zombie?" He grabbed Kai's arm and bit it. Kai screamed as a second student bit the tattoo on his left arm.

Hands cried, "Don't let him bite you! You'll turn into a zombie, too!"

The third yanked Kai's ponytail. "No bite-backs!" He sniffed his neck. "He covered his smell with soap. And he has a zombie tattoo that's bleeding!"

With two jaws clamped on his arms and his head twisted to one side, Kai managed to say, "It's called showering! And that tattoo is just an ocean wave!"

Students jumped, pointed at Kai, and called, "Woo! Woo! Woo!" Kai tried to pull his arms free of the biting lunatics but stopped as their teeth broke his skin.

Blaze, Chopper, and Ram ran to help, pushing students aside. Ram said, "Hold still." She pushed one biter's head into Kai's arm, releasing his jaw, and then repeated this technique with the second. She secured her hand on Kai's forehead and then smashed the student's grabbing hand into the back of Kai's head until his fingers spread and released.

"Zombie Crisis Intervention Training. Funny, always thought I'd use it against zombies."

Kai put one hand on his sore head and let his bleeding, tattooed arm drop. Ram looked at Hands and ripped the shirt off his gigantic chest.

"Hey!" Hands said.

"Well, I wasn't going to rip off mine. Besides, I needed something big. Look at this bleeding Sweetie." She tore the shirt in two and wrapped one of Kai's arms.

Blaze grabbed the mic. "Puddin' Heads, calm down! Open your eyes!" Blaze wiped a smear of Kai's blood on her finger, smelled it, and held it up. The whooping crowd went silent.

Hands yelled, "It's red!"

The crowd sighed but remained skeptical. Blaze licked her finger. Someone dropped an empty puddin' cup, which rattled on the floor.

Blaze nodded. "Human."

The crowd remained unconvinced.

George swiped Kai's blood with two fingers. "His blood *is* red, not blue." He licked it. "It *is* human blood!" (Note to Courageous Readers: Do not try this at home. Nor the biting, head boarding, rock smashing, cymbals, and so on.)

Ram wrapped the second half of Hands's shirt around Kai's other bleeding arm.

"Let the Sweetie human talk," George said firmly. He backed into the three zombie hunters, who peered over his shoulders.

Kai eyed the exit and slowly turned toward it.

Blaze gently gripped his uninjured wrist. "Sorry. We didn't plan that. Or tell you about talking—figured you wouldn't come."

Kai wanted to punch her in the face and sprint to the door. But he took a deep breath, thought of his sister, and turned back to face Blaze. "Of course I'll do this. What Sweetie would turn down an opportunity to talk to a room full of extremist Puddin' Heads, two of whom literally bit me?"

Kai grabbed the mic. With two arms wrapped with red sleeves, a headache, and two thousand Puddin' Heads on edge, Kai broke the silence. "Well, this is terrifying." The crowd chuckled. A group in the back murmured that he didn't look or sound like a zombie.

"I didn't see that one coming. Blaze is always one-upping me and really got me this time." The Puddin' Heads laughed a little harder. Kai gave Blaze the stink eye and took a deep breath.

"So, you might be surprised to learn that we have some things in common. I was taught to hate you, like you were taught to hate me. And I hated Blaze Union more than any other person in this world because of Sugar Falls and . . ." He swallowed. "And what she did

to my sister." The student body let out a sympathetic sigh but
remained on guard.

"It's hard for me to admit this, but Blaze here, has strangely
inspired me. As hard as it is to say this, even to myself, I am partly
responsible for what happened. But I had a good reason! Or . . . so I
thought." He told about students at Sugar Falls needing to work on
the farm to pay his school fees—and then about the Puddin' Head
Middle School and the Puddin' Café attack. "For as long as I can
remember, I was taught Puddin' Heads were the enemy. Some
Sweeties think you eat baby brains when you run out of puddin'!"
Students giggled at this utterly ridiculous idea.

"I made the fighting between our islands worse and this nation
weaker. And now that I'm getting to know Blaze, Chopper, and
other Puddin' Heads, I see that many of my beliefs about you were
wrong—although, it's hard to love someone trying to bite my arm
off."

Some Puddin' Heads laughed. One said, "Sorry about that!"

"I don't get a lot of your ways—and especially the skull-
crushing, rock-throwing thing. But I respect your tenacity. The
bottom line is we all want free, fair, and fabulous schools. And
there's nothing I want more now than to crush MegaCorp."

A slow clap started. Blaze grabbed the mic. "Puddin' Head
friends, now *that* is being strong. That is courage! You know how
hard that was for this big ol' Sweetie? Two of you *bit* him! This kid
is *bleeding*. So, even if you don't like the Sweeties, can we at least
play football with them?" She looked at Hammer, Crusher, Ram,
and then Hands. They shrugged and nodded. She turned to the
student body. "Can I count on you to come to Celebration Island
and cheer us to victory?"

The students applauded, still stunned they'd just met a real-live
Sweetie.

George took the mic. "Well, I don't know about you, but my
head of puddin' is spinnin'. And I'm hungry. These fine, although
long-winded folks have given us a lot to think about. And they're
right. It's time for a change. We *can* have better schools. Some things
we can fix ourselves, but some things are big—like Island Nation
big—and they need our help. Can they count on us?"

Hard Rocks High gave a resounding cheer. Then, they
stampeded out of the gymnasium and sprinted home for puddin'
waiting on the dinner table.

PREGAME PARTY

News and videos of the team's visit to Region 5 spread quickly. Although there was growing momentum and support for a large turnout on game day, various Mega Gossip posts exploited the remaining animosity between Puddin' Heads and Sweeties (Sweeties were zombies, Puddin' Heads ate babies, etc.). Power News and Puddin' Head News questioned whether Blaze had officially gone sweet. But they avoided stating this directly, perhaps fearing another hunger strike.

The cross-island team—coached by Serafina and Jules—not only practiced together on Peace Island, they challenged each other, shared football moves, and improved both individually and as a team. And to my surprise, the coaches demanded excellence and teamwork from everyone, including me. Jules said, "Blaze told me your karaoke crossovers are second to none."

"Uh . . . I don't know about that," I said sheepishly.

"Team!" she shouted. "Everyone line up next to Coach Kosmos. He's going to teach you karaoke drills." And to everyone's surprise, Coach Jules was correct: I smoked all of them in that first karaoke race. Well, except for Wheels. With a newed purpose, I devoted my free time to experimenting and working out. Then, at each football practice, I taught the team new karaoke crossovers, turns, and advances. And guess what? My absurdity neurosis condition improved.

Blaze had learned her lesson about underestimating the opponent and led a discussion on strategies to unite the Puddin' Heads and Sweeties and to beat MegaCorp. She had a winning idea. "Everyone likes a party. Let's throw one for the ages!"

Incredibly, Blaze convinced Scarlet to pony up a lot of money. "Of course!" Scarlet said. "I love parties! And the bigger the crowd, the more people who will see me stomp you." Yet as many resources as MegaCorp provided, TDJP brought more.

Like the Noble Deed Match, on game day, enormous groups of Puddin' Heads and Sweeties poured onto Celebration Island with their red and blue attire, except this time, the crowds were even bigger. People of all regions and backgrounds strolled, skipped, and sprinted toward the stadium. Puddin' Heads and Sweeties; Bigs and

Smalls; athletes, musicians, and artists; the sports fanatics and sports ball haters; the coordinated and the not-so-coordinated; the data crunchers and the chill birds; the rock bashers and the navel gazers with their soft pants. They all came in great waves. Some came to crush MegaCorp. Everyone came to party.

They streamed across the bridge and onto the walkway, through the gateway, and onto the island. But this time, instead of lines divided into red and blue, Citizens for TDJP had painted the walkway, the gateway, and the stadium with blue-and-red checkers. TDJP attendants handed out blue-and-red checkered shirts, blue-and-red face paint, and packages that read, *Warning: Expands Rapidly.* Some fans put on their checkered shirts; many did not. Those who did were most likely TDJP members.

And in case you're wondering, yes, MegaCorp was opposed to selling anything with any semblance of blue *and* red. And yes, there may have been a widespread secret textile worker operation involving Natalina Union to produce thousands upon thousands of checkered shirts.

By midmorning, Puddin' Heads and Sweeties had nearly filled up the island. Blaze's family, including Kuko, joined in the fun. A few surprise guests even stopped by.

"Mr. Peabody?" Blaze exclaimed.

"As hard as this is to say . . . I hope you *crush* MegaCorp!" he snorted and marched away before anyone could respond.

"Didn't see that coming," Blaze said to Chopper.

Moments later, Wheels parents approached Blaze. "Thank you —for giving Wheels a better reason to run."

"Of course! We'll need her speed today!"

Jules strode over, proudly wearing her red and blue coaching shirt. "Good luck out there," she said with conviction. She fist-bumped Blaze and beamed at Chopper and Kai. "You got this."

"Thank you," Blaze said.

Serafina smooched Jules on the cheek.

"What—you're dating a *Sweetie?*" Blaze gasped.

Serafina nodded and smiled.

"And you're dating a *Puddin' Head?*" Kai asked Jules incredulously.

"Uhh. . . Yes," Jules admitted, squeezing Serafina's hand.

Blaze felt goosebumps pop on her arms as she scanned a massive Puddin' Head and Sweetie crowd. "Feel that? Big changes are in the air," she mused.

"Oh, and you might remember School Leader Foster," Serafina said. "He was on Peace Island—"

"Yes, of course! School Leader Foster, I've heard so much about you. We didn't really get to talk."

"Get it done, team. Like Jules said, there are *a lot* of people—on all the islands—counting on you. And by a lot, I mean *a lot*."

The team scanned an island of cheering fans and knew millions more rooted for them from their homes. They gave high fives and filled with determination.

The crowd danced and raged to great music. They tossed each other up and down, and all around. This enormous party—with hundreds of thousands of Puddin' Heads *and* Sweeties—was unlike anything I had ever seen. They partied and did Puddin' Head and Sweetie things I can't mention. But after several hours—with the stadium gates still closed—the crowd became restless. Suddenly, half a million fired up people chanted, "Food! Food! Food!"

Blaze and Kai walked onto an outside platform wearing their checkered jerseys. Blue-and-red paint streaked their cheeks. Screens all around Celebration Island streamed the action. Blaze took the mic. "I don't know about you all, but I could use a snack!"

The audience salivated.

"Does anyone here like snacks?"

The crowd roared, Sweeties hugged, and Puddin' Heads head butted.

Blaze said, "Thanks to our amazing chefs, we have a wide assortment of delicious salads, fruits, nuts, cheeses, breads, spreads, and seafood to tide you over until . . . *dessert!*" (The shiny blue Sweeties had advocated for only eating plant-based food but compromised on dairy and seafood—except for seahorses). The audience cheered and crowded around carts spread across the island.

Moments later, Kai stuck out a bag of crispy kale chips to Blaze and Wheels. "Power food. Try it." Blaze and Wheels exchanged glances and shrugged. But Wheels had a better idea. She pulled out a bag of dynamite chips, smashed the sides, dumped flakes of dynamite chips into the kale bag, and gently shook it. Just before she was about to eat a spicy kale chip, Kai said, "Wait!" He squeezed a tube of honey into the bag and shook it one more time. The trio each tried a spicy honey kale chip, rapidly nodded in approval, and stuffed handfuls into their mouths until the bag was nearly empty. Blaze offered me a chip—and can I just say, *game-changer* for yours truly? Unfortunately, they forgot one thing. "Water!" Kai cried.

After most of the fans had eaten, Blaze and Kai returned to the stage. Kai said, "That was delicious. Now, as for dessert . . . We've had the good pleasure of visiting both main islands. And I've learned something about puddin' . . ." The Puddin' Heads suddenly went wild, waving their spoons in the air. Kai cheered with them.

Blaze waited for the lull, then said, "And . . . I've learned something about cookies and cake!" The cheers shifted like a lightning bolt back to the Sweeties, who danced and group hugged.

"So, we've brought the best chefs on both islands together to make some very special desserts for us today." The entire island cheered, as scores of chefs wearing checkered aprons and chef hats stepped onto the stage and waved.

Scarlet yelled, "Woot! Woot! Time for dessert! Woot! Woot! Time for dessert!"

Blaze announced, "And now, for the first time in the history of this nation, we have a very special surprise. Could I have a Puddin' Head volunteer and a Sweetie volunteer?"

Blaze's sister, Maya, was "randomly" selected as the Puddin' Head volunteer. And Lily, Kai's sister, was selected from among the Sweeties. They stepped on stage. The crowd cheered for the spunky girls.

Blaze said, "Did you like your snacks?"

They nodded.

"Now, I'll bet you're ready for some dessert. Imagine—what if these world-renowned chefs combined the most delicious puddin' with the most delicious cookies?" Blaze paused as millions swallowed with trepidation. "Friends, we have . . . *puddin' cookie crumble*." She pointed at a clear container that held this mouthwatering dessert. "You see, we have delicious cookie crumble on the bottom here and puddin' on top." The cameras zoomed in.

"Now, imagine them swirled together. Would you like to try it?" Jaws dropped across the island.

Lily stammered as half a million people leaned over each other and millions watching at home fell off their sofas. "Uh, I don't know if those things really go together. What about digestive problems?"

Maya backed away. "Yeah, I mean . . . I don't know if that's a good idea."

Chopper sent a group signal to hundreds of student leaders' MC Frames. They chanted, "Eat! Eat! Eat!" The rest of the island shrugged and chanted along with them. The pair had little choice.

The island fell dead silent. Sweat poured down Lily's face. Her checkered spoon dove past the puddin' layer and lifted the cookie crumble, now smothered with puddin'. The crowd watched the enormous monitors like a scary movie right before the bad guy jumps through the window. Lily began to cry. She put the spoon into her mouth. She closed her eyes and swallowed.

Then, Lily's eyes flashed open. She yelled, "Sweet Mother of Sugar Plum Fairies, Sweet Mother of Sweetie Island. *This is incredible!*" She squeezed Maya in a bear hug, hugged her brother, and even hugged Blaze.

Initially struck silent, the crowd erupted into cheers. They urged Maya to "Eat! Eat! Eat!" Maya swallowed and stared at the delicious treat. She ate puddin' off the top without touching the crumble. Then, she looked at the 500,000 Puddin' Heads and Sweeties watching her. She bravely dug out a heaping spoonful of puddin' cookie crumble and stuffed it into her mouth. Her expression turned from trepidation to delight. She grinned from ear to ear. "Wow, that *is* good! Yep, better together."

Exhilarated by her tasty dessert, Lily said two words that few Sweeties had uttered. "Spoons up!" Maya and Lily instinctively clanged spoons and said, "Better together" before gobbling down their cups.

The audience applauded with a mix of anxiety, awkwardness, and mostly excitement. And then, "Heigi hooga!"

"Awesome! We thought you'd like it." Blaze scanned the crowd and sighed. "But now we have a little problem. You see, we have all these different combinations of puddin', cookie, and cake desserts spread throughout this entire island. Desserts like double chocolate puddin' cake, frozen puddin' cookie pops, puddin' cake batter, cookie dough puddin' ice cream swirl, and six-layer puddin' cookie dust mousse." I wondered if that chocolate was produced at Sweetie Experimental High School in Region 4.

Scarlet yelled, "Woot! Woot! Time for dessert! Woot! Woot! Time for dessert!"

The crowd spun around and eyed the dessert carts.

But remembering the puddin' energy crash during the Noble Deed Match, Blaze winked at Scarlet. "But sadly, MegaCorp has locked them all up."

"What?!" Scarlet cried.

The salivating crowd booed loudly. Some shook the carts and locks. Some head butted.

"And the only way to unlock them—and I'm so sorry that you will have to wait—*is to beat MegaCorp!*"

The crowd roared like this made sense.

Blaze ripped off her checkered shirt, which revealed the team's tie-dyed jersey. It had blue-and-yellow waves and swirls with a red flame imprint (why not add the other primary color?). It read, *FFF Schools*, and scripted underneath, *free * fair * fabulous*. Blaze said, "Island Nation, it's time to open the gates. *Who's ready to crush MegaCorp?!*"

The crowd roared again. Thousands flocked into the stadium. Finally! It was time to play *The Match*.

THE MATCH

MegaCorp Stadium was packed to capacity. An estimated 10,000 more snuck in. More than 300,000 cheered outside. About a quarter of the fans in the stadium sat on the right side and wore red. About a quarter sat on the left side and wore blue. About half of the fans wearing red-and-blue checkered shirts spread throughout the stadium. Special guests—including Blaze's family, and myself—stood along the cross-island team sideline where Coaches Serafina and Jules paced, encouraging players to work as a team.

And less than one percent sat in the stands behind the MegaCorp bench. They mostly wore black and white. Blaze was disappointed, but not surprised, to see School Boss J.R. sitting next to the prime minister, who sat next to the football commissioner, who was beyond annoyed to be sitting next to Regional Boss Poppy, who oohed and ahhed all three of them. School Boss J.R. wore all red. "No way I'm cheering for zombies!" he yelled. "I'm a true-red Puddin' Head! Go MegaCorp!" He head butted the prime minister.

No one wanted to beat MegaCorp more than Blaze. She'd waited her whole life for this moment. Now that she better understood the truth behind this absurd world, she wanted to beat MegaCorp even more than she'd ever wanted to beat the Sweeties. She couldn't wait to rack up goal after goal on this national stage. She would prove once and for all that Bigs were just as good as Smalls. Finally, she would become the education minister and improve schools for hundreds of thousands of students across the country. Or so she thought.

Although their odds of winning were 1,000:1, the cross-island team had high hopes due to their strong offense and defense. Yet, the Scarlet-versus-Hands hype dominated sports shows, Mega Gossip, national conversations, and promotional material. Their names and photos and video highlights were everywhere. Despite the odds, Puddin' Head News, Power News, and even Sweetie News said that whoever won this battle would win for their team.

The interest in this game extended beyond Island Nation. Professional football coaches from all over the world sat with MegaCorp. They weren't particularly interested in watching what they assumed would be a blow out win for MegaCorp, but wanted to recruit Scarlet to their teams, and also to see how she would perform against this alleged beast of a goalie. Scarlet remembered Region 5 tryouts and had prepared accordingly. As you can imagine, she had trained nonstop with professional athletes since the announcement of the MegaCorp Match, which by this point was simply called *The Match*.

Just before kickoff, Blaze gave her team a pep talk. "Team, you all know what we're playing for today. You know the stakes. Few think we'll win, but we have almost the entire nation—and nearly this whole stadium of fans—cheering us on. The only way to win is to win as a team. First, I want to thank Chopper, who has been my greatest coach and my best friend. I—*We* wouldn't be here without you. Can I count on you one more time, comrade?"

Chopper filled with pride and saluted the team.

"Offense—Wheels, Ram, Hammer, Crusher—we need your very best today. When you look back on this game, make sure you've left nothing on the pitch! And defense—you must contain Scarlet Pompavich. Root-Woot, you're our left defender. Did you know they built this stadium with thousands of chopped down banyan trees?"

"No!"

"And that Scarlet lives in a mega-mansion made of hundreds of sawed-down banyan trees?"

"No!"

"And she eats baby elephant and endangered seahorses! And most likely, that baby elephant was stolen from the Sweetie Region 3 herd."

"*Nooo*!"

"Can I count on your defense?"

"It would be my highest honor, Blaze." Root-Woot spun and shot out his arms in a defensive stance.

Suddenly, loud booing seemed to erupt from a corner of the stadium. Sweeties in shiny blue robes thundered, "Rooooot Wooooot! Rooooot Wooooot!" as if encouraging their non-leader leader, or perhaps, warning MegaCorp they faced the great defender of creatures and trees. If Root-Woot felt awkward without his robe, he didn't show it. He looked as grounded as the tree tattoos that rose from his feet and branched to his fingertips. Yes, his intricate tattoos included elephants and lovely woodland creatures. Root-Woot nodded slowly to his fan base and whispered a menacing *heigi hooga*, as if promising to deliver on a singular purpose: take down Scarlet Pompavich.

Blaze continued. "Orion, you're our right defender. If you're still hunting for a purpose in your life, let today be the day that you find your answer. You're playing for all of Island Nation! If indeed you are a skillful hunter, then let Scarlet Pompavich be your prey!" Orion clenched his fists, drew his arms back into a bow, and pretended to release an arrow.

"Kai, you're the heart of our defense. Can we count on you to stop Scarlet Pompavich?"

"Of course, you knucklehead."

The team beat their chests.

"Hands, you're the last defense. Remember, the Sweeties are cheering for us; they're not zombies or sea monsters. Can you shut down Scarlet Pompavich once more?"

"I will make her cry." Hands clapped a football that exploded.

Then, Root-Woot asked Blaze, "What about you—are you ready?"

Blaze scanned the massive stadium of cheering fans. "I've never been so excited and terrified in my whole life."

Root-Woot clasped Blaze's hand and pulled her close. "Good. Now let's transform that energy into a victory."

Finally, it was time to play *The Match*.

MegaCorp kicked off. Scarlet wove through players faster than Blaze had once cut through the Sweeties. With newfound inspiration, Orion attacked Scarlet as soon as she crossed midfield. Nevertheless, she faked left, then shot past his outstretched foot.

Root-Woot stormed toward her with swirls, whirls, and twisting twirls. "You ate our baby elephant!"

"What the—" Scarlet tried to juke him left, right, left, right, but it was no use—Root-Woot stuck to her like a tree frog. "No one stops me!" she cried. But she couldn't shake him, dribbling in circles and refusing to pass. The crowd began to laugh. Scarlet screamed, *"I'm winning this match and getting a real pony!"*

"You eat pony, too?" Root-Woot cried.

Sensing a weakness, she barreled into him and said, "Yeah, but it's not as tasty as baby elephant." Root-Woot—who now despised

Scarlet more than any creature in the world—grabbed her wrist, secured her arm, and tossed her a good ten meters. She sailed through the air and landed with a skid.

"Whoa! You can't do that!" an announcer cried.

The crowd gasped.

"Oh no!" Blaze said.

Less than a minute into the game and, the referee had pulled out a red card.

A shiny section of the crowd did boo this time.

Blaze said, "What?! She ran into him!" The referee pulled out a yellow card.

"Blaze!" Chopper yelled.

"Okay!" Blaze stalked away. "I'm good."

Blaze put her arm around Root-Woot and escorted him off the field. He clenched his fist, tilted his head to the sky, and wailed, as if hundreds of trees had just fallen on top of an elephant herd. Blaze locked eyes with him. "It's okay. We got this. We still need you to cheer us on."

Root-Woot nodded, drew in a deep breath, lowered his head, and sulked along the sideline.

Scarlet bounced up and stared incredulously at her green-streaked and scraped hands, elbows, and once-white jersey. "Grass stains?! You ruined my jersey! Payback time!"

Seconds later, now facing a defense short one player, Scarlet sidestepped Kai to shoot between Orion and Chopper. The fans got what they wanted. Scarlet and Hands stared down each other. The crowd fell silent. Millions held their breath.

Scarlet performed flawlessly. She hammered a line drive off the right post. Hands leaned and just missed it. Scarlet drilled the rebound off the left post. Hands spun and dove, grazing the ball with his fingertips, grunting as he landed on his side. Then she did it again. Hands dove to the right, then the left, but still couldn't reach the ball. Scarlet blasted a shot a meter above the goal. Hands leaped, smashing his hands and then his head against the goal post. He wobbled and fell unconscious on top of a tiny MC player.

The ref gave him a red card.

"The giant has fallen! The giant is out!" the announcers cried. Ninety-nine percent of the crowd fell silent. The one percent cheered. Fireworks exploded.

Scarlet flipped off and taunted the quiet crowd, then trotted across the pitch. "I'm getting that pony!"

"What the—" Blaze cried. "Nooo! She did that on purpose! That's a terrible call! This can't be happening!"

But it did happen. Medics carted Hands off on a double stretcher. The coaches had little choice. Kai became the goalie. And they were down to nine players.

The game plan against Blaze was ruthless. Three, sometimes four MC players swarmed her like bees at all times. It was nearly impossible to pass to her. When she did get the ball, other players immediately attacked.

The feisty MC Smalls stole the ball from Blaze. One passed to Scarlet, who scored her first goal. She pretended to eat puddin' with a spoon right in front of Blaze. "All day! All day!" she mocked.

"Hey, that's my thing!" Blaze said.

"Mine now! And that was just the first of many goals."

Blaze received the kickoff pass, but a swarm of MegaCorp players quickly stole the ball. Orion and Kai played magnificently, blocking a barrage of Scarlet's advances and shots. But Scarlet was relentless. She scored again. Power Island launched enormous fireworks. It was 2—0.

"You going to make this a game, big hands?" Scarlet asked Blaze. "Or are you going to be shut out?"

"We only have nine players!"

"Making excuses, already. Just like a Big baby."

The news casters gushed. Coaches drooled. MegaCorp fans shouted. Some of the 99 percent began to boo. Some Puddin' Heads cheered for Scarlet. Blaze and the team began to panic. She yelled for her team to pass the ball, but she was never open. Ram stopped Crusher from head butting Hammer.

Five minutes later, Scarlet scored again. "Do you smell that?" she asked Blaze. "Is that burnt puddin'? No, wait—it's Blaze getting torched! Oh, I love that smell. The smell of a blowout victory."

"This game is getting out of control," Bartle chuckled to Nutt on Puddin' Head News. "Was it over before it began? Did the Bigs ever really have a chance against Scarlet and MegaCorp? And whose idea was it to include Sweeties on a Puddin' Head team?" Nutt smacked Bartle on the back and guffawed.

Blaze was livid. "Someone get these MC fart tarts off of me! How am I supposed to score?!" In frustration, she pushed past an MC defender, nearly knocking him down. Chopper yelled, "Heigi hooga!" The distraction worked—no red card. But the Sweeties stole the ball. The crowd booed louder.

Scarlet scored again. The score was 4—0. She jogged past Blaze, pretending to eat puddin' once again. "All day! All day!" she quipped. Then she galloped on a pretend pony toward the sideline and found Root-Woot. "Mmmm, love me some baby elephant soup," she slurped with a big grin, wiping the side of her mouth. The coaches—and half the sideline—held Root-Woot back from offering another sailing lesson.

"This game is slipping away faster than Sweeties stuff their faces with cake," Bartle said. "Scarlet Pompavich is unstoppable. She looks like a World Cup superstar out there. Root-Woot and Hands are out. Blaze has been snuffed. The cross-island team is out of their league. If they're going to do something, they better do it fast."

"Maybe they could start by advancing close enough for a shot on goal," Nutt chuckled.

Blaze knew what a defeat would mean. She felt her dreams slipping away. She thought of the hundreds of students she'd seen on the tour. She thought of Maya. Blaze locked eyes with the football commissioner and then the prime minister. In unison, they gave her the finger. Blaze randomly thought of Nub, which confused her brain enough to have a crazy idea.

"Put me on defense," she said to Coach Serafina.

"What?" Coaches Serafina and Jules said.

"What?" Chopper said in amazement.

"What?" the rest of the team said in shock.

"We can't win if Scarlet keeps scoring." She paused, as if realizing the power of what she was about to say. "With Orion, Chopper, Kai, and me on defense—together, as a force—I think we can shut her down. At least contain her. And if these MC fart tarts keep trolling me, that'll open up the offense for Hammer, Crusher, Ram, and Wheels."

The plan worked, at least initially. Blaze, Chopper, and Orion triple-teamed Scarlet and either stole the ball or forced her to pass.

Scarlet cursed, then managed to get off a few shots, which Kai blocked. Wheels blew past the defenders and finally scored the cross-island team's first goal. The score was 4—1.

The crowd went wild. New hope emerged. Moments later Wheels, Ram, and Hammer charged down the pitch, passing back and forth. Hammer pounded a header into the goal on a beautiful pass from Wheels. The score was 4—2.

Later in the game, Scarlet bounced a shot off the left post. Blaze retrieved the rebound and blasted a pass to Wheels, who passed to Hammer, who launched a high pass to Ram. Ram rammed a header —not *into* the net, but *through* the net. The entire stadium and nation rose to its feet. "Whoa! Was that ball smoking?!" the announcers cried. "It's 4—3. We have a match!"

The prime minister banged his head on the wall. Once again, he yelled at the football commissioner, who yelled at Scarlet. "Do you want a real pony or not?!" And once again, the football commissioner yelled into her MC Frames. And as you might guess— despite efforts to ensure fair referees—unfair whistles started blowing. Wheels was inaccurately called offside three times in a row. Then, Scarlet scored on a sensational goal off the upper left post moments before halftime. The score was 5—3.

With fireworks exploding and the MC fight song bleating over the speakers, Blaze shouted to Chopper. "Not again!! Why can't they just play fair?!"

Chopper shook his head slowly. "Looks like it's time for Plan B."

Blaze sighed. "I was hoping we wouldn't have to do this."

Chopper grinned. "Yes, you were."

THE MARCH

Now, before we get to this next part, some background is in order. You see, Blaze and Chopper were smarter than the average Puddin' Head. They knew full well that three overlapping, monstrous forces stood in the way of their decisive victory: ridiculous large hand prejudice and discrimination, ridiculous animosity between Puddin' Heads and Sweeties, and an absurdly powerful and corrupt MegaCorp. They knew full well it would take more than overwhelming evidence and disturbing video clips of corruption to overcome these forces.

Of course, a win over MegaCorp could land a fatal blow. But would they even have the chance? Would they be in a position to win as the second half ticked down? Sure, pregame hype, a converted and rowdy following from Region 5, a careful selection of referees, and mixed cookie and puddin' treats could rally a divided nation. But they knew full well it wouldn't be enough.

Blaze had spent many sleepless nights obsessively imagining and searching for an experience so transformative it would band the warring Puddin' Head and Sweetie Islands together to defeat the mighty MegaCorp. Finally, after days and nights of brainstorming and searching and spoon hat head butting, Blaze came across a video clip of The Game—the American football rivalry I referenced earlier. She watched it over and over, unable to tear her eyes away. And suddenly, her tangled nest of confusion exploded into an epiphany.

And yet, now, on the big day, it seemed that these three monstrous forces simply could not be overcome. It was clear that the cross-island team needed this game changer. And they needed it before that second half started. They just wanted the chance to win. The chance to alter the course of Island Nation history. It could work. It had to work.

Minutes later, Blaze asked, "Anything yet?"

Chopper zoomed into the MegaCorp fan section with his MC Frames. The prime minister stood up and danced awkwardly for a minute. He held out his tiny hand and examined it as if he'd never seen it before. Suddenly, he giggled uncontrollably. Then, he scanned the stadium with great confusion, as if living in a silly dream.

Mr. Blunt—who sat a few seats away from the prime minister—nodded at Chopper, grinning.

"Affirmative," Chopper said.

"Silly Sweetie *and* no noggin?" Blaze said.

"Yep. Or as I like to call it, a left right punch."

"How much?"

"Well, schools serve them to elementary students. So, let's just say, enough to get the job done."

Chopper sent a mass group message. Student leaders immediately forwarded it to their teams in the stadium and on Celebration Island. It read, "Sea monsters are not real. But as an extra precaution, wear red *and* blue gear."

An energy shift rocketed through the stands and island. Many fans pulled the blue-and-red checkered shirts over their solid blue or red ones. They slapped red-and-blue paint across their faces. They pulled checkered pom-poms and rapidly expanding foam checkered hands from their packaging. The absurdly large hands surprised and energized the fans. The checkered hands were so large it was as if they were constantly celebrating, trying to scare small children, or mocking the ridiculous idea that large hands were inferior.

No one—not even the news—could ignore or deny the fact that more than half the stadium now sported red-and-blue.

The prime minister was *furious*. He stomped his feet, crying, then giggling, then stomping again.

Oh, and remember Nub, who proudly nipped a fingertip? He made it to *The Match* with several pouty Puddin' Head friends from Region 4. A TDJP source shared several sad video clips of this group with me, including their reaction to the monstrous foam hands. "Checkered large hands—that doesn't even make sense!" Nub scoffed and his friends snickered. They missed the symbolism of the checkered hands altogether, perhaps because they still thought like numbskulls. They still blamed Blaze and the team for their lost opportunities.

And then a strange thing happened. Suddenly, all the fans' MC Frames lit up, not with smiley and frown faces, but with bright-red flames on the right side and bright-blue ocean waves on the left. The crowd cheered and waved their enormous hands.

The MegaCorp fight song abruptly ended. And let me remind

you, MC Stadium and the Celebration Island grounds were tricked out with the highest fidelity speakers this world has ever heard. In the next instant, "Battle Victory March"—the contagious marching song that had originated as a war song and evolved for more than one and a half centuries across regions and countries—blasted throughout the stadium and across the entire island. Trombones, horns, tubas, drums, and, yes, cymbals, played together with such energy, beauty, and force, the fans leaped to their feet with goosebumps, as if ready to fight.

One hundred and fifty shiny-blue-robed, tree hugging Region 3 Sweeties marched into the stadium. I'll bet you can guess the one that marched with the greatest determination. They formed a massive marching battalion behind and around the football goal. They may not have been carrying drums, tubas, or cymbals, but you wouldn't know it from the prideful way they marched together. Sweetie fans groaned. Puddin' Head fans stuck out spoons as if on guard. The announcers were speechless. The prime minister was a hot mess.

Suddenly, at the other end of the stadium, a squadron of 150 shiny-red-robed, tree hugging Region 3 Sweeties marched into rows of battle formation behind and around the opposite goal. The prime minister squinted and scrunched up his face as if he couldn't see or comprehend what was happening, or perhaps he was searching for a genie.

In the next moment, the red battalion hopped up and down, kicked the air, beat their chests, and punched the air as if trying to intimidate the other side. The blue battalion did jumping jacks, flapped their arms, stomped their feet, turned around, and all fell down. They leaped up and reared back on their heels as if they were horses ready to charge. "Heigi hooga!" they warned. They might have stuck their tongues out at each other, but it was impossible to tell because of the hoods draped over their faces.

In a flash, the two battalions charged each other in perfect rhythm to the battle music that blared from the speakers, high-stepping, striding, and waving their arms.

And just when the fans thought these opposing forces would surely ram each other like Puddin' Heads, the marching sides collided into an amorphous sea of blue-and-red swirling circles, which danced around each other like swirling marbles, unable to mix.

The twisting blob suddenly turned into a gigantic recognizable shape and then swirled to form an enormous, polka-dot gesture.

A giant polka-dot hand waved at the east end of the stadium. Instinctively, nearly all the fans in the east end tore out their checkered shirts and gigantic foam hands, shoved them on, and waved back like very excited children. Except for Nub and his not-so-merry band of numbskulls. "I don't get it!"

Giddy and furious, the prime minister was beyond confused. He yelled, "*Stop playing that*—" Then, he turned to see that one end of the stadium appeared to have grown enormous blue-and-red hands. He forgot what he'd intended to say.

The field-sized, polka-dot marching hand turned and waved to the south side of the stadium. These fans pulled on their checkered shirts and hands, too. They waved back with wild abandon. The same happened for the west side. It even repeated on the north side, which also happened to be where the tiny group of MegaCorp executives and senators booed and stomped their feet. But they were easily drowned out by the roaring crowd.

"What am I seeing?" cried a dizzy and giddy prime minister. An entire stadium now waved and saluted and marched in their seats as "Battle Victory March" continued to play.

The enormous marching hand contracted into a compact sphere. In a blink of the prime minister's eye, it exploded into marching rays of perfect red, blue, red, blue formations toward all areas of the fired-up crowd.

The marching army formed an oval around the perimeter of the pitch. Then, they squatted. Suddenly, a red-robed Sweetie and blue-robed Sweetie at the southern midfield line shot into the air and said, "Heigi hooga!" Those next to them immediately sprang into the air. They continued one by one, until—yes you guessed it—they did *the wave* around the stadium. Although Nub still didn't get it, the rest of the stadium did.

Giant waves sped around the stadium. Somehow, these Puddin' Heads and Sweeties even figured out how to send clockwise and counterclockwise waves that crashed down hard on the stadium's north side. The shimmering waves of red and blue—and, increasingly purple—battered the tiny MegaCorp section.

And then, an even stranger thing happened. The red- and blue-oval marched back to the center of the pitch. It formed a giant hand again. But this time, instead of waving, the marchers pulled back their hoods. And without missing a beat, they dropped their robes and kept marching in place. But underneath the robes were not exposed Sweeties, but rather red-and-blue sea monsters—somehow both friendly and creepy. Fake scales, tails, fins, flippers—you name it, they had meticulously put it together, in costumes so real even Hollywood costume designers would be jealous. And much to my delight, some even looked like seahorses.

I can assure you that any fans still wearing either solid blue or red suddenly recalled the message Chopper sent. Indeed, they took no chances. They pulled on their checkered shirts, slapped paint on their faces, and stuffed on the humongous hands faster than Sweeties eat cookies out of the oven, and not the yucky kind. Well, except for Nub and his pouty Puddin' Heads, who were now more confused than ever. "I still don't get it!" Nub cried.

You might think the prime minister would know better, given the zombie trick at the Noble Deed Match. But instead, his eyes bulged. His mouth gaped with great fear. He tried to focus. "They're *real!* I *told* you sea monsters are real!" He shook the football commissioner. The prime minister spun toward the senators in the MegaCorp section. He shoved his tiny finger in their faces. "*Finish that wall!*"

And before the prime minister knew it, three hundred marching sea monsters tightened into an enormous fist—knuckles and all— which sailed triple time toward the tiny MegaCorp section.

"Battle Victory March" blared louder. The fans went wild. They stomped and tried desperately to clench their enormous hands into fists and shake them. But alas, the checkered hands and fingers were absurdly large, and making a fist proved impossible. So instead, they waved their terrible checkered hands and pom-poms in great mockery.

Two tidal waves erupted from the south end of the stadium. One headed east, the other sped west, gaining speed and energy toward the north. As the tidal waves raced, fans leaped from their seats, giving them even more momentum. Fans waved and whipped their hands and pom-poms to the music as if they were conductors directing these shimmering red-and-blue—and seemingly purple— waves like an orchestra toward a fabulous finale.

At the same time the monstrous tidal waves crashed over the top of MegaCorp, the sea monster fist slammed into the wall of the MegaCorp section like surprise left and right cross punches to the face. The prime minister stumbled back into his chair.

Root-Woot leaped, grasped the top of the wall, and easily scaled it. With a flying, twirling and twisting spin, he landed next to the prime minister in a confident, defensive stance. The prime minister shook his head. He looked up in disbelief. Root-Woot—looking remarkably like my classroom's beloved seahorse, Regal—stood within centimeters of the prime minister's face. "Welcome to our home," he said in a creepy sea monster voice.

The prime minister recoiled. He looked at the stadium walls with dread. "Is this . . . *their* house? Are we . . . *in their house*? Run for your lives!!!" He stepped on and over several senators and MC executives, pushed through Puddin' Heads with his tiny hands, bowled over children, and fled the stadium. The football commissioner and several scared MC executives followed close behind. More importantly, several petrified referees fled, too.

"Yes!" Blaze shouted.

"I still don't get it!" Nub cried.

After a head tap to Chopper, Blaze asked, "How long until that wears off?"

Chopper shrugged. "Not sure. Maybe an hour?"

"Then let's make every second count. Now we have a chance."

After smashing the MegaCorp wall, the sea monsters rebounded like footballs. They marched in normal tempo back to their robes. But this time, they turned them inside out. The sea monsters now wore shiny, checkered robes. They scrunched into a tight ball once again. But this time, instead of exploding like a shooting star, they unwound in spirals and marched toward the south end of the pitch, forming a marching, continuous, swirling line.

The non-leader leader—who by now had finally accepted his role as a leader—tore off his hood and placed a tall hat on his Sweetie sea monster head. It had red, yellow, and blue spirals and a bright blue plume. But instead of a baton, you guessed it, Root-Woot twirled a long thin banyan spoon. He high-stepped to the front of the line as the drum major. The crowd went wild. Blaze, Chopper, and Kai hooted and hollered.

Root-Woot high-stepped and sashayed across the pitch to the

east. The battalion of sea monsters followed lock step as if marching for all the people of Island Nation. Nay, they marched with such passion, it was as if they marched for all creatures and life forms in the world—if not the entire universe. Although, perhaps they overlooked—or ignored—the fact that with each step, they crushed hundreds, if not thousands, of bugs and microorganisms.

Root-Woot turned abruptly north. The sea monsters turned sharply, too, like soldiers moving into the battle that would change the course of the war. Root-Woot approached the north sideline, curved, and turned back south, then marched in place as several sea monster soldiers marched past him in a tight line. Suddenly, an enormous marching letter U was formed. The leader continued, connecting the giant U to a cursive "*n*" and then a dotless "*i*" and then a "*t*" and an "*e*" and finally a "*d*." And there it was—a marvelous marching word: *United*. It shone like a bright beacon to the Puddin' Heads and the Sweeties in the MC stadium and across the country.

The crowd roared.

Nub cried, "I still don't get it!"

Chopper saluted Blaze, then Kai. And the least likely of comrades strode behind the high-stepping, spoon-twirling, Root-Woot. Yes, Blaze and Kai dotted the "*i*." They clasped their hands and waved and bowed. They saluted the fans with deep gratitude and pride. And thus began the tradition of *Script United*.

The crowd erupted into wild applause, head butted, and group hugged.

Nub finally understood. "I get it! I get it!" he cried. He had a realization. Then, he had a regret.

For a shining moment, my absurdity neurosis seemed to disappear. I felt bad for the hundreds of Puddin' Heads who had head butted themselves unconscious and therefore missed what happened next.

THE SHOTS SEEN ACROSS THE NATION

"Let's do this!" Blaze and Kai shouted to their team. The second half whistle blew. Keeping to their new strategy, Blaze, Chopper, Orion, and Kai managed to contain Scarlet. With the lightning-fast front line now in sync, Hammer scored midway through the second half. The stadium, the island, and 99.9999 percent of the nation erupted into cheers. Many bowls of puddin' were spilled. Minutes later, Ram rammed a football off the MC goalie's head and then back into the goal. The cross-island team had tied the game, 5—5! The nation celebrated.

Yes, the team had contained Scarlet, but really wanting that real pony, she scored another goal with less than ten minutes to go. She almost scored again, but Orion's attack, Blaze's sliding tackle, and Chopper's toe tip slowed the football down just enough for Kai to block it out of bounds. The crowd and nation let out a deep sigh of relief.

Wheels scorched past five Sweeties to score again. "That kid is ridiculously fast! And she never slows down. Where does she find the energy?" the announcers cried.

Five minutes to go. The game was tied 6—6. The nation was a powder keg ready to blow. Citizens for TDJP hacked the MC Frames again. The flame and the wave lit up the arms, and a delicious *puddin' cookie crumble* flashed across the screens. Fans waved their enormous checkered hands and pom-poms as if they had not eaten in a very long time.

The prime minister stalked back to the game as angry as a Puddin' Head stung on the tongue by a bee hidden in his puddin'. Still in a slight fog, he sometimes randomly giggled, which only made him angrier.

Suddenly, in a last-minute act of desperation, Power News bulletins flashed *Breaking News!* across MC Frames. * *Prime Minister Survives Sea Monster Assassination Attempt * Sea Monsters Steal Three Puddin' Head Children During Prime Minister Coup Attempt * Children Last Seen Wearing Blue-and-Red Checkered Shirts * MC Refs Replaced With Biased Refs in MC Football Game * Stay Tuned for More Breaking News! *

Puddin' Head News confirmed these accounts and added * *MC Football Match Ploy to Turn Puddin' Heads Sweet * No Coincidence Blaze*

*Union Hasn't Attempted a Single Shot on Goal * Blaze Union Proudly Wears Blue Jersey **

Sweetie News had its own *Breaking News! * MC Football Match Scheme Turns Sweeties into Competition Obsessed Puddin' Heads * Sweetie News then showed clips of Sweetie fans cheering wildly after cross-island team goals.

A panic broke out as fast as my absurdity neurosis resurfaced. Puddin' Heads clutched their children. Some ran from the stadium. Some ran for the bridge. Some Sweeties stuffed their faces with cookies and cake. Others switched off their screens, pulled out mirrors, and gazed at their navels.

The MC game clock ticked down.

Blaze ran to the announcer's table. Oh, what she would have done for a guitar. But there was no time. She grabbed the mic. "Island Nation! Tear off your Frames and open your eyes! Do we want to stay imprisoned in the past, to old ways of hating each other, to unfair and harmful schools? Or do we want to free our minds to see a brighter future of free, fair, and fabulous schools?"

She ripped off her MC Frames and held them high in the air. "Do we want to win or lose this match?!" She broke her Frames on the edge of the table.

The crowd tore off their MC Frames, too, shouting "We want to win!" They cheered and stomped their Frames. They tossed broken Frames out of MegaCorp Stadium. The Region 5 section awkwardly tried to chant, "Free, Fair, and Fabulous Schools!" and "Fab-u-lous Schools!" and "FFF Schools!" But those chants didn't work. So, they landed on a more compelling chant, one that many had cheered before. But this time, it meant something very different. "Freedom Schools! Freedom Schools!"

Suddenly, the whole stadium boomed, "Freedom Schools! Freedom Schools!" There was only one problem. The game was still tied. And there were less than two minutes to go.

Scarlet attacked. She juked Orion and Chopper with wicked side steps, fake moves, and counter taps. Orion lunged in the wrong direction. Chopper tripped over himself and fell. Scarlet flew toward the goal with mad determination. Blaze met her just outside the penalty box.

"If you would have *just* gotten that hand surgery," Scarlet said, dribbling with Blaze sticking to her side, "you wouldn't be in this

situation. And you wouldn't have humiliated me and my family!"
Orion returned with a sliding tackle. Scarlet leaped over him, veered
left, less than three meters from the goal. Blaze, Chopper, and Kai
moved with her, seemingly blocking all angles of scoring.

"So, now you need to pay."

The crowd rose to its feet.

Scarlet made a hard fake left, abruptly stopped, then popped the
ball over Chopper, who slid to take away a goal line shot. Blaze and
Kai easily blocked any angle of scoring. But thousands of
specialized training hours had prepared Scarlet for this moment.

She kicked the ball off the post, which ricocheted over Blaze
and Kai. The crowd gasped and grabbed their puddin' and flower
heads. Scarlet sprinted to meet the ball just beyond the center of the
goal area. Now she had options. She nailed a perfect shot into the
lower right corner of the goal, but Kai dove and blocked it with his
outstretched hand on the goal line. The crowd roared. Scarlet
blasted the rebound, which Blaze tipped with her puddin' head off
the goal post. Blaze, Chopper, and Kai watched helplessly as Scarlet
scurried in for the rebound. The crowd roared, then cried as Scarlet
hammered another perfect shot into the left side of the goal.

Orion slid across the goal line to block that third brutal shot.

And that was how close the 99 percent came to losing to the
less than 1 percent.

The crowd head butted and group hugged.

Scarlet screamed.

The prime minister cried, "Those were goals! How did the refs
not call those goals?! The refs are terrible!"

The ball rebounded toward the sideline.

Blaze reached it first and sped down the cross-island team
sideline. She passed Bee Girl, Fist Boy, Four-Armed Stick Boy,
Blueberry Boy, half-conscious Hands, Root-Woot, the
puddin'tender, the mangled Puddin' Head troop of former students,
Coaches Serafina and Jules, Lily, Maya, myself, and the entire cross-
island team, who cheered and ran along the sideline with great hope.
The 99 percent cheered with outstretched arms and enormous
hands.

Chopper pulled Kai up and pushed him forward. "Let's go!"

Kai knew what Chopper meant. "What about defending the

goal?!"

"It's now or never," Chopper said. "Everyone—*charge*!"

And so they did, with what might have been the world's first football karaoke charge. Chopper, Kai, Orion, and the entire team charged down the pitch, while being ever so mindful to avoid being offside—which, as you know, would be a terrible way to end the game. Yes, I was cheering and karaoking down the sideline. The MC players were so confused, someone slipped through their defense.

Blaze weaved around the swarming MC players. Scarlet sprinted behind her, yelling, "Get on Wheels! Someone get on Wheels!"

Chopper yelled, "Pass the ball!"

"I got this!" Blaze yelled back. In a matter of seconds, many thoughts streamed through her mind. *Now is my chance. I haven't scored a goal. I haven't even taken a shot. Finally, after years of big hand discrimination, years of not playing offense, now is my time to prove everyone wrong. This is my chance to make big changes. My chance to be the big boss, the education minister. No one is taking that away from me!*

Thirty seconds.

More MC players buzzed toward Blaze.

"*Pass the ball!*"

But now it seemed that everyone was covered—even the terrific trio that was Wheels, Ram, and Hammer.

Chopper and Kai sprinted with everything they had left. Kai accelerated from karaoke crossovers into cartwheels and back flips. He was now the only person open.

Twenty seconds.

Scarlet ran a half stride behind Blaze. "What's it feel like to be blanked in the biggest game of your life?"

"*Pass the ball!*" Chopper screamed. "*You don't have the shot!*"

"*I have the shot!*"

"*Pass the ball!*"

Blaze knew what Chopper meant. "A *Sweetie* can't score the winning goal!"

"*Blaze, pass the ball!*"

"*I have the shot!*"

It's quite amazing how much Blaze processed in a matter of milliseconds. *Crossing right won't work because of these two annoying MC numbskulls. Crossing left is a tough angle. Scarlet is right behind me. Maybe I can squeeze through the middle here. Ugh, that's not going to work. Maybe if I—no, I can't. Time's running out. It's go time!*

The prime minister screamed, "Offside! Offside! They're all offside!" But too bad, so sad, his MC referee cronies had fled in fear of sea monsters—perhaps most scared of the seahorse monsters.

Blaze made a hard fake right, and with a deft misdirection tap between her legs, the ball shot out to the left. Two players fell for it. Scarlet did not. Blaze and Scarlet sped toward the ball.

"Pass the ball! Please! You can't make that shot!" Chopper pleaded one final time.

"I have the shot!"

Scarlet pushed into Blaze's right side. "You should have joined the MC team!"

"You should have been an ally!"

10 seconds.

Blaze took two more strides, planted her right foot, and said, "This one's for you, Maya." With her left foot, she blasted a spinning line drive across the pitch. It whizzed between two defenders and cleared a leaping defender by a centimeter. The ball blazed toward the upper right goal post.

The shot was wide right.

"She missed it," the announcers said.

"She missed it," the fans cried.

"She missed it," Chopper sighed.

"She missed it!" Scarlet shouted.

"SHE MISSED IT!" the prime minister bellowed. He raised his tiny hands in the air. He waited for the ball to sail out of bounds as time expired. He'd badly wanted a blowout win, or even just a win, but at this point, he would settle for a draw. Or so it seemed.

Blaze fell to her knees, watching the ball head out of bounds.

What happened next remains clouded in great controversy. First, a sudden wind blew across the pitch. The ball spun faster and curved toward the goal. In fact, it now had a chance of scoring. At the same time, Kai had gained ground with his ridiculously fast cartwheels and back flips. There was no doubt he was open. Blaze had known that he was open. And to this day, questions remain about (a) whether Blaze had really intended to shoot or pass, (b) whether a serendipitous wind was ultimately responsible for the game's outcome, (c) other controversies we'll get to later, and (d) whether Blaze would have scored if not for Kai. You see, Kai did a cartwheel to a back flip to a high-flying bicycle kick that, yes, crushed the spinning ball into the net.

For a few seconds, the crowd stood in stunned silence. Throughout the game—if not the decades—they had experienced ups and downs and rising hopes that crashed like tidal waves again and again.

And then . . .

The crowd went no noggin.

They jumped up and down, cheered, head butted, and group hugged like never before. Fans outside waved spoons wildly or strapped them on their heads, head butted each other, and rammed MegaCorp Stadium. Then they group hugged. They flocked to buy checkered shirts, hats, and spoons. Yes, they flocked to the dessert carts and gobbled down the delicious combinations of puddin', cookies, and cake. And as this sweet tooth will attest, those mouthwatering gourmet goodies were ridiculously scrumptious.

Inside the stadium, Blaze, Kai, Chopper, and the entire cross-island team piled on top of each other near the winning goal post. Fans stormed the pitch. They lifted the cross-island team players up over their heads and carted them around the stadium like a train. *Choo! Choo!* All except for Hands, of course, who was simply too heavy to carry. The crowd chanted, "Freedom Schools! Freedom Schools!"

Root-Woot scaled the top of the pitch field wall, where he spun in celebration circles with his shiny robe, hood down. His sea monster comrades cheered him on. The prime minister—who almost bolted from the stadium for a second time—could not resist. He snuck up to Root-Woot, slowly reached out his tiny hand, and touched a scale on his neck. Root-Woot spun and snarled, "Don't touch my scales."

"You *are* real!" the prime minister cried. He tried to push Root-Woot off the wall, but he himself had a great fall. I'm sure you can guess what happened.

The prime minister sailed through the air. The shiny-robed sea monsters caught him and cheered, "Heigi hooga!" Enraged, the top boss charged Root-Woot, and got a similar flying lesson. With the "Battle Victory March" blaring once more, sea monsters bounded across the pitch in a supreme victory lap, tossing a pair of clowns up and down and all around.

The cross-island team had done the impossible. They'd defeated MegaCorp 7—6.

Or so they thought.

THE TRUTH

You may be hoping this very satisfying victory led to a swift, satisfying conclusion to our story. Or perhaps an ending with a reasonable degree of sanity or fairness, given all the absurdity. The cross-island team won. And that was that.

But alas.

Remember that nearly everyone in the stadium—and nearly everyone on Celebration Island, for that matter, including me—had destroyed their MC Frames. And so, we didn't realize until much later that Power News—and its subsidiaries, Puddin' Head News and Sweetie News, and of course, many Mega Gossip posts and shares—had already announced that MegaCorp had won 9—6 in a decisive victory.

At home, Blaze screamed at the screen, turning to Chopper. *"WHAT THE MOLDY FART TART?!"* She could not believe it.

"In the end, MegaCorp was just too good," the prime minister said with strange red, blue, and purple smudges and scratch marks on his face. He tried to be calm but looked unhinged—as if, at any moment, he might be ambushed by sea monsters or seahorses. "The cross-island team played a surprisingly nice game. They played hard for a few minutes. But clearly, they were no match for MegaCorp, and, of course, Scarlet Pompavich. Tremendous performance. Tremendous player. Amazing. What did she have? Nine goals? Amazing."

"What are they talking about? *Nine* goals?!" Chopper yelled.

"And that Blaze character held to zero goals. Tremendous MC defense. But she really wasn't that good."

"*Ahhhhhhhh!*" Blaze shouted. "We won the game! It doesn't matter that I didn't score."

Chopper had to ask. "Did you shoot to score? Or did you mean to pass?"

"What?! Who cares! *More importantly, what is happening?!*"

They had no way of communicating with the others. Blaze tore up her room, looking for an old pair of MC Frames. Chopper ran home and returned with one. But no one answered. "They probably don't have an old set of Frames," Chopper sighed.

"Now, whether you saw the game in person, on Celebration

Island, or at home," Bartle said "you probably don't know about the biased refs, or the fair refs who were kicked out of the game. We didn't even know any of this until the end of the game. And that's why the biased refs 'missed' the final three goals from Scarlet."

The screen replayed video that showed a midfield view of the time Scarlet tried to score at the end of the game, when Kai saved a shot, Blaze saved a shot, and Orion blocked the final attempt. "You can clearly see she scored three times there."

"*What the fart tart?*!" Blaze sprang up and down like a kangaroo on hot coals. "She didn't *score*! You can't tell from that angle! And even if she had scored, she would have scored *once*! But none of that matters because the match is over!"

"Of course, if the referees had fairly counted those three goals, time would have run out." Bartle cocked his head and raised his eyebrows. "And that last goal that so many of you saw of course would not have counted. Everyone was offside anyway. So, there you have it. Unsurprisingly, MegaCorp won in a blowout victory, 9—6. In other news, there is an alarming new idea for Puddin' Head Schools to—get this—learn about the 'positive side' of Sweeties. Folks, can we just ban this ridiculous idea outright? And in case you haven't heard, the supreme prime minister survived a second sea monster assassination attempt. And the sea monster leader named Root-Woot is thankfully in jail . . ."

Blaze was once again literally hopping mad. She jumped up and down and swore. By the time her mom and Maya returned home, she sat angrily in a corner with a spoon helmet strapped to her head, slowly spooning puddin' with chill booster from a bowl. Her mom asked about the large dents in the walls, but instead of answering, Blaze just frowned and growled.

With TDJP help, the team posted to Mega Gossip that the game had clearly ended with a cross-island team victory. They argued that no one—not even the prime minister—can just retroactively count certain goals and discount others. This gained little traction, in part because the posts were quickly taken down. The news continued showing Scarlet's final three "goals" and repeating the narrative of a blowout victory for MegaCorp.

The team knew this was a blatant lie. But after decades of mind-numbing, head-pounding, and navel-gazing education, too many citizens believed the news without question. With the exception of fans in the stadium—who seemed permanently transformed—those who'd seen the three saves and the final goal outside the stadium or at home began to believe the news instead of the evidence of their own eyes.

The team demanded video evidence for Scarlet's alleged three goals and for the alleged offside. The news organizations simply showed the same video footage. Then, someone—who apparently hadn't destroyed her MC Frames—leaked a video that clearly showed Kai blocking one of Scarlet's final shots. It was not a goal. Unfortunately, the person recording had been knocked out with a head butt almost immediately thereafter.

The video was quickly taken down. The "traitor" was thrown in jail.

The team remembered the hunger strike. So, they launched another one. But this time, it was a hunger, news, and MC Frames strike. (The MC Frame strike proved the most difficult.) The protests would last until the news showed relevant evidence to prove who won this epic game.

While the outcome of *The Match* became murkier, the legend of Root-Woot grew. Not only had he magnificently led the first *Script United*, new footage and rumors surfaced about his visit to Puddin' Head Region 3. While Root-Woot regretted tossing both captains of the cross-island team, he single-handedly mowed down half of the Freedom High School student body, and flung some Regional Boss named Poppy into the ocean. And so, obviously, Root-Woot easily had thrown Scarlet Pompavich fifteen or was it twenty meters at *The Match*? Trending Mega Gossip feeds proclaimed that he'd thrown her into the third row of the stands, which was specific, and therefore must be true. Moreover, not only did Root-Woot toss the top school boss onto the pitch, but he had also spun the prime minister like an Olympian throwing the discus, hurling him so high above the pitch that the prime minister broke up a flock of chill birds simply trying to enjoy the post-game celebration. Some said Root-Woot acted in self-defense. Others claimed his attacks were unprovoked—of course he deserved to be thrown in jail.

The peaceful, tree hugger Sweeties marched around the Capitol and the Power Island jail, demanding that *Root-Woot The Legend* be released. The tree huggers easily scaled the walls of the Capitol Building, flinging ropes with grappling hooks onto windowsills and balconies. Scores of tree huggers swung from ropes around the Capitol, bounding off walls and grasping rope after rope like merry-go-round superheroes. The Capitol turned into a high-flying circus with tree huggers tethered to the Capitol carousel, breezing through the air. They showed off ridiculous acrobatic skills, which attracted more gawking and cheering protesters, but confused the prime minister. He stuck his head out the window, waving and thanking the talented, high-flying supporters and gushing crowd. After deafening boos, he had a mini-realization, but not the big one he needed. He slammed the window shut and banged his head on the wall. The tree huggers became more brazen, releasing into towering, twisting, quadruple somersaults, and flips. The crowd gasped, then roared as the soaring tree huggers landed in safety nets held by Sweeties below. "Heigi hooga!"

Regardless, the news refused to show the evidence. Puddin', cookie, cake, and booster sales plummeted once again. News viewership and ratings took a nosedive. Money drained from MegaCorp like water poured out of a ritzy rooftop swimming pool shot full of holes.

The MegaCorp board and senior executives panicked. Power News, Puddin' Head News, and Sweetie News called the team and its sympathetic fans a bunch of sore losers. They interviewed the prime minister, who confidently stated that Scarlet had scored the final goals and those large-handed babies wanted a fake win. The football commissioner said Scarlet scored. Scarlet said she'd scored as she proudly petted ponies on a farm, then pleaded to take more than one home.

But the nation was changing. Gradually, more citizens learned to think for themselves. More citizens recognized biased news and shoddy evidence.

"No evidence, no puddin', no cake!" and "Show us the evidence!" became the rallying cries across the country. Sales of puddin, cake, and cookies slowed to a crawl. Hardly anyone watched Power Island News, or its subsidiaries. TDJP started a small news cast and reported smarter, healthier, and happier people, who were more united than they had ever been.

Despite strong pressure from executives, the prime minister dug in. You see, he was likely suffering from a severe case of *absurdity hypocrisy*. That's where you either (a) accuse others of doing stupid and bad things that you are actually doing or (b) know you are lying about doing stupid and bad things. The prime minister, with the help of the major news networks—who broadcast his every move and sentence—continued to call the cross-island team sore losers, liars, cheats, and scaredy Sweeties afraid to face the truth.

MegaCorp released a video called *The Truth: 100 Video Clips of Scarlet's Final Three Goals*, which the major news networks showed during prime time. MegaCorp created an entire website dedicated to showing this "truth." But as you can imagine, all the video clips were shot from distances or angles from which an objective observer couldn't really tell if Scarlet had scored these alleged goals. Goal line videos were omitted or supposedly disappeared. And as you know by this point in our story, Puddin' Head News anchors did as much critical thinking on this one as Education Minister Pompavich had done before naming School Boss J.R. the top boss.

"So, my fellow citizens," Bartle said in a serious, credible news voice, filled with great concern, "you may have heard about this fabricated video that allegedly was leaked by a fan at the game. But even if that video is real—which is very unlikely, because I heard it was produced by the cross-island crybabies—it is only one very short video. MegaCorp's video shows *one hundred* video clips of what happened in those final moments of the game. Who can deny a mountain of evidence? The truth is, Scarlet scored three times in those final moments. So, get over it, losers!"

But few watched or believed. They wanted real evidence.

The strike continued.

The prime minister refused to admit defeat.

The strike continued.

The prime minister refused to admit defeat.

Kai threw out a wild idea, which was quickly implemented once Puddin' Heads from Region 3 believed they would eat puddin' again. Every fifteen minutes, they posted a video on Mega Gossip of tearing a prime minister statue off the Wall, loading it into a catapult, and launching it into the ocean.

The prime minister head butted many tables and walls (too bad he didn't wear a spoon helmet). In desperation, he ordered the release of Root-Woot from jail. The tree huggers cheered, but the protests continued. The prime minister refused to show the evidence.

The ridiculously long standoff continued.

"We need a Plan D," Blaze said.

"I think we're on Plan E. Or is it Plan F now?" Chopper sighed. "What will it take to end this madness? Just show the evidence already!"

FREEDOM SCHOOLS

Days later, Blaze and the team called Puddin' Heads and Sweeties to gather at Celebration Island. As before, hundreds of thousands of fans packed the stadium. But this time, fans packed the pitch, too. Hundreds of thousands gathered outside the stadium.

Blaze took the mic on a slowly rotating circular stage in the middle of the pitch. Yes, Chopper was proud of his team's staging work. Blaze's lead guitar strap slung over her cross-island team jersey, which she wore along with her game face. "The last time we were here," she said to a very hungry crowd, "this place was called MegaCorp Stadium. But as our good friend Root-Woot—who is on the drums today—reminded the prime minister, this is our house."

Root-Woot twirled banyan drum sticks behind a large shiny red, blue, and yes, purple drum set. Root-Woot pounded the drums, ending with a flurry of cymbal crashes. The crowd roared. Indeed, many came to catch a glimpse of the twirling, whirling, tree-hugging legend who flung foes into the stratosphere with ease.

"And since this is our house, maybe it needs a new name. What do you think about renaming it 'Freedom Stadium?'" Blaze asked. Root-Woot thumped the drums again. The crowd roared louder.

Blaze exchanged looks with Kai, who grabbed the other mic. He tapped a simple yet mighty tambourine, louder and louder. The crowd clapped in rhythm, and the next thing you know, Kai had the ravenous crowd pumping their fists and chanting, "Cake! Cake! Cake!" then "Cook-kie! Cook-kie! Cook-kie!" After they had their musical fill of Sweetie sweets, Kai reluctantly led several enthusiastic rounds of "Pud-din'! Pud-din'! Pud-din'!" He was a team player after all. The rest of the shiny band—that included sublime backup singers and talented musicians on bass guitar, keyboard, and trumpet—swayed behind Blaze and Kai and waited for the signal. Kai nodded back to Blaze.

"Wow, Kai. You feel that energy? That energy makes me hungry." The crowd cheered. "But I have to tell you, I'm not hungry for the puddin' that MegaCorp's been feeding us." The crowd fell silent and exchanged confused glances. "No, I want real puddin' owned and made by Puddin' Heads!" Kai said, "And cookies and cake from the Sweeties!" The crowd erupted into more chants of cake, cookies, and puddin' again.

Blaze raised a spoon and the crowd quieted. "And you know what else? I'm craving something even more delicious. I want something we've been denied for too long." Many Puddin' Heads mouths slowly opened as if asking, *What could possibly be tastier than puddin'?* Blaze pulled a fistful of spoons from her belt and raised them to the sky. "I'm hungry for freedom!" The starving crowd whooped and rumbled. Blaze waited for the right moment and said, "But I don't think the prime minister got the message yet." The crowd booed then shook their fists and jeered toward the Capitol. "So here's a little song that Kai and I wrote to help him understand. It's called, *Freedom Schools.*"

Blaze raised her spoons again and cried, "Spoons Up!" Puddin' Heads raised their spoons with pride and repeated the call to action. Kai raised an eyebrow, shrugged, and led a few rounds of "Heigi hooga!" with Sweeties and a few groups of spoon-waving Puddin' Heads while Blaze holstered her spoons. She ripped a chord that electrified the crowd inside and outside of Freedom Stadium. Backed by their fabulous band, Blaze and Kai belted out the lyrics in Puddin' Head and Sweetie harmony, if there is such a thing.

Two islands in an either-or war.
Bigs versus Smalls.
Left against right.
Puddin' Head red against Sweetie blue.
Maybe it's time for something new.

(Blaze)
Puddin' Head school scripts told us,
Freedom is a board to my puddin' head.
Success is a rock to my face.
Pull on magical bootstraps,
That will make me fly?
I'd rather poke my eye.
March to the MegaCorp writer?
No, I'm a freedom fighter.

(Kai)
Sweetie school scripts told us,

To cooperate—but not with them.
To be community—but not with them.
Sure, I can be kind; I can be fair.
But get rolled over?
I'd rather pull my hair.
Be a push-over Sweetie?
No, I stand strong for solidarity.

The powerful few
Kept us ignorant.
Locked us in boxes
Of us versus them.
Scared us with zombies
And sea monster mayhem.

They told us we are free
But imprisoned our minds
With imaginary binds.
Why is it so hard
To erase made-up lines?
Don't be a dummy,
Just follow the money!

And so we united,
We were no longer divided.
We beat MegaCorp,
Who was not so delighted.

So the big boss, and the news,
And MegaCorp stuffed with pride,
They pouted, cried, and lied.
They said they won.
But they hid the truth,
With evidence so stupid,
You need not be lucid,
To see sore losers.
Threatened power abusers.

(Chorus)
It's time to stop being fools,
It's time to burn this MegaCorp script,
It's time to burn down MegaCorp rules.

Burn it, torch it,
Light it up!
Burn it, torch it,
Light it up!

It's time to stop being fools,
It's time to rewrite the rules.
It's time to write a script united,
You need not be enlightened,
To imagine a vision,
Where all students have,
Freedom Schools,
Freedom Schools.

A nation divided will surely fall.
A lunatic boss cannot be our downfall.
Demand the evidence that matters,
Citizens, we must rise up,
To the tyranny of it all.

(Chorus)

Before the chorus, Blaze shifted the lyrical tirade into a mesmerizing lead guitar solo. Root-Woot countered with a captivating drumming groove. The crowd lurched their heads, danced, waved spoons, and played air guitar. Some waved gigantic foam hands like they did at *The Match*. Others banged spoons on spoon hats like drums. The exhilarating Blaze on lead guitar versus Root-Woot on drums gradually intensified like a gathering storm. The crowd's energy strengthened as the duel transformed into a spectacular musical lightning show. When the bass guitar, then trumpet, then full band finally blasted the chorus, the crowd surged with energy toward the crescendo, bellowing *Freedom Schools, Freedom Schools.* Heads thrashed, bodies slammed, spoons smashed, and hordes of group huggers howled together. And so, when Blaze and the band belted the chorus for the second time, the crowd on Celebration Island, once again, went no noggin.

Given the crowd's demographics, size, and energy, it was shocking that no one was harmed, injured, or started a fire. Perhaps the Puddin' Heads and Sweeties had finally affirmed diversity and learned to be kind and joyful in the pursuit of freedom and justice for all. After many raucous rounds of *Freedom Schools* with hundreds of thousands of Puddin' Heads and Sweeties, the crowd roared louder as if wanting, or expecting a fabulous finale.

And that is exactly what they received. Root-Woot leaped over the drums with a swirling, whirling front flip. Blaze hopped on the drums and bashed out a number while Root-Woot spun and moved into the legendary defensive position. And yes, after each drum roll and cymbal crash, Root-Woot flung a band member into the air with great ease. The crowd loved it. They caught the high-flying rock stars: Kai, the bass player, the keyboard player, the trumpet player, and the backup singers. Only Blaze remained.

Blaze and Root-Woot locked arms and wrestled like yes, professional wrestlers in the match of the century. Then, they danced like yes, professional dancers in the performance of their lives. Root-Woot flipped Blaze into a quadruple backspin. She landed in a superhero crouched position, but in comparison to a ridiculous statue you might remember, Blaze actually looked like a superhero, or perhaps, someone transforming into a superhero. Blaze slowly stood and raised a spoon a final time. The crowd roared once again, filling her with incredible power.

Blaze charged at Root-Woot, who locked her arms again, spun her like an Olympic discus deity, and released. No, Blaze did not land in the third row of Freedom Stadium. Rather, she skyrocketed as though shot from a cannon with one spoon shining like a torch for all to follow to the Capitol. Blaze sailed out of the stadium, then over the Snake Channel and the bridge. In fact, Blaze flew with such force that Root-Woot grabbed her trailing spoon as if hitched to a blazing comet. More impressively, he summoned great creatures to the Capitol. Large flocks of chill birds moved into attack formation and sped behind Blaze and Root-Woot. Elephants and ponies stampeded toward the Capitol. Seahorses grew wings and a horn and yes, transformed into rainbow seahorse unicorns that shot out of the ocean and flew to the Capitol. Oh, it was magical!

Blaze landed on top of the Capitol with her spoon shining brightly. Upon seeing this luminous signal, Puddin' Heads strapped on spoon helmets and rammed through their nation's Capitol doors. Others swiveled on catapults that launched rocks, logs, and flaming dynamite guided by, yes, rocks with googly eyes. Shortly thereafter, tree huggers riding elephants smashed through the beaten down walls. Puddin' Heads charged into the Capitol waving spoons. A few trotted on ponies. Angry birds crashed through windows and chased the corrupt politicians and their cronies outside.

Blaze cried, "I have the power to destroy all who disagree!" A dark cloud suddenly formed and struck Blaze's spoon with lightning, which Blaze hurled at her foes, striking them on their hands and rear ends. Each time Blaze burnt a rump, she laughed, "Because I can!" Kai glided on a mighty seahorse unicorn, thrashing the scurrying scoundrels with a mighty tambourine. Root-Woot and the tree huggers swooped from ropes, easily capturing the smoking and stunned numbskulls, who were mounted on the rainbow seahorse unicorns. These majestic creatures filled the sky and carried the half-cooked, evil villains to the ocean, where they were dropped into the mouths of sea monsters with large, gnashing teeth. And one sea monster was so loud, terrifying, and fearsome, the evil villains died of shock before he chomped them. And his name was Regalzilla.

Oh Courageous Reader, if you cheered on and believed those last few paragraphs, I'm afraid that you fell for the ol' *mean and magical thinking spoon trap*. And sadly, I have faltered as the alter ego of an educator. But not to worry. This was not a high-stakes summative test, but rather a truth-seeking formative assessment from which you can learn. Yes, I know flaming those numbskulls with lightning bolts and feeding them to Regalzilla might be enticing, captivating, and delicious, but nevertheless, there you are: trapped and tangled in a ludicrous web, hanging upside down. Now, quickly release yourself, and reread this entire book before Absurdity gets you! By now, you should be approaching proficiency in the aforementioned standards, not to mention kindness (compassion + action), critical and independent thinking (or even better, interdependent thinking—Blaze has more to say about that later), and the ability to root out the spreading weeds of misinformation. This mindful concoction of skills is essential for building immunity against Absurdity and/or the numbskull virus. Don't let anyone brainwash, trick, or persuade you with half-baked ideas, especially if those ideas look, smell, or taste like yucky cookies, flaming cymbals, flying seahorse unicorns, or banning books with flying seahorse unicorns. Not politicians, your family, leaders, teachers, or even me.

Alas, I can hear your family, leaders, and teachers screaming, "WTK! WTK!" I'm sure a few are even jumping up and down like mad bunnies. So, as a friendly reminder, here is a pro tip: don't be a buffoon who says, "All rules are stupid!" or "Rules don't apply to me," or "The only truth is my egocentric or ethnocentric perspective." That is not empathy, kindness, or critical thinking—it is navel gazing—so don't go there either.

But my guess is that your magnificent mind felt tickled, as if laughing at the absurd notion of Blaze flying like a chill bird or wielding lightning from her spoon. Of course, you were not so easily fooled! (By the way, it is rare for anyone to fall for the *mean, magical, and willfully ignorant spoon trap*. Thus, I didn't bother giving you that assessment. I feel terrible for anyone trapped in that nasty web— escape is nearly impossible. Absurdity can feast for days, if not a lifetime.)

So here is what really happened. Root-Woot did unleash Blaze into the crowd—say five or six meters, maybe seven given the elevated stage. Blaze flew with an arm extended spoon first, her other arm clutching her guitar. The crowd caught and tossed her around a bit. *Heigi hooga!* Blaze made a fast and smooth landing onto the pitch.

And yes, Blaze led the thunderous crowd to Power Island. The crowd sang louder as it crossed the bridge and even louder as they approached the Capitol. The Puddin' Heads waved spoons with great passion. Sweeties, and more and more Puddin' Heads now shouted, "Heigi hooga!" New crowds joined from all directions. These protesters marched around the Capitol, singing *Freedom Schools* over and over and over. Day and night. Day and night.

The prime minister repeatedly stuck his swollen head out the window and yelled at the boisterous crowd. "*STOP SINGING*

THAT SONG!"

Puddin' Heads and Sweeties were thrown in jail.

The band released *Freedom Schools* with a TDJP recording studio, which much to the chagrin of MegaCorp, instantly became a mega hit.

More protesters gathered at Power Island. Tree huggers once again swung on ropes around the Capitol, this time in beautiful, synchronized movement to *Freedom Schools*. Protesters kept marching. They kept singing. Day and night. Day and night.

The prime minister's approval rating plummeted. His numbskull continued to swell. He kept yelling, *"STOP SINGING THAT SONG!"*

The pattern continued over and over to what seemed to be another level of absurdity entirely.

Finally, gratefully, at long last, the prime minister—perhaps influenced by the next election and dwindling popularity—couldn't take it anymore. He arranged a meeting.

The next day, Blaze and Kai walked out of the Capitol looking like leaders.

"Well???" Chopper demanded.

"We have a deal to discuss." Blaze paused and cocked an eyebrow. "They didn't catapult all of those prime minister statutes, right?"

THE DEAL

Blaze, Chopper, and Kai sat at a table in front of the Senate chamber. Senators, MegaCorp executives, news reporters, and select citizens—such as Lily, Maya, Natalina, Jules, Howzin, Foster, and the cross-island team—packed the room. By this point, I had my surly sweet tooth more under control and quietly munched on a bag of spicy honey kale chips, which might have been drizzled with chocolate. Protesters continued marching and singing *Freedom Schools* outside. Live news coverage trained on the prime minister.

Courageous Readers aspiring to be kind, like me, may be wishing that the prime minister finally understood the error of his ways, and quickly ended all this unnecessary pain and suffering, including his own. Perhaps you've been hoping for it all along—*may he please change today*, you've silently cried for him. Perhaps this situation reminds you of a time when you, like me, acted like a numbskull but didn't quite realize it. But thankfully, a courageous friend told you. And you, like me, said, "Wow. Thank you—I was acting like a numbskull," and thus changed and stopped acting like one. Or conversely, perhaps this situation reminds you of someone you know—maybe a dear friend, sibling, or romantic partner—who despite all your kindness and support, is just too thickheaded to change bad behavior, or seems shielded by an impenetrable wall of undisputed pride. Perhaps you've been a little guilty of avoiding, making excuses for, or enabling this bad behavior for all sorts of noble reasons. Perhaps one day you even found the courage to confront this person! Alas, no change. Suddenly—perhaps at this very moment—you realize that you've done everything that you can do. Sadly, there's only one kind action, or non-action, left: to allow this person to suffer the consequences of poor choices, to learn a painful lesson, and hopefully, to grow and change.

And so, perhaps you are hoping that the prime minister transformed like a caterpillar into a loving, beautiful butterfly rather than an insatiable, malicious moth. He was human after all. He once was a little boy, full of hopes and fears and joy and pain I suppose. Despite his generational privilege, perhaps he was harmed because as someone said, hurt people hurt people. Yet, he was an adult now and recently had every opportunity to change. Change beckoned him, practically pounding on his door every day: *Hello! Is anyone home?* Well, peace-loving tree huggers rapped on his window a few times. Even his inner circle of trusted family, friends, and staff members—who surely were more persuasive than acrobatic tree huggers—advised him to face the truth, to admit defeat, and to move on—for the good of the country, if not his own dignity. I'm sorry to share that this did not happen easily or gracefully. Remember what I told you about brainwashed minds? Now imagine one clinging to absurd power.

Judging by his extremely swollen head, the prime minister's absurdity hypocrisy condition had not improved, but rather deteriorated or mutated. Perhaps he also caught the terrible numbskull virus, as if it had returned full circle and clobbered the supreme spreader like an accelerating boomerang. While the prime minister's captive audience tried not to stare at his misshapen dome, he rambled on about the tremendous MegaCorp game, and that MegaCorp had won. However, given the outrageous protests that were destroying the economy, for the good of the country, the prime minister said he'd reached a deal with the co-captains of the cross-island team, Blaze and Kai.

"Because of the very unsatisfactory national consumption of puddin', cookies, cake, and the news—" the prime minister said, then abruptly stopped and snorted. The nation held its breath. He clenched his fists and quickly mumbled, "We will show the goal line footage and final moments of the MegaCorp football game—at some point in the near distant future." Then, he shouted, "More importantly, the sea monster wall is spectacular, but we need more funding—"

"Ahem!" Blaze coughed loudly.

"What?"

"The deal?"

The prime minister snorted again. "No need to publicly—"

"We made a deal."

The prime minister frowned, then suddenly raised his arms as if very offended. "No."

"What?"

"No—we didn't make a deal! I can't believe you are lying in front of the entire nation!" he whined like a gaslighting, defensive dictator, or perhaps a teenager that you might know.

"You *just said* we made a deal!"

"No I didn't. You said that."

Blaze shook her head, flabbergasted. "Your signature is right here!" Blaze held up the signed agreement.

"I don't remember that, so it must be a fake one."

Blaze and virtually the entire room—if not the nation—sighed. Blaze slowly closed her eyes, drew in a deep breath, and exhaled twice as long. She opened her eyes, cocking her eyebrow as if restarting an epic staring contest. She calmly said, "So we should continue protesting. Singing."

"You can't make me!"

Blaze shrugged and belted out a familiar chorus.

It's time to stop being fools,
It's time to burn this MegaCorp script,
It's time to burn down MegaCorp rules . . .

Many in the Senate chamber grumbled, but sang along, nonetheless.

"No! No! No! *Not that song!*" the prime minister pleaded, trying to compose himself. But after watching Root-Woot crack his knuckles while the room sang, he cried, "Ahh! Show the clips!" and banged his head. Then, a strange thing happened. He wobbled and steadied himself on the podium. His noggin somehow continued to swell, becoming absurdly disproportionate to the rest of his body. It was as if instead of transforming into a beautiful butterfly, he was, uh . . . to put it kindly . . . turning into something less dignified. But here's the good news: after millions watched this sad and surprising spectacle continue over the course of the day, head butting, head banging, and head bashing quickly became an embarrassing habit of the past, at least for most Puddin' Heads.

The video—distributed live across the nation on MC Frames and screens in homes—showed Scarlet's three last-minute goal attempts in slow motion. In the first, Kai blocked the shot just in front of the goal line. In the second, the ball grazed Blaze's noggin and hit the goal post, but clearly did not fully cross the line. Besides, it bounced back, so a goal was not logically possible. In the third shot, Orion blocked the football after it had crossed the goal line halfway—which as you know, is not a goal.

The relevant evidence was clear. Scarlet had not scored on any of the three final attempts after all. The crowd outside erupted into cheers and group hugs. Alas, some did head bang. The crowd sang louder. Strangely, Blaze, Chopper, and Kai just smiled.

The final video clips showed the cross-island team's insane final karaoke charge. The cross-island bench ran down the sideline next to Blaze, with great hope on their faces. Tens of thousands of fans with checkered jumbo hands waved and tumbled over each other, wildly cheering in anticipation of what might happen.

No one was offside. No one was even close. And when millions watched the replay of Blaze's ridiculously impossible pass to Kai, and Kai's equally ridiculous last-second goal, they could not help but pause in great awe and quietly gasp, "*What the*—" It was as if this moment suddenly transformed generations of absurd contempt, cruelty, ugliness, injustice, fear, and stupidity into love, beauty, and wisdom. Love, beauty, and wisdom that had secretly remained dormant and hidden all along, for a ridiculously long time.

The crowd outside went ballistic. They sang together louder than they had in their whole lives. Now, you might think that new world records of puddin', cookie, and cake consumption were set in the next few minutes. Surprisingly, you would be wrong. Yes, a strange thing happened. During the "hunger" strike, many Puddin' Heads and Sweeties began experimenting with healthier culinary delights (spicy honey kale chips became a popular choice). As even this sweet tooth now appreciated, better health—and eating desserts in moderation—became the new lifestyle. But let's be real: in this moment some Puddin' Heads and Sweeties lapsed, or just didn't care—they stuffed their faces with puddin', cake, and cookies.

Courageous Reader, this reminds me of a serious idea that I'm still considering as I weigh whether to return to teaching or pursue school leadership. So please allow me a brief bird walk, and not a chill bird one. With my absurdity neurosis subsiding, I tapped into vast reservoirs of astounding energy I didn't even know existed. By this point, I could pump out twenty-nine push-ups, crank out eighty-five jumping jacks (triple time), and speed walk a kilometer in nine minutes, eighty-five seconds, while doing 360-degree karaoke crossovers and turns, thank you very much. And by the time you read this story, I'll probably have surpassed these milestones. Moreover, Root-Woot taught me formidable spins, blocks, and throws. This meteoric increase of strength, speed, and agility made me realize a viable immunity-boosting side hustle: professional wrestling. Imagine me wrestling Absurdity and/or a selected representative as an eternal foe! Ah, but what if Absurdity mutated and doubled, or brought a friend for a tag team match? Root-Woot enthusiastically volunteered himself as a wrestling partner if these epic matches could raise tree and creature awareness. His tree hugging family, friends, and fan base burst with enthusiasm, begging to join such a tour. I could only guarantee raising Absurdity awareness but imagine Root-Woot's joy in slinging Absurdity into the ropes—imagine the rebound! Heigi hooga! On second thought, that sounds ridiculous. But does that mean Absurdity wins? I'll keep mulling it over. Perhaps you have recommendations on who or what to wrestle? Just remember: Absurdity would approve all wrestlers. Hmmm . . . Perhaps I could wrestle Uncle Brute or Brute Jr., and finally heal the trauma of the supernatural rabbits . . . Anyway, I'd love to hear your thoughts. Now, back to our story.

"Are you saying that MegaCorp lost?" a reporter asked the prime minister.

"Huh?" he staggered and pouted. "I'm just saying we have a deal. Island Nation schools will be free, fair, and . . . uh . . . fabulous, or whatever!" Then he mumbled, "By taking funds from the Wall project, if necessary." Then he shouted, "Which it will not!" (As it turned out, the anticipated health care saving from switching to FFF schools—which would substantially reduce student injuries, disease, and other health ailments—far exceeded the funding for the Wall project.)

Blaze, Chopper, and Kai high-fived. The nation roared.

The reporter asked the trio the same question.

"The evidence speaks for itself," Blaze said. "We like the deal."

The prime minister's eyes glazed over, he nodded at the team, staggering and grasping the podium. He spun to the education minister. "You're—"

"Ohhhhh no!" Minister Pompavich charged the podium. "I quit! Mr. *Not-So-Supreme Prime Minister!* I was loyal to you and look where that got me! Now what am I supposed to do?!"

The prime minister, barely able to stand, stuck out his tongue, mocking the education minister like he was seven years old. "Boo hoo. What am I supposed to do?" He laughed at his rhyme, shrugged, and turned to Blaze. "And we have a new education minister! Blaze Union, join me."

The crowd jumped up and down, waving spoons, and cheering, "Spoons Up! Heigi hooga!"

"You have no idea what it's like to be the big boss of education!" the former education minister said to Blaze. "So good luck with this numbskull."

The prime minister scowled, "Can someone get this loser out of here? Blaze, take your leadership position already!"

As Blaze approached the front of the Senate floor, she whispered to former Education Minister Pompavich, "Can you own one thing now? That too many schools have failed too many students?"

"Yes, of course! You think I didn't know that? You have your work cut out for you." Then she spun around and pointed her butt at the prime minister. She plugged her nose, as if expecting something to happen.

It didn't.

"Oh my—thank you!" she cried to Blaze. Then, she had a realization. "Elroy! Scarlet! We need to talk!"

"Can I have a real pony now?" Scarlet pleaded.

"No!"

Scarlet glared at Blaze as if warning her that their brutal rivalry was far from over. *Or was she disguising her transformation into a loving, beautiful butterfly?* Regardless of the answer, in this moment, the Pompavich family slunk from the room.

Blaze took the mic with a trembling, perfect hand. She took a deep breath. Tears rolled down her face. "I know Puddin' Heads aren't supposed to cry. But this has been an emotional day, an emotional week, and an emotional journey altogether. I wanted this opportunity so badly, but never thought it would really happen. I'm so grateful for Chopper and Kai, for the cross-island team, my family—and the great teachers I've had—who put up with my nonsense. Yeah—I put you through a lot." Many people nodded their heads in agreement, then laughed. "And I'm grateful for all the teachers and school bosses and citizens supporting this movement to make our schools great for all kids."

The crowd outside the Capitol thundered. The nation roared.

Blaze looked at Maya. "Because everyone deserves a free, fair, and fabulous education. And as everyone in this room knows, we have a growing number of TDJP citizens and educators working to finalize our FFF school framework. And we have one part ready—"

The prime minister threw his head back, flailed his arms, then slammed his noggin into the podium again. I don't understand how he remained conscious, but there he stood, twitching and wincing. He scanned the room like a spoiled child desperate for attention.

Blaze regrouped. "We have one part ready to vote on today."

"No!" the prime minister pouted.

"I guess we'll launch the last statues."

"No!"

"Or we'll sing again."

The prime minister's brows furrowed. Slowly, his bottom lip curled and then quivered. "Fine! Vote on it!" he blubbered like a distraught toddler.

The senators, who were also sick of hearing *Freedom Schools*, readily agreed.

"As everyone knows, we have an important election coming up," Blaze said. "I know that citizens of this nation will closely watch to see which politicians support free, fair, and fabulous schools. And if not, we know the candidates who will. None of this work means anything if citizens aren't informed and active, or if you fail to vote. Citizens, if you vote for numbskulls, you will have numbskull schools." (Trust me, we had a long discussion on the meaning of an active and informed citizen.)

"Part I of the FFF framework, which you can see in Senate Bill PHS 7412, includes free school for all students, the elimination of hand size rules, the "do no harm" clause, the elimination of school child labor, establishing teaching as a profession, better working conditions, anti-discrimination training, and the national adoption of Puddin' Head Island, Sweetie Island, and TDJP values and principles." (Although, Puddin' Heads and Sweeties good and bad were removed, and the value of *respect authority* was replaced with *respect*, which of course, was more inclusive.)

Kai and Chopper.

"As we worked on this framework," Blaze said, "we also realized it's ridiculous for so much power to rest in the hands of so few. Part

I of the FFF framework includes the creation of a national teacher organization, the requirement that the education minister is an elected position, and also gives the local community authority to hire, or fire, their education bosses."

The prime minister folded his arms, babbled, stuck out his tongue, and closed his eyes as if shutting out reality.

Senator Serafina took it from here. There was much squabbling and arguing, but eventually, the senate voted to approve the bill, 13 —7. And with that—as Blaze and many TDJP citizens knew, and you likely have surmised—everyone had to rethink schools.

"And now, with Part I of the FFF framework in place . . ." Blaze took a deep breath and hung her head for a moment. She exhaled very slowly as if she was about to say something very difficult. Then, after a long moment filled with intense anticipation, she looked up. "With this representative democracy more securely in place, I respectfully resign from my position as the education minister of Island Nation."

The room fell dead silent. Jaws fell open. Chopper and Kai fell out of their chairs.

"I will finish my term, but then I want to . . ." Blaze paused and swallowed. "I want to become a teacher."

The Senate gasped. Teachers cried. I cried. School bosses cried for a different reason.

"What the—" the prime minister sulked with eyes still closed. Then, he plugged his ears.

"Teachers are real superheroes. Teachers are the ones who, yes, teach the students. For better or for worse, they are the ones who make the immediate difference in students' learning and lives."

Jules wiped a tear from her cheek and nodded at Blaze.

"Fellow citizens—a fourteen-year-old in charge of the nation's schools? Think about it—could anything be more ridiculous?" The question hung in the air long enough for me to think of a few contenders.

Blaze continued. "It's ridiculous for someone to be a boss of teachers—or the boss of school bosses, for that matter—when you've never been one yourself. But we don't need bosses—we need leaders, and yes, we need transformative leaders who lead not for mediocre schools, but for fabulous ones. Who lead not for some students, but for all students. The future belongs to transformative leaders, educators, and citizens—not by dividing ourselves or having all the answers—but by learning and working together. Someday I will become a school leader. Perhaps someday I will become the education minister again. But first, I will learn to teach."

Many teachers around the nation cheered. Some did not.

A Sweetie senator asked a critical question. "These transformative citizens—they don't sound very fun. Do they have a sense of humor?"

"Yeah—they sound like sticks in the mud!" another agreed.

"No heigi!" several senators cried.

"Yes, I'm sure they can be very funny!" Blaze said, clearly annoyed.

"Do they know how to laugh at themselves!"

"Heigi hooga!"

"I guess so!" Blaze said, growing more aggravated.

"And what do they eat—cookies, cake, or puddin'?"

Blaze slapped her head.

"That makes me hungry! I could go for a bit of chocolate right now."

Now Puddin' Head senators were excited. "Oh, that sounds good."

"What kind—milk chocolate or dark chocolate? I like mine—"

"Ahhh!" Blaze said. "I'm glad that Puddin' Heads and Sweeties are getting along, but could we talk about something more important!" Blaze grounded herself, winked at Kai, and tapped someone still plugging his ears on the shoulder. "Mr. Prime Minister, remember the other part of the deal. Every school deserves a fabulous football pitch. If they want one, of course."

"No—you're making me angry!"

Blaze started to sing. Most of the room, the marching citizens outside the Capitol, and the nation joined in.

It's time to stop being fools,
It's time to rewrite the rules.
It's time to write a script united—

"Okay!! We'll vote on it! Just *stop singing that song!*" The prime minister banged his head one last time. He slid down the podium, stuck a thumb in his mouth, curled into the fetal position, and cried himself to sleep. While most of the nation had an absurd awakening, the prime minister sucked his thumb and cooed, as if living in a blissfully ignorant dream, or perhaps, Absurdity caught him in a rare spoon trap.

As for the rest of the deal: if you happen to sail past Puddin' Head Horn, and scan the crumbling wall, you can still see one spotter statue and another crouched halfway, as though waiting for sea monsters to arrive any day.

ABSURD BEAUTY

Blaze, Chopper, Kai, their families, and I met on Celebration Island. The adults discussed the changes on the horizon: new schools, new rapidly spreading and delicious cuisines and recipes, and a potential expansion of Union Apparel, the first Island Nation TDJP-affiliated business that Natalina Union now owned and operated. It specialized in red-and-blue clothing that MegaCorp still refused to sell. Today, they considered designs other than checkers and whether to add more colors.

Maya overheard this conversation. "Maybe you should use the whole rainbow," she said with a big smile. Then she and Lily tore off along the shore. They laughed and splashed through small, lapping waves without compression gloves or concerns about their hand size—although Lily still suffered from a mild case of pancake hands.

While I chatted with the adults, the trio of close friends—who'd been enemies not so long ago—walked along the shoreline as the red sun dipped in the blue sky and warmed their faces, which, at least for now, lacked MC Frames. They sat on blankets, admired the sunset, recalled *The Match*, reminisced about the events that had changed the course of their nation's history, and reveled in fulfilling their big changes pact. But then Kai pointed to bite scars on his arms, reminded Blaze and Chopper about that stressful day at Hard Rocks High, and somehow managed to put them both into headlocks while giving double noogies. Yet they quickly discovered Kai's weakness and tickled him with commensurate force. After catching his breath, Chopper shared aspirations for organizing a national solar train project. Now backed with national funding, Kai shocked Chopper with his new plan to start football teams across Sweetie Island. Blaze, of course, already knew.

Blaze dug her fingers and toes into the sand and looked up at the sky. The moon peeked over the horizon. Stars began to twinkle. "Who would have guessed that a Sweetie would promote the expansion of football?" Blaze thought a moment and said, "And you know what else is odd?"

"Besides your face?" Kai smirked.

"Besides this Sweetie's unkind words and ridiculous haircut," Blaze continued without missing a beat. "Not too long ago, we were islands divided because of really stupid reasons. It's like each island thought it was the center of the universe. But when you look at this magnificent sky . . . when you consider the planets, stars, and constellations . . . not to mention how old this planet is . . . not to mention the hundreds of other countries and cultures around the world . . . isn't it ridiculous that *one* island—that one group of people—believed it had the one right way? The only truth? And that it was superior to all the others?"

Chopper said, "Wow, thanks for making me feel small. Thanks for an inspiring celebration."

"I'm just saying maybe we should keep things in perspective and not take ourselves so seriously. It's liberating. When you seek the truth."

"And when you're truthful," Kai said.

"You sound like sweet tarts," Chopper said.

"And I've realized something else." Blaze skipped a pebble across the water, which skimmed the surface and then plunged into the Snake Channel—which, of course, was really a tiny part of the ocean. "Our freedom is interdependent."

"Huh?" Kai said.

"Think of this: Isn't it interesting that you Kai—my enemy— helped me expand my perspective, see my ignorance, and, in a very strange way, set me free? It's as if we were trapped or pulled on opposite sides of a magnet. The more the Puddin' Heads hated the Sweeties, the more the Sweeties hated the Puddin' Heads, and vice-versa. When you showed me not all Sweeties are lazy, brain-eating zombies—" Blaze chuckled, "—it's like I was released from the trap of thinking like a Puddin' Head."

"You got that right. And you might have become even more stupid from all that head butting if not for me. You're welcome. And now I have a magnet image of you and me stuck together. So, *thank you for that*," Kai said.

Blaze punched him in the arm. "Well, then, you missed the teaching point, Sweetie."

Chopper clutched his head with both hands, as if a bright light had suddenly switched on. "Yeah! It's like this mysterious force that even MegaCorp can't escape. They exploit others, but that just crushes their spirits."

Blaze nodded and paused a moment. "Yeah. Our liberation is all tied together."

Chopper raised his eyebrows. "You think any other country has these problems?"

Blaze and Kai laughed. "None as stupid as ours!" they said together.

I reflected on this question later, but I kept my answer to myself. I wonder what you would say. Or if you think those sorts of comparisons mean something.

Blaze grabbed a handful of sand and let it pour through her fingers. She squinted at a grain of sand and blew it away. "But maybe Orion revealed something important. Maybe at a deeper level, we're afraid that we're a meaningless grain of sand in this infinite universe."

Chopper said, "Deep. Please continue, wise teacher."

"Yes, *please*," Kai said sarcastically. Then he said seriously, "No, really, I'm actually interested in your Puddin' Head thoughts."

Blaze gave her first teacher look, which here meant, *don't push it.*

"So, I was thinking, perhaps the greater our fear of meaning nothing—or perhaps of dying, or not existing— the more we armor up with labels like *Puddin' Head, Sweetie,* or *MegaCorp.* It's scary to think about who we are without labels. We armor up, sometimes to survive, sometimes just because we're growing up. But other times, we stack on absurd layers of armor to shield our fear—by seeking obscene power and money, clinging to ridiculous beliefs, or harming others to prove our importance. Perhaps our armor protects us for a little while, but if it becomes too thick or isn't removed, it restricts us from learning and expanding who we are."

Chopper nodded. "Deep."

"Huh . . . A lot of thoughts rolling around in that puddin' head of yours," Kai said. "Where do you come up with these ideas?"

Blaze looked to the sky and said, "That's a bit personal." She scooped up a lump of wet sand lit by starlight. Seagrass silhouettes danced with the waves just below the water's surface. She stacked the sand and said, "Please, join me."

Chopper and Kai shrugged and played along. Chopper built a large, thick perimeter wall and plastered the side facing the ocean with seashells. Kai sculpted a decorative interior with patterns of slanting lines and half spheres across the top of the wall. Blaze molded mini castles inside this playful creation, which quickly evolved into a sand village.

Chopper said, "The tide's coming in. Shouldn't we build farther away from the shore?"

But Blaze just smiled warmly and kept at it. "I haven't told anyone this." She paused as her eyes watered. "After the embarrassment of the Noble Deed Match draw, I climbed Mount Freedom. I thought about Dad and what he would have said. I thought about his death, and how he died." Blaze paused, then explained what happened.

Chopper said, "Blaze, I'm so sorry. Why didn't you tell me?"

"Mom said not to tell anyone. But given everything that's happened, I just can't keep it all inside anymore."

"Yeah."

"And so, I'm looking across Puddin' Head Island, thinking about Dad, and then I thought about Kuko, my twenty-three red cards at school, and why we tied the Sweeties. I thought that I had destroyed my dreams. I'd made Puddin' Head schools worse for everyone. It all seemed so stupid. And I . . ." She swallowed and took a deep breath. "I know what Orion felt—what he was asking. I fell into a dark place. I looked down this cliff. I wasn't sure how I could move on." Tears streamed down her face.

"But as I looked down, this wind blew me back. And something spoke to me— like my inner voice or Dad or the universe was trying to tell me something. The wind knocked me onto my back and blew the breath right out of me. And I swear this voice asked me these questions. And the last one was, *Who is separate?* At the time, it seemed ridiculous. But I just wasn't quite ready to learn."

She swallowed and smiled with great gratitude. "I was emotionally drained, but as I started hiking again, I began to understand. I increasingly felt in awe of the stars, constellations, and then the moon rising over the summit. I felt in awe of this life, and this world. And suddenly, I realized that underneath it all, the Puddin' Heads and Sweeties are connected, not just in a rivalry way, or even in an interdependent way. We're connected at a deep, profound level. It's hard to explain in words. But my awareness shifted I felt this vast freedom. Instead of clinging to my thoughts and emotions—and being overwhelmed by them—they floated by like clouds."

"Fluffy clouds, wispy clouds, or dark and foreboding clouds?" Kai asked.

Blaze laughed. "Come on, I'm trying to share a personal moment here. But they were fluffy ones. And then, a small, thick cloud literally descended into my hand. And a teeny tiny genie stepped out and said in a high-pitched voice, 'You have three wishes.'"

"What?!"

"Are you done?" Blaze smiled. "Or maybe you don't want to know."

"Okay!" Kai said. "Yes, I want to know!"

Blaze looked at the stars twinkling on the ocean surface, exhaled, and recentered. "As my thoughts and emotions dropped like armor and floated away, I had—I don't know how else to say it—this spiritual experience. I felt nothing but pure love, shining within and around me. I felt connected to everything. It wasn't even that I *felt* connected, I *was* connected—to *everything*. The universe was undivided. People, plants, animals, trees, rocks, *clouds*, the ocean, the universe—flowed in a constant exchange of energy. I felt this life force within and beyond humans. That existed before and beyond us, and that was happening right then. Just as it is right now. Just as I am breathing and smelling this air, seeing thousands of stars, feeling this peace, saying these words, and simply *being* right now. Just as we are experiencing this ever-present change, right now. I realized we have no reason to fear change. I realized I still have so much to learn. I knew that our small place in the universe is strangely why we *do* matter. We aren't separate; we are all a part of a larger, unfolding story."

"Wow," said Chopper. "You didn't tell me that, either?"

"I needed to make sense of it myself. It felt weird to share. And we've had a lot going on."

"Yeah. But Blaze, you know you can share anything with me, right?"

"I know."

"Have you had this experience again?"

"Not like that. But it shifted me, you know? I knew I would never be the same."

Chopper nodded.

Kai said, "I can imagine. So, do you have special powers now?

Do you secretly fly at night? Tell the truth: Did you mind control
that game-winning pass to bend—or was it a shot?"

"Kai, come on."

"Can you mind control Scarlet Pompavich into the air and make
her dance and say, 'Heigi hooga!'?"

"Uh . . . no." Blaze laughed. "But that does sound fun."

"So, how do I have this experience?"

"I don't think genies talk to Sweeties. They don't eat cake."

"No, seriously."

"I don't know. I'm still learning. I suspect there are many types
of these experiences and many ways to have them. I suspect anyone
can experience them. But you probably have to stop being a
numbskull first."

"Well said, knucklehead."

The team took this in for some time. They returned to their
playful co-creating. Blaze dug a deep channel from the ocean, which
became a moat that encircled several sandcastles within the sand
village. Chopper built a bridge from driftwood and used stones and
shells to make a grand entrance and walkway. Kai etched animals,
plants, and mosaic patterns along the exterior walls. Kuko, Maya,
Lily, and the adults joined in the fun.

Maya and Lily finished carvings of spoons and flowers and
chased each around the sand village. Maya yelled, "This is the best
day ever!" After they had reached the point of exhaustion, Lily took
a deep breath, smiled at the moon and starlit sky, and winked at
Blaze. Maya suddenly squeezed Blaze and burst into tears. "I don't
want this day to ever end!"

The adults said, "Awww."

Blaze said, "It is a great day, isn't it?"

"Yeah."

"And you know what?"

"What?" Maya sniffed.

"We only recognize a great day because of ordinary ones. Just
like we only know joyful moments because of sad moments, silly
moments because of serious ones, and successful moments because
of failures. They can all teach us something, if we let them. They're
all part of our human experience. None are the same. None last. It's
what makes each one special. I want to experience each moment

fully. I don't want to miss anything, you know?"

Maya shook her head as if she wanted to understand, or she had more urgent things on her mind. "Mom, do we have any more puddin'?"

Of course, Blaze lit a small bonfire to finish the sand village. The team slung their arms around each other. We all stood back and admired this masterpiece in the flickering light.

And then, a strange thing happened. "What the—" we all said in unison. A herd of seahorses coasted into the sand village channel. They bobbed up and down and swam in silly circles. They danced and twirled around the moat in pairs with interlocking tails. In the next instant, a seahorse couple raised their tiny heads out of the water, in the middle of a shimmering, reflected moon, as if to better see these silly land creatures. The seahorses looked at Blaze the same way Blaze had watched seahorses for the first time years ago, wide-eyed and speechless, while snorkeling with her dad.

In many ways, the seahorses were the same as the silly humans watching them. In other ways, they were dramatically different. Yet, underneath it all, the Puddin' Heads, the Sweeties, the seahorses, and myself were interconnected—not on a lifeless planet hurtling through a meaningless universe, but in an absurdly vibrant, complex, and unfolding cosmos. But don't take my word for it. Notice it for yourself.

In the next moment, the seahorse herd swam back into the ocean, as if knowing that my absurdity neurosis had dissolved, as if knowing that silly bet I'd made with my colleague no longer mattered, as if knowing that I felt stronger and more whole, as if knowing that I liked my options, and as if knowing what would happen next. A large shimmering wave approached the shore, curled with awe-inspiring power, and crushed the sand village. It was absurd. It was liberating. And it was beautiful, all at the same time.

Courageous Reader,

Thanks for reading! If you enjoyed this book, please consider leaving an honest review on your favorite store. Reviews make a big difference in connecting readers with new authors and books.

Spoons up! Heigi hooga!
W.T. Kosmos

W.T. KOSMOS
wtkosmos.com

Blaze Union and the Puddin' Head Schools is the debut novel of
W.T. Kosmos. He is the alter ego (pen name) of a life-long educator
who has had the great privilege and joy of serving as a teacher and
school administrator while collaborating with some of the most
fabulous people in the world. W.T. Kosmos lives along the coast of
Paradox, USA, Earth, Milky Way and enjoys reading, writing,
walking the beach, wrestling with his dogs, and snorkeling with
Regal the seahorse. He is also an aspiring professional wrestler.

 wtkosmos

 wtkauthor

wtkosmos

Printed in the USA
CPSIA information can be obtained
at www.ICGtesting.com
JSHW021221121023
49989JS00011B/101